The Rise of SPORTS
IN NEW ORLEANS
1850-1900

DALE A. SOMERS

The Rise of
SPORTS IN
NEW ORLEANS
1850-1900

Louisiana State University Press

BATON ROUGE

To William Ransom Hogan
In memoriam

ISBN 0–8071–0042–0
Library of Congress Catalog Card Number 72–181359
Copyright © 1972 by Louisiana State University Press
All rights reserved
Manufactured in the United States of America
Printed by Vail-Ballou Press, Inc., Binghamton, New York
Designed by Dwight Agner
Chapter ten appeared in a slightly different version
in *Louisiana History,* VIII (Summer, 1967), 219–38.

PREFACE

American society in the past one hundred years has undergone a leisure revolution. Throughout the colonial period and during much of the nineteenth century, Americans adhered fairly rigidly to the gospel of work. Business appeared to be their only interest, and money, their only diversion. Few people would have challenged the observation of the British geologist and traveler Sir Charles Lyell, who expressed great relief when he arrived in New Orleans for the Mardi Gras celebration of 1846: "From the time we landed in New England to this hour, we seemed to have been in a country where all, whether rich or poor, were laboring from morning till night, without ever indulging in a holiday. . . . It was quite a novelty and a refreshing sight to see a whole population giving up their minds for a short season to amusement." [1] Lyell exaggerated the sobriety of American life, but pleasure seeking certainly occupied a low position in the average American's scale of values before the middle of the last century.

Enthusiasm for recreation developed rapidly as the United States shifted from a rural-agrarian to an urban-industrial society. The tremendous, often poorly planned expansion of American cities generated a number of problems that taxed the resiliency and the ingenuity of urban residents and inspired efforts to ameliorate conditions. Improved transportation facilities enabled people to escape the densely populated inner city and thus reduced congestion; beautification crusades relieved urban ugliness with parks, public squares, and tree-lined streets and avenues; slum clearance programs produced better housing; political reforms curbed the excesses of boodling politicians and rapacious businessmen; and the rise of organized

[1] Sir Charles Lyell, *A Second Visit to the United States of North America* (New York, 1849), II, 91.

sports and other commercial amusements provided recreation for city dwellers.[2]

Numerous factors stimulated a boom in leisure-time activities in the second half of the nineteenth century. A reduction in the workday, a rising standard of living, growing concern for the public's physical and mental well-being, and the decline of puritanical notions concerning the value of recreation—all aspects of the new urban-industrial society—were essential to the growth of sports and other amusements. The appearance of organized spectacles and commercialized recreation was also part of a general trend toward specialization in urban communities. As cities expanded, demands for new and better services encouraged merchants, manufacturers, professional men, craftsmen, city officials, and religious leaders to diversify and to improve the quality of their wares; the desire for new services also enabled vendors of pleasure to profit. People in rural areas generally supplied their own pastimes, but many features of urban life—such as regular six-day and sometimes seven-day workweeks, the remoteness of the countryside (especially prior to improvements in transportation), and the temporary loss of any sense of community that affected many newcomers to the city—rendered the simpler, unorganized, often spontaneous diversions of rural America unsatisfactory or inaccessible to many residents of the city. Commercial pastimes and organized activities, such as the theater, the circus, burlesque, vaudeville, and sports, arose to fill this recreational void. Suppliers of commercial amusements, led by P. T. Barnum, realized that people who bought food instead of growing their own; who purchased clothing instead of making it; who rented or bought houses instead of building them would also purchase pleasure, particularly if it were attractively packaged and cleverly sold. Barnum and other promoters prospered because they sensed and exploited a market for leisure outlets in the restless urban masses that increased so rapidly in the nineteenth century.[3]

[2] For accounts of urban growth in the latter half of the nineteenth century, see Arthur M. Schlesinger, *The Rise of the City, 1878–1898*, Vol. X of *A History of American Life* (New York, 1933); Blake McKelvey, *The Urbanization of America, 1860–1915* (New Brunswick, N.J., 1963); Constance McL. Green, *The Rise of Urban America* (New York, 1965); and Charles N. Glaab and A. Theodore Brown, *A History of Urban America* (New York, 1967).

[3] For a general history of recreation, see Foster Rhea Dulles, *A History of Recreation: America Learns to Play* (2d ed.; New York, 1965), especially chapters 5–9 for the beginnings of commercial amusements.

Collectively these changes in the pattern of recreation encouraged the emergence of a leisure-oriented society. By the turn of the century, Lyell's remarks about work-minded Americans no longer seemed valid. In 1905 Lord James Bryce, another Englishman and a keen observer of American urban life, described a vastly changed country. Since Lyell's visit, Americans had developed what Bryce called a "passion for looking on at and reading about athletic sports. . . . It occupies the minds not only of the youth at the universities, but also of their parents and the general public. Baseball matches and football matches excite an interest greater than any other public events except the Presidential election, and that comes only once in four years." As millions of urban residents pursued pleasure, they began to substitute a leisure ethic for the old work ethic; the gospel of work soon yielded to the gospel of play. Work remained important, but people tended increasingly to value it in terms of the leisure it provided. Although the transition from a work-oriented to a leisure-oriented society was not complete at the time of Bryce's visit, it was certainly well advanced; the ultimate transposition of values appeared inevitable. Today, as C. Wright Mills has observed, "work itself is judged in terms of leisure values. The sphere of leisure provides the standards by which work is judged; it lends to work such meaning as work has." This leisure revolution was almost entirely an urban product, for it was in the cities that conditions proved most conducive to change. In rural areas a Protestant-based prejudice against the misuse of time lingered on for a great many years, but in cities, which rural Americans often regarded as centers of vice and wickedness, the gospel of play won widespread acceptance before 1900 and completed its conquest of society in the present century.[4]

Of the many leisure-time activities available to urban residents, none has occupied a more prominent position than organized sports. Sports have played an interesting role in the search for pleasure in America since the colonial period, when the southern gentry rode to the hounds or wagered on their favorite thoroughbreds and a few atypical New Englanders frolicked around the Maypole. But it was not until the latter half of the nineteenth century that sports developed the

---

[4] James Bryce, "America Revisited: The Changes of a Quarter Century," *Outlook,* LXXIX (March 25, 1905), 738–39; C. Wright Mills, *White Collar: The American Middle Classes* (New York, 1956), 236.

characteristics and importance associated with this prominent social institution today. Before the Industrial Revolution and the rise of cities, American sports were mainly unorganized, rural, out-of-doors activities such as hunting, fishing, horse racing, impromptu wrestling matches and foot races, cockfighting, and animal-baiting. The dearth of athletic pastimes led one observer to write in 1901 (with some exaggeration): "Until the middle of the century just closed we were practically without sports." But when industrialization and urbanization caused dramatic shifts in the basic structure of society, sports reflected the transformation. As hundreds of thousands of people made the pilgrimage from farm to city, they experienced a need they had not known in the countryside, a need for formal, organized, commercial recreation. Hence, as they built their metropolises, urban Americans created organized sport as a source of amusement. Its rate of growth was phenomenal. At the turn of the century a writer for the *Saturday Evening Post* announced: "The American love of sports has risen to a pitch never before known. . . . This is the era of sport. Practically every man and boy, every woman and girl, takes part, or wishes to take part, in some branch of it. And it is fortunate that the field is broad enough for all." [5]

As urban society provided the catalysts for the development of organized sports, it also determined most of the characteristics associated with this leisure outlet today. More than many facets of urban culture, such as music, art, creative literature, and science, organized sport is a product of the city. Modern American sports have drawn liberally upon America's rural and frontier background and borrowed freely from abroad, but their most salient features have been determined by the tastes and demands of an urban-cosmopolitan population. Intense organization, commercialization, the proliferation of sporting teams and activities, the development of intercity rivalries, the standardization of rules, the acceptance of amateur and professional classifications, and the growth of spectator sports occurred in the cities.[6]

[5] Both quotes in this paragraph are from Harry T. Paxton (ed.), *Sport U. S. A.: The Best from the Saturday Evening Post* (New York, 1961), 3, 4.

[6] For general accounts of the rise of sports since the colonial period, see John R. Betts, "Organized Sport in Industrial America" (Ph.D. dissertation, Columbia University, 1951); Dulles, *A History of Recreation;* John Durant and Otto Bettman, *Pictorial History of American Sports from Colonial Times to the*

In the course of their development, sports have had a profound impact upon American society. Indeed, few aspects of American life have escaped their pervasive influence, for sports have been enthusiastically and inextricably interwoven into the entire fabric of contemporary society. Sports have given employment to thousands through the manufacture, sale, and professional utilization of sporting equipment; they have encouraged improvements in transportation and communication through the desire to convey players and sporting news from city to city; and they have prompted the addition of an important section to the daily newspaper to slake a seemingly unquenchable thirst for tales of sporting triumphs. Sports have also challenged churches to meet the temporal as well as the spiritual needs of an urban population with an abundance of leisure time; they have lent strong support to the promotion of desirable ethical values through the concept of sportsmanship; and by their very nature sports have tended to obliterate superficial distinctions of economic class, religion, and race. In an editorial for the *Saturday Review*, Richard L. Tobin wrote: "The world of sport has now become, along with the Supreme Court decisions, the civil rights movement, the exploding postwar economy, and world opinion, an undeniable force in moving the United States toward full integration." [7]

As organized sports have permeated and altered society, several scholars have attempted to explain the relationship between the rise of sports and urbanization-industrialization, the value of sports as a leisure-time activity, and the worth of sporting pastimes in democratic societies. Historian Frederic Logan Paxson, an early participant in this discussion, advanced the idea in 1917 that the rise of

Present (New York, 1952); Jennie Holliman, *American Sports* (1785–1835) (Durham, N.C., 1931); John Allen Krout, *Annals of American Sport*, Vol. XV of *The Pageant of America* (New Haven, 1929); Herbert Manchester, *Four Centuries of Sport in America, 1490–1890* (New York, 1931); and Robert B. Weaver, *Amusements and Sports in American Life* (Chicago, 1939).

7 For the impact of sports on society, see particularly John R. Betts, "Sporting Journalism in Nineteenth-Century America," *American Quarterly*, V (Spring, 1953), 39–56; John R. Betts, "The Technological Revolution and the Rise of Sport, 1850–1900," *Mississippi Valley Historical Review*, XL (September, 1953), 231–56; James W. Keating, "Sportsmanship as a Moral Category," *Ethics*, LXXV (October, 1964), 25–35; Robert H. Boyle, *Sport: Mirror of American Life* (Boston, 1963); and Frederick W. Cozens and Florence S. Stumpf, *Sports in American Life* (Chicago, 1953). The quotation is from Richard L. Tobin, "Sports as an Integrator," *Saturday Review*, L (January 21, 1967), 32.

sports gave an industrial nation a new social safety valve to compensate for the closing frontier. "The free lands were used up," Paxson contended. "The social safety valve was screwed down. But the explosion did not come. The reason for continued bearable existence under the increasing pressure generated in industrial society cannot yet be seen from all its sides; but one side is already clear: a new safety valve was built upon the new society. . . . Between the first race for the America's cup in 1851 and the first American aeroplane show of February last, the safety valve of sport was designed, built, and applied." [8]

Other historians share Paxson's conviction that sports help make life endurable in industrial societies. English historian Arnold Toynbee, applying this thesis in an early volume of *A Study of History*, insisted that the passion for sport which developed simultaneously with industrialization "is a conscious attempt at 'recreation' from the soul-destroying exaggeration of the Division of Labour which the Industrial System of economy entails." In *Technics and Civilization*, the American writer Lewis Mumford also explained the rise of sport as a reaction against industrialization, a "corrective to the machine." Mumford wrote: "Since the principal aim of our mechanical routine in industry is to reduce the domain of chance, it is in the glorification of chance and the unexpected, which sport provides, that the element extruded by the machine returns, with an accumulated emotional charge, to life in general." [9]

However, both Toynbee and Mumford concluded that sport, inevitably tainted with the industrial spirit, has provided an inadequate, unsatisfactory corrective to industrialism. Toynbee maintained that the "attempt to adjust Life to Industrialism through Sport has been partially defeated because the spirit and the rhythm of Industrialism have become so insistent and so pervasive that they have invaded and infected Sport itself." Mumford certainly agreed: "Sport . . . in this mechanized society, is no longer a mere game empty of any reward other than the playing: it is a profitable business: millions are invested in arenas, equipment, and players, and

---

[8] Frederic Logan Paxson, "The Rise of Sport," *Mississippi Valley Historical Review*, IV (September, 1917), 145.

[9] Arnold J. Toynbee, *A Study of History* (11 vols.; London, 1934–59), IV, 242; Lewis Mumford, *Technics and Civilization* (New York, 1934), 303, 304.

the maintenance of sport becomes as important as the maintenance of any other form of profit-making mechanism." [10]

The able Dutch historian Johan Huizinga corroborated the conclusions of Mumford and Toynbee. In a brilliant study published in 1938, Huizinga argued that civilization "arises in and as play" and that "genuine, pure play is one of the main bases of civilisation." But Huizinga virtually excluded organized sports from his definition of culture-producing play activities, because, he wrote, "with the increasing systematization and regimentation of sport, something of the pure play-quality is inevitably lost." Sport then

becomes a thing *sui generis:* neither play nor earnest. In modern social life sport occupies a place alongside and apart from the cultural process. . . . The ability of modern social techniques to stage mass demonstrations with the maximum of outward show in the field of athletics does not alter the fact that neither the Olympiads nor the organized sports of American Universities nor the loudly trumpeted international contests have, in the smallest degree, raised sport to the level of a culture-creating activity. However important it may be for the players or spectators, it remains sterile. The old play-factor has undergone almost complete atrophy.

Yet, as Huizinga admitted, sport has helped to introduce the play-spirit into areas of modern life usually regarded as serious, such as business.

The statistics of trade and production could not fail to introduce a sporting side to almost every triumph of commerce and technology: the highest turnover, the biggest tonnage, the fastest crossing, the greatest altitude, etc. Here a purely ludic element has, for once, got the better of utilitarian considerations, since the experts inform us that smaller units—less monstrous steamers and aircraft, etc.—are more efficient in the long run. Business becomes play. The process goes so far that some of the business concerns deliberately instil the play-spirit into their workers so as to step up production. The trend is now reversed: play becomes business.[11]

In such ways sport influences practically every aspect of modern civilization and plays sometimes an indirect and passive and sometimes an active and direct role in the culture-creating process, if we use culture in the broadest sense of the word.

[10] Toynbee, *A Study of History,* IV, 242; Mumford, *Technics and Civilization,* 307.

[11] Johan Huizinga, *Homo Ludens: A Study of the Play-Element in Culture* (Boston, 1955), 173, 5, 197–98, 200.

Another scholar who has expressed serious reservations about the position of sport in modern society is James C. Charlesworth, political scientist and editor of *Leisure in America: Blessing or Curse?* Toynbee, Mumford, and Huizinga insisted only that industrialization and systematization have corrupted sport, but Charlesworth, highly critical of "the present preoccupation with games and sports," contended that modern trends in mass recreation are fraught with dangerous possibilities. With an air of urgency he warned that "mass spectation" poses "a dark threat to American democracy, for, if people are trained to sit and watch professionals in sport and other leisure activities, they will also sit and watch some ambitious busybodies take their government away from them and operate it." He added forebodingly: "Mass-sport spectacles in Central Europe are not unrelated to recurring dictatorships there." [12]

Other analysts of sports have reached less alarming conclusions. John R. Betts, one of the leading historians of sport, takes issue with the idea that sport is merely a reaction against industrialism. Betts has suggested instead that "sport in nineteenth-century America was as much a product of industrialization as it was an antidote to it." In an article published in 1953, he stressed the importance of technology in determining the direction sport took following the advent of the Industrial Revolution. "By 1900," Betts stated, "sport had attained an unprecedented prominence in the daily lives of millions of Americans, and this remarkable development had been achieved in great part through the steamboat, the railroad, the telegraph, the penny press, the electric light, the streetcar, the camera, the bicycle, the automobile, and the mass production of sporting goods." [13] If sport arose as an antidote to industrialism, the disease contributed mightily to the cure.

Others who have studied the rise of organized sports surpass Betts in rejecting the conclusions of those writers who question the value of sport in industrial societies. Foster Rhea Dulles, the only historian who has attempted a full-scale history of recreation in America, contended that in the substitution of new diversions, such as spectator sports and other commercial amusements, for the

[12] James C. Charlesworth, "A Comprehensive Plan for the Wise Use of Leisure," in Charlesworth (ed.), *Leisure in America: Blessing or Curse?* (Philadelphia, 1964), 39–40.
[13] Betts, "The Technological Revolution and the Rise of Sport," 255, 232.

simpler rural pleasures, "a new America, a fumbling, often inept democracy, was feeling its way toward a fuller, more satisfying life for the masses of its people." Frederick W. Cozens and Florence S. Stumpf, in their sociological analysis *Sports in American Life,* have defended the democratizing influences of spectator sports: "In furnishing a common cultural interest, fostering understanding across class lines, and increasing the intimacy of association with different classes, spectator sports have contributed to those integrating forces which are vital and indispensable in the preservation of our democratic way of life." [14]

That the social sciences share a growing interest in the development of sport and its importance as a leisure-time activity is apparent. Professional historians, however, have been laggard in investigating the rise of sports, perhaps because of a conviction that such a lowbrow topic scarcely merits highbrow consideration. But since sports loom so large in the daily lives of millions of Americans, it is increasingly important to examine in depth the origin and the extent of this country's passion for sports. I hope that this history of sports in New Orleans will contribute to an understanding of the role played by sports in American life and of their importance as a leisure outlet in American cities. I have limited this study to the second half of the nineteenth century because it was during this period that sports rose to prominence in the recreational habits of New Orleanians and Americans in general. As the following chapters demonstrate, few organized sporting activities existed prior to 1850, but in the next fifty years the number multiplied rapidly. By 1900 the position of organized sports as one of the city's and the nation's major areas of recreation had been assured. In tracing the growth of sports in New Orleans, I have confined my discussion primarily to organized and commercial activities which seem mainly urban in character—team sports, spectator activities, club functions, commercial vendors of amusement, and the like. For this reason I have discussed such popular unorganized activities as hunting and fishing mainly in terms of their contributions to the development of organized activities, such as rifle clubs and rod and gun associations. Both hunting and fishing were undeniably popular throughout the

[14] Dulles *A History of Recreation,* 99; Cozens and Stumpf, *Sports in American Life,* 299.

South, but my main objective has been to show how highly organized sporting activities for both players and spectators helped to meet the recreational needs of an urban population. I have discussed reasons for the rapidly growing interest in sports, the impact of sports upon life in the city, their importance as a leisure-time activity, and the forms of sports peculiar to various social and ethnic groups. I have also attempted to analyze the formation and proliferation of athletic teams and organizations, the commercialization of sports, the genesis of modern concepts of amateurism and professionalism, the role of Negroes in sports, and the rise of collegiate and intercollegiate athletics—trends important throughout the United States as well as in New Orleans.

Like most people who have written dissertations that subsequently became books, I have accumulated an imposing list of academic and personal obligations which I now gladly acknowledge and freely discharge. My heaviest academic debt is to the late Professor William R. Hogan, of Tulane University, whose own interest in the history of leisure-time activities encouraged the selection of a topic that more "serious" scholars might have dismissed as frivolous and whose careful reading of the dissertation taught me a great deal about historical scholarship. I am also grateful to Professor Robert S. LaForte, now of the Department of History, North Texas State University, who read an early version of this study and made a number of valuable suggestions. The staffs of several libraries also provided crucial assistance. Mrs. Dorothy Whittemore and Miss Betty Maihles of Tulane University; Miss Lora Smith, formerly of East Texas State University; and Miss Jane Hobson and Mrs. Jean Stanley of Georgia State University helped to track down obscure and remote sporting journals and were always willing to submit mounds of requests for books, newspapers, and periodicals in other libraries. Professor Joseph O. Baylen, chairman of the Department of History, Georgia State University, also lent encouragement, particularly by making it possible to complete the last version of this study in Atlanta. My greatest personal obligation is to my wife Sally who read every draft, typed hundreds of pages, proofread hundreds more, and suffered evil moods as cheerfully as could be expected.

CONTENTS

The Rise of SPORTS
IN NEW ORLEANS
1850-1900

Chapter I
THE CITY THAT
CARE FORGOT

Located "upon a site that only the madness of commercial lust could ever have tempted men to occupy," [1] New Orleans was the nineteenth century South's most hedonistic city. Indeed, it had few peers anywhere in the country. "Everybody lives freer, and spends their money more willingly here," a resident who had once lived in New York told Frederick Law Olmsted in 1853. It was a feature of the city that travelers seldom failed to record and that residents freely exploited. When the English traveler James Silk Buckingham visited the city in 1841, he thought its entire mode of life—its shops, hotels, theaters, restaurants, and people—merited comparison with Paris. New Orleans, the country's third largest metropolis, was, said Buckingham, "a city of great gaiety." At the end of the century, the city's relative size had declined, but it retained its reputation for urbanity. Julian Ralph, a well-known travel writer, observed in 1896: "With but little more than a quarter of a million inhabitants, the Crescent City has most of the features of a true capital and metropolis. . . . It is the best of all the American winter resorts, because it has what the others possess (which is to say, warm weather and sunshine), and, in addition, it offers the theatres, shops, restaurants, crowds, clubs, and multiform entertainments of a city of the first class. It is *par excellence* a city of fun, fair women, rich food, and flowers." [2] In a city characterized by commercial pros-

1 "Yellow Fever in New Orleans and Mortality in New York," *Illustrated London News*, XXIII (September 10, 1853), 203, quoted in Robert C. Reinders, *End of an Era: New Orleans, 1850–1860* (New Orleans, 1964), 1.
2 Frederick Law Olmsted, *A Journey in the Seaboard Slave States, with Remarks on Their Economy*, Vol. I of *Our Slave States* (New York, 1856), 588; James Silk Buckingham, *The Slave States of America* (London, 1842), I, 294–394, especially 295, 331, 340, 342; Julian Ralph, *Dixie; or, Southern Scenes and Sketches* (New York, 1896), 44–45.

3

perity, political iniquity, and a highly diverse and cosmospolitan population, residents carefully nurtured a voracious appetite for pleasure.

New Orleans' heterogeneous population traced its roots far into the city's past.[3] Founded by the French in 1718 and ruled by the Spanish from 1763 until 1801, the city became a Latin enclave in a predominantly Anglo-American country after its acquisition by the United States in 1803. The presence of a fairly large number of black residents, both slave and free, and some non-Latin whites gave the city a strikingly cosmopolitan appearance. After the War of 1812, immigrants, both foreign and domestic, increased the variety of the city's population. Thousands of Anglo-Americans, many from the North, poured into the booming port city. Simultaneously cotton ships returning from Liverpool, Le Harve, and other ports deposited thousands of aliens, mainly Irish, German, and French, in the city. This great infusion of people boosted New Orleans to a major position among American cities. By 1850, with 116,375 people, it ranked fifth in the country behind New York, Philadelphia, Boston, and Baltimore. Foreign-born residents comprised nearly 40 percent of the total population and approximately half of the white residents at mid-century; blacks, slave and free, made up almost a fourth of the population. Of the white native-born citizens, nearly one out of four was a migrant from the North, making New Orleans a mecca of moderation in the increasingly belligerent South of the 1850s. The traditional view that the great migration of rude, money-grubbing Americans destroyed the well-developed civilization of the city's cultured Creoles is largely a myth. As Joseph G. Tregle has shown, the word *Creole* was used

3 For general accounts of social, economic, and political developments in New Orleans, see Oliver Evans, *New Orleans* (New York, 1959); Albert A. Fossier, *New Orleans: The Glamour Period, 1800–1840* (New Orleans, 1957); Joy J. Jackson, *New Orleans in the Gilded Age: Politics and Urban Progress, 1880–1896* (Baton Rouge, 1969); John S. Kendall, *History of New Orleans* (3 vols.; New York, 1922); Reinders, *End of an Era;* and Henry Rightor (ed.), *Standard History of New Orleans Louisiana, Giving a Description of the Natural Advantages, Natural History in Regard to the Flora and Birds, Settlement, Indians, Creoles, Municipal and Military History, Mercantile and Commercial Interests, Banking, Transportation, Struggles Against High Water, the Press, Educational, Literature and Art, the Churches, Old Burying Grounds, Bench and Bar, Medical, Public and Charitable Institutions, the Carnival, Amusements, Clubs, Societies, Associations, Etc.* (Chicago, 1900).

before 1865 to describe all natives of Louisiana, whether French, Spanish, American, or German, black or white. Moreover the Latins were no more cultured or sophisticated than other residents; nor were they opposed to making money. Some animosity existed between the various groups in the city, but by the 1840s and 1850s inter-marriage and joint business ventures had erased many of the super-ficial barriers. Thus, as Creoles, foreign immigrants, Anglo-Ameri-can migrants, free Negroes, and slaves mingled, New Orleans developed polyglot features rivaled among few cities of its size.[4]

The city retained its cosmopolitan appearance in the second half of the nineteenth century. Immigration slowed after 1870, but Germans, Irish, French, and, in the 1880s and 1890s, Italians an-nually entered the city in substantial numbers. Native Americans, particularly southerners, also continued to migrate to the commer-cial center of the South. By 1900 the number of residents had grown to 287,104. The city's relative position among American urban centers had dropped to twelfth, but it remained, with the exception of Baltimore, the South's largest metropolis. Although its rate of growth was slower than that of some northern cities, New Orleans experienced the pressures that only a rapidly expanding urban community could generate.

The city attracted great masses of people in the nineteenth century because it was a hustling, thriving, prosperous port. Before the Civil War, it grew fat and wealthy from a rich trade in the agricultural products of the South and West. People of all ranks, from the sweaty longshoreman to the calculating cotton factor, profited as the fruits of national growth and expansion spilled down the Mississippi River for export to the world beyond. An Alabaman who visited the city in 1847 observed "scenes of the most intensely exciting character . . . upon the Levee. The very air howls with an eternal din and noise. Drays and wagons of all descriptions, loaded with the produce of every clime, move on continuualy [*sic*] in one unbroken chain. Ships from every nation, whose masts tower aloft in a dense forest for five miles, with thirty thousand sailors and

---

[4] For interesting and informative accounts of New Orleans' antebellum popu-lation, see Joseph G. Tregle, Jr., "Early New Orleans Society: A Reappraisal," *Journal of Southern History,* XVIII (February, 1952), 20–36; and William W. Chenault and Robert C. Reinders, "The Northern-born Community of New Or-leans in the 1850s," *Journal of American History,* LI (September, 1964), 232–47.

stevedores, busily loading and unloading, stand in your view. Steamboats, and crafts of every make and shape, from every river which empties into the Mississippi, are here mingling in the strife of commerce." For a time in the 1830s and 1840s, the city challenged New York's position as the country's leading exporter. A Scotsman who compared the two cities declared, "New Orleans is the great emporium of the Southern States, as New York is of the Eastern." [5] But the city's share of the western trade began to decline as canals and railroads from the East destroyed New Orleans' natural trade monopoly. Sitting astride a river system that drained a vast area, local businessmen placed too much confidence in their natural advantages and responded too slowly to challenges from rival ports. Not until the 1850s did the business community make adequate efforts to supplement river transportation with railroads. The Civil War interrupted this progress and, as one historian has observed, "destroyed the railroads and shattered New Orleans' commercial empire." [6] Even before Reconstruction came to an end, however, the city had resumed its role as the major port and financial center of the South. New railroads, including the Illinois Central (1873) and the Southern Pacific (1883), made it their southern terminus. And in 1879 Captain James B. Eads constructed a system of jetties that deepened the mouth of the Mississippi River and thereby enhanced the city's value as a port for oceangoing vessels. Manufacturing played a small role in the city's economic growth, as it had before the war, but the great reliance on trade and commerce appeared well founded. The city's economic progress prompted city officials to sponsor the World's Cotton Centennial and Industrial Exposition in the mid-eighties to advertise the present prosperity and the opportunities for growth in New Orleans and the South. Although the South as a whole was not to recover from the Civil War until well into the twentieth century, the local economy proved more resilient. Temporarily blighted by the depression of the nineties, the city had by the turn of the century reached a new level of prosperity.

New Orleans fared less well politically. The city suffered from

[5] Albert J. Pickett, *Eight Days in New Orleans in February, 1847* (Montgomery, Ala., 1847), 19; James Logan, *Notes of a Journey Through Canada, the United States of America, and the West Indies* (Edinburgh, 1838), 177.

[6] Merl E. Reed, *New Orleans and the Railroads: The Struggle for Commercial Empire, 1830–1860* (Baton Rouge, 1966), 130.

corruption and poor administration from the 1840s to the end of the century. The New Orleans *Times* later insisted that the "first organized system of ruffianism for electioneering purposes" was imported in 1848 by a prize-fight promoter. Regardless of origin, rowdyism, malpractice, and maladministration characterized municipal politics for half a century. The Know-Nothings in the 1850s, the Republicans in the 1860s and 1870s, and after that the Democrats, plundered, manipulated, and defrauded in an orgy of political self-gratification. Reform organizations periodically forced improvements in city government, mainly in public finance and in police and fire protection, but reform in New Orleans, as in other cities, proved short lived. Citizens sometimes showed a strong interest in municipal affairs, as they did during the election of 1896 when "political fever . . . wiped out, temporarily, the interest in athletics," [7] but residents usually appeared oblivious to the need for honest and efficient government. In turn, city officials were extremely reluctant to act. Even during periods of great prosperity, New Orleans lagged behind other cities in municipal services. It had few paved streets until well after the Civil War; there was no public lighting system before 1837; and no city-wide system of public sewage disposal existed until 1907. Wharves and warehouses were always in short supply. Public education remained generally poor throughout the nineteenth century, in spite of a generous bequest in the 1850s by the philanthropist John McDonogh for improvement of the city's public schools; higher education languished until Paul Tulane's endowment made possible the creation of Tulane University in 1884.

Whatever the vicissitude of commerce and politics and the inadequacies of public services, residents consistently indulged their fondness for recreation. During the nineteenth century, New Orleans earned and stoutly defended a reputation for amusement and dissipation that set it apart from most American cities. One visitor cautioned readers of his travel account, "Let no one judge of America from New Orleans, for it is altogether *sui generis*." [8]

7 New Orleans *Times,* August 9, 1869; New Orleans *Daily Picayune,* April 20, 1896. For a full discussion of political developments, including reform movements, in the late nineteenth century, see Jackson, *New Orleans in the Gilded Age,* 28–110.

8 James E. Alexander, *Transatlantic Sketches, Comprising Visits to the Most Interesting Scenes in North and South America, and the West Indies* (London, 1833), II, 31.

Residents sought pleasure in a variety of ways. Hotels and restaurants offered fine lodging and excellent cuisine. Private clubs, ranging from the exclusive Pelican, Boston, and Pickwick clubs to the less restrictive fraternal lodges, provided diversion for thousands of persons. Such clubs appeared in profusion in New Orleans and throughout the country in the nineteenth century, as the nation's individual citizens seemed incapable of standing alone in an urban environment. Clubs in New Orleans also reflected racial and ethnic divisions, for there were clubs for Negroes and immigrants as well as for native-born whites. For many people religious organizations offered a leisure outlet. Picnics, bazaars, religious dramas, and concerts were among the activities sponsored by churches and church-related groups of several denominations. Private balls and dinner parties were also popular pastimes, particularly for the well-to-do.

The vast majority of residents spent their leisure hours at public spectacles and commercial amusements. Vendors of pleasure catered to every taste, whether elevated or debased, broad or narrow. The city's several theaters and its opera companies attracted a large share of the more sophisticated pleasure seekers. Indeed, until near the end of the century, few cities in America surpassed New Orleans in the quality of its public arts. Residents fond of dancing attended balls and masquerades, which were scheduled almost nightly in the winter season. Some of the city's balls were formal, exclusive affairs that attracted mainly the bon ton, but others were held in what one observer called "Brothel Ball Rooms" patronized by "the depraved portion of our population." The city also provided a plethora of saloons. Tipplers had a choice of accommodations that ranged from the sleazy waterfront dives where longshoremen and seamen congregated, to the more exclusive bars of fine hotels and restaurants. Throughout much of the century, gambling parlors also abounded in New Orleans. Some were luxuriantly appointed casinos that catered to people of means; others were merely dens where cardsharps separated unsuspecting players from their money. Many men found their pleasure in an evening's dalliance with a prostitute. Again the accommodations varied from lavishly decorated establishments featuring attractive courtesans, to cheap hovels where patrons cavorted with "worn out, false eye-browed, sunken-eyed, disgusting . . . specimens of frail sisterhood." The city council gave formal recognition to this mode of entertainment in the 1850s when it confined prostitution to certain sections of the city, and again in 1898 when it created Storyville, the district set aside for houses of prostitution which became a showplace for, if not the cradle of New Orleans jazz. The centerpiece of the city's pleasure feast was Mardi Gras, the pre-Lenten celebration introduced by the Latin population. Anglo-Americans in the 1850s began to sponsor the formal parades that have characterized the festivities down to the present. By 1900 the Mardi Gras celebration extended over a two-week period.[9]

These numerous diversions amused large segments of the population, but in the antebellum period they began to share the public's attention with organized sports. In the course of the nineteenth century, residents organized clubs and teams to finance and to encourage many sporting activities. Such support quickly produced results. In the space of about fifty years, organized sports rose from a relatively insignificant place in the city's leisure habits to a leading role. By 1900 sports had become the major source of amusement in a city renowned for its varieties of pleasure.

Any leisure activity could easily take root in New Orleans. The city's easygoing moral standards precluded active opposition to any amusement so long as it did not flagrantly transgress the limits of good taste. As one historian has demonstrated, nineteenth century Protestant leaders throughout the country opposed sports and other forms of recreation. "Insolence leads to amusement," they

---

9 Accounts of recreation in New Orleans may be found in Reinders, *End of an Era,* chapters 9 and 10; Henry A. Kmen, *Music in New Orleans: The Formative Years, 1791–1841* (Baton Rouge, 1966); Henry A. Kmen, "The Music of New Orleans," in Hodding Carter (ed.), *The Past as Prelude: New Orleans, 1718–1968* (New Orleans, 1968), 210–32; John S. Kendall, *The Golden Age of the New Orleans Theater* (Baton Rouge, 1952); and in a number of general histories of the city. The quotations describing "Brothel Ball Rooms" are from *New Orleans As It Is: Its Manners and Customs—Morals—Fashionable Life—Profanation of the Sabbath—Prostitution—Licentiousness—Slave Markets and Slavery, &c. &c. &c.* (Utica, N.Y., 1849), 46, and [William L. Robinson], *The Diary of a Samaritan by a Member of the Howard Association of New Orleans* (New York, 1860), 159. The quotation describing prostitution is from the New Orleans *Daily Orleanian,* April 21, 1852, quoted in Reinders, *End of an Era,* 165. The antebellum law restricting prostitution to a certain part of the city is in Henry J. Leovy (comp.), *The Laws and General Ordinances of the City of New Orleans, Together with the Acts of the Legislature, Decisions of the Supreme Court, and the Constitutional Provisions, Relating to the City Government* (New Orleans, 1857), 376–80.

reasoned, "amusement to dissipation, and dissipation to ruin." As late as 1890, a Texas Methodist minister wrote: "Life is short, and no time is to be lost in youth's valuable years. . . . Sport, fun, and frolic, have no chapter in youth's Book of Life in our day; *learning* and *doing* fill up the entire volume." [10] But in sharp contrast to Americans who faithfully followed the gospel of work, New Orleanians were as devoted to amusement as they were to prosperity. The city's gospel of play dictated that if money was worth acquiring, it should be spent freely in the quest for recreation. Neither sports nor other diversions had to contend against the Puritan heritage that retarded their development in other cities.

New Orleans' Sunday habits typified the city's social tolerance. While millions of Americans devoted the Sabbath to worship and meditation, local residents spent the day in the active pursuit of pleasure. For more than a century, Sunday was the city's traditional day for recreation, the day on which military parades, balls, theaters, and sports enjoyed their greatest vogue. Henry Whipple, later Episcopal bishop of Minnesota, noted the unusual approach to the Lord's Day when he visited the city in 1844: "Sunday in New Orleans loses the quiet stillness which hallows the day in New England," he confided to his travel journal. "Here it is a day of leisure not of rest. It is a day of toil, not in business, but in pleasure seeking." Later in the nineteenth century, the contrast between Sundays in New Orleans and in other sections of the country became less obvious, but until well after the Civil War, James Buckingham's sage observation that "the difference of climate between the North and South is not greater than the difference of manners in Boston and New Orleans" remained basically true.[11]

Many visitors expressed shock after spending their first Sunday in the Crescent City. DeWitt C. Roberts, a local journalist in the 1850s, neatly summed up the amazement of Yankee tourists in the "American Paris": "To the stranger . . . who has been reared in

[10] William R. Hogan, "Sin and Sports," in Ralph Slovenko and James A. Knight (eds.), *Motivations in Play, Games and Sports* (Springfield, Ill., 1967), 121–32. The statement by the minister is from H. A. Graves, *Andrew Jackson Potter: The Noted Pastor of the Texan Frontier* (Nashville, 1890), 448, quoted in *ibid.*, 122.

[11] Lester B. Shippee (ed.), *Bishop Whipple's Southern Diary, 1843–1844* (Minneapolis, 1937), 98–99; Buckingham, *The Slave States*, I, 342.

communities . . . where the Sabbath is looked on solely as a day
of rest from labor, and not as a day of rest and amusement combined, New Orleans seems a very wicked, God-defying city." And so
it did. A strait-laced Vermonter who passed through the city in
1848 on his way to Mexico wrote to his niece: "There is a great deal
of business going on here & a great deal of Sin—There seems to be
more Sin committed than I had apprehended." To young Whipple,
who on one Sunday recorded twenty separate violations of the
Sabbath, the city's moral laxity was cause for national concern.
"Well may we blush with shame when such scenes are enacted in a
Christian land," he lamented. "In a land of Bibles. In a land of
sanctuary privileges. Little do the denizens of a quiet northern
village know of the sin & wickedness committed on this day." [12]

New Orleans' refusal to turn Sunday into a day of melancholy
was, of course, a French and Spanish legacy. Many of the immigrants who settled in the city also favored Sunday amusements and
thus bolstered support for the Continental Sunday. But in the minds
of Anglo-Americans, carefree observance of the Sabbath was almost
invariably associated with the Roman Catholic Creole population.
With the exception of young hellions who ignored the "restraints of
home & stifling conscience" and joined the Creoles in what critics
regarded as a mad rush to moral destruction, the predominantly
Protestant American community discountenanced the city's peculiar
Sunday habits. Blue-nosed Anglo-Americans, casting themselves in
the role of "heroic spirits . . . contending manfully against the
vast waves of vice, dissipation, corruption, error and crime," argued
that desecration of the Sabbath was incompatible with the American
way of life and thus, according to an editorial writer for the
intensely anti-Catholic *Semi-Weekly Creole,* "cannot date back to
the time when stern, indomitable men planted the seeds of empire in
the wilderness, or heroes nurtured its growth in the times of revolutionary struggle." Protestant laymen and clergymen alike chided

12 DeWitt C. Roberts, *Southern Sketches; or, Eleven Years Down South, In-
cluding Three Years in Dixie* (Jacksonville, Fla., 1865), 21; G. Loomis to Charity
Loomis, February 23, 1848, G. Loomis Letter (Department of Archives and Man-
uscripts, Louisiana State University); *New Orleans As It Is,* 6; Shippee (ed.),
Bishop Whipple's Southern Diary, 100, 119–20. For similar comments, see George
Lewis, *Impressions of America and the American Churches* (Edinburgh, 1845),
188; and James R. Creecy, *Scenes in the South and Other Miscellaneous Pieces*
(Washington, D.C., 1860), 20–23.

the city for its alleged immorality and urged residents to improve the "moral tone of our city." [13]

Such admonitions had little effect. While strident Protestant voices called for sweeping moral reform, there were also voices of moderation. The liberal Reverend Theodore Clapp criticized narrow-minded Protestants who opposed innocent Sunday amusements: "Such absurd views have invested the Christian Sunday with forbidding gloom and melancholy, darkness and mourning, made it revolting to the glad spirit of childhood, and surrounded it with associations to young minds inexpressibly odious and terrific." Clapp also scoffed at the widely circulated notion that the inhabitants of New Orleans were "more corrupt, or depraved, or worldly, than those who live in Boston and its vicinity." He wrote: "Upon the whole, New Orleans perhaps is rising as rapidly in the scale of moral and religious improvement as could be reasonably expected." [14]

More effective than moderation in overcoming opposition to the Continental Sabbath was apathy. In a predominantly Catholic city, many Protestants preferred to ignore the city's licentiousness as long as it did not interfere with their business. John G. Dunlap, who left his family in Georgia to seek his fortune in New Orleans, wrote to his wife in 1844: "I do not like New Orleans, and nothing but the advancement of my business prospects would on any account induce me to remain in it. To the gay and dissipated, it may have attractions," but the dedicated businessman felt "a degree of isolation . . . that is perfectly chilling." [15] As did many Anglo-American merchants, for the sake of his commercial success Dunlap chose to acquiesce in a social environment of which he disapproved.

Adjusting moral attitudes to accommodate business interests severely weakened opposition to the Creole Sunday. As early as

[13] Shippee (ed), *Bishop Whipple's Southern Diary,* 100; New Orleans *Semi-Weekly Creole,* April 28, February 21, 1855, quoted in Robert C. Reinders, "A Social History of New Orleans, 1850–1860" (Ph.D. dissertation, University of Texas, 1957), 373, 401; Thomas Kelah Wharton Diaries (Microfilm in Special Collections, Tulane University Library; originals in Manuscripts Division, New York Public Library), April 1, 1854. Quotations in this paragraph are in the order cited. See also W. C. Duncan, *Ladies' Pulpit Offering* (New Orleans, 1856), 113.

[14] Theodore Clapp, *Autobiographical Sketches and Recollections, During a Thirty-Five Years' Residence in New Orleans* (Boston, 1857), 383, 253–54.

[15] John G. Dunlap to Beatrice A. Dunlap, December 2, 1844, John G. Dunlap Papers (Special Collections, Tulane University Library).

1859 an English visitor recorded the willingness of some Anglo-Americans to accept Sunday recreation: "When the Yankees first went to New Orleans, with their Puritan ideas and habits, they were shocked at this desecration of the Sabbath, but they did not fail to imitate and exceed it. . . . As the Yankees go to extremes in everything, when they do break the Sabbath they break it into very small pieces." After the Civil War, the contrast between Creole and Protestant-American Sundays all but disappeared. The Englishman George Sala, who toured the city in 1880, remarked: "They have ideas of their own as to the observance of the Sabbath on the banks of the Mississippi. The Roman Catholics go to mass; the Anglo-Americans go to church or to meeting; and, after that, all proved to enjoy themselves to the very fullest extent allowed by custom, and, I suppose, warranted by law." [16]

As the ordinary citizens accepted part of the Creole mores, clerical opposition also declined. The Methodist minister John Mathews, who presided over several congregations in the 1870s and 1880s, regretfully observed: "Public sentiment in New Orleans is very strong in favor of certain doubtful expedients. The German Churches have Sunday picnics, and beer drinking on Sunday, dancing and the like subverting pleasures. The Episcopalians had a mule race to raise money to advance their interests." [17]

Evangelicals continued to man the barricades against desecration of the Sabbath, but their efforts produced little change in the city's leisure practices. In 1882 the Reverend Benjamin M. Palmer, pastor of the First Presbyterian Church for many years before and after the war, encouraged other ministers and laymen to join with him in establishing a Sabbath Observance League, which was active for several years. "Let us arise to our duty as professing Christians and redeem the Sabbath . . . from the desecration over which we mourn," Palmer urged his followers. How well the movement succeeded may be judged by perusing local newspapers of the eighties. In the months and years following the founding of the Sabbath

---

[16] Thomas L. Nichols, *Forty Years of American Life* (2nd ed.; London, 1874), 133; George A. Sala, *America Revisited: From the Bay of New York to the Gulf of Mexico, and from Lake Michigan to the Pacific* (5th ed.; London, 1885), 330.

[17] John Mathews, *Peeps into Life: Autobiography of Rev. John Mathews, D. D., a Minister of the Gospel for Sixty Years* (n.p., 1904), 167.

Observance League, Sunday amusements remained the mainstay and the hallmark of social life.[18] Similarly, when the legislature in 1886 passed a Sunday closing law, which affected not only business establishments but also places of amusement, it had a limited impact on leisure-time activities. Advocates of the measure, including both Protestant ministers and laymen, organized the Sunday Law and Order League to encourage enforcement, but pleasure seekers found ways to circumvent the law. The act served a useful purpose, however, because it ended Sunday work for a number of employees who in the past had been "unjustly deprived of their lawful rest and recreation." [19]

Sunday freedom proved instrumental in the rise of sports in New Orleans. Forced to work long hours in a six-day workweek, many residents had no other day for recreation. Had there been no tradition of pleasure seeking on Sunday, had the city labored instead under the blue-nosed restrictions of a New England Sabbath, the great mass of clerks and workingmen would have been excluded from participation in many of the city's amusements. Sports would have remained almost exclusively an upper-class pastime, becoming a mass movement only after the belated acceptance of the five-day workweek. New Orleans' Continental Sunday, an established tradition long before 1850, acted as a veritable social greenhouse, providing sports a nourishing, invigorating environment in which to grow.

Although recreation was a year-round avocation for many residents, the quest for amusing diversions reached its peak each year in the fall and winter. Throughout most of the nineteenth century, the city was regarded as hopelessly unhealthy and uncomfortably humid in the summer months. From May until October, visitors and well-to-do residents abandoned the city to yellow fever epidemics and muggy weather. The normally gay social life diminished noticeably. But when the temperature cooled and the danger from yellow fever subsided, seasonal residents, planters from the region, and tourists

18 Benjamin M. Palmer, *Sermons* (New Orleans, 1883), 25. See also Benjamin M. Palmer, *The Sabbath Was Made for Man: Sermon* (New Orleans, 1887); and Thomas C. Johnson, *The Life and Letters of Benjamin Morgan Palmer* (Richmond, Va., 1906), 436–38.

19 New Orleans *Daily Picayune*, May 1, 1882; December 20, 1886; February 21, 1887.

returned to participate in the many amusements of the social season. An English traveler who visited the city in January, 1857, wrote: "From all the neighbouring States the planters come in with their wives and daughters, and spend one or more weeks, or even months, in dancing, fiddling, flirting, smoking cigars, and abusing Abolitionists." Places devoted to festivity and entertainment then attracted "thousands of pleasure-seekers, who gather from all parts of the country, and from beyond the sea, to take part in the gay carnival for which our city, in 'the season,' is unequaled by any other on the continent." [20]

Residents forced to remain at home during the summer seldom lacked amusements. In a city so unequivocally committed to recreation, summer lethargy failed to blunt the desire for entertainment. One visitor noted that while wealthy residents spent the summer far removed from the danger of contagious epidemics, "the petty tradesmen and mechanics, who are generally permanent residents, do all they can during the day to earn their dollars, which they seldom fail to spend before the next morning, in having a good time at the theatre, the opera, the circus, the concert, the ten-pin alley, the ball room, the billiard saloon, the cafes, or the unnumbered gambling and drinking establishments." [21] For the sports enthusiast, hastily arranged horse races and sailing regattas also helped to relieve summer boredom.

Although fear of yellow fever prompted an annual summer exodus, the frequent occurrence of epidemics only briefly interrupted the permanent residents' preoccupation with recreation. John Dunlap, the transplanted Georgia merchant, was shocked by the seemingly indecent rapidity with which residents forgot the epidemic of 1847. "You scarcely hear the fever named," he wrote to his wife, "and in a few brief weeks the dead will be forgotten, and the living plunging in hot haste into the deep vortex of dissipation, reckless of the past, and forgetful of the future." Even the great epidemic of 1853, which, in the words of one historian, "literally decimated" the city, only partly curtailed pleasure seeking. John Smith, a local

20 James Stirling, *Letters from the Slave States* (London, 1857; repr. ed., New York, 1969), 150; New Orleans *Daily Picayune,* October 6, 1860.

21 Charles Lanman, *Adventures in the Wilds of the United States and British American Provinces* (Philadelphia, 1856), II, 201.

writer for the *Spirit of the Times*, warned readers not to imagine
that the absence of theaters and balls during the epidemic had cast
a funeral pall over the city. "Mirth has ruled its hours as well as
melancholy, pleasure as well as pain," he noted, "for many have not
had an acquaintance to die or even to be sick, and 20,000 New Orleanians scattered about the coast from here to Mobile have engaged
in their holiday pastimes with more than wonted alacrity." Many
residents treated an outbreak of yellow fever as an accident of nature. When the disease visited the city, as it did so often throughout much of the nineteenth century, those who remained in town
viewed it as a temporary inconvenience. Perhaps like William P.
Riddell, a local scientist, they asked if they could "alter one jot
. . . the laws and course of nature . . . or the decrees of fate," and
concluded, as he did during the epidemic of 1853, that the certainty
of death "this year or the next—or the next, or at least within a
certain prescribed limit," rendered deep concern futile and foolish.
Just as New Orleanians chose to avoid the restraints of a Protestant
Sunday, so too did they resolve that the dangers of yellow fever
would not alter their leisure habits. People of all classes could, on
any day of the week and during all seasons of the year, amuse themselves freely in "the city that care forgot." [22]

22 John G. Dunlap to Beatrice A. Dunlap, October 4, 1847, John G. Dunlap
Papers; John Duffy, *Sword of Pestilence: The New Orleans Yellow Fever Epidemic of 1853* (Baton Rouge, 1966), 167; *Spirit of the Times,* XXIII (October 15,
1853), 410; William P. Riddell Journals (typescript in Special Collections, Tulane
University Library), July 31, 1853. After the Civil War the threat of yellow fever
gradually diminished as a rising standard of living, a more effective drainage and
sanitation program, and an improved quarantine system sharply reduced the
incidence of the disease. John Duffy, "Pestilence in New Orleans," in Carter (ed.),
Past as Prelude, 112–13.

Part One

ANTEBELLUM BEGINNINGS

INTRODUCTION

The rise of organized sports, usually associated with the tremendous expansion of cities after the Civil War, began in the antebellum period. Before 1860 the United States passed through the first stages of the transition from a fairly simple, rural-agrarian society to a highly complex, urban-industrial community. Between 1815 and 1860, cities grew at a rapid rate; proportionately, they increased faster than at any time in the country's history. The process of urbanization, which was to become so strikingly evident after 1865, created a variety of needs, including a need for new forms of recreation.

As people migrated to cities, they found themselves cut off from amusements popular in rural settings. Since urban conditions made it difficult for many residents to provide their own diversions, commercial amusements and organized spectacles arose to provide leisure outlets in the city. The theater, once limited in appeal to the planter and merchant aristocracy, became a democratic institution that drew customers from all ranks of society. "The rapid increase in population in newly formed cities," wrote one observant actor, "produces a style of patrons whose habits and associations afford no opportunity for the cultivation of the arts." [1] Minstrel shows and circuses traveled from city to city, and clever promoters concocted a variety of diversions. No one surpassed P. T. Barnum in sheer ability to amuse the populace. Whether luring wide-eyed gawkers into his American Museum or touting the virtues of Jenny Lind, Barnum proved conclusively that the urban masses represented a lucrative market for organized spectacles.

Whatever the appeal of theaters, minstrelsy, circuses, and dime

[1] William Davidge, *Footlight Flashes* (New York, 1867), 202, quoted in Dulles, *A History of Recreation*, 100.

museums, they were not entirely satisfactory substitutes for the leisure activities associated with rural living. Commercial spectacles, no matter how alluring, could not entirely supplant rural pastimes that encouraged participation and took people into the out-of-doors. Sports thus made great strides in the antebellum period by catering to a desire for participant sports and outdoor activities. Encouraged by organized clubs and teams, urban sports offered some residents an opportunity for active involvement and a great many others the excitement of vicarious participation. As early as the 1820s, crowds of from twenty thousand to fifty thousand thronged grandstands for horse races or pedestrian contests and lined river banks and seashores for rowing matches or sailing regattas.[2] Cities along the Atlantic seaboard pioneered in the development of sporting pastimes, but cities in the South, particularly New Orleans, quickly joined the movement.

Many factors stimulated the rise of sports in New Orleans. The patronage of wealthy planters and merchants, frontier and rural influences, contributions by foreign-born residents, the presence of a large number of northern-born citizens, and the increasing pressures of urban life contributed to the emergence and growth of organized sporting pastimes. People also recognized that the exercise provided by sports had great value for sedentary residents and idle youths. The *Picayune* in 1858 recommended outdoor sports as a means of curbing "precociousness in vice" and of reducing the rising number of "youthful law breakers." The competitiveness of inhabitants further aided the development of sports. Riverboat captains who engaged in impromptu races on the Mississippi; firemen who raced horse-drawn hook-and-ladder trucks when returning from fires; and young turfmen who rode recklessly to the Metairie Course trying to make "2:40 on the Shell road" demonstrated the ability of residents to make play of everyday occurrences. Such people quite naturally welcomed the opportunity to direct competitive impulses into organized outlets.[3]

2 Good summaries of the early development of sports can be found in Holliman, *American Sports (1785–1835)*; Krout, *Annals of American Sport, passim,* but especially chapters 1–5; and Dulles, *A History of Recreation,* chapters 8, 9, and 11.

3 New Orleans *Daily Picayune,* October 10, 1858; Olmsted, *A Journey in the Seaboard Slave States,* 613–14; New Orleans *Daily Crescent,* October 6, 20, 1856;

Sports in New Orleans generally fell into two categories: sports of the upper classes and sports of the masses. Classes in New Orleans and throughout the state were, as Roger Shugg has demonstrated, sharply divided socially, economically, and politically in the 1840s and 1850s.[4] Sports, like other forms of recreation, reflected these divisions. After the Civil War, sports steadily became more and more democratic, ultimately cutting across class lines, but in the ante-bellum period they generally mirrored the caste and class pattern that characterized society in the prewar South. A number of activities, such as horse racing, yachting, rowing, baseball, and cricket, rose to prominence because they received the support of the city's upper class, composed chiefly of the most affluent merchants and planters, and of the upper middle class, which included comfortable business men and merchants and members of the leading professions. As these sporting pastimes became popular, they attracted spectators and sometimes participants from nearly all ranks of society, but before the war they remained primarily upper-class and upper-middle-class amusements. Other sports, such as prize fighting, pedestrianism, animal baiting, target shooting, billiards, bowling, and *raquette,* belonged to the masses. People who either occupied or aspired to high social standing occasionally participated in or observed these activities, but these sports attracted most of their followers from the city's lower middle class, which consisted mainly of clerks and other salaried workers, tradesmen, shopkeepers, and government employees, and from the working class, which included longshoremen, sailors, boatmen, construction workers, and canal diggers. As the following chapters demonstrate, sports existed for people of all classes in 1860, but organized sports as a whole had yet to become a truly democratic leisure-time activity.

James L. Baughman, "A Southern Spa: Ante-Bellum Lake Pontchartrain," *Louisiana History,* III (Winter, 1962), 27.

4 Roger W. Shugg, *Origins of Class Struggle in Louisiana: A Social History of White Farmers and Laborers During Slavery and After, 1840–1875* (Baton Rouge, 1939), chapters 1–6.

Chapter II
MERCHANTS AND
PLANTERS AT PLAY

America's upper classes have always been attracted to sports. Because this country has never had a clear-cut definition of aristocracy and gentility, those who aspire to high social standing have had to resort to what Thorstein Veblen called "conspicuous consumption" and "conspicuous leisure" to advance their claims. These methods of establishing social leadership have taken a number of forms at various stages in the country's history, but sport has consistently given vent to the quest for publicly recognized status. The close relationship between sport and social aristocracy, as historian Dixon Wecter observed, is an Anglo-Saxon concept. "Among Europeans," he wrote, "only the upper-class Englishman really sees in sport a way of life and the cult of gentlemanliness. He may doubt some of the eternal verities, but his blood tells him that to gallop across the downs, to live much with dogs and horses and the smell of the earth, and to feel the salt wind against his cheek as he grips the wheel, are good things and requisite to the salvation of his class." [1]

Claimants to gentlemanliness and social leadership in this country have followed this code of conduct from the colonial period, when horse racing and riding to the hounds were sports of the gentry, down to the present, when polo and yachting, as well as horse racing, are regarded as indications of superior status. By patronizing sports that only people of wealth and leisure can afford to play, America's well-to-do have sought to establish themselves as the social elite. Gentlemen and would-be gentlemen, old-guard social leaders and parvenus, men of established wealth and *nouveau riche* have all attempted to dissociate themselves from the middling and

[1] Dixon Wecter, *The Saga of American Society: A Record of Social Aspiration, 1607–1937* (New York, 1937), 428–29. The subject of gentlemanliness is also treated at length in Edwin L. Cady, *The Gentleman in America: A Literary Study in American Culture* (Syracuse, 1949).

lower sorts through the steady and assiduous cultivation of sports. If ordinary people find the sports of the rich appealing and begin to participate, as has often been the case, the well-to-do move on to other, more exclusive pastimes. In this way upper-class sportsmen have introduced and popularized a number of sports.

Affluent New Orleanians, like people of means elsewhere, also sought to establish high social rank through the patronage of expensive sporting pastimes. This interest in sports, however, was mainly an Anglo-American characteristic. In many respects the city's upper and upper middle classes were close-knit mixtures of Anglo-Americans, French and Spanish Creoles, and some immigrants (mainly French and German), united by intermarriage and the common pursuit of and possession of wealth. But in some ways these groups remained divided, particularly in their leisure habits. French and Spanish Creoles, well known for their devotion to amusement generally confined their pleasure seeking to masked balls, concerts, the theater, games of chance, and the like; they seldom shared the Anglo-American's love of sports. Not until after the Civil War did they begin to feel the sporting impulse that has gripped many of America's affluent citizens since the colonial period. Consequently the emergence of upper-class and upper-middle-class sports before 1860 was almost entirely attributable to Anglo-Americans. Giving freely of their time and money, they made New Orleans a leading center of organized sports.

Horse racing was the first sport to stir great interest among the well-to-do in the lower South. Long a pastime of the wealthy, American thoroughbred racing traced its roots to the seventeenth century. During the colonial period the sport was popular mainly in New York and the southern colonies, but after the Revolution it spread over the greater part of the young republic. Patrons of the turf imported breeding and racing stock and organized jockey clubs to regulate racing and to finance the construction of grandstands; and onlookers by the thousands crowded the multitude of tracks that dotted the country from New York to New Orleans. By the 1820s racing had become more than a pastime for the wealthy few; it was also a great spectator sport. In the East, however, racing's appeal declined sharply in the 1840s, mainly because of a strong anti-gambling crusade. Eastern racing survived, but it failed to regain its former popularity until after the Civil War.[2]

With the decline of turf sports in New York, New Orleans ascended to national leadership. In the twenties and thirties, prosperous cotton and sugar planters of the Lower Mississippi Valley, many of whom were either migrants or the sons of migrants from other southern states where racing was an established pastime for the gentry, began to encourage thoroughbred racing. They purchased racers from Virginia and Kentucky, imported breeding stock from abroad, and organized jockey clubs to build racecourses and to regulate contests. New Orleans soon emerged as the center of turf sports in this section. Its first course was little more than a running track built in 1814 or 1815 on General Wade Hampton's plantation, but in the next decade turfmen constructed several fully equipped racecourses. Early tracks in the city included the Live Oak Course, built between 1820 and 1822 on the plantation of François de Livaudais, just above Canal Street near what is now Race Street; the Jackson Course, completed in 1826; and the New Orleans Course, where races were first run in 1828. These tracks survived only a short time, but they attracted sufficient support to demonstrate the commercial possibilities of racing.[3]

Horse racing's popularity soared markedly in the thirties and forties as professional promoters, experienced turfmen from the upper South, and aspiring sportsmen from Louisiana and Mississippi collaborated to make the sport a sound undertaking. In the late 1830s local and out-of-town turfmen founded three jockey clubs, which financed construction of the Eclipse Course (1837) just outside Carrollton on the site of what is now Audubon Park; the Metairie Course (1838) on Metairie Ridge in Jefferson Parish at the

[2] Krout, *Annals of American Sport,* 34; Charles B. Parmer, *For Gold and Glory: The Story of Thoroughbred Racing in America* (New York, 1939), 90.

[3] For a brief account of racing in New Orleans before 1850, consult John Hervey, *Racing in America, 1665-1865* (New York, 1944), II, 181–93. For information on the city's early tracks, see the item from the New Orleans *Louisiana Courier,* October 4, 1822, in the New Orleans Scrapbook, 1813–1865 (Department of Archives and Manuscripts, Louisiana State University); and New Orleans *Daily Picayune,* March 28, 1880. For example of the interest shown by planters in the acquisition of thoroughbreds, see William J. Minor to John Minor, November 9, 1827, William J. Minor and Family Papers (Department of Archives and Manuscripts, Louisiana State University).

juncture of the Metairie and Shell roads where the Metairie Cemetery is today; and the Louisiana Course (1838) located where the
Pontchartrain Railroad crossed Gentilly Road. The Metairie, which
was to become the city's leading racecourse, had a regulation one-
mile oval and a modest grandstand 250 feet in length. These tracks
thrived for a time, but the depression ushered in by the Panic of 1837
forced the Louisiana and Eclipse courses to close temporarily in the
early 1840s. By that time, however, racing had become a firmly
established pastime, and when economic pressures eased, racecourse
construction resumed. In 1846 Colonel Yelverton N. Oliver, a promoter who had developed successful tracks in several cities and who
had formerly managed the Eclipse Course, joined with Colonel Adam
L. Bingaman, a well-known Natchez turfman and politician, to build
the Bingaman Course in Algiers, a small community across the river
from New Orleans. Evidently convinced by hard times that racing
had to attract a broad following, Oliver announced in January,
1847, that he planned to make the Bingaman "pre-eminently the
people's track," a task that was accomplished in part by reducing
the admission fee from a dollar to fifty cents and by admitting ladies
free of charge. The Bingaman also offered popular entertainment,
such as bull and bear fights and "Welsh Main races," which other
tracks, managed by more conventional turfmen, refused to consider.
Oliver and Bingaman engaged Richard Ten Broeck, an ambitious
promoter from Albany, New York, to supervise the track, which
opened in the spring of 1847. Ten Broeck also purchased an interest
in the Metairie Course.[4]

Ten Broeck arrived in the city at a fortuitous time. The deterio-
ration of turf sports in the East in the forties gave him an opportunity to raise the prestige of racing in the South and to shift the
center of the sport from New York to New Orleans. He proved equal
to the occasion. He first increased the amount of prize money, a policy that attracted the country's leading stables. Although travel

---

[4] *Spirit of the Times*, XVI (January 2, 1847), 534; XXII (March 20, 1852),
54; XXII (July 17, 1852), 259; New Orleans *Daily Picayune*, May 5, 1850; Hervey,
Racing in America, II, 183–85, 188–90. A "Welsh Main race" was a horse race between winners of a series of heat races held throughout the day of the event. In
March, 1852, for example, the Bingaman held a Welsh race which featured a heat
every hour beginning at noon. The winners of five preliminary heats raced at
5 P.M. for a purse of two hundred dollars. *Spirit of the Times*, XXII (March 20,
1852), 54.

facilities were still fairly crude, turfmen from as far away as Tennessee, Kentucky, and Virginia regularly competed in New Orleans. Ten
Broeck next sought to attract more spectators from the city's social
aristocracy by giving racing "a much higher character." He established the Metairie Association, a joint-stock company which purchased full control of the already fashionable Metairie Course in
1851 and provided the funds for a complete renovation of the track's
facilities. He erected new stables, enlarged and beautified the grandstand, and furnished the ladies' stand with parlors and retiring
rooms where female fans could rest between races.[5] Attempts by Ten
Broeck and other turfmen to win the support of women, an indication of respectability and fashionableness, placed them in the van-
guard of those American sportsmen who recognized that commercial
success in almost any sport depended heavily on the feminine seal of
approval.

Ten Broeck's endeavors raised racing enthusiasm to a new level.
His success at the Bingaman and Metairie courses persuaded turfmen to reopen the Louisiana Course in 1851, thus giving the city
three tracks, each of which sponsored week-long spring and fall
meetings. The Bingaman Course closed in the summer of 1852 when
its owners decided to sell the land for town lots, but later in the year
sportsmen laid out the Union Course at the junction of the Bayou
and Gentilly roads. Racing spirit, said one resident, "is so confirmed
here, that scrub races are run on nearly every Sunday during the
interval between the Spring and Autumn meetings of the Clubs." [6]

Racing in New Orleans provided pleasure mainly for well-to-do
citizens. Sunday scrub races attracted mixed crowds, but regular
meetings catered to the affluent. The jockey clubs, dominated by
Anglo-Americans who had yet to accept the Continental Sunday, almost invariably scheduled races for weekday afternoons, thus effectively precluding working-class attendance. Because New Orleans,
like any city, had many inhabitants who might be idle on any day
of the week, such as seasonal workers, newcomers who had not yet
secured work, and professional sporting men, the clubs completed

5 *Spirit of the Times,* XXI (March 1, 1851), 18; XXI (March 22, 1851), 54;
Hervey, *Racing in America,* II, 184.
6 *Spirit of the Times,* XX (June 8, 1850), 186; XXI (May 17, 1851), 150;
XXII (July 17, 1852), 259; XXII (October 9, 1852), 402

the process of social winnowing through seating arrangements at the tracks. Women, who came by invitation, occupied seats in the ladies' stand; members of the clubs and their guests watched from the members' stand; all other spectators were consigned indiscriminately to the public stand or the track infield. Some mingling occurred between races when men of all ranks descended on the barrooms and gambling tables beneath the stands, but in general class lines were rigidly drawn. The one-dollar admission fee at all tracks except the Bingaman also served to discourage working-class attendance because that figure represented a day's wages or more for many of the city's laborers.[7] Racing's social prestige was further assured by its close relationship with the city's leading men's clubs. Throughout the nineteenth century, these associations attempted to uphold the idea of the true gentleman, which involved, among other things, a strong interest in horsemanship and fine blooded horses. At least two clubs, the Orleans and the Gaiety, drew most of their members from the city's avid turf followers, and several gentlemen's associations, including the exclusive Boston Club, encouraged racing by contributing purse money.[8]

Opinions of racing in New Orleans varied widely. At least one English observer found the efforts of local sportsmen pretentious and ridiculous. "The sporting gentlemen of New Orleans," wrote Matilda C. F. Houstoun, "with long hunting-whips in their hands, were clothed in what they seemed, in the ignorance of their hearts, to consider a sort of racing costume; green cutaway coats, with metal buttons, being evidently considered as the 'correct thing' to wear on these *sporting* occasions. The great and knowing men among them, . . . who were looked up to as oracles from having learnt what horse-racing *really was* at New York, had taken possession of the stand, and were laying down the law about a certain 'Lady Sarah' who was to win everything." The scene, she concluded, was a "mockery" of Epsom and Newmarket. But residents and visitors usually expressed altogether different opinions. Despite the exclusiveness of

---

7 *Ibid.*, XX (April 13, 1850), 90; XXI (March 1, 1851), 18.
8 *Ibid.*, XXVIII April 17, 1858), 114; XXIX (April 16, 1859), 115; [William H. Coleman] (ed.), *Historical Sketch Book and Guide to New Orleans and Environs* (New York, 1885), 94–95; Reinders, *End of an Era, 159;* Wecter, *The Saga of American Society*, chapter 7, especially pp. 252–54.

racing, as many as twenty thousand people assembled for races, and most seemed well satisfied. In a report of the spring meeting of 1860, a correspondent for *Wilkes' Spirit of the Times*, a New York sporting journal, observed that "hotels and boarding houses were crowded to their utmost capacity by persons from all sections of the sunny South, and with many representatives from the North." [9]

Antebellum racing differed from the modern sport in a number of ways. Rather than the single dash of today, races consisted of heats at distances of one, two, three, or four miles, a practice designed to develop "bottom" (endurance) as well as speed. Since winning horses had to capture two or three heats (depending on the distance), contests sometimes required as many as eight heats. Fans wagered on a personal basis, for there were no bookmakers or pari-mutuel machines at antebellum tracks. In the absence of modern mechanical devices, jockeys rode their mounts to the starting line; the tap of a drum set them off.

An unusual feature of racing was the light regard accorded jockeys, many of whom were slaves. With rare exceptions, such as the famous professional Gilbert W. Patrick and Duncan F. Kenner's slave Abe Hawkins, few jockeys became widely known for their riding ability. Even the shrewdest of antebellum turfmen placed their confidence in the horse; a well-qualified rider, though desirable, was thought to contribute little to a race's outcome. In the 1850s clubs adopted rules requiring jockeys to weigh before the race and after each heat and to wear high boots, with shirts and caps dyed to represent the colors of his horse's owner.[10] Track stewards ensured honest rides by banning jockeys who deliberately lost. For example, on one occasion the Metairie Jockey Club expelled Abe Hawkins "for plain, positive, and palpable dishonesty—in plain terms, 'throwing

---

[9] Matilda C. F. Houstoun, *Hesperos; or, Travels in the West* (London, 1850), II, 70; *Wilkes' Spirit of the Times,* I (January 21, 1860), 315; Roberts, *Southern Sketches,* 23. For examples of reactions to local racing, see Duncan Shaw Diary (Special Collections, Tulane University Library), April 28, 1852; Gustave A. Breaux Diaries (Special Collections, Tulane University Library), April 1, 1859; Louis A. Bringier to Stella Bringier, January 6, 1858, and April 6, 1861, Louis A. Bringier and Family Papers (Department of Archives and Manuscripts, Louisiana State University).

[10] *Spirit of the Times,* XXII (February 21, 1852), 3; Roberts, *Southern Sketches,* 23; Arvilla Taylor, "Horse Racing in the Lower Mississippi Valley Prior to 1860" (M.A. thesis, University of Texas, 1953), 45.

off' a race which he had already won, by sawing his horse around." [11]

Racing in New Orleans remained consistently excellent primarily because of the single-minded devotion and intense competitiveness of the planter aristocracy that ruled the local turf. Determined to demonstrate the superiority of their thoroughbreds, cotton and sugar planters of the Lower Mississippi Valley brought their stables to the city for every regular meeting. They had little to gain financially, because purses, which were raised by entry fees and contributions from hotels, social clubs, and newspapers, were small by present standards. Moreover trainers' salaries, transportation charges, stabling fees, and other costs cut deeply into apparent profits. But the credo of the gentleman sportsman, which governed the activities of these representatives of the southern gentry as it had turfmen before them, disparaged pecuniary gain. Satisfaction flowed not from monetary rewards but from demolishing the opposition with a great racer. Duncan F. Kenner and Thomas J. Wells of Louisiana, and William J. Minor and Adam L. Bingaman of Mississippi developed the leading thoroughbreds in the area, but invaders from the upper South and lesser-known regional turfmen periodically challenged their domination of the winner's circle. Although not limited to local tracks, this rivalry among southern turfmen produced some of the country's leading racers. By the 1850s New York's *Spirit of the Times*, the nation's leading turf and sporting journal, recognized New Orleans as the national center of thoroughbred racing.[12]

Racing reached its pinnacle in the mid-fifties with a series of three races at four-mile heats between Richard Ten Broeck's horse Lexington, and Lecomte, from the stable of Thomas J. Wells. The first of these races, held April 1, 1854, was the Great State Post Stakes, which brought together horses representing Alabama, Kentucky, Louisiana, and Mississippi. Twenty thousand people, including several governors, mayors, judges, and former President Millard

---

[11] *Spirit of the Times*, XXI (May 10, 1851), 139. Matilda Houstoun also observed an example of this "horse-racing morality." Houstoun, *Hesperos*, II, 72.

[12] *Spirit of the Times*, XX (April 6, 1850), 78; XXI (March 22, 1851), 54; XXI (April 26, 1851), 115; XXI (February 14, 1852), 618; XXII (April 17, 1852), 102; XXII (April 24, 1852), 114–15; XXII (May 1, 1852), 126; XXIII (May 7, 1853), 138.

Fillmore, assembled at the Metairie for the event. "Business seemed
. . . to be suspended," said one observer; "everybody who was anybody, or wanted to be deemed anybody, had gone to the race." Lexington, representing Kentucky, won two straight heats to claim the
purse and a nationwide reputation for speed.[13]

Wells, whose horse Lecomte had run for Louisiana, immediately
requested a rematch. On April 8 another huge crowd gathered to
watch Lexington and Lecomte in what one spectator called "the
greatest four mile race on record." Lecomte more than justified
Wells's confidence. He won two consecutive heats and set a new
world's record of seven minutes, twenty-six seconds for the four-
mile distance. Some critics discounted the record since Lecomte
carried less weight than northern rules specified. Turfmen had periodically attempted to standardize age and weight regulations, because for years the fast times attributed to southern thoroughbreds
had been questioned. Success in this venture came after the Civil War
when travel improvements encouraged more intersectional competition, but in the 1850s regional variations in rules placed a blemish
on Lecomte's record. Nevertheless, most experts recognized Wells's
horse as the country's leading thoroughbred.[14]

Among those who doubted Lecomte's superiority was Richard
Ten Broeck. Contending that Lecomte had won only because Lexington erroneously pulled up after three miles, he offered to race his
stallion against Lecomte's time for ten thousand dollars or against
any horse for from ten to twenty thousand. William J. Minor, who
had backed Lecomte, wrote to Wells: "The Lex. party here are very
sure and very confident—They still think Lex. had Lcte. dead beat
at the end of three miles in the 2d heat of the 2d race." Wells at
first declined a rematch, but two Virginia turfmen bet that Lexing-

[13] The events leading up to this race can be traced in the *Spirit of the Times,*
XXIII (April 2, 1853), 78; XXIII (April 23, 1853), 115; XXIII (May 7, 1853),
138; XXIII (December 17, 1853), 522; XXIV (February 18, 1854), 6; XXIV
(March 25, 1854), 67; and Hervey, *Racing in America,* II, 284. Accounts of the
race may be found in the *Spirit of the Times,* XXIV (April 8, 1854), 90; XXIV
(April 15, 1854), 103; New York *Times,* April 4, 11, 1854; and Eliza Ripley, *Social Life in Old New Orleans; Being Recollections of My Girlhood* (New York,
1912), 245–48. The quotation is from the *Spirit of the Times,* XXIV (April 15,
1854), 103.

[14] *Spirit of the Times,* XXIV (April 15, 1854), 102; XXIV (April 22, 1854),
115; XXIV (May 27, 1854), 174; XXIV (June 10, 1854), 198.

ton would fail to better Lecomte's record run. Soon afterwards, Wells agreed to another race between Lecomte and Lexington.[15]

Ten Broeck scheduled both the time trial and the third Lexing-
ton-Lecomte race for April, 1855. On Sunday, April 1, the day of
the race against Lecomte's record, thousands of residents and visitors
filled the grandstand and spilled out onto the field of the Metairie.
With Gilbert W. Patrick riding, Lexington amazed the onlookers by
completing the four-mile run in 7:19¾. When Ten Broeck's horse
easily beat an ailing Lecomte on April 14, running one of the heats
in 7:23¾, turf enthusiasts everywhere recognized him as the greatest of American thoroughbreds. Amelia M. Murray, an English
traveler who attended the race, observed: "Though I have often
been at English races, I never before saw a horse more graceful, or
more beautifully formed, with such apparent gentleness and good
temper, and yet with such an air of conscious superiority as this
Lexington: he ran like a deer, without either effort or straining, and
his firm, elastic, reaching step in walking, gave one confidence that it
would hardly be possible for any other horse to match him." Soon
after the race, however, Ten Broeck discovered that his horse was
slowly going blind; Lexington retired to Kentucky where he became
the outstanding stud of the last century.[16]

Shortly after the 1855 season ended, Ten Broeck purchased
Lecomte and a filly named Prioress from Thomas Wells and made
preparations to take them to England with his own horse Pryor. The
superiority of English thoroughbreds had long been disputed by
Americans, and Ten Broeck now decided to settle the question on
the English turf. In July, 1856, after selling his interest in the
Metairie Course to Wells, he left for England with a stable representing "the highest and most fashionable racing blood of the United
States." Many observers thought "a better trio could have been
sent to contend for *national* honors," but Ten Broeck, the first

[15] William J. Minor to Thomas J. Wells, June 5, 1854, William J. Minor
Papers; *Spirit of the Times*, XXIV (June 3, 1854), 186; XXIV (June 17, 1854),
210; XXIV (July 8, 1854), 246.

[16] *Spirit of the Times*, XXV (April 14, 1855), 102, 103; XXV (May 5, 1855),
134; Amelia M. Murray, *Letters from the United States, Cuba and Canada* (New
York, 1856), 278; Hervey, *Racing in America*, II, 273.

American turfman to invade England, received unequivocal support from the country's racing fans.[17]

Ten Broeck went from failure to failure in England. Racing on unfamiliar hilly courses and plagued by ailments that attacked his horses because of the change in climate, he won few races in the 1850s. After his first losses American fans, unwilling to admit the inferiority of American horses, openly suggested that foul play had deprived Ten Broeck of victory. The editor of the Brooklyn *Eagle* recommended that Congress investigate the situation, and if the nation's representatives discovered dishonesty, "nothing short of the cession of Canada should satisfy our outraged dignity." [18]

When subsequent seasons proved no more successful for Ten Broeck, interest in his exploits waned. By August, 1858, the *Spirit of the Times* was "thoroughly disgusted with the miserable show which the American horses . . . have made since they have been in England." The *Spirit* now denied that Ten Broeck's invasion of Britain involved national prestige; it was "simply the experiment of an individual." Enthusiasm revived temporarily when Ten Broeck won important victories at Goodwood and Newmarket, but American followers could not overlook or forgive his imposing string of defeats on English tracks. Ten Broeck began to win consistently in the 1860s, but by then his stable included so many English racers that his efforts could scarcely be regarded as a test of American versus English thoroughbreds.[19]

While Ten Broeck was in England, racing progressed as usual in New Orleans. Wells, Kenner, and Minor reorganized the Metairie Association in 1857 and purchased Ten Broeck's interest in the Metairie Course. Improvements to the track, including the first brick and iron grandstand in the United States, helped swell attendance at meetings sponsored by the Metairie Jockey Club, which continued to regulate racing events.[20] Unable to bear competition from the Metairie, the Louisiana Course suspended operations in 1855, and

[17] *American Racing Calendar and Trotting Record* (New York, 1858), 28; *Spirit of the Times,* XXVII (May 23, 1857), 174.

[18] Quoted in *Spirit of the Times,* XXVII (August 22, 1857), 331.

[19] *Ibid.,* XXVIII (August 21, 1858), 330; XXIX (August 20, 1859), 330; *Wilkes' Spirit of the Times,* CXX (December 27, 1890), 873–75.

[20] Hervey, *Racing in America,* II, 240; *Spirit of the Times,* XXVII (April 18, 1857), 115.

the Union Course followed two years later. But racing spirit failed to decline. Southern sportsmen seemed oblivious to the nation's political strife as they turned out in ever larger numbers to watch America's best thoroughbreds race at the Metairie Course. Louis A. Bringier, a sugar planter and minor turfman, wrote to his wife a description of the spring meeting of 1861, which ended only a few days before the firing on Fort Sumter: "The stands were crowded [and] the Ladies were so numerous that the members stand had to be given up to them—I don't think that in the days of Lecompte & Lexington, there were more carriages & vehicles on the grounds of the Metairie. Every spot around the track was perfectly covered with all sorts of conveyances—and they extended way past the half way house," a popular gathering place located midway between the city and the racecourse.[21]

On the eve of the war, racing's position seemed assured. Dedicated turfmen, skillful promoters, and avid fans had made New Orleans the center of American thoroughbred racing in the 1850s. Had the Civil War not intervened, the city's mastery would probably have continued indefinitely, for in 1861 no track in America could consistently duplicate the races sponsored by the Metairie Association. Whatever the shortcomings of the region's planter class, the quality of their thoroughbreds was beyond dispute. Wealth, leisure, and land had enabled them to develop fully the southern gentry's commitment to a sport long identified with the upper classes of England and America. Racing had become a popular spectator sport in the 1850s, but even as jockey clubs attracted thousands of onlookers, racing in the South lost few of its aristocratic trappings. Racing after the Civil War was to become a more democratic and above all a commercial pastime, but the transformation of the sport resulted not so much from any deliberate action on the part of turfmen as from the war-induced decline of the planters who dominated the sport before 1861.

Thoroughbred racing claimed the loyalties of the lower South's planter class, but residents of New Orleans whose business and professional interests confined them to the city found a reasonable substitute for the sport of the gentry in trotting and pacing. Harness

21 Louis A. Bringier to Stella Bringier, April 6, 1861, Louis A. Bringier Papers.

racing, which emerged as a popular American pastime after the Revolution, met strong opposition in the rural South because southern turfmen generally regarded the gaited racer as inferior to the thoroughbred. But in a number of southern cities, notably New Orleans and Mobile, trotting and pacing gained a solid following before the Civil War.[22] Gaited racing flourished in New Orleans for several reasons. First, the city had in the 1840s and 1850s a large community of northern-born residents, many of whom had a knowledge of the sport and did not share the native southerner's hostility to trotters and pacers. Second, promoters and owners from cities where harness racing was well established, such as Cincinnati and St. Louis, helped to stimulate an interest in New Orleans. Finally, the city had many well-to-do merchants and professional men who discovered an appealing diversion in trotting and pacing. Such men perhaps lacked the money, time, or extensive land holdings necessary to successful thoroughbred racing, but they could support gaited racing. Trotting and pacing required neither great stables nor large retinues of trainers, handlers, and jockeys, but they nevertheless offered aspiring gentlemen an opportunity to indulge in sports of the turf.

Harness racing came to New Orleans in the early 1840s when "trotting *amateurs*," as a local correspondent described them, began to compete on the city's running tracks. The sport attracted a steady group of participants and organization inevitably followed. In January, 1843, a Mr. H. Gates, who had managed a trotting track in Cincinnati, came to New Orleans and assisted thirty-five local sportsmen in founding the New Orleans Trotting and Pacing Club, which adopted the rules of the Beacon Course of Hoboken, New Jersey.[23] Poor attendance forced the club to disband after two or three seasons.

Organized trotting and pacing returned to the city in 1849. Charles S. Ellis of St. Louis came South with a stable of the "best bloods" and with the help of several local horsemen, including Francis T. Porter (brother of William T. Porter, editor of the *Spirit of*

22 Dwight Akers, *Drivers Up: The Story of American Harness Racing* (New York, 1938), 75–77.

23 *Spirit of the Times,* XII (March 5, 1842), 6; XII (July 23, 1842), 248; XII (January 21, 1843), 560; XII (January 28, 1843), 572; XIII (April 22, 1843), 85; XIII (April 29, 1843), 102; Taylor, "Horse Racing in the Lower Mississippi Valley," 72–73.

the Times), revived the New Orleans Trotting and Pacing Club. Under Ellis' supervision the association attracted a number of northern and western stables, a development that was soon to make the city a major center of trotting and pacing. The club collapsed in 1851 when Ellis left town, but by that time several top-notch northern standardbreds, including Lady Suffolk, had raced in the city.[24]

For a few years after Ellis' departure, trotting and pacing proceeded on an unorganized basis. Local owners arranged challenge matches throughout the year, and in the winter, when weather conditions closed tracks in other cities, northern and western horses also raced on New Orleans tracks. Organization returned in 1855 with the formation of the Metairie Trotting and Pacing Club. Members held races at the Metairie for several years, but in 1859 the club leased the Union Course, renamed it the Creole Course, and held trotting and pacing races on that track.[25] By the late 1850s, the supporters of gaited racing could regularly see the nation's best racers, such as Flora Temple, Dolly Spanker, Tecumseh, and Pocahontas, and the country's most capable drivers, including Hiram Woodruff of New York, James L. Eoff of St. Louis, and Otis W. Dimmick of Cincinnati.[26] As good horses came from other sections, local stables also improved. In 1849, when Ellis first planned to bring Lady Suffolk to New Orleans, the *Spirit of the Times* had ridiculed the idea, contending that there was no worthy competition in the Crescent City. But in 1861 a trotter owned by Richard K. Bonham of New Orleans demolished Ethan Allen, once described by the *Spirit* as "the pride of New England." [27]

24 *Spirit of the Times, XIX* (January 12, 1850), 558; XIX (January 19, 1850), 570; XIX (January 26, 1850), 582; XX (June 15, 1850), 198; XX (June 22, 1850), 210; XX (November 30, 1850), 486; XX (December 21, 1850), 522; XX (January 4, 1851), 546; XX (February 1, 1851), 594; XXI (March 8, 1851), 30; XXI (March 29, 1851), 66; XXI (May 3, 1851), 126.

25 *Ibid.,* XXII (April 3, 1852), 78; XXII (May 15, 1852), 150; XXII (October 9, 1852), 402; XXIII (July 2, 1853), 234; XXIII (July 30, 1853), 282; XXIV (August 5, 1854), 295; XXVII (August 8, 1857), 306; XXIX (March 5, 1859), 42; New Orleans *Bee,* May 8, 1861; Reinders, "A Social History of New Orleans," 442. The Union or Creole Course became the Fair Grounds Course after the Civil War.

26 *Spirit of the Times,* XXIII (January 28, 1854), 594; XXIII (February 11, 1854), 618; XXIV (February 18, 1854), 6; XXIV (February 25, 1854), 18; XXVII (February 6, 1858), 618; XXVIII (February 20, 1858), 18; XXVIII (March 20, 1858), 66.

27 *Ibid.,* XIX (December 15, 1849), 510; XXXI (March 30, 1861), 121. The

On the eve of the Civil War, harness racing had clearly become a firmly established pastime in New Orleans. Its sponsors probably ranked a notch or two below the patrons of thoroughbred racing, and crowds at the track perhaps stood a little lower on the social scale than onlookers at running races. But the sport had great appeal among well-to-do people whose residence in the city failed to blunt their desire to cultivate some features of the life of the country gentleman.

Horse racing in many ways typified the sporting inclinations of the southern gentry, but it was not the only pastime in which wealth manifested itself. A desire to engage in other pursuits associated with the gentleman sportsman, a nostalgic longing for the country-side, and professions of antiurbanism, which were fashionable at the time, encouraged a number of residents to take up rod and gun in quest of sport. Hunting and fishing ranked among the most popular activities throughout the South, but they assumed special significance in southern cities. As one New Orleans sportsman explained, only people "who are in the habit of walking along dusty and crowded streets, gazing upon endless brick rows, listening with forced patience to the business din and rattling vehicles, of a commercial city, can fully appreciate the pleasure felt, when opportunity enables you to flee these turmoils, for the quietude of a favorite country seat." Another local outdoorsman, quoting William Cowper's familiar line, put it still more succinctly: "As you inhale the health giving air you inwardly exclaim, in thought reverential, 'God made the country, but man made the town!' " [28]

The area around New Orleans abounded in opportunities for such sportsmen. Lakes, bayous, rivers, and the Gulf beckoned anglers, while outdoorsmen who favored what one writer called the "nobler pastime" of hunting could find game of almost every description, including ducks, geese, snipe, deer, and even bear, in the marshes, on the lakes, and in the fields of southern Louisiana. Throughout the antebellum period and until the city expanded to the shores of Lake Pontchartrain, opportunities for hunting and fishing also lay

---

Spirit's description of Ethan Allen is quoted in Akers, *Drivers Up*, 124, but no date is given.

[28] *Spirit of the Times*, XXI (July 26, 1851), 271; XIX (February 9, 1850) 607.

near at hand for local sportsmen. "Surrounded as it is on all sides by an uninhabited swamp," a local observer said of New Orleans as late as the 1880s, "such game as ducks and snipe, and all varieties of fish, both fresh and salt water, are to be caught within the city limits." Rail transportation placed many areas within easy access of urban sportsmen. The "hunter's car" of the Mexican Gulf Railroad carried residents to Lake Borgne in the forties and fifties; and in the fifties the New Orleans, Jackson, and Great Northern and the New Orleans, Opelousas, and Great Western railroads "opened other ranges for the gunner, some of which afford excellent deer, turkey, and quail shooting." [29]

Field sports attracted participants from all ranks of society, but well-to-do sportsmen gave these activities their most distinctive characteristics. Relying on their wealth and leisure, they made hunting and fishing vital parts of their lives. Affluent residents placed themselves apart from the ordinary citizen by the time and money they invested in these sports; they also drew a sharp distinction between "professional hunters," who bagged game for a living, and gentlemen hunters, or "amateurs," who took up the weapons of sport solely for pleasure. Their expeditions into the field often became elaborate undertakings, perhaps drawing them away from the city for several days on end. Hunters sometimes stayed in the homes of planters, such as Isidore G. Szysmanski, "one of those open-hearted, noble souls that are too rarely met with." If a planter's guests sought large game, such as bear, he might provide both slaves and hounds to assist in locating the quarry. Less affluent residents apparently confined their hunting excursions to Sundays. When the Scottish Presbyterian minister George Lewis visited the city in the 1840s, he found to his dismay that his fellow Scots devoted the Sab-

[29] The quotes regarding hunting and fishing and the railroads, in the order cited, are from the *Spirit of the Times,* XIX (February 9, 1850), 607; Coleman (ed.), *Historical Sketch Book,* 245; *Spirit of the Times,* XXI (May 3, 1851), 127; and XXV (December 1, 1855), 499. The construction of these railroads, their antebellum development, and their utility are discussed in Reed, *New Orleans and the Railroads,* 40–42, 88–120. For descriptions of hunting in the area, see *Spirit of the Times,* XIX (July 14, 1849), 247; XIX (February 9, 1850), 607; XX (July 6, 1850), 235; XX (December 7, 1850), 498; XX (December 21, 1850), 522; XX (February 8, 1851), 606; XXI (March 15, 1851), 42–43; XXI (April 19, 1851), 102; XXI (May 3, 1851), 127; XXI (July 26, 1851), 271; XXII (April 17, 1852), 101; XXII (June 12, 1852), 195; XXV (December 1, 1855), 499; XXV (January 12, 1856), 570; New Orleans *Daily Picayune,* September 24, 1858.

bath to pleasure: "Forgetful of all but present enjoyment, they shoulder their gun, and, followed by their dogs, hasten to the woods for a day of field sport and an evening of dissipation." [30]

The efforts of local sportsmen to continue the sporting traditions of the social aristocracy of the South Atlantic states was evident in their dedication to hunting and fishing, but frontier influences gave local field sports some peculiar features. As late as the 1850s, the fringes of settlement were a relatively short distance from New Orleans, and this nearness was reflected in the frontier braggadocio that colored the accounts of many sportsmen. Tall tales and the Big Bear School of Humor, a genre based on exaggeration which flourished in William T. Porter's *Spirit of the Times,* had a number of local practitioners. Hunters from the city frequently contributed stories about great hunts in which phenomenal marksmen downed hundreds of birds in one or two hours. They also recounted the misadventures of "Bagshot," a fictional character who mistook logs for alligators and whose great bear hunt ended when he was chased back to camp by a boy wearing a bearskin. [31] Such stories merely underscored the important place that field sports occupied in the lives of southerners, both urban and rural. Hunting and fishing had amused residents of the South since the colonial period, and these activities lost none of their attractions when sportsmen moved into cities.

For many residents the opportunity to indulge in outdoor activities came primarily in the warmer months when they flocked to various resorts. Every summer thousands of New Orleanians deserted the city. Convinced that they were courting death by yellow fever if they

[30] Examples of the distinction made between "amateurs" and "professional" or "regular" hunters may be found in the *Spirit of the Times,* XXI (April 19, 1851), 102; XXV (January 12, 1856), 570. The description of Szysmanski is in *ibid.,* XXI (April 19, 1851), 102. For an example of a bear hunt in which slaves were used, see *ibid.,* XXI (July 26, 1851), 271. Lewis' remarks are in Lewis, *Impressions of America and the American Churches,* 188. For an interesting collection of stories about hunting in the antebellum South, see Clarence Gohdes (ed.), *Hunting in the Old South: Original Narratives of the Hunters* (Baton Rouge, 1967).

[31] Examples of "great hunt" stories may be found in *Spirit of the Times,* XX (July 6, 1850), 235; XX (December 7, 1850), 498; XXI (April 19, 1851), 102. The tales involving "Bagshot" are in *ibid.,* XX (February 8, 1851), 606; XXI (March 15, 1851), 42–43. This type of humor and the widespread telling of tall tales in the antebellum period have been analyzed in Norris W. Yates, *William T. Porter and the Spirit of the Times: A Study of the Big Bear School of Humor* (Baton Rouge, 1957), especially chapter 6, "Tall Tales in the *Spirit.*"

remained in the "wet grave," some inhabitants sought safety at northern watering places. In the 1840s and 1850s, however, this practice diminished as the sectional crisis deepened. The *Picayune*, militant defender of the South, "ever advocated . . . the policy and propriety of the Southern people patronizing Southern institutions —whether schools, colleges, or watering places." The editor repeatedly urged residents to confine their summer excursions to regional spas "instead of running away to Abolition States and there squandering their hundreds and thousands of dollars." *De Bow's Review*, which as early as 1851 advised proprietors of resorts in the South to "present sufficient inducements *at home*" to "reform our 'distant travel' propensities," reported in 1858 that northern resorts had begun to lose patrons to watering places in the South and predicted that "the contrast between the formal show and the hollow-heartedness, the petty intrigues and the perpetual annoyances of the former, and the quiet ease, the careless abandon, and the habits of home-life of the latter, will secure the future course of summer travel for the South." When well-to-do residents of the lower South reduced their jaunts to the North, Gulf Coast resorts, such as Biloxi, Bay St. Louis, Ocean Springs, Pascagoula, Pass Christian, and Point Clear, rose in importance.[32]

New Orleanians who were unable to leave the city for an extended period of time found temporary respite at suburban Carrollton, which was only a short distance up the river, or in the numerous retreats that dotted Lake Pontchartrain, such as Madisonville, Covington, and Mandeville on the north shore, and West End, New Lake End, and Spanish Fort on the south shore nearer the city. In 1859 one observer noted in his diary that the Fourth of July had passed peacefully because "the gents who get tight and noisy" had "crossed the lake in search of enjoyment & pleasure." Shortline railroads, constructed in the 1830s to strengthen the city's commercial empire, encouraged people to visit local resorts because pleasure-seeking passengers meant the difference between profit and loss. When freight business failed to meet expectations, the Pontchartrain

---

[32] New Orleans *Daily Picayune*, May 28, 1859; *De Bow's Review*, X (March, 1851), 353; XXV (November, 1858), 590; Ruth Irene Jones, "Ante-Bellum Watering Places of Louisiana, Mississippi, Alabama and Arkansas" (M.A. thesis, University of Texas, 1954), 228–32. For similar comments, see New Orleans *Daily Picayune*, July 7, 1850; May 31, July 6, 1852; June 27, 1857.

Railroad developed recreational facilities at the lake, including the Washington Hotel, "one of the most exclusive hotels in the southern country" with bathing facilities for "ladies and gentlemen"; and the New Orleans and Carrollton Railroad built the Carrollton Hotel, which featured a shooting gallery, a bowling green, and a tenpin alley. Railroads, according to a reporter for the *Crescent*, did a "smashing business" during spells of hot weather.[33]

Regardless of location, summer resorts offered similar diversions. They were retreats where careworn, restless urbanites could "pass the warm season healthfully and pleasantly in the way of bathing, fishing, hunting, sailing in fine pleasure boats and mingling in the most refined society." A. Oakey Hall, later mayor of New York during the reign of Boss William Marcy Tweed, gave a clear picture of life at a typical southern resort in his description of the leading hostelry at Pass Christian: "At 'Montgomery's' from early June until late October, there is eating and drinking; bowling and flirting; billiards and snoozing; gossip and toilette; driving and novel reading; sailing and yawning; bathing and mosquito scratching; dancing and music." While men benefited from a wide selection of amusements, Victorian opposition to physical exertion for women hampered young southern ladies during their outings. "Our amusements were simple and distinctly ladylike," Eliza Ripley recalled of summers at Pass Christian. "There was no golf or tennis, not even the innocent croquet, to tempt the *demoiselles* to athletics, so they drifted more to the 'Lydia Languish' style." [34]

Of the aquatic sports available at southern resorts, bathing was the most universally enjoyed. The cost of participation was negligible, and people of all classes and both sexes took part. Men sometimes found the sport appealing because it gave them an opportunity to ogle female bathers. George M. Wharton, a New Orleans journalist, wrote to the *Spirit of the Times* in 1848 about a trip to Tennessee during which he spied upon a bevy of bare-skinned bath-

---

[33] Gustave A. Breaux Diaries, July 4, 1859; New Orleans *Daily Crescent,* June 28, 1858. The descriptions of the Washington and Carrollton hotels are in Reed, *New Orleans and the Railroads,* 43–45.

[34] New Orleans *Weekly Picayune,* May 26, 1856, quoted in Reinders, "A Social History of New Orleans," 432; A Oakey Hall, *The Manhattaner in New Orleans; or, Phases of 'Crescent City' Life* (New York, 1851), 116; Ripley, *Social Life in Old New Orleans,* 142–43.

ers: "You've read about nymphs, syrens [*sic*], and so forth? They couldn't compare. Hair loose, and floating on the waves; arms, &c. &c., glistening in the water. Polly was white as snow. Sue was plump as a partridge in pea-time, and sat in the waves like a bird in its nest. Troup was slim all over, except the upper works. . . . Angeline sported gracefully like a native of the element, and May was a black-eyed houri, coleur de rose, from toe to brow. They splashed, and paddled, and chatted like mad." While young temptresses swam in such daring fashion, a few men also breached the moral code of the period. New Orleans in the 1850s passed a law calling for the arrest of any "person who shall strip naked for bathing . . . in the river Mississippi, or in either of the basins, or anywhere publicly within the limits of the city." [35]

More modest residents confined their swimming to the Gulf retreats or to Lake Pontchartrain. An English traveler observed that "opulent merchants" constructed "villas" on the lakeshore, "and during the summer months, when business is at a standstill, they migrate to the shores of the lake, and refresh themselves by bathing in its salt waters." Less affluent residents patronized the public bathhouses, which were segregated by sex and color. Free Negroes launched an assault on racial segregation in 1833, when "certain colored persons wishing to go to the lake" objected to the Pontchartrain Railroad's policy of ejecting blacks from cars reserved for whites. They "went away and armed themselves, returned and attacked Mr. Reeves, the clerk of the road, by firing pistols at him, &c." Nevertheless, racial segregation continued, not to be challenged seriously until after the Civil War. [36]

Segregation by sex fared less well. An English visitor found to

---

[35] George Michael Wharton's story, under the pseudonym "Stahl," is in the *Spirit of the Times,* XVIII (June 3, 1848), 169. The story is also cited in Yates, *William T. Porter,* 132, but Yates incorrectly attributes the story, which was an original contribution to the *Spirit,* to the New Orleans *Delta,* a newspaper for which Wharton wrote in the 1840s and 1850s. The ordinance regarding nude bathing is found in Leovy (comp.), *The Laws and General Ordinances of the City of New Orleans,* 175.

[36] Matilda C. F. Houstoun, *Texas and the Gulf of Mexico; or, Yachting in the New World* (2 vols.; London, 1844), II, 19–20; New Orleans *Argus,* August 1, 1833, quoted in *Niles' Weekly Register,* XLIV (August 24, 1833), 423. For an interesting account of race relations in the city, see Roger A. Fischer, "Racial Segregation in Ante Bellum New Orleans," *American Historical Review,* LXXIV (February, 1969), 926–37.

his surprise that on occasion "both sexes bathed together." Most Americans considered such conduct improper, but, the account continued, New Orleanians defended the practice:

Creoles often told me how extremely pleasant this sociable way of bathing was, and assured me that the most agreeable moments in the summer were spent in this manner. The bathers are attired in a peculiar dress, mostly of flannel. Whole families walk there together, and young ladies are courted and flirt in the bath with as little inconvenience as in a drawing-room. A little, handsome, black-eyed Creole, in New Orleans, was one day describing to me how much pleasure she found in this recreation, and summed up all she had been saying on the subject in the following words, expressed with perfect ecstasy: *'Mais, Monsieur, c'est charmant, c'est un paradis terrestre!'*

Antebellum bathing costumes, of course, rendered mixed bathing entirely safe. "Bathing suits," Eliza Ripley complained, "were hideous, unsightly garments, high neck, long sleeves, long skirts, intended for water only! . . . How decorous! No *baigneuse decolletée* to be seen on the beach." [37]

Yachting was the chosen aquatic pastime for the city's wealthy residents. This expensive sport had much the same appeal to affluent merchants, cotton factors, and businessmen that thoroughbred racing had to planters. Commanding fleet sailing vessels, like owing fast horses, seemed to qualify men for membership in that vaguely defined class known as gentlemen. Since the colonial period, residents of Atlantic ports had occasionally sailed pleasure craft, but it was not until after 1800 that the sport began to attract a large following. In the early decades of the nineteenth century, a number of prosperous Boston and New York merchants began to commission expensive sailing boats built for speed. Then in 1844 John C. Stevens and several fellow yachtsmen founded the New York Yacht Club to regulate competitive sailing. Organized yachting soon spread to other ports of the Atlantic and Gulf coast. [38]

Fashionable gentlemen in New Orleans quickly followed the example of these northern sportsmen. Sailing first became a popular pastime at resorts on Lake Pontchartrain and the Gulf in the thirties and forties. For example, in 1840 the *Picayune* observed that a local

37 C. F. Arfwedson, *The United States and Canada in 1832, 1833, and 1834* (London, 1834), II, 51–52; Ripley, *Social Life in Old New Orleans*, 142.

38 Krout, *Annals of American Sport*, 59–88, has a brief general history of aquatic sports from the colonial period to the 1920s.

planter would soon launch a yacht comparable to the yachts of New York: "A master boat builder has superintended the work, and her owner designs the yacht for fishing, fowling, and pleasure excursions generally." As the number of sailing vessels increased, interest in founding a sailing association developed. In 1849 several yachtsmen, mostly from New Orleans, organized the Southern Yacht Club at Pass Christian, Mississippi. The influence of northern-born residents was clearly evident, for among the founders were James O. Nixon, a newspaperman from Philadelphia who was soon to become owner of the *Crescent*, and John Egerton, a banker from New York. Several planters also participated, including Thomas S. Dabney of Mississippi, president of the Southern Yacht Club in 1850, and Isidore G. Szysmanski of Louisiana, president in 1860, but the club was dominated by New Orleans businessmen and merchants who could afford to invest heavily in yachts and whose business interests permitted them to devote their summers to competitive sailing.[39]

The Southern Yacht Club, like local jockey clubs, was both an exclusive social organization and a regulatory group. Its purposes, as explained by Egerton, were to encourage "friendly rivalry" among members and to provide a "rational amusement" for residents of the Gulf Coast. The club frequently met its social obligations with a dinner and a ball after a day's racing. Sailing rules restricted participation in regattas to members and invited guests. Competitors and spectators alike were expected to conduct themselves properly. For example, a club rule prohibited betting on sailing contests, presumably on the grounds that gambling and profit-taking detracted from the purity of the sport. To equalize competition the club divided yachts into three classes based on keel length. Owners were honor bound to sail in their proper class. When John G. Robinson, the association's outstanding yachtsman, violated this requirement in July of 1850, members asked him to return his

39 New Orleans *Daily Picayune*, August 18, 1840; Minutes, Southern Yacht Club, July, 1849–July, 1860, entries for July 21, 23, 1849; July 6, 1850 (Southern Yacht Club, New Orleans); Susan Dabney Smedes, *Memorials of a Southern Planter*, ed. Fletcher M. Green (New York, 1965), 83; Chenault and Reinders, "The Northern-born Community of New Orleans in the 1850s," 238, 240. The Southern Yacht Club's history is traced in Louis J. Hennessey, *One Hundred Years of Yachting* (New Orleans, 1949), an "authorized" and highly popularized account.

prize. Robinson angrily complied, but he resigned from the Southern Yacht Club and refused to rejoin until 1853. The seriousness with which local yachtsmen approached their sport was again demonstrated during a regatta in 1857 when a crewman from one of the entries drowned after his boat capsized and foundered. "This sad event," said the *Picayune*, "besides causing a great delay, threw something of a damper upon the joyousness of the occasion. But at length the first gun fired and the boats that had entered for the regatta came gallantly into line." [40]

For several years after the founding of the Southern Yacht Club, sailing followed a well-established routine. Yachtsmen inaugurated each season with a series of races on Lake Pontchartrain and then sailed for Pass Christian, which became something of a southern Newport in the 1850s. For the remainder of the summer, they participated in regattas along the coast from New Orleans to Mobile. Each season ended with a race for the Challenge Cup, the club's most prestigious prize. Historians of yachting have generally dismissed the Southern Yacht Club as an insignificant local club, but its influence on yachting in the lower South was broad. During the 1850s a number of yacht clubs organized along the Gulf Coast; reflecting the influence of the region's dominant association, they generally adopted the Southern Yacht Club's rules. [41]

Yachting remained primarily an out-of-town pastime for New Orleanians until 1857. In that year of business depression, members of the Southern Yacht Club, many of whom were merchants, abandoned their annual trip to Pass Christian and confined their sailing to Lake Pontchartrain, a practice that continued until the Civil War. The club sponsored few sailing contests during the late 1850s, but many well-publicized unofficial regattas attracted large crowds

---

40 Minutes, Southern Yacht Club, entries for July 23, August 4, 6, 11, 18, 22, 1849; November 16, 1850; January 14, 1851; *Spirit of the Times*, XXII (September 4, 1852), 343; XXII (October 16, 1852), 417; John G. Robinson to J. O. Nixon, January 18, 20, 1851, copies of letters in Minutes, Southern Yacht Club, entry for January 20, 1851; New Orleans *Daily Picayune*, August 4, 1857.

41 Regattas, Southern Yacht Club, August, 1849–September, 1857, *passim* (Southern Yacht Club, New Orleans); *Spirit of the Times*, XIX (October 13, 1849), 398; XX (May 4, 1850), 126; XXI (September 27, 1851), 379; New Orleans *Daily Picayune*, July 18, 1852. An article by Captain R. F. Coffin in Frederick S. Cozzens *et. al., Yachts and Yachting* (New York, 1888), 11, described the antebellum Southern Yacht Club as "purely a local organization," which had "no real national influence."

to the lake.[42] Moreover owners of small yachts organized the Crescent City Yacht Club in 1858; this club scheduled several races in ensuing years. But by the summer of 1861 both the Southern and Crescent City yacht clubs had disbanded, casualties of the Civil War. Nevertheless, organized sailing had won a dedicated following in the twelve years after the founding of the first club in 1849; the enthusiasm of these yachtsmen easily survived the martial interlude.[43]

For many residents of the city, rowing rather than yachting satisfied the desire to conquer the elements. Rowing had become a popular pastime in eastern cities after the Revolution; after 1800 it spread to the West and the South. Less expensive than yachting, rowing appealed particularly to middle-class youths who lacked the money and leisure to command expensive sailing boats but who could band together to purchase rowing equipment.[44]

New Orleanians began to express an interest in rowing in the late 1830s. In July, 1837, the *Picayune* published an article urging young men of the city to form a rowing club. When one appeared the following month, the editor commended the undertaking because the city offered so few diversions in the summer: "Lazy inactivity, quarelling, billiard playing, drinking and duelling, are about all the amusements that can be found in this city at present." The efforts of this association evidently inspired imitation, for rowers organized the Wave, Ariel, Lady of Lyons, Algerine, Knickerbocker, Locofo, Edwin Forrest, and Washington boat clubs in the next several years. The first club built its boathouse on the New Basin Canal, but later groups housed their boats on the Mississippi River.[45] Rowers purchased boats and other equipment from the regionally famous

[42] Minutes, Southern Yacht Club, entries for July 15, 16, September 16, 1857; Regattas, Southern Yacht Club, regattas of August 4, September 21, 1857; *Spirit of the Times,* XXVII (August 22, 1857), 329; XXVII (October 10, 1857), 417; XXIX (July 30, 1859), 295; XXIX (August 6, 1859), 308; XXIX (September 24, 1859), 390; XXX (August 11, 1860), 324.

[43] *Spirit of the Times,* XXVIII (August 21, 1858), 325; XXVIII (August 28, 1858), 342; XXVIII (September 4, 1858), 354. This association first took the name Junior Southern Yacht Club but quickly changed to Crescent City Yacht Club.

[44] Krout, *Annals of American Sport,* 59, 77–78; Samuel Crowther and Arthur Ruhl, *Rowing and Track Athletics* (New York, 1905), 6–7.

[45] New Orleans *Daily Picayune,* July 21, August 9, 1837; Coleman (ed.), *Historical Sketch Book,* 232; E. Merton Coulter, "Boating as a Sport in the Old South," *Georgia Historical Quarterly,* XXVII (September, 1943), 233.

John Mahoney of Algiers (who also constructed yachts), or ordered them from New York marine firms that catered to the leading eastern rowing clubs. In 1839 the Lady of Lyons Boat Club selected William E. Chambers of New York to construct a six-oared shell, "one that cannot be beat," at a cost of $275. The depression of the early 1840s, said one member, caused a "scarcity of money in this city as well as in yours" and made it difficult for the club to pay for the boat. Members raised the money by selling an old shell to the Vicksburg Boat Club.[46]

Organized rowing regattas began soon after the founding of the first clubs. In January, 1839, two crews from Mobile and a team representing the Ariel Club of New Orleans held the city's "first regular regatta," a race that ended badly for the local rowers. Soon after the race started, said the *Picayune*, "the Ariel dropped astern and took the position of the Irishman's brag horse, who drove everything before him." Other contests soon followed, including a match in April between crews from Mobile and New Orleans for a thousand dollars. But before rowing fully captured the sporting public's interest, a flood in 1844 washed away most boathouses and destroyed the city's growing fleet of racing boats.[47]

Fifteen years of rowing inactivity followed the flood. In 1859 a group of "gentlemen athletically disposed" revived interest in the sport by organizing the Monoma Boat Club and inaugurating a series of intraclub races on Lake Pontchartrain. Within a few weeks another contingent of young men founded the inaptly named Pioneer Boat Club. Rivalry soon developed, and in the summer of 1860 the clubs agreed to race for a set of oars and the colors of the winning club. Urging residents to go to the lake for the race, the *Crescent* assured people that rowing was "an aquatic sport, bringing out muscle and science, quite as exciting as cricket and baseball on land." After the race, which was won by the Monoma Club, the *Crescent* expressed hope that this "manly sport" would continue in New Or-

46 J. T. Hacher, J. C. Page, J. Saunders, and J. Heyl to William E. Chambers, October 28, 1839; W. G. Dewey to William E. Chambers, April 27, 1840; W. G. Dewey to Henry B. Hart, May 29, 1840, copies of letters in Lady of Lyons Boat Club Book, 1839–41 (Special Collections, Tulane University Library).

47 New Orleans *Daily Picayune,* January 8, April 8, 1839; Coleman (ed.) *Historical Sketch Book,* 233–35.

leans. But the war suspended rowing activity, preventing further contests until after 1865.[48]

Near the end of the antebellum period, summertime pleasure-seekers in New Orleans began to divide their attention between near-by watering places and the city's playing fields. As early as 1841, an article in the *Picayune* observed: "Playing ball is among the very first of the 'sports' of our early years. . . . Who has not played 'barn ball' in his boyhood, 'base' in his youth, and 'wicket' in his manhood? There is fun, and sport, and healthy exercise in a game of ball." Until the late 1850s, young men played these games on an informal basis, mostly for their own amusement, but in 1859 they began to field organized teams to play both cricket and baseball. The press praised the idea: "It is a pleasure to see our young men turning their attention to the healthful and manly sports of the field. Such sports have been too long neglected in New Orleans." [49]

Cricket was a firmly established American sport long before local youths showed an interest in forming teams. Played in this country since the colonial period, the game rose rapidly in popular esteem in the 1850s when American teams played a series of international matches, first with players from Canada and then in 1859 with a visiting eleven from England. These contests stimulated interest to such an extent that for a time it appeared cricket might become America's national pastime.[50]

Players in New Orleans displayed a quickening interest in cricket during the English tour. In the late spring of 1859, several players founded the Crescent City Cricket Club, described by the *Crescent* in 1860 as the "pioneer association in the introduction of this manly game in the South." Another club, the Pelican Cricket Club, appeared shortly thereafter. This eleven, like the Crescent City group, drew its members mainly from the ranks of the well-to-do, a natural development since only young men with ample leisure could devote Tuesdays, Thursdays, and Saturdays—Pelican practice days—to

[48] Coleman (ed.), *Historical Sketch Book,* 235; Reinders, "A Social History of New Orleans," 443; New Orleans *Daily Crescent,* August 30, 31, 1860.

[49] New Orleans *Daily Picayune,* May 22, 1841; New Orleans *Daily Crescent,* August 8, 1859.

[50] Krout, *Annals of American Sport,* 124–26; Frank G. Menke (ed.), *The Encyclopedia of Sports* (3d rev. ed.; New York, 1963), 312–13; Dulles, *A History of Recreation,* 186.

cricket. The *Picayune* once declared: "It has truly been said that cricket stands unrivaled among athletic games, in many important particulars," especially "in uniting all classes; . . . the best men being selected in a match, without reference to position or society." But the willingness of teams to pick the best players regardless of class meant little when the working classes were excluded by their general lack of free time.[51]

The city's cricket teams at first confined their playing to intra-club matches, but in September, 1859, they began a series of inter-club games that continued until the war. In the following May the Crescent City team, featuring the "best ball-players . . . that New Orleans can boast," went to Mobile for the South's first intercity cricket match. The Civil War curtailed cricket activity, but by that time another game had already made permanent inroads into cricket's following. Taking advantage of a latent hostility to foreign, especially English, games and of the inherent drawbacks in the slow-moving sport, baseball had already surpassed cricket in popularity when the war began. Cricket revived after 1865, but it never again challenged baseball for the attention of the city's youth.[52]

Descended from the English game of rounders (and not invented by Abner Doubleday), baseball in some form has been played in America since the late eighteenth century. In the 1840s Alexander Cartwright, the true founder of modern baseball, suggested that a group of New York gentlemen form the Knickerbocker Baseball Club. This organization, the first of many in the East, wrote the initial rules of modern baseball. Many of these regulations are still fundamental to the game today, but they were not universally adopted for several years. Regulations varied from team to team and section to section. This confusing situation made clarification of the rules mandatory, an idea supported vigorously by the *Spirit of the Times*. Pointing out that "the Germans have brought hither their Turnverein Association . . . and various other peculiarities have

51 The quotes in this paragraph are from the New Orleans *Daily Crescent*, March 19, 1860; and the New Orleans *Daily Picayune*, June 30, 1859. References to the formation of cricket clubs are in the New Orleans *Daily Crescent*, September 20, 1858; June 27, 1859; and New Orleans *Daily Picayune*, June 27, 1859.

52 New Orleans *Daily Picayune*, August 11, September 15, 17, 1859; New Orleans *Daily Crescent*, April 16, 18, 23, October 1, 1860; *Spirit of the Times*, XXIX (September 24, 1859), 391. The description of the Crescent City players is in the New Orleans *Daily Crescent*, April 23, 1860.

been naturalized," the *Spirit* argued that there "should be some one game peculiar to the citizens of the United States." Although attempts to standardize rules had not succeeded when the Civil War restricted baseball activity, the game progressed rapidly in the 1850s, gaining adherents in all sections of the country.[53]

New Orleanians began playing baseball on an organized basis somewhat later than young men in other cities. Dozens of nines were already playing in the East when the city's first team, the Louisiana Baseball Club, began to play intraclub games in July of 1859. But baseball soon attracted a strong local following. By the end of the year, there were seven teams in the city, including the Empire, Southern, Magnolia, Melpomenia, Washington, and Lone Star baseball clubs. In the following year, volunteer fire companies organized the Liberty and Home teams, which raised the number of clubs to nine.[54] Most players, like the cricket enthusiasts, came from the middle and upper classes. The formation of these teams demonstrates that there is no basis in fact for the hoary myth that Union soldiers introduced baseball to the South.[55]

Teams at first amused spectators with a series of intraclub games, matching the bachelors against the "Benedicts" (married men), but within a short time all nine teams were engaged in spirited competition for the city championship. Interclub rivalry soon led to standardization of local rules. Some teams at first insisted on following Massachusetts regulations, which permitted ten players, the additional man being a fourth outfielder. By 1860, however, when the Empire players captured the city championship, all nines played under the Knickerbocker, or New York, rules.[56] Spectators came prepared to spend the day. Although scheduled for nine innings,

[53] Robert W. Henderson, *Ball, Bat, and Bishop: The Origin of Ball Games* (New York, 1947), 169; Harold Seymour, *Baseball: The Early Years* (New York, 1960), 4–9, 15–20. For a recital of the confusion regarding rules, see, in addition to Seymour, the account by Carl F. Wittke, "Baseball in Its Adolescence," *Ohio State Archaeological and Historical Quarterly*, LXI (April, 1952), 111–27. The quotation is from the *Spirit of the Times*, XVI (January 31, 1857), n.p., quoted in Wittke, "Baseball," 121.

[54] New Orleans *Daily Picayune*, July 30, August 20, September 15, 1859; November 18, 1860; New Orleans *Daily Crescent*, August 22, 29, September 20, October 10, December 12, 1859.

[55] This myth is found in a number of accounts, including Krout, *Annals of American Sport*, 119; and Frederick G. Lieb, *The Baseball Story* (New York, 1950), 34.

[56] New Orleans *Daily Crescent*, August 13, 1859; May 14, 1860.

games sometimes ended after as few as four or five innings because teams scored so many runs. Newspapers occasionally commented on a team's "peculiar bowling" (pitching), but pitchers were expected to toss the ball across home base so that it might be hit easily. Scores such as 55–14 and 53–29 were fairly common.[57]

Baseball and cricket appealed mainly to the city's upper classes. Club members made elaborate preparations to assure the comfort of spectators, who often came by invitation. They provided tents to shade ladies from the sun and to protect the refreshments, which were given by the "thoughful care of the club to their numerous invited guests." A witness at a cricket club match recalled: "Three fine tents were pitched for the accommodation of the ladies, and three smaller ones, containing sundry suspicious-looking baskets and rows of bottles, on which the gentlemen kept up a very spirited attack." Not all baseball and cricket games were conducted in such an aristocratic setting, but when the antebellum period ended, there were few indications that either of these sports would become a truly democratic pastime. Some residents from the lower ranks played baseball, but for the most part both games furnished amusement mainly to middle- and upper-class residents. Baseball, which the *Picayune* called the "national game" as early as November of 1860, ultimately became popular with all classes, of course, but the masses generally turned elsewhere for amusement before the Civil War.[58]

57 New Orleans *Daily Picayune,* July 30, 1859; New Orleans *Daily Crescent,* October 3, 1859. The phrase "peculiar bowling" is from the New Orleans *Daily Crescent,* December 12, 1859.
58 New Orleans *Daily Picayune,* September 3, 1859; *Spirit of the Times,* XXIX (September 24, 1859), 391; New Orleans *Daily Picayune,* November 1, 1860. Quotations are in the order cited.

Chapter III
SPORTS FOR
THE MASSES

While the city's nabobs cheered blooded horses and trim yachts or gathered sedately under white tents to watch society's future leaders master the challenges of ball and bat, ordinary citizens patronized other sporting diversions. Rank-and-file residents occasionally attended horse races, regattas, and ball games, but they were more likely to while away their leisure hours playing billiards, watching professional runners, or yelling for first blood at a prize fight. These and other activities flourished partly because they required less money and leisure time than the sports of the wealthy. People of limited means could not afford to buy thoroughbreds and yachts or to attend baseball and cricket matches on working days, but they certainly could patronize gas-lighted billiard parlors after working hours or watch animal baiting contests and prize fights staged on Sundays. Less affluent residents were thus in large measure responsible for encouraging a variety of sports that came to be regarded as typically urban pastimes. Restricted in time, space, and spending power, they sought their pleasures almost entirely within the confines of the city.

Another factor that influenced the growth of mass sports was the preponderance of males in antebellum New Orleans. Like many thriving, rapidly growing urban communities, the city attracted more male than female migrants. In 1840 adult white men between the ages of twenty and fifty outnumbered white women of the same age group by 21,230 to 10,686. Twenty years later the gap had narrowed noticeably, but still adult white males between the ages of twenty and fifty outnumbered adult white females in the same age bracket by 41,607 to 34,163. Moreover, as one scholar has demonstrated, the marriage rate was much lower in the nineteenth century, particularly before 1860, than it is today. As a result New

Orleans and other cities had a great many unmarried adult males who comprised a "confirmed-bachelor subculture." The presence of so many adult males committed to remaining single had a great impact on the city's leisure habits. It was this group that regularly visited professional prostitutes and sustained all-male gathering places like gambling parlors and saloons. They also cultivated their own sporting pastimes, which ranged from billiards and bowling to target shooting. A few daring women might attend such activities, but in antebellum New Orleans the sports of the masses were predominantly male events.[1]

Prize fighting was among the most popular sports of the city's workingmen. Professional boxing had emerged as a semirespectable sport in eighteenth century England, where it found favor with the sporting aristocracy, and then crossed the Atlantic, probably brought to this country by wealthy young southerners who encountered the sport abroad. In the early decades of the nineteenth century, the "sweet science," despite its upper-class origins, won a great following among America's rowdier elements.[2] Its popularity rose markedly in the 1830s when waves of Irish migrants gave the sport a rapidly expanding audience. Prize fighting then as now appealed to members of an oppressed minority group who saw in the sport a way to profit and to win social recognition. Just as Negroes and Puerto Ricans have become prominent in the ring in the twentieth century, the Irish became the masters of prize fighting in the nineteenth century.

Whatever its appeal to the Irish, prize fighting occupied a low place in the minds of many Americans. Its association with society's roughest elements, particularly with the professional sporting men, a wild, gambling crowd known as the "fancy," placed it beyond the

1 United States Bureau of the Census, *Sixth Census* (1840): *Compendium of the Enumeration of the Inhabitants and Statistics of the United States, as Obtained at the Department of State, from the Returns of the Sixth Census, by Counties and Principal Towns* (Washington, D.C., 1841), 60–61; United States Bureau of the Census, *Eighth Census* (1860): *Population of the United States in 1860; Compiled from the Original Returns of the Eighth Census, under the Directorship of the Secretary of the Interior* (Washington, D.C., 1864), 188, 195; Paul H. Jacobson, *American Marriage and Divorce* (New York, 1959), 21–22; Ned Polsky, *Hustlers, Beats, and Others* (New York, 1969; Anchor Books ed.), 21–24.

2 Alexander Johnston, *Ten—And Out! The Complete Story of the Prize Ring in America* (3d rev. ed.; New York, 1947), 5.

approval of "respectable" people. Defenders of the prize ring, such as Frank Queen of the New York *Clipper,* assailed to no avail "the unfounded and unreasonable objections entertained by certain classes against pugilists and sparring exhibitions." [3] Prize fighting escaped the active hostility that greeted some English pastimes in this era of rampant nationalism, but it met with continuing resistance among those people who abhorred what they regarded as boxing's barbaric features and the raucous, seemingly atavistic ruffians who supported the sport.

Objections to prize fighting's crudities possessed some merit. The London Prize Ring Rules, which governed contests after 1838, permitted a great deal of violence. Regulations prohibited gouging, butting, kneeing, and hitting a downed opponent, but fighters were still allowed to wear shoe spikes, and rounds ended only when one of the fighters went down. Moreover the contest continued until one of the men could no longer come to "scratch," a line drawn in the center of the twenty-four-foot ring. Governed by these harsh rules, ring bouts in England and America often ended only when a fighter was beaten into bloody unconsciousness. [4]

In spite of the opposition of moralists, prize fighting became increasingly popular in the United States. Championship matches involving James "Yankee" Sullivan, Tom Hyer, John Morissey, John C. "Benecia Boy" Heenan, and the Englishman Tom Sayers inspired widespread public interest. Although few antebellum ring heroes aroused mass enthusiasm as John L. Sullivan was later to do, they often fought before thousands of fans, many of whom journeyed long distances to witness a championship fight. A few New Orleanians even went to New York to see the fight for the American championship between Morissey and Heenan in 1858. [5] But traveling so far to see a bareknuckle "mill" was unusual; most Crescent City fans restricted their viewing to local matches.

Pugilistic encounters occurred irregularly in New Orleans before the 1850s. Sam O'Rourke, expatriate champion of Ireland, opened an athletic club to sponsor bouts in 1835, but fight promoting proved difficult and financially unrewarding. Relying primarily upon local

3 Quoted in Robert M. DeWitt, *The American Fistiana, Showing the Progress of Pugilism in the United States, from 1816–1873* (New York, 1873), 80.

4 Johnston, *Ten—And Out!,* 14–15.

5 Betts, "Sporting Journalism in Nineteenth-Century America," 45.

talent, O'Rourke offered fans a sporadic diet of mediocre contests. He achieved some success in 1837 when he fought a pair of matches with James "Deaf" Burke, the English champion. Burke had traversed the United States seeking opponents before O'Rourke, who styled himself the champion of America and Ireland, agreed to fight him in New Orleans. The Englishman gave O'Rourke adequate cause to regret his decision, thrashing him soundly on two occasions and thus establishing a tenuous claim to the championship of America, for there was no champion at the time. The second contest, like the first, drew an immense crowd. When Burke again humiliated O'Rourke, who had become something of a hero among the local fancy, the Irishman's friends "introduced bowie knives and pistols, by way of an Irish-American commentary on the main text of pugilism." A reporter observed: "This was something new to the Deaf 'Un, but he was not slow to learn. Some trusty friends procured him an immense 'Arkansas toothpick' and a fast horse." Burke then "cut" his way loose. O'Rourke, deprived of his championship, soon faded from the local sporting scene. Burke stayed in the city and opened a club "for the purpose of teaching the scientific and manly art of Self Defense, whereby gentlemen, after taking a few lessons, will be enabled to chastise those who may offer insult, and protect themselves against the attack of the ruffian." [6]

Prize fighting languished after the Burke-O'Rourke fights until Chris Lilly of New York began to promote matches in the 1840s. Lilly relied mainly on local Irish toughs, but he supplemented this supply of fighters with English- and Irish-Americans imported from New York, described by one reporter as "flash boys from Gotham, rejoicing in the fancy titles of Lusty Joe, Dandy Jim, Cock-eyed Jack, and the like expressive cognomens, and wearing a flashy, fantastic costume, embracing red topped boots, figured cravats, and illustrated vests." Although Lilly apparently improved the quality of boxing contests, residents remembered him in later years not as a promoter of fights but as the man who imported the city's "first organized system of ruffianism, for electioneering purposes," a

---

6 DeWitt, *The American Fistiana*, 9; New Orleans *Daily Picayune*, March 4, 1837; Nat S. Fleischer, *The Heavyweight Championship: An Informal History of Boxing from 1719 to the Present Day* (New York, 1949), 42–44; Johnston, *Ten—And Out!*, 6.

practice prevalent in New Orleans for the remainder of the century.[7]

Despite Lilly's efforts, public disfavor retarded the development of prize fighting in New Orleans until a few years before the Civil War. In 1852 the *Daily Orleanian* dismissed the sport as a "demoralizing, vulgar and brutal vice, occasionally practiced in the 'Bloody Third,' " adding that "such disgraceful exhibitions are rare here." The city placed legal barriers in boxing's path in 1856. Few fights had been held before then, but the city council wished to suppress growing interest in this repugnant sport.[8]

Legal restrictions failed to impede the development of prize fighting once it gained a following. To circumvent the law, fighters practiced their occupation across the river or in adjacent Jefferson Parish beyond the jurisdiction of the city ordinance. When "John McLaughlin, of the New Orleans fancy" and "Dan Callaghan, of the New York fancy" fought a three-hour, one-hundred-and-sixteen-round contest at the Metairie Course in February, 1857, the *Crescent* observed: "Our police would probably have interfered, had not the fight taken place on that part of the race course which lies in the parish of Jefferson." Prize fighting where the sport was illegal, on the other hand, usually brought a quick reaction. On September 18, 1857, St. Tammany Parish police frustrated an attempt by James Lafferty of St. Louis and John Dillon of New Orleans to fight across Lake Pontchartrain in Mandeville. After posting peace bonds of five hundred dollars, the pugilists and their fans crossed the lake to Metairie Ridge where Lafferty required only seven rounds to teach Dillon the folly of evading the law.[9]

Besides occasionally inconveniencing prize fighters, official bans tended to confine the popularity of professional boxing to the fancy. Because support came almost exclusively from this libertine group, rowdyism understandably accompanied many contests. Reporting a fight in 1860, a writer for the *Crescent* observed: "The liveliest feature of all was a row between the opposing partisans, some fifteen or twenty of whom jumped over the ropes and engaged in a grand

---

[7] New Orleans *Daily Orleanian,* February 13, 1852; New Orleans *Times,* August 9, 1869; May 11, 1870.

[8] New Orleans *Daily Orleanian,* February 13, 1852; Leovy (comp.), *The Laws and General Ordinances of the City of New Orleans,* 176.

[9] New Orleans *Daily Crescent,* February 16, September, 19, 1857; DeWitt, *The American Fistiana,* 52.

impromptu plug-muss. . . . This was stopped by two peacemakers in broadcloth, who, jumping into the ring, drew their revolvers, cocked them, and swore that they would kill the man who struck the next blow." Convinced by this sound argument, the battling rowdies withdrew and allowed the professional fighters to continue. Such disturbances, which occurred fairly regularly, alienated peaceful, law-abiding citizens. Prize-fight enthusiasts periodically claimed that people "of all classes" attended fights, but only the lower classes consistently patronized the sport. For example, in 1856 the *Picayune* reported a fight attended by two thousand "abandoned men and women." Normally a male pastime, boxing also found favor among members of the frail sisterhood whose virtue had long since disappeared.[10]

Although prize fighting appealed mainly to the under classes, matches in the late 1850s drew hundreds and sometimes thousands of onlookers. Since fighters depended on contributions from spectators as well as their own side bets, fighting in New Orleans became a lucrative pursuit that attracted many local and out-of-town pugilists eager to reap the fruits of the sport's rising popularity. To facilitate the quest for profit, two predominantly Irish sporting associations, the St. Mary's Market and Gallatin Street clubs, took charge of the sport. These clubs arranged bouts between local fighters for the city championship, which Jim Burns won in April of 1858 and retained for the remainder of the period. These groups also classified fighters as "invincibles" and "beaten bummers" and imported pugilists to battle them. Improved transportation facilities in the 1850s made it possible for fighters from other cities to compete frequently in New Orleans.[11]

Some fights were also promoted from as far away as New York. Jack Looney and Joe Cole, who fought "at a snug retreat about five miles from New Orleans" on March 14, 1858, had arranged the bout at the New York Clipper Saloon only a few days before.[12] Insufficient evidence makes it impossible to determine how often such

10 New Orleans *Daily Crescent,* April 9, 1860; DeWitt, *The American Fistiana,* 89; New Orleans *Weekly Picayune,* March 17, 1856, quoted in Reinders, "A Social History of New Orleans, 1850–1860," 449.

11 New Orleans *Daily Crescent,* April 16, 1858; January 23, 1860; DeWitt, *The American Fistiana,* 55.

12 DeWitt, *The American Fistiana,* 67.

bouts occurred, but the number of imported fighters performing in the city indicates that local promoters had established effective relations with New York sportsmen. When prize fighting encountered strong opposition in the North after the Civil War, these ties with tolerant New Orleans proved vital to the development of the American prize ring.

Fights involving visiting boxers gave local fans an opportunity to see some of the country's best and most flamboyant fighters. Among the battlers who appeared in the city were Barney Aaron, who was later to win the "championship of the light weights in America," and Hen Winkle, both of New York. When Winkle fought Dan Kerrigan, also of New York, in February, 1858, he bolted into the ring with an American flag tied round his waist, in the manner of James "Yankee" Sullivan who had acquired his nickname by following the same ritual. Winkle's appeal to patriotism proved futile; Kerrigan, "after informing the crowd . . . that he did not intend to fight the flag, but the man . . . walked into him and used him up in four rounds." [13] When local fighters met such invaders, fans showed their civic pride. In April, 1860, on the Metairie Course two thousand fans, including "a thousand levee laborers" who had "bivouacked there after 'footing it' from New Orleans the previous night," saw Jerry Donovan, "a caulker at Algiers," pummel Steve O'Donnell, a "bruiser from Chicago." [14]

In addition to staging bouts in the city, local pugilists also capitalized on prize fighting's increasing appeal by joining the fighters' tour. Pete Gallagher of New Orleans journeyed to St. Louis in 1858 for a fight with "Shanghai" Conners who battled Gallagher for eighty-two rounds before delivering a "neck blow for the *coup de grace*." The following year Jim Burns, who had defeated Conners in New Orleans in March of 1858, also traveled to Missouri to fight "Shanghai." Burns was fifteen pounds lighter than his opponent, but was once again thrashing Conners until he lost on a foul in the thirteenth round. Cutting short a rousing fight, the referee's decision infuriated the fans, who responded with a general

<hr>

[13] *Ibid.,* 57, 35; New Orleans *Daily Crescent,* February 22, 1858; Johnston, *Ten—And Out!,* 24.

[14] DeWitt, *The American Fistiana,* 89; New Orleans *Daily Crescent,* April 9, 1860.

brawl that resulted in at least one death and several serious injuries. Although occasionally hazardous, hopping around the country was apparently profitable, for the number of vagabond boxers increased rapidly.[15]

The proliferation of local and intercity matches testified to the ring's ascending popularity. At the close of the antebellum period, prize fighting claimed a large nucleus of rabid fans who scorned the opposition of polite society and poured cash in the countless passing hats to support America's nineteenth century gladiators. War interrupted the sport's progress, but it had gained a firm foothold among American pastimes. In less than twenty-five years, prize fighting had developed into one of the major sports locally and throughout the country.

People who gathered around the prize ring to watch men flail-away at one another also supported several violent animal sports. Throughout much of the antebellum period, cockfights, dogfights, bullfights, and bull and bear contests regularly drew large crowds. City ordinances banned all of these sports except cockfighting in the mid-fifties, but until then they amused thousands of residents. Respectable people found animal contests revolting, but New Orleans, like other large cities, had what a writer for the *Spirit of the Times* called "a pack of keen fellows pandering and catering to the low, useless, depraved, and unchristian tastes of man." Contests that reduced the elements of life to an essential struggle to survive seemed to have a strong appeal to the city's poorer classes who were themselves engaged in a day-to-day effort to prevail.[16]

Animal sports catered to a variety of tastes and nationalities. Bullfights, which occurred nearly every Sunday in the 1840s and 1850s and which often featured *matadores* and *banderilleros* from Mexico, were "very common with the city's Spanish and Sicilian population." [17] Samuel J. Peters, Jr., the son of a Connecticut Yankee, spoke for many Anglo-Americans when he described a bullfight in 1848 as "a most disgusting sight. The 'butchers' tortured the Bulls

15 DeWitt, *The American Fistiana,* 56, 71.

16 Leovy (comp.), *Laws and General Ordinances of the City of New Orleans,* 176–77; *Spirit of the Times,* XXII (June 19, 1852), 212.

17 Roberts, *Southern Sketches,* 23; *New Orleans As It Is,* 34, 48; John G. Dunlap to Beatrice A. Dunlap, December 22, 1844, John G. Dunlap Papers.

. . . & made them suffer death in an awful manner. I never witnessed a Bull fight before nor will I again I hope."[18] The popularity of dogfights, which were held in cockpits, cut across ethnic divisions. Ordinarily, however, only rowdier citizens watched dogs tear at one another. The leading promoter of this activity was Sam Banks, who matched his fighting dog Sweep against all challengers.[19] Cockfighting was reportedly a favorite amusement of the "Bloody" Third District, where gamecocks attacked each other with natural spurs. When a reporter for a Mobile newspaper suggested that cockfighting was universally enjoyed in New Orleans, the *Daily Orleanian* described it as the sport of Americans and Spanish immigrants and emphatically denied that Creoles pursued this pastime. But the distribution of cockpits throughout the downtown area indicated that cockfighting drew support from most ethnic and social groups.[20]

Bull and bear contests attracted larger crowds than other animal sports, for bloodlust ran high when promoters scheduled this type of entertainment. On the occasion of a contest between Dr. C. W. Hall's grizzly bear General Jackson and a Mr. Honore's bull Columbus at the Bingaman Course in May, 1852, five thousand people attended "to see two brutes tear and mangle each other; and to incite, provoke and drive them into a fight, for which their natural instincts were not sufficiently savage." Outraged by this spectacle, the *Picayune* dismissed the affair as a "disgusting sight, and a humiliating theme to speak of in this age which assumes to be civilized," and expressed the hope that "the scenes of yesterday will never be attempted again." But the contests continued. A fight the following year attracted the attention of the New York *Illustrated News*, whose editor reluctantly published an account "so calculated to blight the good name of a sister city." Local authorities, stung by such gibes, soon took action. Consequently bull and bear contests, as well as other animal sports, declined. By 1860 only cockfighting,

18 Samuel J. Peters, Jr., Diary (Department of Archives and Manuscripts, Louisiana State University), July 4, 1848.

19 *Wilkes' Spirit of the Times*, II (August 25, 1860), 396; III (September 8, 1860), 12; III (September 22, 1860), 37; III (September 29, 1860), 61; *New Orleans As It Is*, 51.

20 New Orleans *Daily Orleanian*, February 13, 1852; Shippee (ed.), *Bishop Whipple's Southern Diary*, 101, 119; Reinders, "A Social History of New Orleans," 448.

which the city regulated and taxed, claimed much of a following.[21]

For residents whose desire for vicarious competition was satisfied by less violent demonstrations, foot racing was a popular pastime. This sport won a large following in the quarter century before the Civil War as scores of speedy runners staged races around the country. Pedestrians, as they were called, were usually professionals (and thus not gentlemen), who earned their livelihoods by betting and by charging admission to their exhibitions. Oliver Wendell Holmes once observed that "society would drop a man who should run around the Common in five minutes," but thousands of people gathered to watch professionals perform.[22]

Pedestrianism became a popular sport in New Orleans in the 1840s and 1850s. The general pattern followed locally was that established on the national level. Dozens of runners flocked to the city seeking quick, easy money, and residents aided the "peds" by turning out in massive numbers for special running events. When John Gildersleeve of New York promoted his own ten-mile race in 1845, an observer said he ran before the largest crowd ever seen on the Metairie Course. "The stands were full, and the interior of the course presented an immense number of carriages, equestrians and pedestrians." The most acclaimed runner to visit the city was William Jackson, who ran in New Orleans in 1846 and again in 1850.[23] Jackson's fifteen-mile hurdle race in 1850 demonstrated the appeal of the sport. According to the *Delta:* "The affair . . . drew together the most miscellaneous crowd of men, women, and children, loafers, wharf rats, Fourierites, Agrarians, gentlemen, niggers, vagabonds, and outside barbarians, that have rejoiced in fresh air and the sight of green fields, since the day when Adam mounted his first pair of breeches!"[24]

21 New Orleans *Daily Picayune*, May 23, 25, 1852; *Spirit of the Times,* XXII (June 19, 1852), 212; New York *Illustrated News,* April 23, 1853.

22 Oliver Wendell Holmes, "The Autocrat of the Breakfast Table," *Atlantic Monthly,* I (May, 1858), 881; *Spirit of the Times,* XX (June 15, 1850), 193; New Orleans *Daily Picayune,* March 28, 1857; Dulles, *A History of Recreation,* 143–44.

23 *Spirit of the Times,* XV (April 12, 1845), 74; XV (February 14, 1846), 602; XV (February 21, 1846), 614; XX (April 27, 1850), 114.

24 New Orleans *Delta,* April 8, 1850, quoted in *ibid.,* XX (April 27, 1850), 114. For examples of other visiting runners, see *ibid.,* XV (February 14, 1846), 602; XVI (March 14, 1846), 30; XVII (May 8, 1847), 124; New Orleans *Daily Picayune,* March 28, 1857; New Orleans *Daily Crescent,* April 2, 1860.

Local runners also sought to capitalize on their speed. Fire companies, centers of athletic activity in the 1850s, produced several excellent runners. William O'C. Donnell, a fireman in the First District, and John Kingman of the Third District, "the fleet fireman who has won several silver trumpets by his running in circuses," were the best known. Foot races between local contestants often occurred as side attractions at horse races because local runners usually lacked the prestige necessary to attract large crowds.[25]

Foot racing became so popular in New Orleans that the anti-feminist sentiment of the period temporarily fell before its appeal. In January, 1858, three women overlooked polite society's opposition to female athleticism and joined the ranks of professional runners. Mademoiselle Eugenie LaFosse of Paris, Miss Lucy Reynolds of Liverpool, and "the fleet and celebrated Indian squaw Ba-tu-uch-o-ua-ra, of the Cherokee tribe," agreed to race in Jackson Square for a set of jewelry.[26]

At the same time that foot races entertained residents who preferred outdoor amusements, billiards and bowling provided recreation for people who wished to pass their time indoors. These activities did not invite public observation, but more than pedestrianism, horse racing, and prize fighting, billiards and bowling encouraged widespread participation. St. Charles Street, the Bourbon Street of the nineteenth century, served as the center of these sports. Describing the street during the winter season of 1857, the *Picayune* observed:

Lights glare out of its palaces, dedicated to Bacchus, far into the midnight watches. The banquettes and the saloons are thronged with crowds of the most diverse characters, coming one knows not from whence, and flitting away, at late hours, one knows not whither. There are eating houses and drinking houses, coffee saloons and shooting galleries, billiard rooms and ten-pin alleys, whose din like that of Babel when language was confounded, astonishes the stranger. . . . St. Charles street is the theater of a perpetual carnival.[27]

25 New Orleans *Daily Crescent*, April 20, 1857; *Spirit of the Times*, XX (June 8, 1850), 186; XXII (June 26, 1852), 222.
26 New Orleans *Daily Picayune*, January 9, 1858.
27 *Ibid.*, December 26, 1857. St. Charles Street refers to the blocks between Canal Street and Tivoli (now Lee) Circle. St. Charles Avenue, mainly a residential thoroughfare, developed after the Civil War and is that part of St. Charles that runs uptown from Lee Circle.

Bowling at pins (as distinguished from lawn bowling) was introduced to colonial America by the Dutch and in the early nineteenth century became a popular tavern sport. Originally played with nine pins, bowling acquired a tenth pin in the 1830s after Connecticut outlawed "bowling at 9 pins" in a misguided effort to eliminate gamblers from the sport. From Connecticut the new game of tenpins spread to New York and then to the rest of the country. In August, 1843, New York's *Spirit of the Times* reported the sport's growth: "Within a few years, Bowling Alleys have increased beyond precedent; at this time there are not less than two hundred, probably, in this city, while in Boston, Philadelphia, Mobile, and New Orleans, the number is constantly increasing." As bowling's appeal broadened, the public ceased to associate it with the gambling fraternity. Instead, all classes adopted tenpins; it even became a fashionable pastime for both sexes at exclusive resorts like Newport. As early as 1843, the *Picayune* noted: "We recollect when it was esteemed essentially a vulgar game; now almost every gentleman can make his 'ten strike' in the course of an evening." [28]

Residents of New Orleans quickly discovered the appeal of bowling. "A great game is this 'ten-pins,'" the *Picayune* informed its readers, "whether you play the 'cocked hat,' or the 'nine-ball game;' —the 'single string' or the 'match'—'on and off,' or 'roll out.' If you will only go into it with a rush, you can get more exercise in an hour—good wholesome exercise of every part of the system—than in any other amusement which we know of in twice the time." Several years later the *Picayune* returned to the subject of bowling's respectability when comparing the American sport to the English game of skittles: "In England it is considered rather a vulgar game, as it is commonly indulged in by the lower classes of society. . . . Here playing at ten-pins is a favorite amusement, and, affording excellent exercise, is indulged in by all classes of society." The statement seemed accurate. The downtown amusement area featured

[28] The quotes in this paragraph are from the *Spirit of the Times,* XIII (August 12, 1843), 282; and New Orleans *Daily Picayune,* n.d., quoted in *ibid.,* XIII (September 9, 1843), 330. For bowling's legal problems, see Frederick Marryat, *A Diary in America, with Remarks on Its Institutions* (Philadelphia, 1839), I, 107; II, 174–75; and Menke (ed.), *The Encyclopedia of Sports,* 209–10. See also *Spirit of the Times,* XVIII (November 11, 1848), 451; and Dulles, *A History of Recreation,* 6, 33, 36.

a number of bowling establishments, such as Caldwell's, Murphy's, and Johnson's, which attracted patrons of all ranks. Gulf Coast resorts, including Pass Christian, also had tenpin alleys and regularly advertised bowling as a pastime for summer visitors.[29]

Bowling in the forties and fifties was in the process of acquiring the main characteristics of the modern sport. By the early forties, tenpin alley everywhere featured smoothly polished lanes made of narrow wooden planks, as well as gutters and ball-return lanes. Moreover, as one New Orleans bowler observed: "At the extreme end of the alley is a small, ragged urchin, placed there for the purpose of setting up the pins." These features of bowling remained unchanged until the advent of automation a century later. In other respects, however, the game differed from city to city. The length of the lane, the method of keeping score, the size of balls and pins, and the number of balls rolled in a complete game varied to such an extent that the *Spirit of the Times* once conceded that "it is difficult to estimate the comparative skill of the bowlers" in different cities.[30]

The *Spirit of the Times* encouraged bowlers to adopt uniform rules and equipment by publishing accounts of bowling matches throughout the country. If players rolled games on short alleys or with oversized bowling balls, they risked the scorn of fellow keglers everywhere. When a New Orleanian reportedly scored ten successive strikes on a substandard alley in Cincinnati, the editor of the *Spirit* dismissed the feat with the observation that "he couldn't make such a game any where else, and has been repeatedly beaten by a gentleman, formerly of this city, who wouldn't roll us for 'the outside shadow of a continental d——n,' without large odds, and we don't 'sit up for shapes' as a crack player." [31] On another occasion,

29 New Orleans *Daily Picayune,* n.d., quoted in *Spirit of the Times,* XIII (September 9, 1843), 330; New Orleans *Daily Picayune,* n.d., quoted in *ibid.,* (XVIII December 23, 1848), 521; New Orleans *Daily Picayune,* May 18, 1850; *Spirit of the Times,* XII (September 24, 1842), 349; XVIII (December 23, 1848), 521; XIX (July 14, 1849), 247; XXIII (October 5, 1853), 410.

30 New Orleans *Daily Picayune,* n.d., quoted in *Spirit of the Times,* XVIII (December 23, 1848), 521; *Spirit of the Times,* XIII (August 12, 1843), 282. For articles indicating differences in rules and regulations, see *ibid.,* XII (September 24, 1842), 394; XIII (August 12, 1843), 282; XIII (September 9, 1843), 330; XIII (September 30, 1843), 361; XIV (October 26, 1844), 414; XV (May 3, 1845), 106; XV (February 14, 1846), 602; XVI (January 2, 1847), 534; XVII (July 24, 1847), 254; XVIII (December 23, 1848), 521.

31 *Spirit of the Times,* XVI (January 23, 1847), 570; XIV (October 26, 1844), 414.

when the *Spirit* reported that New Orleans bowlers used a large ball "measuring 7½ inches in diameter, with which it is perfectly sure to get a strike if you can govern it so as to hit the head pin," a self-ordained expert wrote: "I do not consider the *game* of Ten Pins worth a red cent where that kind of ball is used." [32] Under such prodding bowlers began to accept standard rules and regulations. By 1850 they had agreed on lane lengths, scoring procedures, and the number of balls to be rolled in a game.[33]

Bowlers in New Orleans played an important role in the acceptance of uniform regulations. When local keglers adopted the sport in the 1840s, they began to submit accounts of games to the *Spirit*. This correspondence facilitated the adoption of nationwide standards and ultimately helped to produce a distinctively American sport. When Charles Styles, proprietor of a bowling establishment in New York, went to England to open Styles' American Bowling Saloon in Liverpool, the Liverpool *Chronicle* described tenpins as an "American game." Said the *Chronicle:* "This species of sport, the national one of America, promises, from the success which has attended its introduction into England, to be equally popular with us." [34] Bowling soon lost its tenuous status as the national sport of the United States, but the reception given the game in England underscored the process of acculturation by which a number of games, including baseball as well as bowling, had been taken from the Old World and fashioned along New World lines. Drawing freely on their European heritage, bowlers had begun with ninepins, added an extra pin, and, with the aid of a national sporting journal, adopted rules and regulations recognized throughout the country. The result was a new "national" sport.

This trend toward standardization doubtless would have progressed further, but bowling's popularity dwindled in the 1850s.

---

32 *Ibid.,* XIII (September 30, 1843), 361.

33 *Ibid.,* XII (September 24, 1842), 349; XII (November 12, 1842), 238; XIII (August 12, 1843), 282; XIII (September 9, 1843), 330; XIII (September 30, 1843), 361; XV (February 21, 1846), 614. The present method of scoring, described in the 1840s as "off and on" scoring, was adopted at least as early as 1843. See *ibid.,* XIII (September 9, 1843), 330; XIII (September 30, 1843), 361; XV (February 21, 1846), 614. The second of these references suggests that off and on scoring was first used in New Orleans.

34 Liverpool *Chronicle,* January 27, 1849, quoted in *Spirit of the Times,* XIX (February 24, 1849), 6.

Tenpin alleys continued to attract patrons, but players showed little interest in events in other cities. Even the *Spirit*'s enthusiasm declined; the editor published only a few scores in the 1850s.

An important reason for the waning appeal of bowling was the fascination that another indoor sport—billiards—held for game players in the decade before the Civil War. First introduced to America by colonial aristocrats, such as William Byrd of Westover who once boasted of copulating with his wife on his billiard table, the game became in the late eighteenth century a popular tavern sport, which John Adams denounced as a pastime for "rakes and fools." In the early years of the nineteenth century, billiards attracted support at all levels of society. Charles Francis Adams, grandson of the redoubtable John, played the game while a student at Harvard in the 1820s and considered it "the most delightful of all mere amusements." Billiards reached its antebellum zenith in 1859 when Michael J. Phelan beat John Seereiter for the national championship before a fashionable Detroit audience that included several ladies.[35]

New Orleanians had a long-standing interest in the sport. As early as 1723, only five years after the founding of the town, the Superior Council of Louisiana found it necessary to prohibit billiard playing on Sundays and feast days or at late hours.[36] By the 1850s the game had a large following among both the well-to-do and the humbler folk. As was true elsewhere, billiards in New Orleans was played on two distinct social levels. Upper-class players generally confined their participation to tables in their homes or in the rooms of private men's groups, such as the snobbishly aloof Boston, Louisiana, and Pelican clubs. Even members of less exclusive clubs, such as the Odd Fellows, insulated themselves from the masses by purchasing their own tables.[37] Rank-and-file citizens, on the other hand, played in the city's many public parlors, which were "fitted up . . . in the neatest manner, with everything appertaining to a gen-

35 Louis B. Wright and Marion Tinling (eds.), *Secret Diary of William Byrd of Westover, 1709–1712* (Richmond, Va., 1941), 207; Durant and Bettman, *Pictorial History of American Sports,* 330 (for John Adams' description of billiards); Aïda DiPace Donald and David Donald (eds.) *Diary of Charles Francis Adams* (Cambridge, Mass., 1964), I, 187

36 Charles L. Dufour, *Ten Flags in the Wind: The Story of Louisiana* (New York, 1967), 85.

37 New Orleans *Daily Picayune,* September 12, 1852; December 16, 18, 1860.

teel Billiard Saloon." [38] It was in their support of these facilities that the "confirmed-bachelor subculture" demonstrated most noticeably its desire for all-male gathering places. The popularity of billiards rose steadily for as long as the city's population contained a preponderance of males. Gambling establishments, Gulf resorts, and hotels also had tables for their patrons. In 1853 the rebuilt St. Charles Hotel, which had burned in 1851, exceeded the expectations of guests when it included "a billiard room neatly and tastefully fitted up, and designed expressly for ladies." [39]

Billiard playing was normally a casual pastime, but players periodically arranged formal matches. Contests sometimes involved itinerant billiard experts who, like pedestrians and prize fighters, toured the country to exhibit their skill with the cue.[40] In other matches local "knights of the cue" played for the city championship or to fill the pockets of contestants. On one occasion, when the French national champion was staging exhibition games in New York, the *Picayune* observed: "There is 'some billiards' played in this city in the course of a season, and we think we risk nothing when we say that there are a few players here who would be ready and happy to 'knock the balls about' a little with the new champion from over-sea." [41] One of the most lucrative local duels matched the "Algiers Bull" with the "Bayou Lafourche Mule" for a purse of five thousand dollars. "Rumors of the affair having gone abroad," a reporter said, "an immense throng of spectators were present, and many of the prominent sporting characters in attendance had come from as high up as Julia Street." [42]

In the decades before 1861, the South became increasingly militant. Military schools and organizations multiplied and flourished; hunting and horsemanship received support not only as sports but also as training exercises; thousands of southerners entered the army and by the 1850s dominated its command structure; and private citi-

38 *Ibid.*, November 20, 1853.

39 *Ibid.*, January 9, 1853. For accounts of the various places that provided billiard equipment, see Buckingham, *The Slave States of America,* I, 327; Joseph Holt Ingraham, *The South-West. By a Yankee* (New York, 1835), I, 127; New Orleans *Daily Picayune,* May 18, 1850; May 28, June 25, 1859; January 8, 1861; *Spirit of the Times,* XIX (July 14, 1849), 247; XXIII (October 15, 1853), 410.

40 New Orleans *Daily Picayune,* December 16, 1860.

41 *Ibid.*, October 20, 1860.

42 *Ibid.*, December 5, 1857.

zens and public leaders became ever more bellicose. The South prepared for war years before the actual conflict began.[43] In southern
cities this militancy took a variety of forms, including widespread
interest in the sport of target shooting.

Residents of New Orleans proved themselves genuine southerners
in this respect. To be sure, not every person who engaged in target
shooting was a potential soldier, but the rising interest in this
sport on the eve of the Civil War was no mere coincidence. Volunteer
military organizations, such as the socially elite Washington Artillery and Continental Guards, scheduled rifle practice regularly as
well as full-dress military parades.[44] Citizens who belonged to no
military association sharpened their abilities with rifle and pistol at
the numerous shooting galleries in the main part of the city.[45]
Located chiefly on St. Charles and Perdido streets, these galleries
reportedly attracted men of all ranks, but they probably relied
mainly on middle- and working-class patrons. Some residents also
practiced shooting in open spaces on the outskirts of the city or
across the river. The English traveler Matilda Houstoun described
shooting as the favorite pastime of inhabitants. "Thousands flock to
the ground where the performance takes place," she wrote, "and
great is the emulation excited among the aspirants for fame." The
Georgia merchant John Dunlap informed his wife that matches in
New Orleans "are somewhat different from the shooting matches of
Carolina and Georgia—Instead of shooting for beef, they collect
large droves of Turkeys and shoot for them." [46]

The city achieved national prominence in 1852 when John Travis
constructed a pistol gallery in the downtown area. Recognized as
America's champion pistol shot, Travis built "the most beautiful
shooting-gallery ever seen in the Southern country." Financed by
ten-dollar subscriptions from two hundred people, it was attended
nightly by a "great number of gentlemen." Travis advertised the
advantages of practice by performing a number of remarkable feats

[43] John Hope Franklin, *The Militant South, 1800–1861* (Cambridge, Mass.,
1956), *passim.*

[44] New Orleans *Daily Picayune,* July 10, 1859; Reinders, "A Social History
of New Orleans," 279–85.

[45] *Spirit of the Times,* XXIII (February 26, 1853), 18; New Orleans *Daily
Picayune,* December 26, 1857.

[46] Houstoun, *Texas and the Gulf of Mexico,* II, 46; John G. Dunlap to Beatrice A. Dunlap, December 22, 1844, Dunlap Papers.

in the 1850s. Once for a bet of a thousand dollars, he agreed to shoot an apple off the head of a man standing thirty-six feet away. After locating a man with the heroic qualities of William Tell's son, he met with several witnesses on Tiger Island in St. Mary's Parish in May, 1854. Substituting an orange for the apple, Travis splattered the fruit on the first shot. "Some of the best sportsmen and acknowledged best shots in the country were present," a witness reported, "and all express themselves fully satisfied that Mr. Travis is the *best pistol shot in the world*." [47] Employing his reputation to make his fortune, Travis spent the remainder of the decade establishing shooting galleries in New York, Louisville, and other cities.[48]

The sports discussed thus far cut across ethnic and, to a lesser extent, racial and class lines in popularity. But in antebellum New Orleans there were also sports identified with specific racial and national groups. These sports sometimes attracted spectators of all descriptions, but participation seldom appealed to people outside the group that introduced the sport. Until after the Civil War, sports such as gymnastics, *raquette, les quatres,* and Irish football were the sports of well-defined groups of people.

Gymnastics, an athletic pastime fostered by *Turnvereins,* was the sport of German-Americans. The *Turnverein* movement, which began in Prussia in the early nineteenth century, combined physical training with intellectual development in an effort "to realize the ideal of an all-around human being." The first American *Turnvereins* were founded in the 1820s by political refugees, but the movement gained real strength in this country only after the mass influx of Germans in the 1840s and 1850s. Stressing gymnastics based on the Greek system, energetic German-Americans organized more than 150 societies by 1860.[49]

Two *Turnvereins* were organized in New Orleans, the first in 1850 and the second a few years later. In addition to encouraging exer-

47 *Spirit of the Times,* XXII (January 8, 1853), 558; XXIII (February 26, 1853), 18; XXIII (September 3, 1853), 342; XXIV (May 20, 1854), 162.

48 *Ibid.,* XXV (April 7, 1855), 90; XXV (July 14, 1855), 258; XXV (February 9, 1856), 618; XXVI (December 13, 1856), 522; XXVIII (February 27, 1858), 30.

49 Augustus J. Prahl, "The Turners," in Adolph E. Zucker (ed.) *The Forty-Eighters: Political Refugees of the German Revolution of 1848* (New York, 1950), 79–92; Carl F. Wittke, *Refugees of Revolution: The German Forty-Eighters in America* (Philadelphia, 1952), 147–51; Krout, *Annals of American Sport,* 209.

cises on parallel bars, ropes, and the padded horse in their gymna-
iums, these associations began in 1853 to sponsor jointly an annual
Volksfest, the equivalent of a county fair.[50] Held in May, this spectacle at first attracted mainly nostalgic Germans eager for reminders
of the fatherland. But by the latter part of the decade, the *Maifest*,
as it was sometimes called, appealed to the entire citizenry. Attracted
by an "army of tents and booths," a "flying-horse machine," Chinese
jugglers, Turkish magic women, "Ethiopian minstrel bands," and the
youthful gymnasts, thousands of people turned out annually for this
great German bazaar where they found themselves amazed by gymnastic feats performed "in a manner which might shame any circus."
Contented visitors agreed with the *Crescent* when it announced: "The
Volksfest is a German institution—but hereafter the Germans will not
be able to monopolize it. The thing is contagious, and the indications
this year have been such to warrant the prediction that the whole
population more or less, will join in the festival hereafter." Whether
held on the Union Course, the Creole Course, or the Delachaise
Grounds in Jefferson City (a suburb of New Orleans), this German
pastime had become "exceedingly cosmopolitan in spirit and detail." [51]

German insistence on physical well-being also contributed to an
interest in physical training in the city's schools. "We are glad to
perceive that the Directors of our public schools and the professors
in private institutions of learning have of late turned their attention
to the development of the physical powers of the rising generation
as well as to the enlargement of their mental capacities," the
Picayune announced in November, 1857. Concerned that sedentary
scholars, in common with the majority of the city's population, got
too little exercise, both Boys' High School and the University of
Louisiana (later Tulane University) had erected "gymnastic ma-
chinery." Soon "the scholars were busily engaged in climbing, and
swinging, and sliding, and going through those other performances
in which boys so much delight." [52] The introduction of physical edu-

[50] New Orleans *Daily Crescent,* February 23, 1869, Reinders, "A Social History of New Orleans," 462.

[51] New Orleans *Daily Crescent,* May 10, 18, 1858; May 17, 1859; May 8, 1860;
New Orleans *Sunday Delta,* May 20, 1860.

[52] New Orleans *Daily Picayune,* November 7, 1857.

cation in local schools may be attributed in large part to the influence of the *Turnvereins*, which demonstrated the efficacy of an eminently satisfactory remedy to the physical inactivity of urban dwellers.

Raquette, an activity peculiar to New Orleans, was the only ball game played by organized teams in the city before 1859. Described by the *Crescent* as "the ancient game of the lower end of the city," *raquette* probably originated with the Choctaw Indians. A visitor who saw *raquette* played in 1850 said the game "much resembled one I had previously seen played by the Munseytown Indians, in the western part of Canada; and I have no doubt that it had been adopted from some of the Indian tribes." At an early though indeterminate date, local Negroes appropriated *raquette* and formed two teams, the Bayous and the LaVilles, which popularized the sport. *Raquette* was played on a field varying in length from two hundred yards to a half mile. Two poles, across which canvas or paper was stretched, were set at each end of the field as goals. Each player carried a spoon-shaped *raquette*, eighteen to twenty inches long, with which he threw or carried a leather ball, two inches in diameter, in a frantic effort to hit the opponent's goal. There were no rules to limit team sizes, and often more than eighty youths played on each side. Under such conditions *raquette* amounted to little more than organized mayhem; scoreless draws, highlighted by many bruises, were common when the Bayous and LaVilles clashed.[53]

Despite the indecisiveness of the contests, *raquette* fascinated people of all ranks and both colors. For Sunday games as many as three or four thousand people gathered at the *raquette* grounds, the area now bounded by Galvez, St. Bernard, North Claiborne, and Elysian Fields. Cake booths, beer and ice-cream dispensaries, and other refreshment stands bordered the field for the comfort of the spectators who came to see the half-naked young Negroes battle for the honor of their teams and for prizes that might total a hundred and fifty dollars.[54] Whites sometimes played the game but usually not on Sundays, a day reserved for the Bayous and LaVilles. In 1859

[53] New Orleans *Daily Crescent*, August 8, 1859; Arthur A. T. Cunynghame, *A Glimpse at the Great Western Republic* (London, 1851), 223; Henry C. Castellanos, *New Orleans As It Was: Episodes of Louisiana Life* (New Orleans, 1895), 298–99.

[54] New Orleans *Daily Crescent*, August 16, September 13, 1858; June 6, 1859.

the American Racket Club and the Third District Racket Club placed white participation on an organized basis, but Negroes continued to draw the largest crowds.[55]

Other ball games played in New Orleans included *les quatres* and Irish football. *Les quatres* is an obscure game, which was probably similar to lacrosse. Despite the name, it was played mainly by the Irish. In 1859 players founded four teams—the Apollo, Variety, Washington, and Ne Plus Ultra clubs. The city's first Irish football team was organized in 1859 by residents of Jefferson City. Players issued special invitations asking ladies to be present for their games. *Les quatres* failed to survive the war, but the attraction of Irish football, a game similar to soccer, persisted; though the sport was never to become a major pastime, interest increased in the 1870s.[56]

By 1860 New Orleans had become the sporting center of the Old South. In the quarter century before the war, and particularly in the 1850s, the Crescent City, in common with urban communities around the country, witnessed the speedy development of organized sports, which fully demonstrated their appeal, their vitality, and their utility in a city whose residents found themselves cut off from the open spaces and the traditional pastimes of a rural existence. Many of the prominent features of modern American sports, such as intense organization, an increase in spectator interest and blatant commercialism, had appeared before the Civil War temporarily interrupted the progress of sporting pastimes. Inchoate though some of these developments were, the importance of the antebellum experience can be fully grasped only after considering the impact of the war. As will be seen, some sporting activities continued, in restricted form, throughout the war; others resumed soon after peace returned as if there had never been a military conflict.

55 *Ibid.,* August 20, 1858; August 8, 22, 1859.
56 *Ibid.,* December 12, 1859; New Orleans *Daily Picayune,* October 2, 1859; Reinders, "A Social History of New Orleans," 445.

Chapter IV
CIVIL WAR
INTERLUDE

A common assumption about the significance of the Civil War is that it rigidly delineates the Old and New South. On the distant side of this civil cataclysm, so the hypothesis goes, lies a South wedded to agriculture and slavery and all that these institutions implied; on the near side lies a New South, gradually and somewhat reluctantly industrialized and modernized by a technological way of life imported from a section that had proved its superiority by force of arms. Politically and economically, the idea has some validity; socially, the argument requires qualification. The Civil War wrought few profound changes in the South's religious attitudes, in its assumptions regarding racial stratification, or in its uses of leisure time. Following the martial interlude, these and other salient characterstics of southern society developed along guidelines laid down during the antebellum period.

Sport in New Orleans fits this pattern. While conflict substantially reduced the public's desire and ability to engage in sporting pastimes, the four-year interruption did not determine, except very indirectly, the direction sports took in the ensuing thirty-five years. After 1865 sports in the Crescent City (and the country in general) changed in a number of ways, but the changes resulted less from the shock of war than from other pressures that were brought to bear in the postbellum period. Continuing urban growth after the war, rather than the war itself, produced new developments in organized sports.

New Orleans played two roles during the Civil War. Until April, 1862, the city belonged to the Confederacy; from then until the conflict ceased, it was an occupied city, Captain (later Admiral) David Farragut's contribution to Union control of the Mississippi River.[1]

---

[1] For a comprehensive account of New Orleans during the war, see Gerald M. Capers, *Occupied City: New Orleans Under the Federals, 1862–1865* (Lexington, Ky., 1965).

In each of these periods, military necessity and economic depression placed severe limitations on the city's social life. But even in the midst of military strife residents found time to pursue pleasure, if not as actively as before the war, at least with vestiges of the studied abandon that characterized leisure before 1861.

During the year of the city's active support of the Confederacy, sporting pastimes and other leisure-time pursuits declined gradually as residents surrendered to the lilt of martial tunes. "There is no mistaking it," the New Orleans *Bee* declared on April 9, "the martial spirit is paramount in our city now, and the military excitement is 'all the go.' Every evening the sound of fife and drums, or the stirring strains from brass instruments tell of volunteer companies drilling and parading in every direction." An anonymous woman diarist confirmed this opinion: "War, war! is the one idea. The children play only with toy cannons and soldiers; the oldest inhabitant goes by every day with his rifle to practice; the public squares are full of companies drilling, and are now the fashionable resorts." Not all sports terminated abruptly, but with so many men absent or constantly drilling with local militia units, the peak of interest in sports reached before 1861 could not be maintained. Whatever their appeal to the entire population, many sports foundered when the young men who organized teams and arranged games flocked to military standards.[2]

Baseball and cricket teams, gymnastic societies, and yachting and rowing clubs dissolved within a few months after the onset of hostilities. Southerners quickly recognized that young men with athletic interests had physical assets necessary to the development of a superior army. When the German *Turnvereins* organized a military company of eighty men in April, 1861, a reporter observed: "The gymnastic and athletic proclivities and practices of the Turners will render them equal to the best Zouaves in the world, should hot and heavy work come on." On the occasion of their final game in the same month, members of the Louisiana and Crescent City cricket clubs received their share of appreciation for pursuing an exercise so well suited for "fitting our young men for the duties of a soldier's life."

2 New Orleans *Bee,* April 9, 1861; George Washington Cable (ed.), "War Diary of a Union Woman in the South," in *Famous Adventures and Prison Escapes of the Civil War* (New York, 1893), 7.

Similarly the only regatta of the Crescent City Yacht Club in 1861 drew commendation not because it furnished amusement but because "if the military spirit of our people has been very largely encouraged in every possible way, it must be confessed that we have somewhat neglected our naval resources, seeming to forget the battles of our independence may have to be fought on sea as well as on land." Women also were encouraged to enlist sport in the services of the southern cause. In May, 1861, the *Crescent* reported that "patriotic ladies of the Fourth District . . . under the prevailing spirit of the day" had organized a pistol shooting club. "Let the pirates of the North ever seek this city for its 'booty and beauty,' and they will find that our beauty can do something in its own defense." The report continued confidently, "But the Crescent City will never be invaded." [3]

While most sports enthusiasts submerged their interests in favor of the common goal, some refused to acknowledge the necessity of curbing recreation. In May, 1861, only a few days after the war began, patrons of the prize ring journeyed to Kenner where Mike McCool "took the conceit out of big Tom Jennings in 27 rounds; time 33 minutes; called 'rattling work' by 'the fancy.' " Several weeks later thousands of residents assembled to watch Negro *raquette* players, "in the full tide of their usual summer sport," vie for a flag bearing Jefferson Davis' picture bordered by eleven stars.[4] Turfmen also ignored the spirit of the times. Trotting and pacing continued through the summer of 1861, and the Metairie Jockey Club, loath to abandon its popular and successful pastime, proceeded with arrangements for the regular winter meeting in December. In "a spirit of patriotic liberality," the club agreed to donate all proceeds to the city's "gallant volunteers in the field, and their families at home." The folly of the enterprise became apparent on the first day; attendance was far below "the brilliant assemblages in the piping days of peace." The *Picayune* related: "War's alarms . . . have had a great effect in calling to other stirring scenes many whose faces were

---

[3] New Orleans *Daily Crescent,* April 20, 22, 1861; New Orleans *Daily Picayune,* September 4, 1861; New Orleans *Daily Crescent,* May 14, 1861. Quotes are in the order cited.

[4] New Orleans *Daily Crescent,* May 3, June 17, 1861.

sure to be seen in peaceful times on our far-famed race ground." [5]
Ignoring the limited public response and the small number of entries,
the jockey club persisted, laying plans for a spring meeting in 1862.
Before March, however, turfmen bowed before an insistent fate. The
halcyon days of the Metairie had come to an end.[6]

By the spring of 1862, sports of almost every description had
followed the same route. For a brief time patrons and promoters
ignored the war, but ultimately they abandoned their pastimes and
waited for a more propitious time to reorganize. As war tightened
its grip on the city in the winter of 1861–1862, New Orleans stag-
nated economically and languished socially. Mardi Gras of 1862,
normally the highlight of the winter and spring season, "passed off
with a quietness probably never before known in New Orleans. No
masks on the street, no revelry or intoxication, as is to be seen by
the absence of all serious cases from our police records." A few days
later, officials placed New Orleans under martial law because an attack
on the city seemed imminent. Military authorities also imposed a cur-
few requiring saloons, billiard parlors, gambling establishments, and
other places of amusement to close each night at eight. Recreation
had all but deserted the beleaguered city of pleasure.[7]

Federal occupation shook the city from its doldrums. Ironically
the influx of Union soldiers soon made the war seem more remote. The
possibility of liberation existed until 1864, but the relative security
of occupation permitted a partial return to traditional patterns of
life. Even under the rule of General Benjamin F. Butler, known in
local lore as "the Beast," the city began to reclaim its position as
the capital of recreation in the South. George H. Devol, a river-boat
gambler for forty years, later recalled that during Butler's occupation, from May until December, 1862, "Money was very plentiful,
and of course everything was lively." [8] Under Butler's successor,
General Nathaniel P. Banks, economic recovery accelerated and
social life began to assume aspects of its antebellum vigor.

[5] New Orleans *Daily Picayune,* June 22, July 5, 29, 30, December 11, 15, 1861.
The quotes regarding the Metairie's season, in the order cited, are from *ibid.,*
December 15, 11, 1861.

[6] *Ibid.,* January 23, 1862.

[7] New Orleans *Daily Crescent,* March 5, 1862; New Orleans *Bee,* March 15,
April 3, 4, 1862.

[8] George H. Devol, *Forty Years a Gambler on the Mississippi* (2d ed.; New
York, 1892), 221.

Complete revival was, of course, impossible. Since the city was an important center of Union military operations, some restrictions on social freedom were unavoidable. For example, until the end of the war, military commanders forbade jaunts to Gulf resorts even after these spas fell into Federal hands.[9] Moreover Union officers and chaplains made a systematic effort to bring the city's lax Sabbath habits into line with those of New England. In 1864 self-righteous army chaplains founded the Union Ministerial Association of New Orleans, a group dedicated to the abolition of Sunday amusements as well as to the advancement of the city's general moral purification. The group compared New Orleans with Boston to promote its cause. Boston, where residents rigidly observed the Sabbath, remained loyal to the Union, while the Crescent City, where Sunday was "a day of sports, of theatres, horse-races and amusements of kindred character," had supported the Confederacy. This difference, in the eyes of Union ministers, demonstrated "the results of ignoring the Christian sabbath, and rejecting the divine law." [10] Military authorities concurred in the attempt to purify local customs. In 1862 Abraham Lincoln had enjoined military leaders to encourage observance of the Sabbath, and Banks belatedly published General Orders Number 179 in December, 1864, forbidding attendance at "Theatres, Billiard Rooms, and other places of amusement on Sunday." Most residents objected to these restrictions but to no avail; the order remained in force until several months after the return of peace.[11] With the exception of this sustained effort to alter the city's leisure habits and the prohibition regarding Gulf resorts, the city enjoyed a large measure of social freedom.

Sports recovered as rapidly as any form of entertainment in the city. Before the war's end, many forms of athletic recreation had been restored. "Out-door rambles" to lake resorts attracted large numbers of people who apparently agreed with the *Times*'s suggestion that "if we place ourselves out of the sight of soldiers, we can easily forget the miseries of devastating war." Early in 1863 the *Picayune* recommended baseball, cricket, and other outdoor sports as games that "may be prudently enjoyed without injury and with

9 New Orleans *Daily Picayune,* May 3, 1865.

10 New Orleans *Times,* May 5, 6, 17, 1864.

11 *Ibid.,* January 3, October 29, 1865.

positive benefit to mind and body." By the end of the summer, the local press reported renewed interest in these sports: "During these healthful bracing days, the boys in the upper portion of the city resort to the old Delachaise commons, where they very sensibly pass the evening in playing ball." Renewing competition for the city championship, several social clubs formed teams to play both cricket and baseball.[12]

Indoor sports also resumed during the years of Federal occupation. For animal lovers, the Spanish Pit on St. Claude Avenue featured cockfights and an occasional scrap between "Sporting Dogs." St. Charles's shooting galleries offered amusement "for all lovers of the art of Pistol Shooting" from nine in the morning until eleven at night. Roper's Gymnasium, founded during the war, catered to the more athletic with boxing and fencing lessons and a fully equipped gymnasium open "from daylight to 9 o'clock P.M., Sundays excepted." An advertisement assured prospective patrons: "An hour a day spent in exercise is three hours clear gain in vigor of life." [13] Billiard parlors and bowling alleys also prospered during Federal occupation. New billiard saloons opened, and old ones, "determined to comply with the demands of the public," imported up-to-date equipment like "PHELAN'S CELEBRATED PREMIUM ELASTIC CUSHION BILLIARD TABLES." The Phoenix House, the "oldest established Saloon in New Orleans," offered patrons a bowling alley with six new tenpin lanes and an oyster bar and restaurant featuring old wines and liquors "to which the Proprietor begs to draw the attention of good judges." [14]

Turf sports probably drew more patrons than any other sport during the Civil War. In the absence of socially prominent jockey clubs, clever promoters resuscitated thoroughbred and standardbred racing after New Orleans fell to the Federals. With a string of nineteen trotting, pacing, and running horses, gambler George Devol operated a lakefront racecourse and later claimed to have made "big money." There were also races of all types on the track at the Mechanics' and Agricultural Fair Grounds (formerly the Union or

12 *Ibid.,* September 28, 1863; New Orleans *Daily Picayune,* May 17, 1863; New Orleans *Times,* October 12, 19, 1863; February 1, 1864. Quotations in this paragraph are from the first three citations in the order cited.

13 New Orleans *Times,* October 16, 24, November 9, 1864; April 23, 1865.

14 *Ibid.,* April 11, October 21, 28, 1864.

Creole Course), which was leased by several promoters during the war. Usually these races were impromptu contests arranged by issuing challenges through the press. Given sufficient notice, as many as five thousand people attended such races.[15]

Visitors to the track soon discovered that racing had declined greatly in quality. The fine thoroughbreds that brought fame to the Metairie had disappeared. Some had become cavalry mounts, others had been killed, and still others had been sold. The stables of Duncan F. Kenner, a member of the Confederate Congress, and of planter William J. Minor were confiscated and sold at auction. Among the buyers was George W. Wilkes, the New Yorker who edited *Wilkes' Spirit of the Times*. Wilkes sent the horses North for "improvement in the breed for the turf, the saddle and for general purposes." While some turfmen were driven from local courses by the loss of their racing stock, at least one local sportsman deserted the city to pursue his interests abroad. When the Louisiana writer James S. Zacharie attended Paris' Chantilly Course in September, 1863, he recorded in his diary: "Saw the famous horse 'La Touques' (a French mare of much renown) win a prize of 10,000 francs. This fine mare is the property of Montgomery of New Orleans otherwise styled here Alfred Comte de Montgoméry." [16]

Deprived of experienced turfmen and superior thoroughbreds, local fans settled for races featuring slow-footed horses entered by Union cavalry officers and promoters like Devol who saw a chance to acquire a few greenbacks. By offering large purses (sometimes as high as two thousand dollars), selling pools on the races, and charging from fifty cents to one dollar for admission, shrewd managers found racing a profitable enterprise.[17] Although the quality of racing had declined, the frequency of contests and public response testified to the popularity of the sport, whatever its merits.

The resumption of horse racing and other sports and the revival of other amusements, such as the theater, balls, gambling, and the

15 Devol, *Forty Years a Gambler,* 221; New Orleans *Daily Picayune,* June 17, 1862; May 2, 26, September 6, 1863; New Orleans *Times,* September 4, 24, 25, 28, October 12, 20, November 26, 27, 1864; January 1, 1865.

16 *Wilkes' Spirit of the Times,* VIII (April 11, 1863), 92; New Orleans *Daily Picayune,* March 22, 1863; James S. Zacharie Diary (Department of Archives and Manuscripts, Louisiana State University), September 20, 1863.

17 New Orleans *Times,* September 4, 25, 28, 1864.

circus, indicate that the traditional portrayal of civilian hardship in occupied New Orleans is misleading. The city could not return completely to the gaiety of antebellum days, but the extent of recovery from 1862 to 1865 belies the tales of suffering at the hands of Federal soldiers passed down to postwar generations of New Orleanians. Contemporary observers described Butler as a beast, a ruffian, "the Pontiff of Brutality," and even as a man so nearly "insane on the subject of enriching himself" that "he opened several graves, supposing that gold had been hidden in them." His administration of the city, said one observer, was "a perfect reign of terror." Banks fared little better in the eyes of some witnesses. Julia LeGrand grudgingly noted: "There is a difference even among devils, it seems, as some of Banks' people do try to be kind to us, while Butler's were just the reverse." [18] These views, generally shared by later historians, [19] suggest that the city suffered dreadfully during the three-year Federal occupation. But such was not the case. Indeed residents so successfully sought and found amusement during the occupation that one Protestant minister complained: "There is a soiree here to-night and the young girls seem to have forgotten everything else—They dance beneath the very flag that has been the death of their friends & relatives—The Federals did a good thing in abolishing Sunday Theatres—Sunday balls &c—Would that they would abolish them altogether." Some suffering seems to have been in large measure

[18] Thomas C. DeLeon, *Four Years in Rebel Capitals: An Inside View of Life in the Southern Confederacy, from Birth to Death; from Original Notes, Collated in the Years 1861 to 1865* (Mobile, 1892), 173; Kate Mason Rowland and Mrs. Morris L. Croxall (eds.), *The Journal of Julia LeGrand: New Orleans, 1862–1863* (Richmond, 1911), 222; William Watson, *Life in the Confederate Army; Being the Observations and Experiences of an Alien in the South During the American Civil War* (London, 1887), 401; Rowland and Croxall (eds.), *The Journal of Julia LeGrand,* 77. Quotations are in the order cited. See also Sarah Morgan Dawson, *A Confederate Girl's Diary* (Boston, 1913), 97.

[19] See, for examples, Jefferson Davis Bragg, *Louisiana in the Confederacy* (Baton Rouge, 1941), 97–138, especially 112; E. Merton Coulter, *The Confederate States of America, 1861–1865,* Vol. VII of *A History of the South* (Baton Rouge, 1950), 368, 370; John Rose Ficklen, *History of Reconstruction in Louisiana (Through 1868)* (Baltimore, 1910), 33; and John D. Winters, *The Civil War in Louisiana* (Baton Rouge, 1963), 125–48, especially 127. Capers, *Occupied City,* presents a more balanced view of Butler and the Federal occupation generally, particularly in chapter 4, "The Rule of the Beast, May to December, 1862," 77–97. The classic defense of Butler is James Parton, *General Butler in New Orleans: History of the Administration of the Department of the Gulf in the Year 1862: With an Account of the Capture of New Orleans, and a Sketch of the Previous Career of the General, Civil and Military* (New York, 1864).

self-induced. Sarah Morgan Dawson's diary, which has numerous passages agonizing over Confederate defeats, contains a highly revealing passage written in August of 1863: "Doomed to be bored! To-night Miriam [Sarah's sister] drags me to a *soirée musicale*. . . . What a bore! What a bore! And she looks as though it was a pleasure to go out! How I hate it!" But for those residents who, unlike Sarah Dawson, chose to resist melancholia, the city offered a variety of amusements.[20] As a mitigating factor during the occupation (and also during Reconstruction), amusements have been given too little attention. In a time of political stress and economic privation, sports and other forms of recreation made life endurable, even pleasurable for the majority of the city's residents.

With the return of peace, conditions improved even more noticeably. Economic recovery went forward rapidly as trade returned to normal channels. Early in 1866 the *Picayune* reported that wharves were being rebuilt and that longshoremen were returning to work at increased wages. "Crowded streets, crowded hotels and boarding houses may still be reported," one journalist noted. "The great influx of strangers to our city is one of the principal reasons that our amusement resorts are nightly filled. These resorts, however, are ample for all whose inclinations lie in that direction. We have theatricals, operatic performances, concerts, balls, museums, billiard saloons, and—shall we write it?—gambling hells." In the midst of the first full social season since the end of the war, the city seemed well on the path to recovery. Political and economic difficulties lay ahead, but the city bustled as it had in "the piping days of peace." [21]

20 Charles W. Hilton Diary (Special Collections, Tulane University Library), February 14, 1865; Dawson, *A Confederate Girl's Diary*, 405–406.

21 New Orleans *Daily Picayune*, January 7, 1866.

Part Two

THE RISE OF
SPORTS, 1865-1900

INTRODUCTION

Organized sports came fully into their own in the thirty-five years after the Civil War. Cities grew very rapidly during this period as the transition from a rural-agrarian to an urban-industrial society accelerated. In 1860 one out of six Americans lived in cities; by 1900, 40 percent of the population—more than thirty million people—had left the countryside behind for the close quarters of an urban community. The expansion of cities intensified the need for commercial recreation and planned spectacles. Thus, as the modern American city emerged after 1865, organized sports, together with skyscrapers, incandescent lighting, electric streetcars, and telephones, became an everyday feature of urban life. At the turn of the century, sports had risen to a preeminent position among leisure-time activities.

Sports in New Orleans joined the city's surge toward peacetime readjustment. Within a few years after the end of the war, those sports popular during Federal occupation and those which had languished since 1861 enjoyed a greater vogue than they had in the 1850s. In ensuing years the city's sportsmen also welcomed many new activities, including cycling, tennis, golf, and eventually the most popular of them all, American football. Theater, opera, balls, concerts, social clubs, saloons, houses of prostitution, and, until legal restrictions intervened, gambling and the Louisiana Lottery provided diversions for thousands of residents, but against this backdrop of generally well-established amusements, sports increased in popularity until they surpassed all rivals. As early as January, 1882, the *Picayune* observed: "New Orleans is fast becoming one of the most prominent sporting cities of this country. Her yachtsmen have won fame in Northern waters; her oarsmen have snatched many laurels from their muscular Northern competitors; and her riflemen have upheld her honor nobly." Furthermore, the account continued, the John L. Sullivan-Paddy Ryan prize fight, scheduled for the following month, "will tend to make New Orleans the fair field of the most famous sporting people in the country for some time to come." [1] Sports had clearly become the major source of recreation in a city renowned for its varieties of pleasure. By the end of the century, organized sport was a major enterprise involving thousands of participants and spectators and tens of thousands of dollars.

Interest in sports expanded to such proportions for a number of reasons. The growth of the city and attendant urban pressures, the appearance of appealing new sports in other parts of the country, and a further decline in the workweek played vital roles in the sporting boom. Sports profited also from widespread recognition of the salubrious effects of physical exercise. In 1869 a New Orleanian wrote to *Wilkes' Spirit of the Times* that "athletic sports are becoming more popular. It is what we need, for I believe with due exercise of the body the ills we delight in nursing will fade away, and an energy we so much need take their place." Finally, residents appreciated the ability of sports and other pastimes to draw attention away from worldly problems. In an age of rapid and frenetic change, punctuated by complex issues of economic and political adjustment, sports provided a sense of order and continuity as well as timely relief from workaday cares. In March, 1874, during Reconstruction, the *Picayune* extended its appreciation to the city's social and sporting clubs: "It seems as if they wished to dissipate some of the troubles and anxieties of these hard times, to detract our minds from the dark realities of life and afford us pleasure and relief from care." The ability of sports to divert attention from the perplexities of political and economic problems remained important after Reconstruction came to an end. When baseball activity began in the spring of 1879, the *Picayune* observed: "The B. B. season having opened, there is still ground for hope that there is life in the old land yet, and that whatever be the condition of the State debt or the Texas Railroad, the sweet consciousness remains that the base ball business is being properly attended to." [2]

1 New Orleans *Daily Picayune*, January 15, 1882.

2 *Wilkes' Spirit of the Times*, XXI (September 11, 1869), 53; New Orleans *Daily Picayune*, March 15, 1874; March 10, 1879. For other expressions of the value of sports as a diversion from the cares of everyday life, see New Orleans *Bulletin*, January 23, 1875; and New Orleans *Daily Picayune*, December 9, 1876.

Locally and nationally, the development of sports after the war generally followed antebellum trends. Commercialism, spectator interest, the formation of teams and sporting organizations, intercity rivalries, and the standardization and nationalization of rules—all features of sports that appeared before the war—became even more pronounced after 1865. Organized sports also acquired some new aspects in the postwar period. Participation in athletics by women of all ranks, greater interest in sports among Negroes, the rise of collegiate and intercollegiate athletics, technological improvements in equipment, and the acceptance of modern concepts of amateurism and professionalism were among the prominent developments in the period 1865 to 1900.

Negro participation in sports was particularly important, for it raised questions about the ability of sports to bridge class lines and racial divisions and about the nature of black-white relationships in the post-Civil War South. As portions of the following chapters demonstrate, the idea that American sports have been and are genuinely democratic is debatable. In recent years organized professional and amateur sports have assumed an important role in encouraging acceptance of racial integration; but in the late nineteenth century, sports in New Orleans and elsewhere too often merely reflected the social and political pressures that made rigid racial segregation an established practice in the South and, to an only slightly lesser extent, in the North.

The development of modern definitions of amateurism and professionalism also posed interesting questions about the democratic character of sports. Creeping professionalism, a minor problem before the war, became a major issue after 1865. In the antebellum period, sportsmen defined a professional as a man who made a profit from participation in sports; an amateur, by contrast, was a gentleman sportsman who played for the pure love of sport. This definition, borrowed from England where custom and practice rigidly separated gentlemen from other players, generally restricted the amateur class to America's sporting gentry whose wealth and leisure permitted them to indulge in sports with no concern for financial reward. This basically undemocratic distinction between amateurs and professionals broke down in the 1860s and 1870s, when participants who regularly followed other types of work began to play for money in such large numbers that they seemed likely to dominate most sports. Billiard players, bowlers, baseball players, yachtsmen, rowers, and other athletes often spiced their contests with side bets or competed for cash prizes. Many of these athletes were workingmen or members of the lower middle class who neither wanted nor qualified for designation as gentlemen amateurs. But many players also came from the upper middle and upper classes and had no wish to tarnish their claims to gentlemanliness by playing sports for money. By the seventies many observers agreed that amateurism and professionalism had to be defined more clearly; otherwise, it was believed, gentlemen players would be driven from the field altogether. Baseball escaped the control of gentlemen soon after the war, but simon-pure amateurs made a strong effort to protect the purity of other sporting pastimes, such as rowing, track and field, and cycling. Their determination to enforce concepts of amateurism and professionalism that discriminated against low-income players who could ill afford the self-abnegation of wealthy sportsmen ran completely contrary to the democratizing tendencies in sports during the late nineteenth century. Consequently the attempt to win approval of such definitions was not entirely successful. Nevertheless, vestiges of this athletic exclusiveness are still evident in American sports and remain a problem for modern competitors.

In spite of the failure of sports to eradicate racial prejudice or to eliminate class cleavages, the democratic impulses in sports were clearly present after 1865. Increased participation by women and Negroes (even though often segregated by sex and by race), the failure of upper-middle- and upper-class participants to retain exclusive control of some sports, such as baseball and horse racing, and the inability of these same classes to monopolize new sports, including roller skating and American football, indicated that organized sports in the late nineteenth century were in the process of becoming truly democratic pastimes. This trend toward democratization reflected political realities. The abolition of slavery and the extension of the suffrage to poor white farmers and laborers in the Louisiana Constitution of 1864 and temporarily to blacks in the Constitution of 1868 made politics in New Orleans and Louisiana theoretically more democratic. Class divisions remained, as the revolt of low-income farmers and laborers near the end of the century indicated, but the control of planters and merchants had been weakened.[3] In sports, as in politics, class divisions remained, but the lines were blurring as sportsmen in New Orleans moved slowly toward a time when sports of nearly every description would be open to people of all social and economic backgrounds. A few sports, such as yachting, remained permanently beyond the reach of ordinary citizens because of their cost, but others, such as tennis, merely resisted democratic pressures. At century's end the capitulation of these activities seemed primarily a matter of time.

Old and new trends taken together constituted the story of the rise of sports in New Orleans and throughout the country. In the century since the Civil War, Americans have submitted to the attractions of this leisure-time activity with an enthusiasm unmatched by any nationality, with the possible exception of the British. As the following chapters indicate, the conquest was virtually complete by 1900. New Orleans had sustained its interest in sporting amusements throughout the war; in succeeding decades it yielded to the triumph of organized sports as willingly as any city in the country.

[3] Shugg, *Origins of Class Struggle in Louisiana,* chapters 6–9.

Chapter V
THE SPORT
OF KINGS

Horse racing, once an exclusive diversion for the social aristocracy, became a pastime for the masses after the Civil War. In New Orleans and throughout the country, racing, like a number of other leisure-time activities, experienced great changes in response to the urban populace's demand for new forms of recreation. In the antebellum period, urban residents who lacked the time or means to provide their own entertainment had experimented with several commercial amusements and had generally found them acceptable substitutes for the casual activities of the countryside. The practice of buying pleasure became even more firmly entrenched after 1865. Theaters, vaudeville and burlesque, circuses and museums, and playing fields and sports arenas attracted thousands of observers who were eager for entertainment and willing to pay handsomely for it. No sport showed the impact of this desire for spectacles more than horse racing, which became increasingly popular among ordinary city dwellers. The planter and merchant aristocracy that dominated the sport in New Orleans and other cities gradually lowered or eliminated the barriers that had formerly discouraged the support of the urban masses. Participation generally remained the prerogative of the well-to-do, but crowds included people of all ranks. The sport of kings thus became a pastime for all levels of the social structure. By 1900 the two-dollar bettor had become a regular and an indispensable patron of the American turf.

Racing's ascendancy as a popular sport began during the war. Although generally dormant in the Confederacy, organized racing claimed a strong following in the North. Track promoters, aided by war profits and the public's desire for temporary escapes from the gloom of war news, offered racing on an extensive scale. John Morissey, once the heavyweight champion of America, established the pattern for racing for the remainder of the century when he made Saratoga a showplace for turfmen during the war. After 1865 some of the country's wealthiest men and shrewdest promoters joined forces to develop great stables and to construct elaborate tracks such as Jerome Park, Pimlico, Monmouth Park, Churchill Downs, Washington Park, Gravesend, Belmont Park, and the Fair Grounds in New Orleans. This group soon transformed racing from a sport controlled by the gentry for its own amusement into a commercial venture with vast earning potential and broad popular appeal. Spacious grandstands, lucrative purses, fast horses, and fans addicted to racetrack gambling made the Gilded Age the heyday of the turf.[1]

With the restoration of peace, patrons of racing in the South revived their favorite pastime. Despite a paucity of money and fine horses, turfmen joined in the South's campaign to resurrect old social patterns. Perhaps, like a writer for *Wilkes' Spirit of the Times*, they believed that racing "was to be a means rather than an effect of recuperation at the South." Jockey clubs in Memphis, Mobile, New Orleans, and Charleston reorganized soon after the war and laid plans for racing meets. When sportsmen in Mobile sponsored the South's first postwar meeting, *Wilkes'* predicted that "a grand revival of horse-racing may be looked for in this section, commensurate with that which began at the North some years ago." [2]

Fans in New Orleans also hoped for a speedy recovery of racing. For several months after Appomattox, just as during Federal occupation, racing consisted mainly of challenge matches and charity races arranged by *ad hoc* associations.[3] But in December, 1865, the Metairie Jockey Club, reactivated by a group of turfmen that included former Governor P. O. Hebert, G. S. Mandeville, Henry B. Foley, and C. H. Slocomb, announced plans to resume regular spring and winter meetings. This group sponsored semiannual meets at the Metairie Course until 1872. Ownership of the track remained in the

1 See Parmer, *For Gold and Glory*, 113–73, for a fairly comprehensive history of racing after the Civil War.

2 *Wilkes' Spirit of the Times*, XVIII (May 9, 1868), 194; XIV (April 7, 1866), 92; New Orleans *Daily Picayune*, December 30, 1866; Krout, *Annals of American Sport*, 35.

3 New Orleans *Daily Picayune*, June 9, 14, 23, September 16, December 29, 1865; New Orleans *Times*, August 13, 18, 1865.

hands of the Metairie Association, which had purchased the track in 1851.[4]

Resumption of jockey club races met with an enthusiastic reception. "Puritanism may grimly smile at the idea of calling men engaged in the unholy amusement of horse-racing public benefactors," the *Crescent* noted in 1868, "but we think that the verdict of the thoughtful men of the world will be that were such trials of fleetness and endurance more frequent—were men to find their enjoyments in the open air, and their pleasures in the discussion of pedigrees and blood, of muscle and wind—society would be better." The *Picayune*, concerned more with a healthy economy than with a healthy society, stressed the financial advantages of organized racing. "Every branch of trade is helped by the attractions of a well conducted race course," a reporter contended. "The hotels, steamboats, railroads, merchants, theatricals, stable keepers, hackmen, and even the ragged boot-blacks, are greatly benefited by the visitors drawn here to witness the racing." [5]

Anticipation of a successful racing revival proved premature by several years, for prosperity eluded the Metairie Jockey Club during its brief postbellum existence. The club sponsored thirteen meetings before its dissolution in 1872; of these, only the last three could be regarded as financially profitable. For these later meets, the club tried to attract additional stables by increasing purses, a liberal policy that brought better horses to the city, including the first northern stable to race in postwar New Orleans. The outstanding feature of the club's meetings in 1871 and 1872 was the success of Lexington's offspring. In April, 1871, the blind sire's get won several important races, including the Bingaman Stakes, which went to T. G. Moore's Foster; and the Club Purse, a race of five-mile heats won by D. Swigert's Pilgrim, "a fine dark bay, and one of the most beautiful animals we have ever seen upon the turf." In December, 1871, and again

4 New Orleans *Daily Picayune*, December 31, 1865. When local sportsmen first reorganized a club to sponsor regular meetings, they took the name Fair Grounds Jockey Club, intending to schedule races on a track that had become popular during the war. By the time of the spring meeting, however, they had adopted the name Metairie Jockey Club and had made arrangements with the Metairie Association to run races on the Metairie Course.

5 New Orleans *Daily Crescent*, November 29, 1868; New Orleans *Daily Picayune*, December 18, 1866.

in April, 1872, M. H. Sanford of New York dominated racing at the Metairie with a stable of Lexington's thoroughbreds led by the highly rated Monarchist, a horse that subsequently performed well on tracks in the East. But soon after the Metairie had apparently found a formula to pump life into thoroughbred racing, the South's most illustrious jockey club disbanded. After the spring meeting of 1872, the track where notable steeds like Lexington and Lecomte had thrilled American racing fans by the thousands was sold, to become the Metairie Cemetery. *Wilkes' Spirit of the Times* lamented that "the scenes which have long been so famous for exhibitions of rare pluck and gallantry, for life and gaiety, and game and resolution in horse and man and 'ladye fayre,' will now be devoted to the sad but pious offices of the bereaved to their beloved departed." [6]

An acrimonious struggle for control of local racing caused the club's collapse. Sometime after the Metairie Jockey Club reorganized, a schism developed between younger members, led by Gustave A. Breaux and Robert W. Simmons, who believed that racing would prosper only if the club recruited spectators from all ranks of society; and older members wedded to the traditions of a glorious past, who wished to preserve racing as a sport for the social aristocracy. The conflict became open and bitter in 1871 when the rebels attempted to bring Charles T. Howard, director of the state lottery and patron of several sports, into the club. Because Howard, as head of the lottery, was closely linked with the state's much despised Republican government, his application aroused the anger of the old guard, who quickly blackballed his request for membership and thus precipitated a crisis.

Howard persuaded several members of the Metairie Jockey Club to resign and to join him in founding the rival Louisiana Jockey Club. Gus Breaux became president of the association, which purchased the Fair Grounds and made it one of the country's most attractive racecourses. In the antebellum period, the Fair Grounds track, then known as the Union Course, had been popular with the city's turf fans, but since the war it had fallen into disuse except for occasional match races. Members of the Louisiana Jockey Club proposed to revitalize the track, which was located in the midst of an ex-

6 New Orleans *Daily Picayune,* April 9, 16, December 5, 7, 24, 1871; April 9, 12, 1872; *Wilkes' Spirit of the Times* XXVI (May 11, 1872), 201.

tensive tract of land covered with magnificent oaks. They refurbished existing buildings and constructed, at a cost of $25,000, a three-tiered grandstand with a seating capacity of five thousand. For the fashion-conscious there was a promenade at the rear of the grandstand. The structure, said the *Picayune*, "rises, in its handsome crowned roof, from among the trees and buildings of the grounds like a monarch among his creatures." Today the Fair Grounds is the third oldest racecourse in the country, antedated only by Saratoga and Churchill Downs. In a spirit of revenge, Howard completed the ruin of the Metairie Jockey Club by purchasing the Metairie Course from the Metairie Association, which had, according to one report, fallen into "the hands of speculators, who care little for racing." When Howard offered $128,000 for the course, "a great deal more than the grounds are really worth," the association eagerly accepted. Howard then transformed what had once been the nation's liveliest racecourse into a graveyard. A member of the Louisiana Jockey Club later justified Howard's action on the grounds that the Metairie club had "dry rot in it." The "racing interests of the South," he went on, "cannot be subservient to any little clique of people. The new club is on a broad and noble foundation, and if there is peace and prosperity in our borders they will accomplish a great work." To take advantage of the Metairie's efforts to attract turfmen to the city, the Louisiana Jockey Club scheduled its first spring meeting to begin immediately after the conclusion of the Metairie's last racing meet. Thus did the old give way to the new.[7]

During its management of the Fair Grounds, the Louisiana Jockey Club broadened racing's following appreciably. The Metairie

---

[7] New Orleans *Daily Picayune,* April 5, 1872; *Wilkes' Spirit of the Times,* XXVI (May 11, 1872), 197; XXVIII (March 1, 1873), 34. When the Metairie Jockey Club dissolved, the local press neither reported the issues involved in the struggle nor mentioned the men who participated in the quarrel. Historians have reflected this lack of information. Louis J. Hennessey said only that financial difficulties and personal squabbles forced the collapse of the Metairie Jockey Club, but he gave no names. Hennessey, *The Fair Grounds Race Course: A Time-Honored American Institution* (New Orleans, 1947), 10. Walter S. Vosburgh contended that "personal spite on the part of one man" led to the rupture, but he did not name the man. Vosburgh, *Racing in America, 1866–1921* (New York, 1922), 62. The account presented here is gleaned from several sources, particularly *Wilkes' Spirit of the Times,* XXVI (May 11, 1872), 197, 201; XXVIII (March 1, 1873), 34; LXXXVI (October 18, 1873), 231; CIX (February 14, 1885), 84; New Orleans *Daily Picayune,* September 17, November 12, 1871.

Jockey Club, both before and after the war, was an exclusive social club devoted to racing. From the general public, members expected only the price of admission to offset rebuilding and operating costs. To avoid direct contact with the *hoi polloi* (and to protect the flower of southern womanhood), club rules required that the grandstand be divided into three separate sections—one for ladies (who received formal invitations), one for members, and one for the general public. Even as it admitted the public, the Metairie exercised an economic veto by charging twenty dollars for a quarter-stretch badge for a six-day meet and two dollars for daily admission to the "democratic portion of the stand." [8] Members of the Louisiana Jockey Club, conscious of their own high social standing, retained the practice of dividing the stand, but they attempted to attract large crowds by setting the price of general admission at one dollar and by allowing people into the infield for fifty cents. One reporter noted in approval of this policy that "there are a great many to whom a stroll in the open field, with a view of the crowd, and the enjoyment of fresh air, green fields and a respite from city drudgery, are as attractive as the incidents of the race course itself, exciting as these may be." Formerly the high cost had barred such spectators from the races. In other respects the new club, like its predecessor, remained an exclusive social organization. Members had access to an elaborately appointed clubhouse on the grounds of the racecourse, which was the scene of fashionable parties and musical entertainments during the racing season and throughout the year. At the end of each racing day "the members of the club retired from the arena, escorting their lady guests, through the handsome rear entrance of their Club-House grounds, to the Club House itself." [9]

The Louisiana Jockey Club sought to attract fans of all ranks, but members only partly reversed one restrictive policy begun by the Metairie Jockey Club—racial segregation. Negroes in New Orleans had long been interested in the turf as jockeys, as spectators,

---

8 *Rules and Regulations for the Government of Racing, Trotting, and Betting, as Adopted by the Principal Turf Associations Throughout the United States and Canada* (New York, 1866), 225–27; New Orleans *Times,* April 11, 12, 1866; Metairie Jockey Club Invitation, 1870, in Joseph P. Horner Papers (Department of Archives and Manuscripts, Louisiana State University). The quotation is from the New Orleans *Daily Crescent,* April 10, 1869.

9 New Orleans *Daily Picayune,* April 14, 1872.

and even as owners of race horses.[10] Before 1871 the city's race-courses had admitted black fans to any part of the track except the members' and ladies' stands, which were also closed to most white spectators. Racial harmony evidently prevailed at the track, if not in society at large. In December, 1873, the *Times* said of the jockeys: "The darkies and whites mingle fraternally together, charmed into mutual happy sympathies by the inspiriting influence of horse talk." But the efforts of Radical Republicans to safeguard the political and civil rights of blacks, a movement that gathered strength after the adoption of the Constitution of 1868 and the passage of a state civil rights act in 1869, elicited an angry response from many recalcitrant whites. In April, 1871, the *Louisianian*, a Negro newspaper, reported that "for the first time, there has been erected a separate stand on the ground [of the Metairie Course], to prevent the mingling of whey faces, and *sang melées*. . . . The managers of the course have pandered to the ignoble passions and prejudices of those who possess no other claim to superiority, than the external shading of a skin." The editor urged Negroes to boycott the races, to withhold their support from a club "which takes your money, and gives the value of it to others." Economic pressure brought a partial reversal of the policy of segregation. After the Louisiana Jockey Club assumed control of racing, it admitted Negroes to the public stand, but it barred them from the quarter stretch, a stand at the finish line. In May, 1874, two black fans filed suit against the club, charging that it had violated the law of 1869, which guaranteed equal access to public accommodations, by refusing to sell them quarter-stretch badges. The *Louisianian* encouraged the plaintiffs "in their effort to sustain the manhood of their race," but the suit evidently failed. When Reconstruction came to an end, pressure for equal seating arrangements at the Fair Grounds eased for the remainder of the century.[11]

The most farsighted change in racing practices introduced by the Louisiana Jockey Club was the acceptance of new methods of gambling. The Metairie, catering to wealthy spectators, had never pro-

10 For an example of a race involving horses owned by Negroes, see New Orleans *Semi-Weekly Louisianian*, March 26, 1871.

11 New Orleans *Times*, December 14, 1873; New Orleans *Semi-Weekly Louisianian*, April 9, 1871; New Orleans *Weekly Louisianian*, May 2, 1874.

vided adequately for the small bettor. Before 1873 fans bought auction pools on the night before the race or made side bets at the
track.[12] These methods, which often required large amounts of
money, appealed to few small wagerers. In December, 1873, the Louisiana Jockey Club introduced "Paris Mutual Pools," which had been
imported to New York's Jerome Park by Leonard Jerome two years
earlier. With minimum bets of five dollars, pari-mutuel pools were
"especially adapted to the requirements of that class of pigmy specu-
lators who are inclined to sing small at the pool box." Advocates of
the new system also saw in pari-mutuel wagering a leveling influence.
According to the *Times:* "The young gallants who went out behind
spanking pairs and dashing trotters, jostled and bought pools with
the great unsorted who had struggled and labored on the journey
by cars." [13] At the following spring meet, the Fair Grounds' management completed the renovation of betting procedures when it permitted the selling of auction pools, as well as pari-mutuel pools, at
the track. The club also abolished all gambling not connected with
racing, such as faro, monte, chuck-a-luck, and roulette.[14]

Early meetings of the Louisiana Jockey Club indicated that racing had recaptured the prosperity it had enjoyed in "the palmy days
of Lexington and Lecomte." The club attracted few entries from
other sections, but the colors of additional southern stables began
to appear at the Fair Grounds.[15] The most successful turfman in this
period was William Cottrill, a wealthy Mobilian who brought his
stable to the city for two decades after the war. Year after year
Cottrill's thoroughbreds made him the leading winner at meetings of
the Louisiana Jockey Club and its successor the New Louisiana
Jockey Club. In April, 1880, for example, his horses captured the
Pickwick Stakes, the Momus Stakes, the Walker Stakes, and the
Howard Stakes. A four-year-old named Bucktie won two of these
events, including a two-mile dash which the *Picayune* described as "a
most interesting contest, where the horses displayed their racing
qualities, and the jockeys their expert riding." [16] In 1874 Charles T.

---

12 New Orleans *Daily Crescent,* April 21, 1866.
13 New Orleans *Times,* December 14, 21, 1873.
14 New Orleans *Daily Picayune,* April 12, 1874.
15 *Ibid.,* April 14, November 24, 1872; November 18, 28, 1875; March 19, 26,
1876; New Orleans *Bulletin,* March 14, 1875.
16 New Orleans *Daily Crescent,* January 3, April 12, 1868; New Orleans

Howard, "the main man at the helm" of the Louisiana Jockey Club, attempted to stimulate greater local interest by purchasing several horses to organize a "home stable" for New Orleans. The enterprise temporarily aroused enthusiasm, but a series of disastrous reversals in 1875, including the death of one thoroughbred and the crippling of another, forced Howard to abandon the undertaking.[17]

However, the club attracted public support. Crowds ranging in size from a thousand to five thousand were common throughout the 1870s, and special races drew as many as twenty thousand. City officials cooperated in November, 1875, by "doing all in their power to improve the roads leading to the Course." [18] In a city noted for its poor streets, the effort was a tribute to racing's popularity. The country plunged into a depression in the mid-seventies, but racing profits mounted steadily. In 1873, when pessimists predicted failure on account of the "great financial crash," the club cleared four thousand dollars from the winter meeting. After the spring meet of 1875, members counted nine thousand dollars above expenses.[19]

Statistics, however, told an incomplete story. Behind the façade of prosperity, financial obligations slowly crushed the Louisiana Jockey Club. Since the organization borrowed heavily to buy and to renovate the Fair Grounds, the club, of necessity, had to extract handsome profits from each meet. To increase the returns, the club periodically reduced purses, until by 1878 it offered total prizes of only sixty-six hundred dollars, a tremendous drop from the thirty thousands dollars given to winners at the first spring meeting in 1872. Faced with the need to slash purses still more—a decision that would have further lowered the quality of racing—the club chose to relinquish control of the turf. After the spring meet of 1878, the Louisiana Jockey Club disbanded.[20]

Less than a year later, "a number of public-spirited citizens" led

---

Times, April 9, 1869; December 9, 1874; New Orleans *Daily Picayune,* April 4, 1869; December 2, 1874; April 11, 25, 1875; March 26, 1876; November 25, 1877; April 30, 1878; March 31, April 2, 4, 7, 1880; April 25, 1882; April 7, 1885.

17 *Wilkes' Spirit of the Times,* LXXXVI (October 18, 1873), 231; LXXXVIII (October 3, 1874), 190; New Orleans *Times,* September 20, October 11, 1874; April 17, 1875.

18 New Orleans *Times,* April 13, 1873; New Orleans *Bulletin,* November 28, 1875; New Orleans *Daily Picayune,* April 16, 18, 1875; April 25, 26, 1878.

19 New Orleans *Daily Picayune,* December 28, 1873; June 6, 1875.

20 *Ibid.,* April 9, 1872; April 30, 1878.

by R. W. Simmons and G. W. Nott organized the New Louisiana Jockey Club to continue thoroughbred racing. Instead of sponsoring fall and winter races, the new club restricted its activities to a week-long spring meet, thereby enabling the association to apply all its resources to the success of a single season. Initial meetings demonstrated the efficacy of this approach. After only three spring campaigns, the club cleared enough money to buy the Fair Grounds from representatives of the Louisiana Jockey Club.[21]

Like its predecessor, the New Louisiana Jockey Club continued to democratize racing in an effort to broaden its commercial appeal. At its first meeting, the club made the track infield available to fans free of charge. Deviating from earlier habits, members briefly sponsored Sunday races, heretofore the exclusive domain of fly-by-night promoters and working-class social organizations. The *Picayune* praised this innovation because it made racing available to "the many who cannot attend during the working days of the week." Catering to this same group, the New Louisiana Jockey Club experimented with night racing. The managers of the Fair Grounds installed "forty Brush electric lights" in 1881. "If the expectations of the promoters of the scheme are realized," it was pointed out, "it will be possible to begin the races at a late hour in the evening, thus permitting all classes to attend and enjoy the magnificent sight, as well as escaping the heat of the day." However, after one trial conscientious judges abandoned racing under the lights because they found it impossible to distinguish the colors of the various riders across the track. Successful night racing had to wait upon further improvements in electric lighting.[22]

When the New Louisiana Jockey Club demonstrated the potential of racing in New Orleans, turfmen from other sections looked upon the Fair Grounds with a fresh appreciation. In 1882 W. A. Engeman, a well-known promoter who had helped to develop racing at Coney Island and Brighton Beach, initiated a project that determined the future course of local racing. Proposing to sponsor a long season while cold weather idled tracks in the North, Engeman leased the Fair Grounds for five years in December, 1882. Prolonged bad

21 *Ibid.*, February 9, 18, 21, 23, 1879; April 27, 1881.

22 *Ibid.*, April 14, 18, 1879; February 20, April 17, 1881. The quotations are from the issues of April 18, 1879; February 20, 1881.

weather forced him to surrender his lease, but the idea appealed to the jockey club. Since Engeman had sent notices to many northern stables, the members simply appropriated the scheme.[23]

Scheduling races every Tuesday, Thursday, and Saturday, the New Louisiana Jockey Club began the city's first winter season on January 27, 1883. After seventeen days of racing, the longest meet held in the city up to that time, opinions varied as to the practicability of winter racing. T. Atcheson, a reporter for *Wilkes' Spirit of the Times*, gloomily predicted that, although the climate offered advantages, there was "not a very bright outlook for racing at the Crescent City. The point is isolated, away out of the live racing current." Consequently, he continued, "the better class of animals, outside of a few, will not come here, and thus the *eclat*, the crowds, the enthusiasm, which you find further north, where the cracks of the turf are entered for competition, are wanting here." Nevertheless, optimism prevailed locally. Attendance at the races fell below expectations, but encouraged by the presence of several northern stables, members of the club laid plans for the next winter meeting. "New Orleans is a splendid point for wintering horses," the *Picayune* declared in 1884, "and many prominent stables will make this their annual meeting place in the future."[24]

For all the initial confidence, winter racing passed through a series of convolutions before it became a well-established institution. After two financially unrewarding experiments with the extended season, the club retreated to the womblike safety of its spring meeting.[25] A group of professional pool sellers, including Leon Lamothe and Ira E. Bride, then leased the Fair Grounds from the club and began to hold winter races in January of 1885. During a three-year period, they extended the meeting to more than forty days. Attendance periodically declined, partly as a result of bad weather and partly because flagrant cases of dishonesty sometimes discouraged fans, but Lamothe and his associates offset reverses at the turnstiles with gambling profits and bookmaking fees. Lamothe also attracted fans (and

23 *Ibid.*, December 24, 1882; January 25, 1883.
24 *Wilkes' Spirit of the Times*, CV (April 14, 1883), 288; New Orleans *Daily Picayune* April 20, 1884. See also New Orleans *Daily Picayune*, January 28, March 18, April 4, 1883.
25 *Wilkes' Spirit of the Times*, CVI (January 5, 1884), 685; CVI (February 2, 1884), 20.

thus bettors) shunned or alienated by the Metairie, Louisiana, and New Louisiana jockey clubs. In January, 1887, the Negro newspaper *Pelican* announced that "in keeping with Mr. Lamothe's liberal spirit . . . every person will be admitted free of charge." Admission fees were charged on most days, of course, but the Fair Grounds now admitted Negroes on a nondiscriminatory basis.[26] The policy helped racing to prosper. After losing ten thousand dollars during the season of 1885, the management of the Fair Grounds began to show a profit. Atcheson of *Wilkes' Spirit of the Times* recanted his earlier pessimism and admitted that "judging from the results up to date . . . winter racing can be made successful and profitable at the Crescent City." [27]

As winter racing prospered, gamblers also sought to revive trotting and pacing. For twenty years after the war, a few amateurs, some gamblers, officials of the state fair, and social and benevolent clubs had attempted with little success to resurrect harness racing.[28] Nevertheless, the good fortune of gamblers at the Fair Grounds aroused new interest in the commercial possibilities of trotting and pacing. In 1886 Ira E. Bride headed a group that opened a trotting track at Oakland Park, then a popular spot for Sunday excursions. Primarily a gambling enterprise, the track's first "improvements" consisted of a pool stand and a bookmaking stall. The Oakland venture collapsed when the matches drew few entries and small crowds.[29] George W. Wintz, another gambler-turned-promoter, then opened the Brooklyn Race Course in Algiers where he scheduled both running and trotting races.[30] After this track closed in 1887, the Audubon

26 New Orleans *Weekly Pelican,* January 8, 1887. P. B. S. Pinchback, lieutenant governor during the Reconstruction period, attended the races regularly. "Pinchback is probably more at home on the racecourse than anywhere else," one reporter wrote, "and he is certainly a model racegoer, being singularly well-bred and gentlemanly in his demeanor, without a suggestion of the rough, uncouth or ill-mannered." *Wilkes' Spirit of the Times,* CXVI (January 5, 1889), 862.

27 *Wilkes' Spirit of the Times,* CIX (March 14, 1885), 202; CX (January 9, 1886), 715; CXIII (April 9, 1887), 341; New Orleans *Daily Picayune,* April 13, 1887. The quote is from *Wilkes' Spirit of the Times,* CX (January 16, 1886), 750.

28 New Orleans *Times,* May 13, 14, 1865; New Orleans *Daily Crescent,* December 14, 1866; April 14, 1869; New Orleans *Daily Picayune,* December 3, 25, 1865; June 13, October 5, 1869; January 30, 1870; April 24, 1872; April 25, 1873; May 31, July 26, August 30, 1875; February 27, 1876; February 9, 18, 1879; April 26, 1880; May 8, 1882.

29 New Orleans *Daily Picayune,* April 1, 3, 16, 18, 19, 1866.

30 *Ibid.,* October 18, November 15, December 20, 1886.

Driving Club, a pale imitation of the gentlemen's driving associations in other urban centers such as Chicago and Cleveland, sponsored Sunday trots at Audubon Park. For several years a succession of mediocre races and the opportunity to participate in pari-mutuel pools attracted as many as a thousand people to the races, but interest in harness racing waned after 1890. By December, 1891, the track had ceased to operate.[31] Another effort to resuscitate standardbred racing in the mid-1890s also failed.[32] The competition of thoroughbred racing and other commercial pastimes, the declining size of the city's northern-born population (which had sustained the sport in the 1850s), and the introduction of new modes of transportation, including bicycles, electric streetcars, and later automobiles, had made the roadhorse an increasingly unpopular source of amusement, at least in New Orleans.

In the meantime the New Louisiana Jockey Club had temporarily regained control of thoroughbred racing at the Fair Grounds. Convinced that Lamothe had begun to mine a racing bonanza, the club terminated his lease and resumed management of the winter season in November, 1887. Deprived of the gambling profits on which Lamothe had relied, the club lost money for four years. When racing concluded in the spring of 1891, disillusioned members permanently relinquished control of winter racing to professional gamblers and promoters. Until the state legislature outlawed racing in 1908, a syndicate headed by Lamothe, Charles Bush, and P. A. "Bud" Renaud directed the winter meet. These "enterprising local sporting men" took charge of winter racing in January of 1892 and in the following December organized the Crescent City Jockey Club to supervise and to regulate the Fair Grounds' winter season.[33] The New Louisiana Jockey Club sponsored spring meetings until 1908, but these week-long events were primarily social gatherings where the city's nabobs watched inferior programs of "cheap selling races." [34]

While the spring meet slowly declined in importance, the winter

---

31 *Ibid.,* January 31, February 7, 14, 28, March 7, April 4, 1887; March 19, 1888; April 1, 22, 1889; January 5, 1890; December 25, 1891.

32 *Ibid.,* June 2, 3, August 26, November 18, 1895; July 6, 1896.

33 *Wilkes' Spirit of the Times,* CXIV (December 3, 1887), 613–14; CXXII (January 9, 1892), 951; New Orleans *Daily Picayune,* January 5, December 11, 1892.

34 New Orleans *Daily Picayune,* March 25, 1898.

season rose in both local and national estimation. In the 1890s the members of the Crescent City Jockey Club, aware that New Orleans could compete with the East only by racing in the winter, took steps to revitalize local turf sports. They extended the season to more than one hundred days between November and March, enlarged track facilities to provide stables for a thousand horses, added a mechanical starting machine, and increased purses to a total of approximately $150,000 for each meeting. The managers also sponsored special races each year in the manner of the Kentucky Derby. In 1894 the club introduced two such features—the St. Patrick's Day Handicap, in honor of which the stand was decorated in green and a band played "a medley of Irish airs," and the Crescent City Derby, a race for three-year-olds traditionally run on the last day of the season for the club's largest purse.[35]

As a result of the Crescent City Jockey Club's progressive management, more stables came to the Fair Grounds in the 1890s than at any time in the past. In the season that ended in March, 1899, more than two hundred owners from throughout the country participated in the races.[36] The Fair Grounds could not consistently attract the country's leading thoroughbreds, because many owners preferred to rest their animals during the winter, but some outstanding horses raced in New Orleans in the 1880s and 1890s. Running times for all distances compared favorably with times on other tracks, and at two distances, one and seven-eighth miles and two and one-sixteenth miles, thoroughbreds established the national records at the Fair Grounds in February, 1900. In March the local record for a two-mile race was set at 3:30¾ by S. J. Charles's chestnut gelding Rush Fields in one of the Fair Grounds' most exciting races: "Rush Fields and Banquo II fought it out every foot of the last three-eighths in the long-distance event. Banquo II set the pace for the first mile and a half, when Rush Fields moved up and joined him. At the sixteenth pole it was hard to tell which would win. Rush Fields was the better horse, but Banquo II had much the strongest rider up. Pete Clay rode the latter like a demon, but try as he would he could not stall off Rush Fields, and the

---

[35] *Ibid.*, October 23, 1893; April 1, 1894; March 2, 29, 1896; March 28, 1897; March 24, 1898; March 18, 1900; *Wilkes' Spirit of the Times,* CXXVII (March 24, 1894), 331; CXXXIII (April 3, 1897), 336.

[36] New Orleans *Daily Picayune,* April 3, 1899; March 7, 1900; Frank H. Brunell (ed.), *The American Sporting Manual for 1901* (New York, 1901), 21, 35.

latter beat him out by a head. It was a pretty finish for a two-mile race." By the turn of the century, it was clear the Crescent City Jockey Club had realized its ambition to make the Fair Grounds one of the country's leading tracks. James A. Macdonald (alias "Colonel" John R. Stingo, the "Honest Rainmaker"), a turf reporter for the New Orleans *Item* in the 1890s and later for New York's *Evening Sun* and *Evening Journal*, told his biographer in the early 1950s that before the turn of the century "New Orleans offered the most important winter racing in America." Atcheson of *Wilkes' Spirit of the Times,* who reported all major racing meets on the western circuit, surpassed MacDonald's assessment when he observed in 1899: "New Orleans has developed into a racing point of the first class, and its meetings will compare with the best of those in the West." [37]

While the Crescent City Jockey Club attracted America's leading turfmen and many fine horses, it also won the support of racing fans. To make all classes feel welcome at the Fair Grounds, managers abandoned the ritualistic practice of setting aside certain portions of the grandstand for preferred groups. Instead the club simply charged fifty cents for general admission and admitted women free of charge. At the same time, the club demanded "rigid enforcement of the proprieties—the small amenities of life that help to make ladies thoroughly at home with the surroundings." [38] Other improvements included a restaurant managed by "the well-known caterer" Tony Licazzi, a "reporters' apartment" near the finish line, and a press room below the stand "where the newspaper fellows can do their principal work." Accommodations for the press attracted not only local reporters but also at least two writers from New York City dailies, Frank Bryan of the *Evening Journal* and Frank W. Thorp of the *Evening World,* who brought the Joseph Pulitzer-William Randolph Hearst rivalry to the lower South. A reporter for *Wilkes'* expressed the attitude of sports writers when he observed in December, 1895: "Probably on no other track are race reporters more considerately treated than at the Fair Grounds. But then, after all, what would racetracks amount to if it were not for the newspapers?" Efforts to at-

---

37 Abbott J. Liebling, *The Honest Rainmaker: The Life and Times of Colonel John R. Stingo* (Garden City, 1953), 184; *Wilkes' Spirit of the Times,* CXXXVIII (December 16, 1899), 540.

38 *Wilkes' Spirit of the Times,* CXXVI (December 16, 1893), 697; New Orleans *Daily Picayune,* April 3, 1894; December 18, 1900.

tract spectators succeeded beyond expectations. After lowering social barriers and improving the track's facilities, the Fair Grounds
drew from five to ten thousand fans on many racing days. Winter
racing had clearly become a successful enterprise.[39]

Conversion to the winter season, aside from restoring to New Orleans part of its antebellum eminence, substantially altered local racing. As northern turfmen mounted a full-scale invasion of the Fair
Grounds, practices of many years' standing yielded to the forces of
change. Gambling procedures, racing styles and regulations, the
status of jockeys, and the control of racing underwent significant al-
terations between 1883, the year of the first winter meet, and 1900.
Changes in racing in this period in many ways paralleled changes
that occurred in other enterprises of the late nineteenth century. Intense competition, monopolistic practices, and bribery appeared in
thoroughbred racing as well as in other business ventures. Together
with other adjustments since the war, these new developments completed the transformation of southern racing from an exclusive pastime for the planter aristocracy to a commercial amusement for people
of all ranks and a profitable business for those who managed the sport.

Winter racing first of all hastened the acceptance of bookmaking
as the public's favorite method of losing money on the ponies. Although bookmakers had attended local races since the 1860s,[40]
auction and pari-mutuel pools remained the preferred forms of
wagering until the 1880s. Required to pay track officials as much as a
hundred dollars a day for the privilege of taking bets, transient bookmakers needed a long campaign to justify a trip to New Orleans.
Winter racing made the journey profitable. In 1887 eight bookmakers took bets at the track; in 1898 fifteen set up stalls; and by
1900 nineteen operated daily at the Fair Grounds.[41]

Bookmaking posed some serious problems for track officials,
problems that clearly illustrated the growing desire for profit. In the
late 1880s, bookmakers throughout the country, following economic
trends of the era, organized two associations to regulate their

---

[39] *Wilkes' Spirit of the Times,* CXXX (December 14, 1895), 705; CXXXVI
(December 10, 1898), 518; New Orleans *Daily Picayune,* December 8, 1895; January 10, November 25, 1898.

[40] New Orleans *Daily Picayune,* March 28, 1869.

[41] *Ibid.,* April 12, 1887; January 10, 1898; *Wilkes' Spirit of the Times,*
CXXXIX (January 27, 1900), 44.

trade and to win concessions from track officials, the Association of Western Bookmakers and the Eastern Alliance of Bookmakers. A majority of jockey clubs agreed to bar members of these groups and thus crushed the bookmakers' associations as effectively as industrial magnates destroyed unions. In the 1890s the Crescent City Jockey Club compensated bookmakers at the Fair Grounds by arranging with Western Union not to furnish racing results to local poolrooms. This arrangement granted track bookmakers a betting monopoly and gave Western Union the exclusive right to dispatch results to gamblers and pool-sellers in other cities. Local pool-sellers protested this situation, but to no avail.[42]

Greedy gamblers also made dishonest racing, an infrequent nuisance since the early days of the sport, a major problem in the eighties and nineties. As early as the first winter meeting, reports of the races contained veiled suggestions that lagging attendance resulted from a widespread suspicion that the races were not fairly contested.[43] Fair Grounds' officials constantly endeavored to ferret out individuals guilty of rigging races: jockeys who pulled up their mounts; owners who bet against their own entries and then instructed their riders to lose; and bookmakers who bribed jockeys to "throw off" races.[44] In the 1890s the Crescent City Jockey Club created a Board of Racing Stewards and employed a special force of track police to investigate charges of fraud.[45] When officials detected dishonesty, they speedily expelled culpable parties, thus barring them from all tracks in the country except for a few "outlaw" courses. For a time in the 1880s, the Fair Grounds suffered from a reputation for dishonest racing, but in 1893 Atcheson of *Wilkes' Spirit of the Times*

---

42 *Wilkes' Spirit of the Times,* CXVI (December 1, 1888), 671; CXXXII (January 2, 1897), 748.

43 New Orleans *Daily Picayune,* February 21, 1883. One historian of the turf has contended: "The South was not besmirched by the same gang of gamblers which cursed the East with their presence. It had comparatively little gambling." Parmer, *For Gold and Glory,* 159. This view is not only demonstrably false and absurd; it ignores one of racing's primary appeals: the desire to bet.

44 New Orleans *Daily Picayune,* April 11, 12, 1883; February 13, 1887; December 13, 1892; December 31, 1900; *Wilkes' Spirit of the Times,* CX (January 2, 1886), 682; CXI (March 27, 1886), 264; CXV (April 7, 1888), 357; CXVI (December 1, 1888), 671; CXVI (December 29, 1888), 826; CXIX (February 1, 1890), 41; CXXIV (December 17, 1892), 794; CXXV (February 4, 1893), 88; CXXXVI (December 24, 1898), 574.

45 *Wilkes' Spirit of the Times,* CXXV (January 21, 1893), 8; New Orleans *Daily Picayune,* December 31, 1900.

said: "I do not know of a race-course in America where there is more thorough vigilance exercised than right here, in the interest of honest sport." Nevertheless, crooked racing occasionally plagued the Fair Grounds for the remainder of the century. In 1900, for example, track and city police exposed "one of the most daring gangs of turf wreckers that have developed in years." [46] Despite the vigilance of track officials, dishonest gambling sometimes escaped their notice. As the idea grew that all race-track gambling was basically crooked and immoral, outraged citizens persuaded the Louisiana legislature in 1908 to place a six-year ban on racing. When the sport resumed on January 1, 1915, the Fair Grounds' management adopted controls even more stringent than those employed before 1900 to guard against dishonesty.

Bookmaking, of course, bore only part of the responsibility for increasing fraud at the Fair Grounds. Racing's integrity declined in large part because control of the sport shifted from the planter aristocracy to professional sportsmen. Until the introduction of winter racing, most of the men who raced thoroughbreds belonged to that same class of men who had dominated southern racing before the war. Duncan F. Kenner, for example, remained active in local racing until the 1880s. Moreover meetings sponsored by the Metairie, Louisiana, and New Louisiana jockey clubs had retained many of the aristocratic trappings that had characterized racing before the Civil War. The exclusive Boston and Pickwick clubs continued to sponsor races; ladies who attended the races selected "brilliant toilettes" "almost as elaborate as those seen upon fashionable nights, at the Opera"; and jockey clubs presented their traditional dinners and balls. To maintain a proper atmosphere during the races, club rules "positively prohibited" smoking on the members' stand and stated that "ladies and gentlemen will be required to keep their seats during the running of the races." And while society's rulers watched blooded horses, "young darkies" tended their carriages, "old bandanaed Creoles" sold "indigestible refershments," and "curiously dilapidated old Uncle Toms . . . slouched about dusting . . . coats and saying, 'How d'ye, Massa.' " As long as racing remained the sport of the South's aristocrats, it was widely believed, deception

---

[46] *Wilkes' Spirit of the Times*, CXXV (February 11, 1893), 136; New Orleans *Daily Picayune*, December 31, 1900.

rarely occurred. The *Times* in 1880 observed: "It is . . . all important that the control of the New Orleans turf be kept, as it now is, in
the hands of gentlemen who will tolerate nothing bearing the shadow
of resemblance to trickery." [47] But winter racing attracted a new
type of owner to the city—professionals to whom racing represented
not merely a pleasant and traditional pastime for the well-to-do but
also a lucrative business. Each successive winter meet made it more
apparent that southern racing was no longer an exclusive pursuit
for the social elite. Incorporated stables, acquisitive businessmen,
and professional turfmen permanently wrested control from the
planter and merchant aristocracy that had dominated the sport since
its inception in New Orleans. In the late 1880s and throughout the
1890s, races attracted turfmen like George E. Smith, better known
as "Pittsburgh Phil"; the Dwyer brothers, one of whom was ruled
off the course in 1898 for "attempted jobbing schemes"; and Frank
James, laconically described by one reporter as "a somewhat noted
Missourian," who brought a stable to the city in 1894. Professional
turfmen of this sort, more than the aristocrat of the turf, discovered
that bribery insured returns on their investments. By the nineties
racing had obviously ceased to be merely a means of asserting social
leadership; it had become a commercial enterprise that amused the
populace and rewarded horsemen. [48]

Another change that resulted from winter racing was the acceptance of northern styles of racing. In the early postwar meetings,
local turfmen predictably followed the successful patterns of the
past. Jockey clubs elsewhere converted to dashes, but heat races at
distances up to four miles remained standard fare in New Orleans.
Northern sportsmen, however, gradually accepted speed rather than
endurance as the best measure of a thoroughbred. Reluctantly acknowledging this trend, the Metairie Jockey Club slowly began to

47 The quotations, in order cited, are from New Orleans *Bulletin*, April 2,
1876; New Orleans *Daily Picayune*, November 27, 1869; April 4, 1880; New Orleans *Times*, November 28, 1869; January 4, 1880. Other information in this paragraph was taken from the New Orleans *Times*, April 11, 1875; April 12, 19, 1882;
April 7, 1885; and Metairie Jockey Club Invitation, 1870, and Louisiana Jockey
Club, Bill of Fare, for the DINNER Given by Edward A. Yorke, to His Friends,
Wednesday, Feb. 5, 1873, in Joseph P. Horner Papers.

48 The quotations are from *Wilkes' Spirit of the Times*, CXXVII (March 3,
1894), 222; CXXXVI (December 24, 1898), 574. Other information is from *ibid.*,
CXVI (January 19, 1889), 934; CXIX (February 8, 1890), 98; CXXIX (February 23, 1895), 177; CXXXVI (January 21, 1899), 676.

sprinkle its racing program with dashes.[49] The Louisiana Jockey Club returned to heat races to "restore to the thoroughbred his failing powers of endurance," [50] but efforts to block short races failed when both the New Louisiana and Crescent City jockey clubs accepted the dash. Turfmen of the old school disdained the total emphasis on speed, but commercial promoters, purse-conscious owners, and inveterate race-track gamblers preferred six or seven dashes a day rather than one or two heat races. Selling and handicap races, long staples of the eastern turf, also became popular in New Orleans when Yankee horsemen came to the city.[51]

As the Fair Grounds' managers acceded to national styles, they also came under the sway of national regulations. For some time before the war, turfmen in all sections had periodically attempted to standardize rules, but little was done until the late nineteenth century when the quest for uniformity led to the formation of several regional associations, such as the Western Turf Congress. A *national* organization was conspicuously lacking until fifty turfmen founded the Jockey Club in 1894 to regulate racing on all New York tracks. This association soon established reciprocal relations with other turf groups and by 1900 was well on the way to achieving recognition as the highest arbiter of American racing.[52]

Local acceptance of Jockey Club standards came relatively soon after the club's formation. Early acquiescence was made possible by a sporadic campaign to standardize racing rules that began before the war and resumed in the late 1860s. At that time the Metairie Jockey Club joined a short-lived Turf Congress to encourage "concert of action in the South and West; and have, as far as possible, uniform weights for ages, etc., etc." R. W. Simmons, who officiated at many tracks in the East, continued the crusade for standard racing regulations in the 1880s. At a Louisville conference of southern and western jockey clubs in 1883, he informally committed local

49 *American Turf Register: A Correct Synopsis of Turf Events in the United States, Embracing Running, Trotting and Pacing, for 1870* (New York, 1871), 25–30; *American Turf Register and Racing Calendar: A Correct Synopsis of Turf Events in the United States and the Dominion of Canada, Embracing Running, Trotting and Pacing, for 1871* (New York, 1872), 10–13, 289–91.

50 New Orleans *Daily Picayune*, September 17, 1871; December 17, 19, 1875; April 23, 1876.

51 *Ibid.*, December 31, 1886; April 4, 1893.

52 Parmer, *For Gold and Glory*, 139.

sportsmen to a uniform schedule of weights and a code to discourage dishonest racing and other "corrupt and fraudulent practices." Formal acceptance of regional uniformity came a few years later when the New Louisiana Jockey Club joined the Western Turf Congress, which in turn accepted the rules of the Jockey Club after 1894. The Crescent City Jockey Club chose not to join the Western Turf Congress, but it was "closely identified" with this regional organization and thus followed national racing rules.[53]

Winter racing also brought greater recognition to jockeys. For several years after the war, the jockey's status in New Orleans remained essentially what it had been in the 1850s. Most riders became permanently attached to one stable and few achieved any measure of fame for their ability. Racing accounts seldom mentioned riders unless they suffered injury or the reporter believed the jockey's "carelessness or criminality" resulted in an unnecessary defeat. As the *Times* demonstrated in describing the races of April 8, 1871, a thief was more likely to see his name in the racing news than a jockey: "Beyond the throwing of a rider, who was not seriously hurt however, and the arrest of the notorious Pete Munday, for picking pockets at the gate, nothing additional of unusual interest transpired." Prior to the 1880s the only local rider to receive more than cursory notice was "the renowned jockey, Abe, a black boy, formerly owned by Colonel Kenner . . . who still clings to his old master now that he is free." The report continued: "He is probably the best rider on the continent, is a dwarf in size, but well formed, and 'knows the ropes like a book.' "[54]

Northern sportsmen introduced new attitudes toward the diminutive riders. At the first winter season: "It was suggested that the names of the jockeys be posted with those of the horses at the pooling stand, as a number of betting men say they would invest more did they know who would ride." In contrast to racing experts of the past who bet almost solely on the merits of the horse, the new breed of

[53] New Orleans *Daily Picayune*, March 14, 1869; June 20, 1880; December 7, 1883; *Wilkes' Spirit of the Times*, CXVI (December 29, 1888), 827; CXXXIII (February 27, 1897), 179.

[54] New Orleans *Daily Crescent*, April 4, 1869; New Orleans *Times*, April 9, 1871; April 12, 1866. Quotations are in the order cited. Abe Hawkins occasionally rode at tracks outside New Orleans, and in 1866 he won the Travers Stakes at Saratoga, one of the leading races for three-year-olds. Menke (ed.), *The Encyclopedia of Sports*, 586.

race-track gamblers often placed their money in the belief that a really clever jockey could win on a second-rate mount. The Fair Grounds began to extend recognition to outstanding jockeys in 1885 by giving a medal to the season's best rider.[55]

Jockeys found themselves in a seller's market. Able riders auctioned their services to the highest bidders, often agreeing to ride for several stables in the course of a meeting.[56] They also traveled from track to track, a practice that enabled New Orleans to attract many outstanding riders, such as Todhunter "Tod" Sloan, Fred Taral ("America's premier jockey"), "Snapper" Garrison, Tommy Burns, Winnie O'Conner, Isaac Murphy, and Jim Boland. Some of these riders first rose to prominence at the Fair Grounds; two New Orleans' products, Sloan and O'Conner, later became internationally famous jockeys who made fortunes riding in England. Sloan also enhanced his reputation by popularizing a new riding style—the crouch. Jockeys had formerly ridden upright with long stirrups, but by 1900 Sloan's style had been accepted by most American riders.[57]

The financial rewards of racing made riding a means of social and economic mobility for members of disadvantaged social groups. Young men who might have found it impossible to move upward otherwise advanced economically and probably socially by becoming jockeys. The names of many jockeys, including some of those listed above, suggest that Irish youngsters frequently tried this avenue of escape from poverty. Negroes, treated harshly throughout the country, also turned to riding. Black jockeys rode regularly at both the Metairie Course and the Fair Grounds, apparently without incident. At least one black rider of this period, Isaac Murphy, achieved a nationwide reputation. A white resident who saw Murphy and other Negro jockeys later recalled that "no discrimination" existed at the track in the eighties and nineties. Indeed, as late as 1893, when social pressures and Jim Crow laws were forcing Negroes into a rigidly segregated existence in New Orleans and elsewhere, the "crack

55 New Orleans *Daily Picayune*, February 21, April 1, 1883; April 6, 1885.

56 *Ibid.*, April 4, December 26, 1883; December 22, 1885.

57 *Ibid.*, March 7, 1889; January 15, 1895; January 24, 1898; April 3, 1899; March 25, 1900; *Wilkes' Spirit of the Times*, CXXIX (January 19, 1895), 3; CXXIX (March 23, 1895), 324; Parmer, *For Gold and Glory*, 28. Four of these jockeys—Sloan, Taral, O'Conner, and Garrison—were elected to the Jockeys' Hall of Fame when it was founded in the 1950s. Menke (ed.), *Encyclopedia of Sports*, 541.

jockey" at the Fair Grounds was "a bright mulatto youth" named Sargent. "In the matter of honesty and integrity he is simply above suspicion," one reporter noted. After the turn of the century, racial prejudice forced the vast majority of black jockeys off American tracks, but before 1900 riding thoroughbreds served one of the functions that professional sports have traditionally served—it provided an egress from poverty and humiliation for members of afflicted minority groups.[58]

Although jockeys achieved a large measure of independence, they remained under the close scrutiny of track officials. Stewards at the Fair Grounds disciplined jockeys not only for outright cases of dishonesty, such as pulling up their mounts or taking bribes, but also for committing any act that might affect adversely the outcome of a race. Officials ruled a rider off the track in 1896 for using an "electric saddle" designed to increase the speed of his mount. Stewards in the following year expelled one jockey for "unmercifully beating a horse he was exercising," and another for brutally whipping his mount over the head during a race. Officials also regulated the personal conduct of jockeys. *Wilkes' Spirit of the Times* reported in December of 1898: "Jockey Coombs was indefinitely suspended during the week for pistol practice in the jockey room, with alleged deadly intent." [59]

All of the changes that affected local racing after the war, from the growing emphasis on attracting spectators to the rising prominence of jockeys, focused on one central theme—after fifty years as a sport of the wealthy, thoroughbred racing had emerged as a commercial amusement for the masses. As early as 1870 the *Times*, concerned about the future of racing, warned: "Old fashioned exclusiveness must now be set aside in a measure, and the turf in this city assume to a greater degree the characteristics of other and more metropolitan communities." Under the supervision of the Louisiana, New

58 New Orleans *Times*, April 12, 1866; December 14, 1873; New Orleans *Daily Picayune*, April 19, 1879; January 23, 1884; *Wilkes' Spirit of the Times,* CXVII (March 16, 1889), 289; CXVII (March 30, 1889), 382; CXXV (April 1, 1893), 418; CXXXI (February 22, 1896), 156; Parmer, *For Gold and Glory*, 150. The quotations are from Allen Bruce Blakemore, interview conducted by D. Clive Hardy, January 18, 1960 (Tape recording of interview in Department of History, Tulane University); and *Wilkes' Spirit of the Times*, CXXV (April 1, 1893), 418.
59 *Wilkes' Spirit of the Times*, CXXXI (February 22, 1896), 156; CXXXIII (March 27, 1897), 308; CXXXVI (December 24, 1898), 574.

Louisiana, and Crescent City jockey clubs, patrons of racing reluctantly at first, and then enthusiastically, accepted this suggestion. As they sought to improve the sport, they became the agents of far-reaching reforms. An awareness of racing's economic benefits also stimulated support for the commercialization of this activity. "Horse owners must live, horses must eat, betting men generally enjoy themselves," the *Picayune* noted on one occasion, "and a winter meeting, bringing all these here, puts considerable money into circulation." The *Times-Democrat* in 1896 estimated that a winter season pumped two million dollars directly into the city's economy and indirectly a great deal more.[60] There was indeed an air of business and business efficiency about racing at the turn of the century that made it vastly different from the trials of speed and endurance that had enthralled society in the 1850s and 1860s. A hypothetical modern-day fan, who would have been befuddled by events on an antebellum track, would have felt completely at ease amidst the urban masses at the Fair Grounds in 1900. Participation remained a rich man's enterprise, but neither a clerk nor a longshoreman needed a retinue of trainers, grooms, and jockeys to sit in the grandstand and place two-dollar bets. If the halcyon days of the Metairie had passed forever, the transformation of thoroughbred racing had opened new vistas in urban recreation.

[60] New Orleans *Times,* December 4, 1870; New Orleans *Daily Picayune,* November 21, 1886; New Orleans *Times-Democrat,* April 8, 1896.

Chapter VI
THE NATIONAL
GAME

Baseball came of age in New Orleans and throughout the country after the Civil War as people of all ranks eagerly adopted what Albert G. Spalding said was a game "too lively for any but Americans to play." [1] While horse racing reflected a desire for pastimes that catered mainly to paying spectators, baseball met a need for sports that invited participation as well as observation. Played on a large, open field, the game may have evoked memories of the countryside and of a simpler rural existence, as Bruce Catton once suggested, but baseball was primarily an urban institution. In New Orleans and other cities, the presence of tens of thousands of people encouraged the formation of numerous teams; transportation improvements facilitated the creation of intercity leagues; and the relative brevity of games (as compared with cricket matches) appealed to spectators of virtually all occupations, however limited their leisure time. Consequently baseball became one of the Crescent City's most popular pastimes. Players organized scores of teams; promoters brought professional baseball to the city in the 1880s; and fans by the thousands attended games on diamonds scattered throughout the city.

Baseball soared in popularity after 1865 because it became both a democratic pastime and a pleasing commercial spectacle. Moreover it seemed to capture the essence of the thought and deeds of the period. "Baseball," Mark Twain accurately observed, "is the very symbol, the outward and visible expression of the drive and push and struggle of the raging, tearing, booming nineteenth century." [2] The urban upper classes who had introduced and popularized the game in the forties and fifties lost their monopoly after 1865 as baseball pro-

---

[1] Albert G. Spalding, *America's National Game* (New York, 1911), 10.

[2] Twain's description is quoted in Boyle, *Sport: Mirror of American Life,* 17. For Catton's views, see Bruce Catton, "The Great American Game," *American Heritage,* X (April, 1959), 16–25, 86, especially 17.

gressed from a sport for gentlemen amateurs to a game dominated by professional players and finally to a successful business enterprise managed by team owners or "magnates." On the national level, the owners of major league teams controlled the sport; in New Orleans and elsewhere in the South, the owners and managers of Southern League teams became the principal figures in baseball. Upper-class players lost control of the game partly because baseball, with its emphasis on individual ability and equality of opportunity, was incompatible with social exclusiveness and partly because players of superior talent began to play for pay and thus drove gentlemen from the field. The National Association of Base Ball Players, founded in 1858, tried to restrict competition to simon-pure amateurs, but soon after the organization of the professional Cincinnati Red Stockings in 1869, the association conceded defeat. Two years later management of the game passed to the National Association of Professional Base Ball Players, which was in turn replaced by the National League of Professional Base Ball Clubs in 1876.

By applying techniques developed by other businessmen in the Gilded Age, National League team owners made organized baseball a highly profitable, monopolistic enterprise. They eliminated competition by destroying rival leagues or by forcing rivals to accept their business practices; they proved themselves capable of treating players as harshly as workers in any industry by crushing revolts and by their use of the reserve clause; and finally, they brought minor leagues, such as the Southern League, under their jurisdiction. Reluctantly sharing control of major league baseball with the American Association (1882–92), the Union Association (1884), the Players' League (1890), and the American League (1903–present), the National League pioneered in developing a structural form that has been widely imitated in the twentieth century by other professional sports like football, hockey, and basketball.[3]

When professionals assumed control of the sport in the 1870s,

---

[3] For accounts of baseball after 1865, see David Q. Voigt, *Baseball: From Gentleman's Sport to the Commissioner System* (Norman, 1966); Seymour, *Baseball: The Early Years;* Dulles, *A History of Recreation,* 185–91, 223–26, 263–64; Spalding, *America's National Game;* Arthur Bartlett, *Baseball and Mr. Spalding* (New York, 1951); Robert Smith, *Baseball in America* (New York, 1961); Lieb, *The Baseball Story.*

amateur baseball in the strict sense of the term all but disappeared. Baseball was far and away the country's most popular participant sport, but few genuine amateurs played the game. Most "amateur" clubs played for side bets and gate receipts or unabashedly employed wandering professionals to strengthen sagging teams. Amateur baseball regained its antebellum standards only when it became a popular sport in high schools, colleges, and gentlemen's athletic clubs. Developments in New Orleans clearly illustrated the confusion surrounding baseball for several years after the Civil War.

Stimulated by the revival of a few teams during Federal occupation, local interest in baseball rose rapidly after 1865. Clubs appeared in such profusion that in 1869 the *Picayune* observed: "Baseball has become a national game, and it is, perhaps, the best that can be devised for exercising the entire body, and, at the same time, diverting the mind." The *Picayune* also stressed the game's importance to the moral health of the city's youth. "No parent will object to his son taking up bat and ball in preference to the dice, the cards or the glass," a reporter contended; nor would a parent object to his son joining other youths on the playing field rather than "at the gambling table, or at other assemblages more seductive yet more vicious, and more dangerous to the impressionable minds of the rising generation than ever a trial of manly muscle in the open air can be." [4]

In New Orleans, as elsewhere, the game attracted players from all levels of society. Firemen, telegraphers, typographers, railroad workers, factory hands, longshoremen, brewery workers, journalists, and federal and state employees organized many of the city's teams, and Sunday excursions sponsored by middle- and working-class social clubs almost always featured baseball matches. The names of teams frequently reflected the occupations of players and sometimes their political views as well. Firemen took names like Screw Guzzles and Red Hots, while telegraphers organized the Morse Baseball Club and postal workers formed the Ubiquitous team. Players also established the Quickstep Baseball Club, perhaps as a reminder of a malady common to soldiers during the Civil War. In the waning days of Reconstruction, players fielded the Ku-Klux Baseball Club and the Regulators. Cycling enthusiasts played under the names of Headers

4 New Orleans *Daily Picayune*, August 29, 1869; October 17, 1871.

and Anti-Headers.[5] Baseball also became a common pastime for the city's various ethnic groups. German citizens founded the Schneiders, Laners, and Landwehrs, and Irish players formed the Fenian Baseball Club. Exhibitions of baseball occurred regularly at picnics arranged by ethnic clubs, such as the French Society, the Hibernian Benevolent and Mutual Aid Association, and the Tiro al Bersaglio Society, an Italian group.[6] Upper-class residents played baseball, but not as frequently as in the 1850s when they dominated the game in New Orleans. Reports of contests involving the city's most prominent and exclusive social associations indicated that baseball had indeed become a sport of the masses and that society's elite no longer played regularly. When players from the Pickwick and Louisiana clubs met for a game in 1885 to promote interest in the Cotton Centennial and Industrial Exposition, the press described the event as "the social sensation of the season" and commended the players for aiding the city by "casting aside their dignity for a day and working hard with ball and bat, which none of them had handled for years." On the occasion of a charity game between the Pickwick and Boston clubs in 1895, a reporter noted that the players "are all business men, and it required a good deal of effort on their part to array themselves in the awfulness of baseball costumes, and appear upon the diamond as pleasing spectacles for a thousand eyes." [7]

So pervasive was baseball's appeal that prejudice against female athleticism partially yielded to its pressures. In the last quarter of the nineteenth century, several female nines competed in the city. A "large crowd of miscellaneous people" went to the Fair Grounds in 1879 to watch a team of girls who refused to play until each received ten dollars. The *Picayune*'s reporter concentrated on a description of the players in his account of the game: "Their dresses somewhat resembled the Greek costumes of men, being white, trimmed with blue and red, and having skirts that reached to the knee. The players were

[5] *Ibid.*, July 4, August 17, September 28, 1869; June 26, September 11, 1870; March 5, 1871; July 2, 1872; September 19, 1875; March 10, September 15, 1879; June 13, 1881; May 16, 23, June 6, 29, 1886; August 31, 1891; New Orleans *Daily Crescent*, June 25, July 9, September 24, 1867; New Orleans *Times*, August 17, September 28, 1869; May 4, 1874; New Orleans *Times-Democrat*, July 23, 1887.

[6] New Orleans *Daily Crescent*, May 12, June 2, 1868; New Orleans *Daily Picayune*, July 12, 1870; June 19, 1881; June 8, 1884; New Orleans *Times*, June 7, 1870.

[7] New Orleans *Daily Picayune*, December 4, 6, 1885; May 11, 1895.

all of home talent, none of them beautiful, and of ages reaching from childhood to middle age." Near the end of the century, a traveling female team, the Bloomer Girls, also played in New Orleans. "For women they play well," the *Picayune* conceded, "their handling of the ball, of course, being in that style that is characteristic of the feminine sex—a side and hip throw." [8]

By far the most notorious women's club to appear locally was Harry H. Freeman's nomadic team of "buxom beauties," who visited the city several times in the mid-eighties. These "short-skirted ball tossers" played poorly, said one reporter, but he added: "The girls try and play hard even if they do not succeed better than girls are expected to with the national game." Reports of Freeman's last trip to the city strongly implied that he was recruiting girls for a profession considerably older than baseball. In May, 1886, local officials arraigned Freeman "on the charge of being a dangerous and suspicious character" after a number of complainants accused him of "inducing young girls to leave their homes and parents to join his troupe of base ball players." One of the plaintiffs was the father of Florence Harris, whom Freeman had spirited out of town after cutting off her dark hair and substituting a blond wig.[9]

One of the best proofs of baseball's broad attraction was Negro participation. In the late sixties and early seventies, black employees of the Boston and Pickwick clubs organized nines and took the names of their employers' exclusive clubs. Several other Negro amateur teams, including the Orleans, Dumonts, Aetnas, Fischers, and Unions, joined the Boston and Pickwick players in the eighties. These teams played frequently, and the better nines periodically arranged matches to decide the Negro championship. Games often featured brass bands that played "to encourage the boys to victory." [10]

8 *Ibid.,* June 16, 1879; April 16, 1899; February 19, 1900.

9 *Ibid.,* December 27, 1884; January 4, April 19, 1885; May 5, 9, 1886. Quotations are in the order cited.

10 *Ibid.,* December 12, 21, 1869; March 1, 1880; August 15, 1881; May 29, 31, 1885; October 8, 1888; New Orleans *Times,* December 21, 1869; July 20, 1874; New Orleans *Bulletin,* June 18, 1876; New Orleans *Weekly Louisianian,* May 7, 14, 1881; New Orleans *Weekly Pelican,* December 4, 1886; April 23, May 28, July 30, 1887; March 23, April 13, 27, May 18, 25, June 1, 8, 1889; Stuart O. Landry, *History of the Boston Club* (New Orleans, 1938), 150; Dorothy R. Eagleson, "Some Aspects of the Social Life of the New Orleans Negro in the 1880's" (M.A. thesis, Tulane University, 1961), 96–97. The quotation is from the New Orleans *Weekly Pelican,* April 13, 1889.

For almost a quarter century after the war, Negro and white teams played against each other regularly. Good will ordinarily prevailed at these contests and both blacks and whites attended. The Negro newspaper *Pelican* reported on a game in May, 1887, in which the Pickwicks defeated a white team: "The playing of the colored club was far above the average ball playing and elicited hearty and generous applause from the large crowd in attendance, which was about evenly divided between white and colored." Another example of the camaraderie among ball players of both races was a game played by the Pickwicks and another black team for the benefit of William F. Tracy, a white sportsman who had been a founder of the Lone Star Baseball Club, one of the first white teams to play matches with Negroes.[11]

After twenty years of amicable competition, attitudes toward interracial contests changed swiftly in the 1880s. In July, 1885, two white teams protested a proposed Negro-white game and threatened to boycott white players who crossed the color line. The *Picayune* warned that any white club competing with a black team "will have to brave considerable opposition on the part of the other clubs." [12] Under this threat, other teams restricted themselves to lily-white competition. In the late 1880s, the city's professional Southern League team, the Pelicans, played Negro teams,[13] and the Ben Theards, the "champion amateur white club," played a few games with the Pinchbacks, the "colored champions," before crowds "composed of the best elements of both colors," [14] but these contests were exceptional. By 1890 interracial baseball activity had ceased, a victim of the increasingly harsh racial attitudes in the South. Negroes continued to play ball, but only on a segregated basis. The failure of the national game to bridge racial divisions in the South (and elsewhere, for that matter) indicated that it lacked, along with other

[11] For examples of interracial games, see New Orleans *Daily Picayune*, December 21, 1869; March 1, 1880; August 29, September 12, 1881; September 18, 1882; May 29, July 20, 1885; New Orleans *Bulletin*, June 18, 1876. The quotation is from the New Orleans *Weekly Pelican*, May 28, 1887. This paper, incidentally, said little about games between Negroes and whites. The benefit for Tracy is mentioned in the New Orleans *Daily Picayune*, February 10, 1878.

[12] New Orleans *Daily Picayune*, July 4, 1885.

[13] *Ibid.*, July 8, 1889; New Orleans *Weekly Pelican*, July 6, September 21, 1889.

[14] New Orleans *Daily Picayune*, November 5, 1888; New Orleans *Weekly Pelican*, July 13, 1889.

sports, some of the democratic tendencies ascribed to it by admirers. Even when Negroes and whites played against each other, the competition scarcely occurred in a completely democratic setting. The initiative lay always with the whites, who specified the time and circumstances of interracial matches. The drawing of the color line in the 1890s in a sense merely underscored the inability of sports to provide at that time an adequate tool for the destruction of racial prejudices.

As baseball became a popular pastime for people of all classes, both black and white players founded hundreds of teams in the postwar era. Many teams existed for only a single season, but the city also had a nucleus of well-established teams that entertained fans year after year. Until the organization of a professional club in the mid-eighties, fans divided their loyalties among scores of teams that pursued the game with varying degrees of aptitude and interest. Most nines played on a relatively unorganized basis, challenging one another with no end in mind save their own amusement. Games of this sort usually drew spectators only from a particular section of the city, but as many as a thousand people attended matches between minor teams.[15]

Clubs organized on a permanent basis competed in a more orderly fashion. Before New Orleans fielded a professional team, amateurs founded three separate leagues to govern contests for the city and state championship—the Louisiana State Base Ball Association (1868–73), the Crescent City League (1880–84), and the New Orleans Amateur League (1884–86). All three associations suffered from internal dissension, a problem that led to the collapse of the first two organizations. Quarrels among members threatened to dissolve the Amateur League also, but the creation of the intercity Gulf League killed this group before it could throttle itself.

Loose organization characterized the Louisiana State Base Ball Association. Clubs played no regular schedule, but instead determined supremacy through a challenge system during the championship season, which lasted from February 1 to November 1 each year. Beginning in 1870 teams played at a new baseball park on St. Charles Avenue, midway between the main part of the city and the suburb of Carrollton. A reporter who came to the city with the Chicago White

15 New Orleans *Daily Picayune*, May 28, 1877.

Stockings described the stadium, which held four thousand people, as "the finest arranged base ball park in America." [16] Squabbles over infractions of association rules and lack of interest among players brought an end to this league in 1873. When players failed to appear for association games in October, 1873, the *Picayune* warned that "unless more energy is used we will relapse into supineness in the field." The *Times* took the diagnosis one step further in November and announced that baseball was dead in New Orleans.[17]

Baseball activity declined for several years after the collapse of the Louisiana State Base Ball Association. The depression of the mid-seventies left many fans without money for games and promoters without funds to build and maintain playing fields. Spectators had to settle for hastily arranged matches involving seasonal teams or nomadic professional and amateur nines. Toward the end of the 1870s, however, as financial pressures eased, interest in baseball revived. The Hop Bitters, a professional team owned by Asa T. Soule of Rochester, New York, completed the resuscitation of the game with a series of contests in January and February, 1880. Soule, creator of "Hop Bitters, the Invalid's Friend & Hope," allegedly gave each player a teaspoonful of his nostrum before every game, proclaiming, "We shall march from victory to victory." When the team lost, he doubled the dosage. Local promoters formed a Park Association to finance construction of the Crescent City Baseball Park (later Sportsman's Park), where the Hop Bitters played before thousands of fans who paid twenty-five cents apiece to watch good hitting, flawless fielding, and "forcible pitching." [18]

After the Hop Bitters and the Park Association demonstrated the commercial possibilities of baseball, five teams formed the Crescent City League to sponsor Sunday games. Each team played a schedule of twenty matches to determine the city championship. With from one thousand to two thousand people attending games, the association presided over four successful seasons from 1880 through

---

[16] New Orleans *Times,* April 5, 22, 1870; September 7, October 12, 27, 1873. The quotation is from the Chicago *Tribune,* May 7, 1870.

[17] New Orleans *Daily Picayune,* October 27, 1873; New Orleans *Times,* November 30, 1873.

[18] Samuel H. Adams, *Grandfather Stories* (New York, 1955), 209, 215; New Orleans *Times,* January 1, 1880; New Orleans *Daily Picayune,* January 5, 25, 28, February 9, 11, 12, 13, 22, 1880.

1883. Charging twenty-five cents admission, the league used gate receipts to rent the Crescent City Baseball Park and to pay winning players, who were almost invariably described as amateurs.[19]

Despite sound indications of prosperity, the Crescent City League suffered from serious problems, mostly of its own creation. Lackadaisical players who refused to appear for games, scheduling difficulties, and inadequate supervision by officials of the association undermined interest in league games and crowds began to dwindle. For defeating the Brennans in April, 1884, the Lone Stars received only $2.70 after paying park rental. Other teams fared as poorly, forcing the Crescent City League to disband before the season was fully under way. It revived briefly in the fall, but unruly players who refused to honor league commitments and competition from visiting professionals soon brought an end to the association's existence.[20]

While the Crescent City League languished from lack of interest during the 1884 season, several independent junior clubs (teams composed of younger players) formed the New Orleans Amateur League, which functioned sporadically until 1886. The Amateur League attracted athletes from the Crescent City League and by May, 1885, included what one writer called the city's "leading amateur players." Reverting to the challenge system of competition, the Amateur League drew large crowds in 1884 and 1885, a development of importance to the "amateurs" who divided gate receipts. Friction occasionally flared within the association over division of money and the pirating of players, but members usually resolved these problems without difficulty because, as they candidly admitted, baseball under such circumstances "was not as profitable as the games when harmony existed and thousands attended each game." However, in 1886 the Amateur League faced a problem for which it had no solution— the competition of an intercity professional association.[21]

Although each of these leagues lasted only a short time, collectively they contributed substantially to the development of baseball. They proved particularly important in hastening acceptance of the trend toward the democratization and commercialization of the na-

19 New Orleans *Daily Picayune,* March 18, April 18, 26, June 20, 1880; March 14, August 22, 1881; September 4, 25, 1882; October 8, 1883; April 19, 1884.

20 *Ibid.,* April 22, October 14, 1883; April 19, November 10, 14, 1884.

21 *Ibid.,* May 31, September 23, 1885. See also *ibid.,* June 8, 1884.

tional game, a trend that was altering the sport throughout the country. For some time after the war, players in New Orleans, with the aid of many fans and the press, endeavored to preserve baseball as a pastime for the upper ranks of society. They performed in the same aristocratic settings that had characterized games in the 1850s. When a "gallant body of young men," "animated by an *esprit de corps* and a desire to cultivate a spirit of courteous and generous rivalry," fielded teams, ladies assembled under tents and "by their patronage and encouragement" gave baseball "a fashionable standing and permanent popularity." Teams frequently scheduled games for weekdays, thus preventing both participation and observation by the working class. Players honored visiting nines with banquets or a "grand dress, fancy dress and masquerade ball." [22]

Such practices gradually disappeared in the seventies and eighties. Efforts to keep baseball as an exclusive pastime for the well-to-do failed when people of all ranks invaded the playing field and when baseball leagues began to emphasize profit rather than fashionableness. The Louisiana State Base Ball Association, the Crescent City League, and the Amateur League played most of their games on Sundays, a day when virtually all residents could attend. Although the Louisiana Association encouraged the attendance of ladies by building a special grandstand for them, the other leagues displayed less enthusiasm for this traditional ritual. The Crescent City League reserved a stand both for women and their escorts, while the Amateur League made no special provisions for female fans. Promoters introduced ladies' days in New Orleans at least as early as 1880, but their purpose was to attract paying customers rather than to give the game an elevated social standing. By the mid-eighties gamblers, such as Marsh Redon, a successful pool-seller, had become prominent in the staging of league games, a sure indication that baseball was no longer merely a diversion for the upper classes. These changes in baseball emphasized the increasing interest in the profitability of the game. When great masses of people played baseball and also demonstrated a willingness to pay for the privilege of watching others per-

22 *Ibid.,* August 1, 1869; January 10, 1866; New Orleans *Times,* April 30, 1870; New Orleans *Daily Picayune,* December 24, 1869. Quotations are in the order cited. See also New Orleans *Daily Picayune,* March 6, June 8, 1869; New Orleans *Times,* June 8, 1869.

form, promoters quickly rose to the occasion and made the sport a commercial amusement. "Baseball," said the *Picayune* in 1883, "is becoming more of a paying business . . . and the gatekeeper is kept busy handling the tickets of admission." It was altogether fitting that the national game should become a profitable enterprise in an age of unchecked capitalism.[23]

Amateur leagues also provided promising players opportunities to advance into professional ball. Before minor leagues became well established, the major leagues had no formal system for recruiting new players. Professional teams sometimes employed talented youngsters from their immediate area or from amateur teams they encountered while on tour. Teams also dispatched scouts to various parts of the country to ferret out aspiring athletes. As early as 1871, for example, the Chicago White Stockings sent a man with the unlikely name of John Barleycorn to New Orleans to recruit players. These methods of filling professional ranks apparently worked well, for in the 1870s and 1880s several local players, including Joe Ellich and Denny Mack of the Robert E. Lees, James J. Woulffe of the Brennans, and Frank Graves of the Eckfords, found positions on major league teams in Louisville, Buffalo, Cincinnati, and St. Louis. Ellich also spent the 1884 season as manager of Chicago's Union Association team. Local leagues thus contributed to the development of what was later to become one of baseball's most salient features: the game's ability to facilitate the economic and social elevation of athletes from scorned and deprived groups, such as the Irish and Negroes. Baseball, like horse racing, failed to fulfill its potential in this regard, however, for the major leagues barred black players from the 1890s until the 1940s. Nevertheless, the game enabled many young men to move upward. Owners of professional teams unwittingly contributed to the democratization of baseball because in their determination to field teams that would attract paying customers, they employed players from all ranks of society and from many ethnic groups.[24]

23 New Orleans *Times,* April 22, 1870; New Orleans *Daily Picayune,* April 22, 1870; January 28, 1880; September 23, 1885. The quotation in this paragraph is from the New Orleans *Daily Picayune,* September 17, 1883.

24 New Orleans *Times,* August 28, 1871; April 25, 1875; New Orleans *Daily Picayune,* August 22, 1880; May 2, 1881; November 6, 13, 1882; March 17, 1884; March 8, 1886; *The Baseball Encyclopedia: The Complete and Official Record of Major League Baseball* (rev. ed.; New York, 1969), 804, 905, 1150, 1670.

The commercialization of baseball, which the "amateur" leagues accelerated, was also aided by intercity competition. Improvements in transportation, which permitted teams to travel freely, made intercity matches commonplace occurrences after the Civil War. Amateur and professional teams frequently came to New Orleans, and local nines often traveled to other cities. These games attracted thousands of fans and soon created a desire for a professional team to represent New Orleans against other cities. Intercity competition also encouraged teams to accept standard national regulations and improved the quality of play.

Interurban games, which at first involved only teams from nearby communities such as Mobile and Vicksburg, became national in scope in the late 1860s. The Southern Baseball Club visited several cities in the upper South and the Midwest in 1869 to "show the base ball players of those districts the metal [sic] of our Crescent City clubs." The Southerns won every game until they encountered the recently organized Cincinnati Red Stockings in August. "Their defeat by the Red Stockings was to have been expected," the *Picayune* conceded, "as the latter club has been severely trained, and are what are known as 'professionals'—that is to say, they make a business of pleasure." In succeeding years several other teams, including the Lone Stars, the Lees, the Remy Clarkes, and the Brennans, traveled to other cities. At the same time, players from the upper South, the East, and the Midwest appeared in New Orleans. Private contributions, fundraising festivals, and gate receipts financed these trips.[25]

Negroes also joined the ranks of nomadic baseball players. Teams of black athletes from St. Louis and Memphis came to the city in the late 1880s, and local Negroes traveled to Mobile and Natchez for contests. These teams evidently developed strong rivalries, for in 1889 a Memphis nine played the P. B. S. Pinchbacks for "the championship of the South." Black promoters attempted to

---

[25] The quotations are from the New Orleans *Daily Picayune*, August 8, 29, 1869. For examples of intercity games involving teams from New Orleans, see New Orleans *Daily Crescent*, April 13, 1867; March 6, 7, 1869; New Orleans *Times,* August 24, 1869; August 15, 18, 1870; January 8, 9, 10, 1871; August 23, September 7, 1874; New Orleans *Daily Picayune,* December 22, 1866; August 1, 17, 18, 21, 22, 24, 1869; November 8, December 27, 1870; July 28, September 26, 1871; November 9, 12, 1874; July 26, 1880; July 4, August 15, November 14, 1881; July 3, 6, 11, 24, 1882; August 10, 12, 15, 19, November 18, 1883; October 5, 6, 1884.

bring professional ball to the South in 1886 by forming the Southern League of Colored Base Ballists, but the association collapsed after a few games. Games between Negro teams were popular with fans of both races and sometimes drew more than a thousand spectators.[26]

Professional teams understandably evoked the greatest response from local fans. They featured well-known players, who were expected to "expound the beauties of the game in a most scientific manner." The first professionals to play locally were the New York Mutuals, a team composed of men employed by New York City expressly to play ball during the reign of "Boss" Tweed. Shortly before the arrival of the Mutuals in December, 1869, the *Picayune* urged residents to attend the games because "the gentlemen composing the Mutual Club are all good Democrats, who did splendid service in the late election in New York, and helped to rescue the State from Republican rule." Several months later the Cincinnati Red Stockings and the Chicago White Stockings also played in the city.[27]

The success of these teams in New Orleans established a pattern for other professional nines. For the remainder of the century, the city was the most popular spot in the South for professionals on tour in the winter and early spring. Clubs representing the National League, the American Association, and the Players' League performed regularly on local diamonds. Players at first stayed only a short time, because they preferred to travel from town to town gathering money to supplement their regular incomes. But teams that played winter ball in New Orleans and elsewhere in the South in the 1870s and 1880s popularized the idea of a preseason training period. Professional athletes concluded that the South's temperate climate best prepared players for the rigors of a long season and began to stay in a single city for several weeks. In December, 1894, the New York Giants announced plans to train in New Orleans in the early spring of 1895. "The trip will undoubtedly be of great benefit to the team," the New York *Sun* observed, "and the boys should return to

26 New Orleans *Daily Picayune*, August 13, 23, 24, 28, 31, 1885; June 7, 17, 22, September 14, 1886; October 22, 1888; New Orleans *Times-Democrat*, August 26, 1885; New Orleans *Weekly Pelican*, June 8, 1889.

27 The quotations are from the New Orleans *Daily Picayune*, March 12, 1871; December 12, 1869. See also *ibid.*, December 24, 28, 29, 30, 1869; January 1, 4, 1870; April 26, 27, 29, 30, May 1, 7, 10, 12, 1870; New Orleans *Times*, December 30, 1869; April 26, 27, 30, May 8, 10, 1870; Chicago *Tribune*, May 7, 9, 1870. Seymour, *Baseball*, 52, 183, discusses Tweed and the Mutuals.

begin the fight for the pennant in the very pink of condition." Several years later the Cincinnati Red Stockings also selected the city as a "training ground." The *Picayune*, commending the sagacity of Cincinnati's manager, noted: "The trainers who have had experience in this city claim this is the greatest climate in the world to fit athletes for a hard season." Although spring training camps had not become an established practice with all major league teams by the turn of the century, the seed of an idea had been planted by professional teams that came South after the war.[28]

Contests with professionals and amateurs from other cities compelled local players to accept national rules. Teams throughout the United States yielded first to the National Association of Base Ball Players and then to the professional organizations to revise and amend regulations, but the success of these groups as supervisory agencies depended on the willingness of teams beyond their immediate authority to accept their decisions. Baseball rules changed frequently in the postwar period, a situation that sometimes hindered complete standardization of the game. Teams in New Orleans generally adopted new regulations after reading about them in journals such as *Sporting Life* or in official baseball guides.[29] But if local players disliked a rule, they might disregard it until forced to accept it in intercity matches. As early as 1858, the National Association of Base Ball Players permitted umpires to call batters out for not swinging at good pitches; the association strengthened the rule in the 1860s. But New Orleanians apparently ignored this regulation until the Lone Stars went north in 1870. The *Times*'s account of their game with the St. Louis Empires said: "The umpiring was very strict; in fact, our New Orleans friends would stare at the rapidity with which St. Louis umpires call *balls* and *strikes*." By the following year, this practice had filtered southward. In May, 1871, the *Times* complained that a game between the Lees and the Lone Stars was devoid of interest because the umpire enforced "the absurd

28 New York *Sun*, December 13, 1894; New Orleans *Daily Picayune*, January 30, 1900. See also New Orleans *Daily Picayune*, March 12, 1871; November 21, 1881; February 5, 1883; March 27, 28, November 1, 1887; March 5, 22, 1888; March 10, 23, 1890; March 26, 1893; March 20, 1894; March 12, 1900; and Seymour, *Baseball*, 184.

29 New Orleans *Daily Picayune*, February 8, 1884; New Orleans *Weekly Pelican*, May 28, 1887; Eagleson, "Some Aspects of the Social Life of the New Orleans Negro," 96.

law requiring all balls, after the first one pitched, to be called a ball or strike." The reporter expressed hope that the rule would be ignored, but it remained in effect in later games.[30] Baseball was thus to a great extent nationalized and standardized only after teams began to travel for competition. Advanced technology gave the country an extensive system of transportation, which in turn assured the complete nationalization of the national game.

Intersectional rivalry also exposed New Orleans enthusiasts to advanced techniques of play which, like rules, changed rapidly in the late nineteenth century. A second baseman for the visiting St. Louis Empires treated local spectators in 1871 to "a handsome double play, by purposely dropping a fly ball, stepping on second to force the runner from first, and directly touching his man just in the act of returning to second." On another occasion a team of Chicago professionals gave an exhibition of place hitting while defeating a New Orleans team, 12–1: "The visiting professionals batted the balls all over the field, putting them just where they wanted." When the Pittsburgh Pirates came to the city in 1893, they demonstrated another stratagem that has since become commonplace. "Pittsburgh has five left-handed batters, and bats them all in a row," a reporter said. "It puzzles a pitcher and yields runs." Local athletes soon demonstrated the benefits of contact with accomplished players. Reports of games for several years after the war had often chided players for poor fielding or "muffinism," but as athletes profited from the intercity matches, complaints subsided. The *Picayune* reported in 1880 that a pitcher named Lorch "acquired a good deal of the 'science' while on his Northern tour, but his pitching is now so effective that it will be a difficult matter to catch for him." Pitching for the Wrights, who made only one fielding error, Lorch defeated the Crescents, 1–0, on September 19, 1880. Scores were not always so low, of course, but thirty or more runs in a game, a frequent occurrence in baseball's early decades, became increasingly rare in the eighties and nineties as play improved.[31]

30 New Orleans *Times,* July 28, 1870; May 22, August 21, 1871. This rule is discussed in Wittke, "Baseball in Its Adolescence," 121–24; and Seymour, *Baseball,* 62.

31 The quotations are from the New Orleans *Times,* September 21, 1871; New Orleans *Daily Picayune,* November 21, 1881; March 26, 1893; September 5, 1880. The Wright-Crescent game is reported in the New Orleans *Daily Picayune,* Sep-

Besides speeding the acceptance of standardized rules and better methods of play, intercity competition generated enthusiasm for a professional team to represent New Orleans in an interurban league. Promoters periodically attempted to form a professional league beginning in the seventies, but their efforts brought no results until the mid-eighties. In the autumn of 1884 and again in 1885, managers of the World's Cotton Centennial and Industrial Exposition hired several professional players to organize the New Orleans Expositions and also imported professional teams from New York, Chicago, St. Louis, and other major league cities. All teams played in the New Orleans Base Ball Park, which was built expressly for the professionals. The highlight of the Centennial season was a series of games in November, 1885, between the New York Giants and the St. Louis Browns, champions of the American Association. As many as three thousand people attended weekday games, and a Sunday contest drew eight thousand. "In the crowd were many prominent citizens," the *Picayune* said, "judges, lawyers, doctors, merchants, laborers, politicians, and representatives of every other class which goes to make up the population of a large city." [32]

The success of the Centennial's professional season spurred the movement to create a professional team to represent the city during the summer months. After two unsuccessful attempts to secure a franchise in the recently founded Southern League, promoters in New Orleans and Mobile organized the Gulf League with two teams from each city—the New Orleans Baseball Club, the Robert E. Lees, the Mobile Baseball Club, and the Acid Iron Earths. This last team was named for a popular extract described as a "great natural blood purifier" that would allegedly cure everything from chronic diarrhea to female complaints. The Gulf League soon demonstrated the feasibility of membership in an intercity association. "To-day marks a new era in base ball," the *Picayune* proclaimed on the day of the

tember 20, 1880. "Muffinism" was a term used frequently until the 1880s to describe poor playing. According to Seymour, *Baseball,* p. 65, it had been used since the 1850s to denote "unskilled or inept players." When beginners organized teams, they sometimes took the name Muffins or Muffers. For examples of this use of the term in New Orleans, see the New Orleans *Daily Picayune,* October 4, 1870; June 19, 1881.

32 New Orleans *Daily Picayune,* November 20, 1885. See also New Orleans *Times,* March 2, 29, 1874; New Orleans *Daily Picayune,* November 2, 4, 10, 24, 1884; April 5, October 9, November 14, 17, 18, 23, 27, 30, December 21, 30, 1885.

league's first game. "For the first time in the history of the game in this city a league which includes clubs from other cities has been formed." Playing each Sunday, the association regularly attracted two or three thousand onlookers to its contests.[33]

Encouraged by the success of the Gulf League, promoters redoubled efforts to enter New Orleans in the more prestigious (and presumably more profitable) Southern League. In December, 1886, Toby Hart, who had been involved with several of the city's leagues, secured a franchise in the Southern League for 1887. The new club would play teams from Memphis, Nashville, Savannah, Mobile, and Charleston. Preparations for this ambitious enterprise included a thorough renovation of Sportsman's Park, which increased its capacity to more than five thousand and provided the Pelicans, as the team was called, a field with lines "correct to the hundredth of an inch." While construction progressed, Hart and his associates recruited athletes from throughout the country. Paying a total of $1,740 a month to fourteen players, New Orleans had "about the cheapest team in the league." [34]

Residents greeted the arrival of the Southern League enthusiastically. Urban rivalry was a major factor in the growth of cities in the nineteenth century. The creation of a league with teams representing other southern cities gave New Orleanians an opportunity to supplement economic competition with ersatz battles on the playing field. The Pelicans' first game attracted a "patriotic crowd" of five thousand people who "applauded every good play, and almost went wild when the nine took a decided lead." Game after game, on weekdays as well as on Sundays, drew large masses of fans who came to see the Pelicans demolish the representatives of rival southern cities. After a defeat residents "left the grounds looking as if they had sustained great personal losses." But if New Orleans won, the crowd "poured out of the grounds with a step as if marching behind lively music and a feeling as if it had just arisen from a feast at which good digestion had waited on appetite." When the Pelicans com-

---

33 The quotes describing the Acid Iron Earth nostrum and the first day of play are from the New Orleans *Daily Picayune*, June 13, 20, 1886. See also *ibid.*, January 4, October 17, 1885; January 31, April 26, June 14, 21, August 9, October 4, 1886, for the efforts to join the Southern League and for the formation and operation of the Gulf League.

34 *Ibid.*, December 19, 1886; April 17, May 9, 1887.

pleted the schedule of 111 games firmly in first place, the future of professional baseball seemed assured.[35]

But for all the interest aroused by the first season, the Southern League occupied an unenviable position in organized baseball. Founded in 1885 the league struggled through two financially disastrous years before New Orleans obtained a franchise. League officials anticipated improvement after adding the Pelicans to the association, but conditions remained pretty much the same. Plagued by financial difficulties, scheduling conflicts, feuds between members, an insouciant public, and other problems of varying magnitude, the Southern League hovered constantly on the abyss of failure.

The most important figure in local baseball then was Abner Powell. Born in Shenandoah, Pennsylvania, in December, 1860, Powell played briefly in the major leagues before coming to New Orleans in 1887 to manage and to pitch for the city's first Southern League team. He remained in New Orleans until his death in 1953. As player, manager, and owner, Powell made every effort to keep the Pelicans and the Southern League solvent. At one time in the 1890s, he owned Southern League teams in four cities—New Orleans, Atlanta, Nashville, and Selma, Alabama—in an attempt to prevent the association's financial collapse. "That is something that don't happen today," he later wrote; "I had to do it to keep the league going. That was real campaigning for the good old game."[36] In spite of Powell's personal commitment, the league fared poorly before the turn of the century. Through 1900 there were seven years (1886, 1888, 1889, 1893, 1894, 1898, and 1899) in which the league collapsed before the end of the season, and four (1890, 1891, 1897, and 1900) when it did not organize at all. The association completed play in 1885, 1887, 1892, 1895, and 1896, but its membership fre-

35 *Ibid.,* April 18, August 8, October 11, 1887.

36 *Sporting South* (New Orleans), March 3, 1888; New Orleans *Daily Picayune,* August 8, 1853; *The Baseball Encyclopedia,* 1362. According to local legend, Abner Powell introduced both ladies' day and rain checks, but these practices were in employ in New Orleans and elsewhere before Powell came to the city. The New Orleans *Times,* April 30, 1870, reported the use of rain checks, and the New Orleans *Daily Picayune,* February 16, 1880, mentioned a "ladies' day." Powell apparently devised the idea of a detachable stub for a rain check in 1899 because, he said, "a lot of fellows would climb the fence or get into the park without paying. Then it would rain and they'd all get tickets for the next game." New Orleans *Daily Picayune,* August 8, 1953.

quently changed during each season. By 1900 a total of eighteen cities, including Evansville, Indiana, had at one time or another been members of the league.

Each year financial difficulties loomed as the most ominous obstacle blocking the Southern League's quest for stability. Poor attendance, travel expenses, and burdensome payrolls often crushed members of the association. Even New Orleans, which usually fared better than its rivals, periodically encountered financial problems. During the abbreviated season of 1888, the club reportedly lost four thousand dollars. To ease the economic crush, league officials periodically adjusted the division of gate receipts. From 1885 through 1887, all receipts went to the home team, but in October, 1887, members of the association agreed to give 30 percent of the proceeds to visiting clubs. When this division proved inadequate, the league agreed in 1892 that gate money should be shared equally by host and guest teams. New Orleans consistently had the largest total attendance, so it paid the greatest price to assure the welfare of the association.[37]

League magnates also took steps to lighten operating costs. Many expenses, such as monthly dues to the association, could not be reduced because the Southern League had to employ umpires and to pay for the protection of the national agreement, but other costs were slashed severely. Like other businessmen of the period, owners first reduced the cost of "labor." Southern League magnates in 1888 placed a limit of two thousand dollars a month on players' salaries, or a total of twelve thousand dollars for each team for the six-month season. They later lowered this ceiling by steps from two thousand to twelve hundred and finally to eight hundred dollars a month. The *Picayune*, whose editors tended to regard professional baseball players and other employees as commodities to be purchased at the lowest possible price, contended that salary reductions did not seriously weaken teams, that smaller pay checks merely eliminated "the wreckers and the swelled head men." But the South's baseball barons apparently concluded that the reduction in pay brought a reduction in talent, which in turn discouraged fans. In 1894, despite the pressures

37 New Orleans *Daily Picayune*, November 1, 1887; June 30, August 8, 1888; June 18, 1889; February 22, 1892; June 24, 27, 1894; July 29, 1895; July 13, 1896.

of the current economic depression, they raised the total monthly payroll to a thousand dollars, which was still only half the amount paid in 1888.[38]

The player-workers had little choice but to accept the limits established by their employers. Southern League teams, like other minor league organizations, received the protection of the "national agreement," an arrangement which permitted a minor league to reserve all its players by paying fifteen hundred dollars annually to the National League and, until its demise, the American Association. At the end of a season a player could move to another club, hopefully in the major leagues, or he might advance in mid-season with the consent of his employer, sometimes referred to as his owner. In 1889, for example, a New Orleans player named Ward moved to Philadelphia's National League team. "The matter was arranged in a sensible way," the *Picayune* reported. "Ward is loaned for a month and gets $150 and expenses. If he turns out well Philadelphia will buy him." By expediting the movement of young men into the major leagues, the Southern League soon acquired a self-proclaimed reputation for producing excellent players. A reporter for the *Sporting South*, a New Orleans weekly, contended: "No minor league in the country has been more proficient in the development of young blood than the Southern." While a well-developed farm system remained years away, New Orleans assumed one of the major functions of a minor league team soon after it joined the Southern League. But this system had its drawbacks. The national agreement and the reserve clause clearly empowered club owners to oppress their employees by eliminating competitive bidding for the services of players. In a period when employers were unlikely to deal generously with workers, baseball players lacked an adequate means of redress. When major league players tried to improve their position by forming their own teams in 1890, National League team owners ruthlessly crushed what was called the "players' revolt" and thereby kept athletes' salaries at the lowest possible level.[39]

---

38 *Ibid.*, June 19, 1888; January 22, 1889; February 22, 1892; February 18, 1894.

39 *Ibid.*, June 6, 1889; *Sporting South*, March 3, 1888. The national agreement is mentioned in the New Orleans *Daily Picayune*, November 8, 1887.

Reducing expenses proved of little benefit to the Southern League. Officials repeatedly urged owners to cultivate patience because baseball teams required careful development. When league magnates met in December, 1888, to make arrangements for the next season, the *Picayune* announced: "In the formation of the new league there will be strictly business principles adhered to. . . . It requires experience to run a club economically and to make money." Franchises, the *Picayune* cautioned on another occasion, were long-range investments that would increase in value only after the league proved durable over several seasons. But the warnings went unheeded. Clubs collapsed with a lamentable regularity as flagging attendance and transportation tolls made it impossible for many aspiring magnates to bear the financial obligations of management, however light these burdens were.[40]

Bitter relations between league members further marred the Southern League's reputation. Some rivalry was, of course, beneficial to the league. But as teams representing cities that were themselves economic rivals struggled to win the pennant, urban tempers flared easily and sometimes produced financially costly results. The Pelicans refused to complete a three-game series in Charleston in October, 1887, because Abner Powell, the manager, objected to the Charleston umpires. Players on the opposing teams attacked each other after Powell reportedly reflected unkindly upon the marital status of one umpire's parents. That night the umpire and several friends cornered Powell in a local restaurant and demanded an apology. When the Pelicans' manager refused, the umpire beat him while his allies prevented Powell's players from coming to his rescue. After this incident the Pelicans "left Charleston in the dead of night, in fear and trembling, in order to escape the brutality of the Charleston mob." When they arrived in New Orleans at seven in the morning, a thousand fans and a brass band met them at the depot. Five years later, when Birmingham and New Orleans were engaged in a close race for the league championship, bitterness erupted after the *Picayune* accused other teams of playing halfheartedly so that Birmingham rather than New Orleans would win the pennant. The closing games, an enraged reporter scoffed, "were farcical to an extreme." This

40 New Orleans *Daily Picayune,* December 8, 1888; July 23, 1893.

kind of dissension inevitably weakened the association, for any suspicion of dishonesty resulted in waning public support.[41]

Player conduct also discouraged spectators. "Ball players are professional athletes," one writer declared. "They are supposed to be in training while they are playing ball." But many Pelicans chose to ignore this admonition. Professional ball players have always been as dedicated to Bacchus as to baseball and the New Orleans nine proved no exception to this rule. "More Lushing by the Home Team," a *Times-Democrat* headline proclaimed in July, 1887. In the story that followed a witness reported seeing the Pelicans "pretty well tanked up" in a local bar. On another occasion the players went to West End on the eve of a game, "and they did not spend their whole time out there in listening to music and breathing fresh air." Reports of drunkenness among players throughout the association undermined public confidence and contributed to the league's difficulties.[42]

Taken together, the tribulations confronted in the eighties and nineties effectively frustrated efforts to establish a solvent Southern League. Better days lay ahead in the next century, but by the late 1890s disgust characterized the attitude of many former association supporters. When the league prematurely failed in 1898 for the sixth time, the *Picayune* regarded the collapse as "a benefit to the sport in this city, for dirty politics have been infused in the organization almost from the time of its birth. . . . Over and again New Orleans has kept the league together by its generous support. Yet whenever this city asked for the slightest favor a snarl was given." [43]

Despite overt dissatisfaction with the league, fans demonstrated an interest in professional baseball that transcended temporary indifference. New Orleanians ordinarily supported their team enthusiastically, and twice, in 1887 and 1896, the Pelicans responded by winning the pennant. Feigned unconcern about the future of organized baseball in the South quickly faded at each attempt to resuscitate the Southern League. When the association secured a firm footing in the twentieth century, it enjoyed a long period of prosperity

41 *Ibid.*, October 3, 1887; September 21, 1892.
42 *Ibid.*, July 2, 1892; New Orleans *Times-Democrat*, July 24, 1887; New Orleans *Daily Picayune*, July 2, 1892. Quotations are in the order cited.
43 New Orleans *Daily Picayune*, May 22, 1898.

before falling to the fate of many minor leagues after World War II. The experience with professional baseball from 1887 to 1900 thus completed the transformation of baseball from a pastime for gentlemen amateurs to a commercial amusement for all urban residents. "In the north, east and west baseball is a business like any other," the *Picayune* once noted, "and when a man puts his money into it he wants some return. It should be so in the south." [44]

While the Southern League fell short of the financial solvency and the stability it so assiduously sought, amateur baseball remained popular among participants and spectators. Rowers, gymnasts, social clubs, cycling enthusiasts, and white- and blue-collar workers organized scores of teams in the late 1880s and throughout the 1890s.[45] Some played without affiliation but many nines formed interclub associations. Promoters periodically resurrected the Crescent City League (sometimes called the Amateur or City League) at the end of the professional season or when the Southern League momentarily faltered.[46] At various times players also founded a Catholic league, a jewelers' league, a commercial league, a rowing club league, and an association of gymnastic clubs. Finally, the city had collegiate teams, which were particularly active at Tulane University.[47]

The formation of nines by rowing and gymnastic clubs and by college players brought about a revival of genuine amateurism. For two decades after the Civil War, amateur teams in the modern sense of the term scarcely existed. The *Bulletin* estimated in 1875 that the United States had approximately fifteen hundred baseball teams, "of which number not more than fifteen can be strictly classed as professional." [48] At the same time few teams could be *strictly* classed as amateur. Teams described as amateur clubs played for money and hired vagabond professionals.[49] "Amateur" players often competed

44 *Ibid.*, December 8, 1888.

45 *Ibid.*, October 18, 1886; May 21, June 19, 1888; September 6, 1890; July 7, 1892; November 13, 1893; New Orleans *Times-Democrat*, July 23, 1887.

46 New Orleans *Daily Picayune*, September 17, 1888; October 6, 1889; May 13, 1894; April 6, 1897; June 27, 1898.

47 *Ibid.*, May 21, October 14, 1888; April 9, May 19, 1889; October 27, 1890; May 6, 28, 1895. Collegiate and intercollegiate baseball are discussed in chapter 11, "The Day of the Athletic Club," below.

48 New Orleans *Bulletin*, March 28, 1875.

49 New Orleans *Times*, September 6, 1870; April 28, 1873; May 23, 1875; New Orleans *Daily Picayune*, October 10, November 1, 8, 1880; December 5, 1881; March 6, June 19, 1882; October 23, 1883; September 23, 1885.

as professionals and then returned to amateur nines.[50] Popular definitions of amateurism and professionalism did little to dispel the confusion. An amateur, while he might occasionally play for money, regularly pursued another occupation, but a professional made "a business of pleasure." Teams composed of both amateurs and professionals were described as "semi-professional." [51]

Rowers, gymnasts, and college students brought clear concepts of amateur competition to the baseball diamond, concepts based on the well-established credo of the gentleman amateur. Rowing clubs had rigid definitions of amateurism which they applied to baseball as well as to sculling; athletic organizations, such as the Southern Athletic Club and the Young Men's Gymnastic Club, subscribed to the amateur regulations of the Amateur Athletic Union, organized in 1888; and after 1894, Tulane belonged to the Southern Intercollegiate Athletic Association, which had rules of amateur competition similar to those of the Amateur Athletic Union and the Intercollegiate Association of Amateur Athletes of America.[52] Each of these groups prohibited amateur players from profiting in any fashion from athletic activities. The introduction of these standards in the eighties and nineties eliminated the confusion regarding amateurism and professionalism. By the turn of the century, three classes of players had emerged: amateur, professional, and semiprofessional. Amateurs avoided contests from which they might derive profit; professionals played ball for a living, either for a Southern League team or for touring major league teams. Between these extremes there existed a large group of semiprofessional players who belonged to clubs and leagues that offered side bets and gate receipts to participants.[53] The newspapers usually referred to these players as amateurs, but the contrast presented by comparing them with the legitimate amateurs made it apparent that they no longer deserved this distinction. This tripartite division of players had not yet become

50 New Orleans *Times,* September 4, 1871; New Orleans *Daily Picayune,* August 22, 23, 1880.

51 New Orleans *Daily Picayune,* August 29, 1869; December 30, 1885; December 4, 1887.

52 *Ibid.,* October 15, 1893; Arthur G. Nuhrah, "History of Tulane University" (typescript in Special Collections, Tulane University Library), 777. The credo of the gentleman amateur is treated at length in chapter 11, "The Day of the Athletic Club," below.

53 New Orleans *Daily Picayune,* March 22, 1890; April 12, 1896.

permanent, but the outlines of the modern system of classification were clearly present.

Baseball's growing public, of course, cared little about distinctions between amateurism and professionalism. To the spectator the general attraction of the game assumed paramount importance, and by 1900 baseball's appeal as a participant sport and a commercial amusement had been conclusively demonstrated. Since its introduction in New Orleans, baseball had changed in a number of ways. A pastime for gentlemen players had become a game for all citizens; casual play had yielded to a highly organized system of teams, associations, and intercity leagues; and an exclusively amateur activity had become a business enterprise. As the game changed, its popularity grew apace. At the turn of the century, hundreds of people played the game, and thousands attended contests of all types—professional, amateur, and semiprofessional. Baseball, said the *Picayune* in 1898, "is the cleanest sport of the day, and is fraught with brilliancy, activity, skill and daring. Unlike the coarser sports, there is no fear of dishonesty, and the teams cannot help but battle their best in a contest." [54] As participants and spectators, Americans demanded little more of their national game.

[54] *Ibid.,* April 14, 1898.

Chapter VII
WHITE SAILS AND RACING SHELLS

Although well-to-do residents in New Orleans and other cities failed to preserve sports such as baseball and horse racing as their exclusive pastimes, other leisure activities submitted only partially to the urban populace's growing demand for commercial spectacles. Aquatic sports of the last century fall into this category. Watering places attracted people from all levels of society, as they had before the Civil War, and some diversions at these resorts, such as swimming, enjoyed general popularity. Rowing and yachting, on the other hand, appealed to a smaller and sometimes more select group. The same influences that contributed to the democratization and commercialization of horse racing and baseball touched these sports and for a time seemed likely to make rowing a pastime of the masses. But some characteristics of rowing and yachting, including the cost of participation, the inability of participants to sustain interest among spectators, and the efforts of those who engaged most actively in these sports to maintain an aura of social exclusiveness, made the democratization of these activities difficult. Water sports occupied an important position in the leisure habits of many New Orleanians, but the predominantly middle- and upper-class rowers and yachtsmen generally showed little concern for the leisure preferences of rank-and-file citizens.

Interest in aquatic pastimes revived in New Orleans soon after the war. During Federal occupation military authorities had permitted residents to go only to the south shore of Lake Pontchartrain; the city's pleasure-seekers were barred from the north shore of the lake and from all Gulf resorts. But the return of peace brought an end to all restrictions, and people soon revived the practice of leaving New Orleans behind as summer enveloped the city.[1] By the summer of

[1] New Orleans *Daily Picayune,* May 3, 1865; May 25, June 1, 1869; New Orleans *Daily Crescent,* March 24, 1866; New Orleans *Times,* July 23, 1865.

1870, almost a score of resorts at Bay St. Louis, Pass Christian, Mobile, and other Gulf towns were advertising regularly in New Orleans papers. In February, 1871, the Morgan Line announced plans to offer continual service from the lake to the principal resorts on the Mississippi Gulf Coast. Spas in the upper South also sent notices of their attractions. In an age of easy cures, Yellow Sulphur Springs in Virginia modestly recommended itself to travelers as the "best sanitorium in America for delicate females and children. Children carried there on pillows, suffering from that terrible scourge, Cholera Infantum, get well at once without medicine." [2]

Endeavoring to keep residents and their money at home during the summer, the local press repeatedly urged lakefront resorts and city railroads to make retreats more appealing to people of all ranks. "There is no wonder that people run away from New Orleans in the summer season, when it is taken into consideration the inducements offered to keep them at home," the *Picayune* lamented in 1869. "During the heated term, when baths become a necessity with those who do not indulge in them at other seasons, the expense attending a plunge into the water is actually so great as to make those in moderate circumstances hesitate before taking it." A thirty-cent bathhouse fee, in addition to the railroad fare, the *Picayune* concluded, placed cleanliness, much less sport, beyond the reach of all too many residents. On another occasion the *Bulletin* predicted that Milneburg, a retreat on the south shore, would become "the most popular summer resort of our own pent-up city residents, if the means of access to the lake are made at once cheaper and more frequent." [3]

Despite the sometimes poor travel accommodations and the relatively expensive bathing fees for public bathhouses, local resorts attracted a larger proportion of summer pleasure-seekers than before the war. As early as 1872, the *Picayune* noted that more people were finding recreation near the city each summer as the danger of yellow fever epidemics diminished and as spas on Lake Pontchartrain improved their facilities. Thus, a practical-minded reporter added, "much of the money which has hitherto been spent elsewhere will be

2 New Orleans *Bulletin,* June 21, 1874; New Orleans *Daily Picayune,* July 17, 1870; February 5, 1871.

3 New Orleans *Daily Picayune,* July 8, 1869; New Orleans *Bulletin,* June 28, 1874.

kept at home." Many New Orleanians, particularly the well-to-do, continued to seek summer amusement far from the city, but thousands turned to lakefront resorts at West End, Spanish Fort, and Milneburg, or to the numerous parks that dotted the fringes of the city. The Census Bureau observed in the 1880s: "During eight months of the year . . . both Spanish Fort and West End are nightly patronized by thousands, including those of all classes of society and of both sexes." Julian Ralph, the travel writer, reported in 1895 that West End featured "dance platforms, shooting galleries, candy and tobacco shops, drinking-saloons, nickel-in-slot machines, and all the queer paraphernalia of a Southern Rockaway." At the end of the century, a guidebook listed the three watering places on the lake and Audubon Park as the city's favorite retreats.[4]

Watering places usually welcomed all residents, but in the 1870s Negro citizens began to encounter a rigid color line. Blacks had shown a quickening interest in the attractions of local spas after 1865, mainly because the abolition of slavery gave them a freedom of movement that even free Negroes had not known before the Civil War. During the Reconstruction period, black residents apparently confronted few racial barriers. In 1872, for example, the *Louisianian*, a Negro newspaper, carried an advertisement for Stoke's Hotel in Bay St. Louis and noted that the owners were "ready to accommodate all who desire to patronize them." On another occasion the newspaper reported an excursion to Biloxi sponsored by Negro Odd Fellows: "The day was spent in agreeable recreation; fishing, bathing, boat-sailing, dancing, speech-making incident to the occasion and contesting for the prizes, filling up the time." But the collapse of Reconstruction and a corresponding decline in efforts to safeguard the political and civil rights of black citizens invited the adoption of racial segregation. The *Louisianian* reported in May,

---

4 The quotations in this paragraph are from the New Orleans *Daily Picayune,* March 20, 1872; United States Bureau of the Census, *Tenth Census* (1880): *Report on the Social Statistics of Cities,* Vol. XIX, comp. George E. Waring, Jr. (Washington, D.C., 1887), 275, hereinafter cited as Waring (comp.), *Report on the Social Statistics of Cities;* and Julian Ralph, "Two Early Southwestern Beach Resorts," *Harper's Weekly,* XXXIX (September 21, 1895), 891. For other information on resorts, see New Orleans *Daily Picayune,* June 26, July 10, 1876; Lady Duffus Hardy, *Down South* (London, 1883), 248–49; and *Picayune's Guide to New Orleans* (6th ed.; New Orleans, 1900), 172–75.

1880, that during an excursion to Mobile, black passengers had been assigned to special railroad cars. Racial separatism evidently had not assumed the rigidity of later years, for the editor noted: "Of course decent colored people will leave these special cars alone"; instead they could sit where they chose. Nevertheless, the practice of providing Jim Crow coaches, once begun, soon became firmly established. Segregation laws of the 1890s merely reinforced prevailing customs that had been forced on the black community in the 1880s.[5]

Of more immediate concern to local Negroes was the discrimination they found at lakefront facilities. In 1880 and 1881, the *Louisianian* conducted a campaign against segregation policies at both Spanish Fort and New Lake End. The editor's protests at first brought some improvement. In June, 1880, the newspaper announced: "The warning relative to the ostracism of colored people at Spanish Fort has been heeded. Mr. J. A. Brett has opened a fine saloon and restaurant, called the 'Sea Breeze,' where all can be entertained in first-class style, without distinction of color. The bath houses and pic-nic grounds are delightful, and convenient for pleasure seekers. Mr. Brett should be liberally patronized." By the following year, however, segregation had returned. The *Louisianian* complained in June because the "most respected colored citizens of our community are deprived of the pleasures and benefits of these resorts by the glaring insults offered them, by bluntly refusing to accommodate them to refreshments in common with others"; but at the same time "the most despicable, or depraved white man or woman, can enjoy the hospitalities as bountifully as our most respected white citizen" and "the blackest servant girl is allowed to sit majestically beside her little white wards, and sip daintily at her ice cream, lemonade, or beer." Several weeks later the editor reported: "The idea [of segregation] becomes more ridiculous when we observe that upon the cars, in the gardens, and along the walks there is no distinction whatever, but as soon as a glass of refreshment is ordered, the politest answer you can get is, 'we don't sell to colored people.'" At the suggestion of R. L. Desdunes, Negroes planned to form an Equal Rights Association "for rescuing our liberties from the jaws of prejudice,"

[5] New Orleans *Weekly Louisianian,* September 7, 1872; July 25, 1874; May 1, 1880.

but further protests proved useless. Negroes continued to visit local and regional resorts, but only on a racially segregated basis.[6]

For residents of all classes, black and white, swimming was the most popular sport at all watering places. Since the relatively low cost of plunging into the lake, Gulf, or river barred few people from participation, thousands swam during the summer. Women alone encountered mild opposition. Female bathers had enjoyed the sport since long before the Civil War without in any way compromising themselves, but lingering prejudice against female athleticism occasionally manifested itself after 1865. As late as 1891, an article in the *Picayune* warned: "Beautiful Women . . . Take Their Lives in Their Hands When They Go for Their Daily Dip in the Ocean." The writer went on to explain that improper "sea bathing" led to "the accumulation of flesh and sinew, the toughening of the skin, and the quickening of the surface circulation of the blood." [7] Such fears seem to have had little effect in discouraging female swimmers.

Swimming, like other sports, underwent a degree of organization in the late nineteenth century. L. F. Gery, described as "a distinguished and expert French swimmer," and several local athletes founded the New Orleans Swimming Club in the 1870s and began to sponsor races for both amateurs and professionals.[8] These contests and others arranged by independent promoters indicated that swimmers, in common with participants in a number of other sports, lacked clear definitions of amateurism and professionalism. With few exceptions, swimmers, whether classed as professionals or amateurs, vied for money. Local swimmers evolved no rigid amateur standards, but most people understood that a professional depended mainly on his athletic prowess for his livelihood; an amateur, though he sometimes received cash prizes, regularly followed another occupation. In 1874 "Professor" John T. Clarke, a professional who sometimes worked as a longshoreman, swam against Gery, an amateur, for a purse of four hundred dollars. The press classified Clarke as a professional because, unlike Gery, he traveled throughout the United

---

6 Quotations in this paragraph are from *ibid.*, June 19, 1880; June 18, July 23, 1881. For other editorials regarding segregation at lakefront resorts, see *ibid.*, May 1, 1880; June 25, July 30, 1881.

7 New Orleans *Daily Picayune*, August 20, 1891.

8 *Ibid.*, September 7, 1874; June 26, 1876; June 3, 1878; New Orleans *Times*, September 7, 1874; New Orleans *Bulletin*, October 5, 1875.

States and Great Britain for matches. John L. Henderson defeated "Professor" Clarke in July of 1891 "for a purse and the championship of the south." Although he took money, the *Picayune* said a few days later, "Mr. Henderson is not a professional swimmer in the strict sense of the term, as he does not swim for a living." [9]

Of the many swimming contests held in New Orleans, the only purely amateur matches (in the modern sense of the term) were those of the Southern Athletic Club in the 1890s. When this association held meets for its members, it gave medals rather than money to the winners. Despite the club's emphasis on amateurism (which will be discussed at length in chapter 11), professionals dominated swimming in the city throughout the latter part of the nineteenth century.[10]

After the war yachting remained the favorite aquatic sport for the upper class. As wealthy residents settled into their familiar routine of summer holidays, those who stayed near the city soon showed an interest in reviving yachting clubs and in resuming organized sailing matches. Members of the city's antebellum yacht clubs began to sponsor regattas on Lake Pontchartrain and along the Gulf Coast in 1867. The success of these outings encouraged J. O. Nixon and other yachtsmen to reorganize the Crescent City Yacht Club in 1869.[11] This association sponsored or sent representatives to scores of races along the Gulf Coast for several years. Given fair weather, large crowds gathered at the lake to watch regattas and on occasion boarded steamers to Mississippi resorts for sailing contests. The *Picayune* observed that at one regatta "there were quite a respectable sprinkling of those who have a genuine love for aquatic sports, and not a few who affect a sentiment which is foreign to their nature in order to be in the fashion. It is quite the thing, you know, to don white linen suits, jaunty little hats, to put on a certain swagger when walking, and to throw as many nautical phrases as possible into the conversation." [12]

9 New Orleans *Times,* September 7, 1874; New Orleans *Daily Picayune,* September 7, 1874; June 26, 1876; July 27, August 2, 1891.

10 New Orleans *Daily Picayune,* July 3, 1891.

11 New Orleans *Daily Crescent,* July 2, September 4, 11, 12, November 5, 6, 7, 1867; New Orleans *Daily Picayune,* June 20, 27, July 2, 1869.

12 For examples of Crescent City Yacht Club regattas, see New Orleans *Daily Picayune,* July 16, 17, August 13, 17, 1869; July 22, August 28, 31, 1870;

Whatever its fashionableness, interest in organized yachting soon waned. By the mid-seventies the Crescent City Yacht Club had dissolved, probably a victim of the financial panic and depression of that decade. A few yachtsmen continued to schedule races, but most commodores preferred private pleasure cruises. The paucity of formal regattas prompted one reporter to complain: "With our breezy afternoons it is a pity our yachtsmen could not entice a crowd from the heated city to indulge in the pleasure of witnessing a closely sailed race." In New York, another reporter gibed, "the bay is alive with the snowy sails, and the races are held almost daily." Residents who desired to witness yacht races generally had to travel. In August, 1875, for example, several hundred New Orleanians took an excursion train to Bay St. Louis for a regatta. "There was a lively exhibition of enthusiasm when the victorious boats shot by the winning stake," the *Picayune* reported, "and also quite a variety of grum looking faces, for the way money changed hands was a caution to the city boys." [13]

Organized sailing resumed in New Orleans in May, 1878, when several prominent citizens met at Hawkins' Saloon to reestablish the Southern Yacht Club. Drawing its members from the city's leading merchants and professional men, this association fully restored competitive sailing in succeeding years. According to one of its charters, the club existed "to encourage athletic and other exercises of its members and to foster and to encourage social intercourse among its members." During the twenty-two years after its reorganization the club lived up to its objectives. Described locally as "the best organization of its kind in the South," the association dominated yacht racing in New Orleans and along the Gulf Coast. It sponsored regattas on Lake Pontchartrain and also arranged and participated in sailing contests in Mississippi and Alabama. To fulfill its social obligations, the club built a clubhouse at West End in 1879. When the growth of the association rendered this building inadequate, members replaced it with a larger structure in 1900.[14]

July 21, 29, 1871; New Orleans *Times,* July 14, 16, 17, September 8, 1869. The quote is from the New Orleans *Daily Picayune,* July 17, 1869.

    [13] New Orleans *Daily Picayune,* July 14, 20, 1873; August 17, 1875.

    [14] The quotes in this paragraph are from the *Charter, By-Laws, Table of Time Allowances, Racing Rules, Etc. of the Southern Yacht Club, of New Orleans, La.* (New Orleans, 1892), 4; and New Orleans *Daily Picayune,* May 25,

The Southern Yacht Club succeeded where the Crescent City Yacht Club had failed because it attracted the support of many wealthy residents. Competitive yachting has always flourished only when well-to-do people freely invested time and money in the sport. The Crescent City Yacht Club revived during the Reconstruction period when money was in short supply and usually not available for such "frivolous" enterprises. In 1871, shortly before the dissolution of the Crescent City Club, the *Picayune* attributed declining interest in yachting to two groups: yacht owners who refused to race for the club's small prizes and businessmen who spent their money elsewhere. Such men, said the *Picayune*, were "destitute of that public spirit which activates gentlemen in other cities to further, in every possible way, all sports and amusements for the entertainment of the general public, even though such furtherance may entail personal expense." Indeed the Crescent City Yacht Club found only a handful of men, including J. O. Nixon, the club president; John Mahoney, the "famous architect of swift yachts"; and Charles T. Howard, director of the state lottery, willing to accept the financial burden of yachting. Howard was a particularly avid yachtsman, perhaps because his support of this sport, like his ownership of thoroughbred horses, offered a possibility of social acceptance which his connection with the lottery and the state's Reconstruction government denied him. He entered three yachts in the Crescent City Club's first regatta in 1869 and manned them with a crew of "thirty-two skilled yachtsmen" and a "marine band" consisting of a drum and fife. While two of his boats sailed to victory in the first and second classes, Howard invited members of the club aboard another of his yachts "to get a better view of the race, and to investigate the contents of some very curious bottles which had been smuggled aboard." Howard's enthusiasm alone, however, could not save the club.[15]

When the Southern Yacht Club reappeared, conditions proved

1879. Information about the reorganization and progress of the club may be found in the New Orleans *Daily Picayune,* May 8, 15, 1878; May 25, 1879; May 27, 1900; and Hennessey, *One Hundred Years of Yachting,* 10. For references to Southern Yacht Club regattas, see New Orleans *Daily Picayune,* June 25, 26, July 21, 1878; June 12, 1879; June 28, 1882; August 26, 1883; June 24, 1885; June 27, 1890; July 2, 1891; August 13, 20, 1893; June 17, August 26, 1900.

15 Quotations in this paragraph are from the New Orleans *Daily Picayune,* July 21, 1871; and July 16, 1869. The "marine band" is mentioned in the New Orleans *Times,* July 16, 1869.

more favorable. More people had money; and more people of wealth stayed in the city. This moneyed class turned naturally to yachting to satisfy their desire for summer pleasure. "To those who love not the sport it would be impossible to describe the feelings of the owner of a crack yacht," the *Picayune* once informed its readers. "Only monarchs and those who have all they can wish for can understand his feelings." Racing may have been a secondary consideration for those who bought yachts, but men who invested large sums of money in sumptuous floating palaces found that regattas offered a socially acceptable method of exhibiting their princely possessions.[16]

Competitive sailing offered yachtsmen little compensation other than social prestige. The Crescent City Yacht Club had given small cash prizes, and the Southern Yacht Club followed this practice for a time. Both clubs also sponsored annual races for a Challenge Cup.[17] In the late 1880s, the Southern Yacht Club abandoned money rewards altogether and began instead to present silver cups donated by members to the winners of all races.[18] The conversion from money to loving cups underscored the idea that yachtsmen raced not for a financial return but rather because regattas enabled them to demonstrate publicly their high social and economic standing. Yachting thus provided well-to-do merchants and professional men an entree to the local aristocracy.

Whatever the inducement for races—silver cups, small cash prizes, or the opportunity for public display of yachts—Southern Yacht Club regattas stimulated strong rivalries among club members. Alexander Brewster dominated the association's races in the 1880s when his fleet sailing craft repeatedly won the Challenge Cup, but other yachtsmen began to dispute his supremacy in the 1890s. Brewster's *Mephisto*, Sidney Ranlett's *Nyanza*, John Rawlins' *Nydia*, and Charles P. Richardson's *Nepenthe* engaged in a series of

---

16 New Orleans *Daily Picayune*, June 18, 1888.

17 New Orleans *Times*, July 16, 1869; New Orleans *Daily Picayune*, September 14, 1869; July 21, 1871; July 28, 1878; June 12, 1879; July 6, 1880; June 6, 28, 1882; June 29, 1887; May 18, June 29, 1888; June 3, 1891.

18 *Charter . . . of the Southern Yacht Club* [1892], 39; *Charter, By-Laws, Racing Rules, Table of Time Allowances, Sailing Directions, Etc., of the Southern Yacht Club of New Orleans, La.* (New Orleans, 1901), 42–47; *Charter, By-Laws, House Rules, Racing Rules, Sailing Directions, Etc., of the Southern Yacht Club of New Orleans, La.* (New Orleans, 1905), 45–51; New Orleans *Daily Picayune*, June 25, August 13, 1893; August 5, 12, 1900.

spirited and closely contested matches for the Southern Yacht Club's cups. From 1893 until the end of the century, for example, Brewster's *Mephisto* and Ranlett's *Nyanza* sailed against each for the Walker Cup, but neither could win the three consecutive victories necessary to gain permanent possession of the trophy. Richardson won permanent possession of the Brewster Cup in June, 1894, by defeating his rivals for the third straight year. "The cup had been won twice by the Nepenthe," the *Picayune* reported, "and it was hoped by many that some other boat would get it this time, in order to prolong the contest, but the beautiful and costly Richardson yacht had too firm a grip on Mr. Brewster's cup to give it up, and she won in one of the prettiest races seen on the lake this summer." [19]

Aside from the interest they contributed to yachting, cup races helped to solve a problem that had troubled yachting since its introduction in New Orleans. Before and after the war, the sport was dominated by wealthy citizens possessing the means to buy large yachts and to employ the best professional seamen. The Southern Yacht Club attempted to solve this problem by scheduling contests both for amateurs (men who sailed their own boats) and for professionals (those who received money to sail for others). This solution was not completely satisfactory, however, because professionally manned yachts continued to dominate challenge cup races while small boats settled for inferior prizes. The introduction of a full schedule of cup races in the 1890s eliminated this problem. Donors of the cups usually specified that they were to be given for competition involving certain classes of yachts. At the turn of the century, to cite a few examples, the club offered the Sully Cup for cabin sloops under thirty-two feet, six inches; the Scooler Cup for cabin sloops under twenty-five feet; and the Oliveri Cup for cat boats. Cup races placed amateurs in competition with professionals, but only within well-defined classes. Given ability as a seaman, an amateur could defeat a professional if the yachts were of equal size and structure. [20]

Members of the Southern Yacht Club saw no necessity for formal and rigidly enforced definitions of amateurism and professionalism,

19 New Orleans *Daily Picayune,* June 28, 30, 1882; June 29, 1887; June 18, 1893; June 27, 1894; June 21, August 9, 1896; June 20, 1897; June 19, 1898; June 17, 1900.

20 *Ibid.,* May 23, 26, June 8, July 6, 1880; June 6, 7, 9, 1882; *Charter . . . of the Southern Yacht Club* [1901], 43–47.

because the club was composed mainly of men dedicated to defending the credo of the gentleman sportsman, men who sailed primarily for pleasure. Unlike the owners of thoroughbred racers, who had occupied an equally lofty position before they made horse racing a commercial pastime, yachtsmen showed little concern for prize money and no interest in attracting paying spectators. Ordinary residents were free to attend races, but only members of the club and their invited guests could watch from the clubhouse, which was the best vantage point. For many members the most important facet of the club was its social life. The clubhouse furnished a retreat where members could attend the "usual hop" that followed each regatta, play cards (for drinks only, because house rules emphatically informed the gentlemen members, "No money stakes will be permitted"), or engage in any of the myriad activities normally associated with membership in an exclusive club. Members were generally free to do as they chose as long as they followed basic rules, such as the one that admonished: "No gentlemen shall be permitted to enter the Ladies' Dressing Room." The club's handbook indicated that members led a gay life, for the "Notes on Treatment of Simple Ailments" by Fleet Surgeon John B. Elliott gave prominent attention to a remedy for delirium tremens. Elliott suggested fifteen grains of chloral hydrate and thirty grains of bromide of potash. "If there is much depression," he added, "an occasional dose of whiskey can be given." [21]

Although the social life associated with the club resisted change, other aspects of postwar yachting altered rapidly. Toward the century's end, yachtsmen introduced steam yachting, which was to change the future course of aquatic sports in the twentieth century. Steam-driven boats had been an important type of water transportation in America for years, but the idea of using steam vessels for sport occurred to few people before the 1880s, except on the occasion of exciting riverboat races such as the contest between the *Robert E. Lee* and the *Natchez* in 1870. In 1884, however, *Outing* magazine reported that the recent regatta of New York's American Steam-Yacht Club had awakened great interest in steam yachting. This interest soon spread southward, and by 1892 at least three members of the Southern Yacht Club owned steam yachts. Before the end of the

[21] *Picayune's Guide* [1900], 173; New Orleans *Daily Picayune,* August 12, 1900; *Charter . . . of the Southern Yacht Club* [1892], 19, 53.

century, the club had established racing classifications for both steam yachts and "motor yachts." Mechanized boating was in its infancy and was doubtless scorned by purists, but the growing appeal of motor boats betokened an era of mass participation in "yachting" in the twentieth century. Following a pattern common to many sports, the upper class first introduced this phase of boating.[22]

If yachtsmen had initiated the loss of their sporting monopoly by embracing a type of boating that was to stimulate widespread participation, it was scarcely apparent as the Southern Yacht Club entered a new century. Yachting in 1900 remained a rich man's pastime as it had been in 1849, the year of the club's founding. More people owned yachts and belonged to the club at the end of the century simply because wealth was more widely dispersed. Yachting filtered down to the middle class only as the general standard of living climbed and as mass production lowered the cost of boats of all sizes.

For many residents rowing was the favorite aquatic sport. Throughout the United States the years following Appomattox saw a great revival in this activity. By the 1870s the country had more than two hundred clubs, many of which looked to the National Association of Amateur Oarsmen for supervision. Founded in 1873 through the efforts of Philadelphia's Schuylkill Navy, the association attempted to reserve rowing for gentlemen amateurs by guarding against professionalism in any form. It also sponsored annual regattas for national championships in several categories. For a generation after the war, rowing ranked among the country's most popular participant sports.[23]

Rowing resumed in New Orleans in the summer of 1872 when some of the city's "first and best young men" formed the St. John and Pelican rowing clubs, built boathouses on Bayou St. John, and began to schedule regattas. Their success encouraged other rowers and by 1874 the city had at least a dozen clubs. For the remainder of the century, one or two rowing associations appeared nearly every year. Some existed only a short time, but more than thirty

22 New Orleans *Daily Picayune,* July 6, 1870; *Outing,* V (November, 1884), 138; *Charter . . . of the Southern Yacht Club* [1892], 7; New Orleans *Daily Picayune,* April 26, June 17, 1900.
23 Crowther and Ruhl, *Rowing and Track Athletics,* 151; Menke (ed.), *The Encyclopedia of Sports,* 768.

clubs organized before 1900. They constructed clubhouses and boat docks throughout the city—on Bayou St. John, on the New Basin Canal, and on Lake Pontchartrain. Rowers also occasionally practiced their skills on the Mississippi River.[24]

Clubs that engaged actively in rowing over a period of years often invested heavily in equipment. Postwar competition, much more specialized than in the 1840s and 1850s, required a large number of boats, including single- and double-scull craft and four-oared shells, gigs, and wherries. Some clubs acquired as many as thirty boats, which they bought from local builders like John Mahoney, "the prince of boat builders," or from marine architects in New York or England. Although rowing clubs spent freely, the cost to individual members was relatively small because the club collected dues from several score young men. In the mid-seventies, for example, the New Orleans Rowing Club, which received only two dollars a month from each member, spent hundreds of dollars each year for boats, maintenance, and a boathouse.[25]

Since young athletes could become active rowers at very little cost, the appeal of the sport spread to nearly all classes. In the 1850s participation had been limited mainly to the upper levels of society; to some extent this exclusiveness continued after the war. The Pelican Rowing Club, according to the *Picayune*, included "many of our first and best young men, full of vim and ambition, and determined to make for themselves a reputation in the rowing arena." The same newspaper in 1875 described the St. John Rowing Club as "a club of high social standing—perhaps the highest occupied by any club in New Orleans. Its members are chiefly young gentlemen of polish and attainments and fashionable proclivities whose associations are with the first people of the city." As was the case with many sports, the bon ton soon lost its monopoly. Some clubs continued to enlist only "young gentlemen of polish and attainments," but others existed for rowers of all ranks. Employees of the city's cotton presses founded the Orleans Rowing Club in 1873, and the

24 New Orleans *Daily Picayune,* May 14, August 25, November 17, 1872; August 9, 1874; August 13, 1876; August 30, 1877; *Charter and By-Laws of the St. John Rowing Club of New Orleans* (New Orleans, 1884).

25 New Orleans *Bulletin,* October 5, 1875; June 11, 1876; New Orleans *Times,* March 7, 1873; New Orleans Rowing Club: Account Book and Membership Rolls, 1873–1877, *passim* (Special Collections, Tulane University Library).

Riverside Club, also organized in 1873, drew most of its members from metal foundries. In the 1870s firemen, always eager for sport, formed several rowing associations, including the highly successful Hope and Perseverance clubs. The city's outstanding oarsman in the 1870s and 1880s, Frank J. Mumford, who rowed for the Perseverance Rowing Club, worked as both a fireman and a cotton weigher. A common fondness for athletic rivalry temporarily cut through social distinctions, attracted adherents from virtually all economic levels, and thereby democratized rowing.[26]

Competition among clubs assumed many forms. Interclub matches, anniversary regattas, and state championship races comprised the majority of rowing events, but local oarsmen also had opportunities to compare skills with rowers from other sections. As transportation facilities improved, local athletes regularly attended races in the Northeast and Midwest, and rowers from other sections journeyed south to row in the Crescent City. In 1875, 1880, and 1885, the St. John Rowing Club held elaborate regattas that attracted outstanding rowers from New York, Chicago, Detroit, Charleston, Galveston, Mobile, and small towns in Michigan and Iowa. The events won the club an impressive amount of space in newspapers and sporting journals throughout the United States. However, the regatta of 1885 was a financial failure, and the club soon abandoned its efforts to promote intersectional competition.[27]

While outstanding rowers from other cities came to New Orleans, local oarsmen made frequent trips to regattas in the North. Several clubs, including the Hope, Perseverance, St. John, and West End, sent representatives to city, regional, and national regattas. James O'Donnell, who placed second in the single-scull race at a Detroit regatta in 1877, was the first New Orleans rower to compete outside the city. When he returned, "The Hope Club received their popular member at the Jackson depot with a band of music and

---

26 New Orleans *Daily Picayune,* August 25, 1872; May 7, 1875; June 23, 1900; New Orleans *Times,* July 14, 1873; New Orleans *Bulletin,* September 12, 1874.

27 New Orleans *Daily Picayune,* July 16, 17, 18, 20, 1875; June 4, 5, 6, 1880; May 26, 27, 28, 29, 30, 1885; New Orleans *Times-Democrat,* May 25, June 17, 1885. For indications of the national coverage of the St. John regattas, see New York *Times,* July 20, 1875; June 4, 5, 1880; May 26, 27, 28, 1885; New York *Herald,* May 26, 27, 28, 29, 30, 1885; Chicago *Tribune,* June 4, 1880; May 27, 28, 29, 30, 1885; *Wilkes' Spirit of the Times,* XCIX (March 27, 1880), 181; CIX (June 6, 1885), 578.

escorted him through the principal streets." Frank J. Mumford, champion of the South in the late 1870s and early 1880s, was by far the most capable local oarsman to participate in distant regattas. He won the single-scull championship at the regatta of the National Association of Amateur Oarsmen in 1879 and 1880. He also dominated regional rowing events, twice winning the single-scull championship of the Mississippi Valley Rowing Association. On the occasion of his first victory in 1880, *Wilkes' Spirit of the Times* called him "the finest oarsman who has ever pulled in the Association." A generation later one of Mumford's students, C. S. Titus, won the national single-scull championship in 1901, 1902, and 1906.[28]

Intersectional competition in rowing, as well as in other sports, was regarded as a great benefit to a country recently torn by civil war. When a local club won the national double-scull championship in 1878, *Wilkes' Spirit of the Times* declared: "The 'Solid South' were universal favorites, and their success was extremely popular." The New York *Sun* supported this contention in its report of the victory: "Intense excitement existed among the thousands on the banks, who cheered the Southerners as warmly as the others." At the presentation of prizes, a representative of the national association said that "of course all could not win; but he was glad our friends from Dixie had carried off something." A belief in the power of athletic competition to heal festering sectional wounds found even more lucid expression at the St. John regatta of 1880. In presenting the awards to winners from Michigan, New York, and New Orleans, Congressman R. N. Ogden assured rowers that "these are the contests we desire, contests of manly skill, and powess, embittered by no sectional prejudice, inflamed by no political animosity, contests of brotherly love, where the best man wins." [29]

For all the enthusiasm aroused by intersectional contests, regat-

28 New Orleans *Daily Picayune,* August 8, 23, 1877; August 21, 22, 26, 1878; July 10, 11, 12, 27, 1879; June 26, July 4, 10, 1880; August 11, 1884; July 3, 5, 1885; July 15, 1888; July 17, 24, 1898; July 30, 1899; July 20, 21, 22, 1900; New York *Herald,* August 22, 23, 1878; New York *Times,* July 12, 1879; *Wilkes' Spirit of the Times,* XCVII (July 5, 1879), 545; XCIX (July 10, 1880), 585; CI (July 2, 1881), 602; Menke (ed.), *The Encyclopedia of Sports,* 769. The quotations in this paragraph are from the New Orleans *Daily Picayune,* August 23, 1877; and *Wilkes' Spirit of the Times,* XCIX (July 10, 1880), 585.

29 *Wilkes' Spirit of the Times,* XCVI (August 24, 1878), 68; New York *Sun,* August 22, 1878; New Orleans *Daily Picayune,* August 26, 1878; June 6, 1880. Quotations are in the order cited.

tas for the state championship were most popular with local fans. Soon after the first clubs appeared, rowers evinced an interest in a parent organization to sponsor races for the state championship. This desire for regulated rivalry led to the formation of four separate groups in the postwar period—the Louisiana Rowing Association (1873–74), the Louisiana Amateur Rowing Association (1875–84), the Pontchartrain Regatta Association (1881–93), and the Southern Amateur Rowing Association (1898–1900).[30] Although troubled by internal dissension, these organizations sponsored regattas nearly every year from 1873 to the end of the century. The first three associations attracted only local rowers who competed for the state championships, but in 1894 a club from Pensacola, Florida, joined the Southern Amateur Rowing Association. For the remainder of the period the association scheduled annual races in either New Orleans or Pensacola for the "southern championship." [31]

The existence of these rowing associations prevented the development of serious problems regarding professionalism. All four groups accepted the authority of the National Association of Amateur Oarsmen, which defined an amateur as "any person who has never competed in any open competition for money, or under a false name, or with a professional for any prize, or where gate money is charged, nor has ever, at any time, taught, pursued, or assisted in athletic exercises for money or for any valuable consideration." One club, the St. John, remained independent of state associations for most of this period, but it was a member of the Mississippi Valley Rowing Association and therefore accepted national regulations.[32] Such was the effectiveness of attempts to maintain athletic purity that only

---

30 New Orleans *Times,* August 10, 1873; New Orleans *Daily Picayune,* August 9, 16, 1875; September 26, 1877; June 16, 1886; April 16, 1893; May 23, 1897; June 22, 1900; *Wilkes' Spirit of the Times,* CII (September 10, 1881), 178.

31 New Orleans *Times,* September 2, 1873; September 15, 1874; New Orleans *Daily Picayune,* July 18, 19, 1876; September 25, 26, 1877; July 16, 17, 1878; July 29, 31, 1879; August 22, 23, 1882; July 25, 1883; July 31, 1884; June 16, 1886; July 22, 1887; June 14, 1888; June 20, 1890; June 17, 18, 1891; June 19, 1892; March 1, April 16, 1893; June 27, 1894; June 26, 1896; June 25, 1897; June 14, 15, 1898; July 7, 1899; June 22, 23, 1900.

32 New Orleans *Daily Picayune,* August 9, 1874; March 28, 1881; February 16, May 2, 1885; June 24, 1895; *Constitution of the Pontchartrain Regatta Association* (New Orleans, 1889), 13; Edward James, *Manual of Sporting Rules* (12th ed.; New York, 1877), 84. The National Association of Amateur Oarsmen's definition of amateurism is taken from the New Orleans *Daily Picayune,* March 22, 1885.

one Crescent City rower ever ran afoul of the amateur code. In 1884 the national association barred Frank Mumford from amateur competition "for rowing crooked." [33]

Both the purity of the sport and the enthusiasm of participants made rowing a highly popular sport in the 1870s and 1880s. Regattas on the lake or river attracted as many as ten or fifteen thousand people who cheered enthusiastically for their favorites. When the West End Rowing Club held its fifth anniversary regatta in June, 1885, the *Picayune* reported: "A great many ladies graced the clubhouse balcony, and the oarsmen had the additional encouragement of a band of music, which played lively airs at the start and finish of each race." Journalists met prominent visiting oarsmen at railroad depots or at the docks and published full accounts of their training procedures, records, and aspirations. The sport also invaded the language and even the scientific thought of the late nineteenth century. A New Orleanian who vacationed at Saratoga in 1875 reported: "Young women no longer ask for an arm; it is, 'Give me your starboard oar, please.' . . . In the evening, not a waltz, but 'a double-scull race' is suggested." Moreover, he added, "The 'Origin of Races' is asked for in the bookstores, and the impression prevails that the Darwinian theory solves the vexed question of the winnin' stroke." Ladies were reportedly more susceptible to the rower's charm than other fans, for, said the *Picayune*, "Women, who are by nature weak, delight to gaze upon the evidences of strength in the other sex. The brawny arm and sinewy frame, which the oarsmen develop to the utmost, are objects of the deepest admiration to them. The victor in the athletic struggle finds his sweetest reward in the bright glance and smiles of approval from their eyes and lips." [34]

[33] New Orleans *Daily Picayune,* August 12, 1884. Mumford had been suspected of dishonesty several years earlier. In 1880 the National Association of Amateur Oarsmen appointed a committee to investigate the "hippodroming of races in the interest of poolroom gangs." The committee suspended Mumford for a time, but he was exonerated in 1881. The suspension of 1884 lasted until 1898 when J. J. Woulfe of the Young Men's Gymnastic Club persuaded the association to reconsider the case. Mumford then returned to amateur rowing, but while training for a regatta in 1900 he developed pneumonia and died. *Ibid.,* October 11, 1880; April 25, 1881; June 23, 1900.

[34] Quotations in this paragraph, in the order cited, are from the New Orleans *Daily Picayune,* June 21, 1885; New Orleans *Bulletin,* August 15, 1875; and New Orleans *Daily Picayune,* June 4, 1880. For examples of large attendance at rowing regattas, see New Orleans *Daily Picayune,* July 20, 1875; July 16, 1878; Sep-

By the 1890s, however, many residents had lost interest in rowing and rowers. As other sports, such as baseball, summoned spectators and participants, many clubs dissolved. In particular, rowers from the working and lower middle classes abandoned the sport, thus allowing it to fall once again under the control of athletes from the upper levels of society who showed little desire to revive popular enthusiasm for the sport. Members of the city's most prominent clubs, the St. John and West End, were, like yachtsmen, dedicated to preserving the sport as a pastime for gentlemen and to providing the amenities of an exclusive social club. The West End rowers in May, 1890, announced plans "to make the club as prominent in social affairs as it is in boating, so that those who have not time nor inclination for rowing will find leisure in the attractions offered." Both clubs showed little interest in the comfort of spectators at regattas. The St. John Club had constructed in 1885 a huge grandstand equipped with bar, poolroom, and seats for five thousand people, but after the financial failure of its intersectional regatta in that year, the club allowed the grandstand to deteriorate; by 1900 it had rotted away. In the 1890s only close friends of the rowers were encouraged to attend races; they entered the clubhouses "by card from the members." By that time clubs limited their activities to state championship races each year and to annual regattas to celebrate their founding.[35]

Although rowing had declined sharply in the 1890s, it was an important factor in sustaining general interest in aquatic sports. Boat clubs disappeared after the turn of the century when upper-class youths also abandoned the sport, but the tradition of seeking recreation at nearby watering places remained. If yachting and, to a lesser extent, rowing resisted the pressures that made baseball and horse racing commercial pastimes, it was less an indication of the unpopularity of aquatic sports than of the determination of some

tember 10, 1879; May 26, 1885; New Orleans *Times-Democrat,* July 22, 1887. The interest of journalists in rowers is mentioned in the New Orleans *Daily Picayune,* May 15, 16, 1885.

35 Quotations in this paragraph are from the New Orleans *Daily Picayune,* May 25, 1890; and *Picayune's Guide* [1900], 172. For indications of the dissolution of clubs and the relatively small number of associations still active in the 1890s, see New Orleans *Daily Picayune,* June 20, 1890; June 27, 1894; June 26, 1896; July 17, December 3, 1898; June 17, 1900. The grandstand is described in the New Orleans *Daily Picayune,* May 25, 1885; June 21, 1900.

sportsmen, particularly yachtsmen, to participate in leisure activities that were beyond the reach of ordinary citizens. Class divisions remained more pronounced in aquatic sports than in other activities, but rowing and yachting, together with swimming, picnicking, dining, dancing, and drinking, helped to make local spas popular resorts that offered amusements of one type or another for people of all ranks.

Chapter VIII
A RELIC
OF BARBARISM

Prize fighting occupied a unique position among American sports in the postwar period. It never entirely eluded the shadow of social disfavor that had crept over it soon after Americans imported the sport from England. But while society paid lip service to condemnations of the ring, people of all classes idolized prize fighters and gave professional boxing the support that allowed it to achieve near respectability and a high level of popularity. Outwardly loathing the brutality and barbarity of the "sweet science," Americans who matured in the 1880s and 1890s were inwardly proud that the United States could produce John L. Sullivan and James J. Corbett.[1]

New Orleanians expressed a particularly strong interest in prize fighting and prize fighters because the sport's rise to national prominence in the late nineteenth century was closely related to developments in the Crescent City. In the final analysis, the American prize ring prospered because fighters and fans flouted laws prohibiting the sport and because one city ignored the prevailing national sentiment. Elsewhere, self-appointed guardians of the public weal denounced fighting as a relic of barbarism and erected legal barriers that nearly eliminated the sport, but New Orleans, long renowned for its moral laxity, became the national center of prize fighting as local fans, promoters, and pugilists openly encouraged the sport. They either ignored objectionable municipal ordinances and state laws or persuaded officials to repeal or amend them. As a result, New Orleans in the 1880s and 1890s offered an atmosphere conducive to the prosperity of prize fighting.

In addition to the support given by New Orleans, prize fighting flourished after 1865 for several reasons. As before the war, it offered

[1] For accounts of boxing after the Civil War, see Johnston, *Ten—And Out!;* and Fleischer, *The Heavyweight Championship.*

young men from disadvantaged groups an opportunity to elude poverty and discrimination. For this reason, Irish pugilists continued to dominate the sport, but toward the end of the century, black fighters also turned to the prize ring to escape squalor, deprivation, and the hostility that everywhere confronted black faces. Prize fighting also thrived because, like other activities, it helped to satisfy the urbanite's growing appetite for commercial spectacles. It attracted support not only from those rowdy fans who had sustained the sport in the antebellum period but also from respectable citizens who had once scorned it. The prize ring spanned the gulf between lower- and upper-class enthusiasts because it appeared to capture better than most sports the spirit of the age. In an era dominated by rugged competition in politics and business, which was justified by "scientific" slogans such as "the struggle to survive" and "survival of the fittest," prize fighting rose in popular esteem by reducing the values of American society to a pair of gladiators meeting in the ring for a fight to the finish. When the prize ring produced men capable of beating all rivals in such rigorous, primeval struggles, it seemed to justify America's competitive system and to prove the value of the system's scientific underpinnings. After one of Sullivan's victories, the New York *Sun* called him "the most phenomenal production of the prize ring that has been evoluted during the nineteenth century." Professional boxing also flourished because it restored a sense of individualism to national life. As the tempo of industrialization and urbanization accelerated, America became a mass society composed of people whose lives were governed increasingly by the machine and the time clock, and whose individual accomplishments were dwarfed by the collective efforts of all. The prize ring seemed to reverse this process by glorifying champion fist-fighters who had risen far above the ranks. A writer for the New York *Herald* found still another explanation for the ring's appeal in an urban community where the rapidly increasing and deepening tensions of daily life required outlets: "There is in every man a trace of original savagery, and it is probably no worse to gratify this by looking at a fight than by scolding one's wife, kicking the family cat or trying to bulldoze a Legislature in the interest of Tammany." [2]

Prize fighting resumed in New Orleans soon after the restoration

[2] New York *Sun*, February 9, 1882; New York *Herald*, February 8, 1882.

of peace. For approximately twenty-five years after the war, a municipal ordinance prohibited the sport, but poor enforcement and a little ingenuity enabled fighters to practice their trade with a minimum of interference. In 1866 pugilists began to pummel each other on the outskirts of the city beyond the halfhearted reach of Orleans Parish officials.[3] Respectable elements protested in vain as professional boxers from New York, Philadelphia, Chicago, and St. Louis followed a trail to New Orleans blazed by their antebellum predecessors.[4] Fights often attracted large crowds, particularly if local fighters battled invaders. In May, 1866, when Tom King of New Orleans fought William Farrell, "a 'professional,'" who "came to N. O. expressly to fight," a crowd said to be "probably the largest ever assembled at a prize fight in this country" saw what *Wilkes' Spirit of the Times* called "a thorough give-and-take fight, in which neither of the parties exhibited much science, but both displayed a fair amount of game."[5]

Public organs generally opposed "these brutal exhibitions of merely animal skill, courage and endurance," but as the *Times* explained, "so long as these meetings are permitted to take place, duty as a public journal requires us to record the event." Reports of matches were sometimes unduly brief, like the *Crescent*'s account of the Farrell-King bout: "The contest was of the most exciting description, but we do not deem it of sufficient interest to our readers to give a detailed account of the fight." But occasionally the press performed its loathsome responsibilities with undisguised pleasure as reporters succumbed to the lure of the ring's colorful argot. The *Crescent* in 1867 offered its presumably outraged readers a round-by-round analysis of a fight between King and Jim Turner. King in one round administered "a regular right-handed rib-bender" that sent Turner "to grass on his bumbazine"; Turner retaliated with "a small one in the breadbasket" and a few rounds later "planted a stinging left hander on the kisser, which rattled Tom's ivorys [*sic*]."[6]

3 New Orleans *Daily Picayune,* February 13, 1866; New Orleans *Daily Crescent,* April 5, May 14, 1866; New Orleans *Times,* May 1, 14, June 26, 1866.

4 New Orleans *Times,* May 1, 14, June 26, 1866; January 19, 1868; April 3, 1871; New Orleans *Daily Crescent,* May 14, 1866; December 29, 1868.

5 New Orleans *Times,* May 14, 1866; *Wilkes' Spirit of the Times,* XIV (May 26, 1866), 196.

6 New Orleans *Times,* May 1, 14, 1866; New Orleans *Daily Crescent,* May 14, 1866; July 4, 1867. Quotations are in the order cited.

That New Orleans had a broad reputation for tolerance was fully demonstrated when Jem Mace selected the city as the site for two of his championship fights in this country. One of England's greatest bareknuckle fighters, Mace had few peers in the twenty-four-foot ring under the London Prize Ring Rules. When he came to the United States in 1869, the Gypsy, as he was known to contemporaries, was generally recognized as the champion of the world.

Mace's first fight in New Orleans restored a degree of order to prize fighting in America. At the time of the Gypsy's arrival, three men—Joe Coburn, Mike McCoole, and Tom Allen—claimed the American championship, and each was reluctant to fight either of the other claimants. Soon after Mace reached the United States, he and Allen agreed to fight in or near New Orleans on May 10, 1870, for twenty-five hundred dollars and the world championship. Rufus Hunt, referee for the match, said the fighters chose the Crescent City because it was "the only place where a fair show for both sides could be had." A better explanation was the outspoken opposition to the fight that prevailed in other cities. When news of the proposed bout first became public, the New York *Herald* warned: "If these men are determined to fight, as no doubt they are, we hope that it will not be in this vicinity, but as far away as possible—some place where the laws will not be violated and where they can pummel each other to their hearts' content." Whatever the reason, the pugilists' decision to fight in New Orleans outraged the city's respectable elements, who resented bitterly what the *Times* called the "sudden irruption into our city of a population of men in which the animal predominates over the intellectual." [7]

Notwithstanding the opposition, the fight occurred with little difficulty. Hawkins' Saloon, traditional gathering place for local sporting men, handled ticket sales for the affair, which was held a few miles west of the city at Kennerville, a site reached easily and quickly by way of the Jackson Railroad. On the morning of the fight, a thou-

---

[7] The quotations in this paragraph are from William E. Harding, *Jem Mace of Norwich, England, Champion Pugilist of the World: His Life and Battles, with Portraits and Illustrations* (New York, 1881), 17; New York *Herald*, January 8, 1870; New Orleans *Times*, May 11, 1870. The confusion regarding the American championship can be traced in Harding, *Jem Mace*, 16; John L. Sullivan, *Life and Reminiscences of a 19th Century Gladiator* (Boston, 1892), 57; *Wilkes' Spirit of the Times*, XX (June 19, 1869), 276–77.

sand people, including General Philip A. Sheridan, commander of the Fifth Military District, and John C. Heenan, former American champion, entrained for Kennerville. "Here and there through the crowd stalked men whose broad shoulders and stalwart forms gave unmistakable evidence that they were disciples of the P. R.," the *Picayune* reported, "but by far the larger proportion were cultivated and refined gentlemen who had evidently determined to break through the strict and formal rules of etiquette to go once to see a prize fight." Interest in the fight was so widespread that several out-of-town newspapers, including the New York *Herald*, the New York *Sun*, the Chicago *Tribune*, and *Wilkes' Spirit of the Times*, sent reporters. "No event of the period has caused such excitement in pugilistic circles since the Heenan-Sayers mill in England some years ago," said a writer for the New York *Herald*.[8]

Mace required only forty-four minutes to demonstrate his ring mastery. "After a little turkey-cock strutting about the ring for effect," Mace showed "real science" in defeating his opponent. His strategy, a reporter observed, was "to shut off Allen's head-lights." The fight ended suddenly in the tenth round when Mace clamped Allen's head "in chancery and slashed away at it with serious effect. . . . The struggle was fearful." William E. Harding, sporting editor of the *National Police Gazette*, related in his biography of Mace: "Like giants they swayed backward and forward, but Mace was too fine a wrestler for his game opponent. Holding Allen firmly in his vise-like grasp, slowly but surely he bore his head to the ground and threw him a complete somersault, alighting upon his right shoulder with great force, nearly dislocating it, Mace falling heavily upon him. Allen gave an awful groan, and all around the ring rose to their feet, thinking his neck had been broken." Allen "was carried off the ground with a face mutilated out of all semblance to humanity." Mace, by contrast, returned to New Orleans "looking as fresh as though he had been a spectator instead of the victor in one of the most scientific encounters ever witnessed."[9]

8 New Orleans *Daily Picayune,* May 11, 1870; New York *Herald,* May 11, 1870; New Orleans *Times,* May 11, 1870; Chicago *Tribune,* May 5, 11, 1870; New York *Sun,* May 11, 1870; *Wilkes' Spirit of the Times,* XXII (May 14, 1870), 201; DeWitt, *The American Fistiana,* 145.

9 New York *Sun,* May 11, 1870; New York *Herald,* May 11, 1870; New Orleans *Times,* May 11, 1870; Harding, *Jem Mace,* 18; New York *Herald,* May 11,

Age soon relaxed the Gypsy's grip on the world championship. Thirty-nine years old when he defeated Allen, Mace had passed his prime as two fights with Joe Coburn soon indicated. The first of these contests, which took place in Port Dover, Canada, on May 11, 1871, was a farce. Both men stood in the ring for an hour and sixteen minutes without striking a blow. The "fight" ended when a company of Canadian militia dispersed the crowd.[10] Coburn immediately issued another challenge, and Mace agreed to fight once again near New Orleans.

The second Mace-Coburn match left spectators as disappointed as the first. After the Port Dover fiasco, fans expressed little enthusiasm for the bout, which was held in Bay St. Louis, Mississippi, east of New Orleans, on November 30, 1871. Through eleven rounds neither fighter inflicted much damage on his opponent. In the twelfth and final round, the fighters "stood looking at each other for nearly an hour, Mace only going up to the scratch when ordered by the referee to do so, and at once retreating again, amid the hisses of the crowd. Coburn, although he had everything his own way now, was apparently afraid to force the fight to a close." The disgusted referee declared a drawn fight. Mace retired immediately after the match and returned to England where he died in 1907.[11]

Following the Mace-Coburn debacle, pugilism temporarily lost much of its following in New Orleans. Few fights occurred in the 1870s, partly because public officials enforced laws against prize fighting more stringently and partly because fans displayed little enthusiasm for the sport.[12] National interest also declined as Tom Allen, Mike McCoole, and other fighters staged a series of disputed and generally unsatisfactory contests for the American championship. However, in 1880 Paddy Ryan, a young Irishman from Troy, New York, established a clear claim to the title.[13] In the meantime a young Boston Irishman, John L. Sullivan, was cultivating a reputation by annihilating all comers. Ryan at first refused to fight him, but at length he

---

1870; New Orleans *Daily Picayune,* May 11, 1870. Quotations are in the order cited.

[10] Harding, *Jem Mace,* 19; Sullivan, *Life and Reminiscences,* 57.

[11] Harding, *Jem Mace,* 20; New Orleans *Daily Picayune,* December 1, 1871; *Wilkes' Spirit of the Times,* XXV (December 9, 1871), 261; New York *Herald,* December 1, 1871; Chicago *Tribune,* December 1, 1871.

[12] New Orleans *Daily Picayune,* May 31, June 3, 1880.

[13] Fleischer, *The Heavyweight Championship,* 74.

agreed to meet the twenty-three-year-old Sullivan near New Orleans on February 7, 1882, for the championship. Ryan's decision to battle the Boston Strong Boy revived national interest in the ring and set in motion a succession of events that catapulted New Orleans to the forefront as a center of American prize fighting.[14]

The Sullivan-Ryan fight provoked great enthusiasm in New Orleans and throughout the country. Both fighters trained in the city, Sullivan at Carrollton and Ryan at West End. When they stopped their preparations a few days before the bout, the *Picayune* reported that Ryan, who weighed 190 pounds, was in "splendid form" and that Sullivan, 180 pounds, had muscles "as hard as iron." A city ordinance prohibited prize fighting and the promoters decided to stage the match in Mississippi City, a watering place easily accessible by railroad. The *Picayune*, professing surprise that prize fighting "should have so long survived the downfall of barbarism," reported that scores of residents queued up at the office of the Louisville and Nashville Railroad for tickets. Responding to the fight's importance, many of the country's leading newspapers, including the New York *Herald*, the New York *Sun*, the Boston *Globe*, and the *National Police Gazette*, sent reporters. Richard K. Fox, the editor of the *National Police Gazette* and a leading patron of the ring, promised readers an eight-page supplement with pictures "engraved in the highest style of art . . . faithful in every detail." Out-of-town visitors also included a number of famous and infamous characters such as Red O'Leary, a bank robber; Dan O'Leary, the pedestrian; Nat Goodwin, a well-known actor; Frank and Jesse James; and Harry Hill, whose New York saloon was a traditional gathering place for pugilists in the late nineteenth century.[15]

14 For accounts of Sullivan's career and importance to the American ring, see D. B. Chidsey, *John the Great* (Garden City, 1942); R. F. Dibble, *John L. Sullivan: An Intimate Portrait* (Boston, 1925); and Nat S. Fleischer, *John L. Sullivan: Champion of Champions* (New York, 1951). For Sullivan's efforts to arrange a bout with Ryan, see Sullivan, *Life and Reminiscences*, 43; and Richard K. Fox, *Life and Battles of John L. Sullivan* (2d ed.; New York, 1891), 15–18.

15 Quotations in this paragraph, in the order cited, are from the New Orleans *Daily Picayune*, February 6, 7, 1882; and the *National Police Gazette*, XXXIX (February 4, 1882), 2. For other information about the fight, see *National Police Gazette*, XXXIX (February 18, 1882), 17–24; New York *Herald*, January 30, 31, February 7, 8, 1882; New York *Sun*, February 3, 4, 5, 6, 7, 1882; Chicago *Tribune*, February 2, 6, 7, 1882; Boston *Globe*, January 22, 25, February 5, 7, 8, 1882; Cincinnati *Enquirer*, February 1, 2, 5, 6, 7, 1882; New Orleans *Daily Picayune*, February 5, 6, 7, 8, 1882; Fleischer, *John L. Sullivan*, 45.

As America's sporting population inundated the city, opponents of fighting protested vigorously. The Reverend J. William Flynn urged city officials to prevent the match because "a disreputable class of people from all parts of the country always swarm to witness these scenes, and when our youths are seduced into the temptation of mingling with such company the contact must soil them and leave a moral stain on their lives." The *Picayune*, regretfully acknowledging its journalistic obligation to report the fight, agreed with Flynn: "The better elements of our city view with disgust and shame the rallying of the crowd here that attends upon a prize fight, and every good citizen must regret that there is no legal remedy to avert the disgusting spectacle." [16] City officials could only force promoters to stage the fight outside Orleans Parish.

For all their vehemence and asperity, the outraged portion of the citizenry failed to diminish the popularity of the match. On the morning of February 7, a special train left the Louisville and Nashville terminal bound for Mississippi City. "No more orderly crowd ever started for a Sunday School picnic," a reporter related. "A conference of clergymen couldn't have been more staid." [17] At the site of the bout, fifteen hundred fans representing all classes—merchants, businessmen, professional men, sporting men, and reporters—assembled for what Richard Fox later called "the most important battle ever fought in the annals of pugilism in America." [18]

At midday Ryan and Sullivan entered a makeshift ring located in front of the Barnes Hotel. Like most fights under bareknuckle rules, the Sullivan-Ryan meeting was a mixture of wrestling and boxing. The Boston Strong Boy quickly demonstrated his supremacy in both phases of the sport. Ryan surrendered his title in the ninth round "after one of the fiercest and most determined battles of modern times." He later confessed: "When Sullivan struck me I thought a telegraph pole had been shoved against me endways." The new champion, said the *Picayune*, "bore his honors modestly." When told he was "now the greatest fighter in the world," Sullivan's "characteristic answer" was, "Not the greatest, but one of them." After only eleven minutes in the ring with Ryan, the great John L. had begun his ten-

16 New Orleans *Daily Picayune*, February 5, 1882.
17 Quoted in Dibble, *John L. Sullivan*, 23.
18 Fox, *Life of . . . Sullivan*, 19; Johnston, *Ten—And Out!*, 57.

year rule as heavyweight champion of America, a reign that elevated prize fighting to a position of semirespectability and made Sullivan one of the country's foremost folk heroes.[19]

Cities throughout America reported unparalleled interest in the fight. Crowds gathered in front of bulletin boards at newspaper offices everywhere to receive instantaneous reports of the battle. Sullivan's victory dominated conversations from the lowest level of society to the highest. "The most remarkable thing about yesterday's prize-fight," the New York *Times* editorialized, "is, not that it should have been allowed to take place on American soil, but that it should have excited very general public interest in all parts of the country and among all classes of men." [20]

While writers reported and analyzed popular enthusiasm for the fight, Louisiana and Mississippi took steps to prevent a recurrence of the fistic antics that had enthralled the nation. Prior to 1882 neither state had laws specifically prohibiting prize fighting; officials could only enforce statutes against unlawful assembly and riot. Since these laws had proved totally ineffective, the legislatures of both states passed new legislation calling for the imprisonment of persons found guilty of prize fighting.[21] In a few years, patrons of the sport would find clever ways to circumvent these laws, but legislative action temporarily erased prize fighting from the city's list of sports.

While boxing's appeal reached low ebb, wrestling, which had first attracted a small following in the 1870s,[22] temporarily provided amusement for ring-minded sportsmen. "Wrestling is a sport not often seen here," the *Picayune* said in January, 1883, "and from the interest taken in it by the amateur gymnasts it bids fair to become popular." Matches sometimes attracted several hundred people, a fair showing for a new pastime. The best-known local grappler was Theodore George, a Greek-American identified by the press as the

[19] Fox, *Life of . . . Sullivan*, 26, 25; New Orleans *Daily Picayune*, February 8, 1882; Sullivan, *Life and Reminiscences*, 82.

[20] New York *Times*, February 8, 1882; New York *Sun*, February 8, 1882; New York *Herald*, February 8, 1882; Boston *Globe*, February 8, 1882; Chicago *Tribune*, February 8, 1882; Cincinnati *Enquirer*, February 8, 1882.

[21] New Orleans *Daily Picayune*, June 8, 1882; William H. Adams, "New Orleans as the National Center of Boxing" (M.A. thesis, Louisiana State University and Agricultural and Mechanical College, 1950), 8.

[22] New Orleans *Daily Picayune*, October 31, 1875; March 13, 1876; January 22, 1877; New Orleans *Bulletin*, August 20, 1876.

champion of Ohio, Michigan, Illinois, and the South. In February, 1883, "Greek George," as he was called, defeated a seaman named Thaurel Olsen who claimed the championship of South America. George later traveled extensively for matches and ultimately gained a national reputation.[23]

Promoters soon sought to capitalize on the sport by bringing William Muldoon to the city. Muldoon, who had won the Greco-Roman championship of America in 1880, led an international entourage of touring wrestlers in the 1880s. With athletes from England, France, Germany, Japan, Scotland, Spain, and Switzerland, the "Solid Man of Sport" came to New Orleans on several occasions. The costumes of Muldoon's protégés moved the *Picayune* to suggest that they appeared "almost naked," but this outspoken opponent of prize fighting heartily endorsed the sport. "A wrestling match is one of the most commendable of athletic exhibitions," a reporter noted in 1883, "as there is but little brutality connected with it, and agility, coolness, strength and science are the winning points." [24]

Unfortunately, from the *Picayune*'s point of view, the sport failed to arouse permanent interest. By the mid-eighties promoters of prize fighting were cautiously reviving their chosen pastime, and wrestling could not compete for the spectators' dollars. One reporter lamented: "The science necessary for wrestling does not seem to interest the public here as well as men pounding each other with their hands encased in pillows." In later years athletic clubs periodically sponsored amateur wrestling, but these contests attracted few fans.[25]

Prize fighting returned to New Orleans because of the vagueness of local and state laws. An old city ordinance of the 1850s merely forbade the staging of any "pugilistic contest," while the more recent state law of 1882 outlawed "personal combat with fists." Sportsmen, as usual, availed themselves of the law's imprecision; in the summer of 1884, promoters began to conduct bouts under the Marquis of Queensbury rules, which required combatants to cover their fists.

[23] New Orleans *Daily Picayune*, January 20, 24, February 5, 1883; April 10, 1885.

[24] Quotations in this paragraph are from *ibid.*, January 11, 1884; May 2, 1883. See also *ibid.*, May 1, 1883; May 11, 19, 1884. For Muldoon's career, see Edward Van Every, *Muldoon, the Solid Man of Sport: His Amazing Story as Related for the First Time by Him to His Friend Edward Van Every* (New York, 1929).

[25] New Orleans *Daily Picayune*, March 9, 1885; February 3, October 12, 1890.

Gloves had been used occasionally since long before the Civil War, but fighters and fans alike generally scorned such battles. Faced with legal extinction, however, pugilists reluctantly sheathed their hands. So long as fighters wore either "hard gloves" (four ounces or less) or "soft gloves" (more than four ounces), municipal authorities allowed fights to occur. Reporting a prize fight in June, 1884, the *Picayune* noted that although several policemen attended, they permitted the match to proceed after learning that gloves were to be used.[26]

When local officials sanctioned glove contests, prize fighters once again invaded the city. Early in 1885 Jere Dunn, a noted promoter from New York, set up headquarters in New Orleans and imported a number of prominent pugilists. In March, 1885, Jack Dempsey, the Nonpareil, who had won the middleweight championship in 1884, defeated Charles Bixamos before a thousand people. The *Picayune* reported: "For the first time a number of the fairer sex looked on at such a contest here." Dunn even tried to entice women into the ring. In February, 1885, the paper announced: "Annie Lewis, of Cleveland, 5 feet 6 inches tall, weighing 155 pounds, and 28 years of age, and Hattie Stewart, of Norfolk, Va., 23 years of age, 5 feet 6½ inches, and weighing 140 pounds, have signed articles in New York to fight eight soft glove rounds in New Orleans, on February 22." The bout never materialized, but the proposal underscored the newfound popularity of prize fighting.[27]

Despite the growing appeal of pugilism, severe opposition remained. Alarmed by the influx of fighters in the early months of 1885, the city council updated its ordinance against the sport by declaring that fighting with or without gloves was "contrary to good order." For the next several years, city officials followed an exceedingly equivocal course. Local law specifically prohibited prize fighting, but the mayor often issued permits allowing fights to occur.[28] This policy sometimes presented problems, as Jere Dunn explained when he left the city in March, 1885. Dunn complained about the "many obstacles

---

26 Leovy (comp.), *The Laws and General Ordinances of the City of New Orleans,* 176–77; New Orleans *Daily Picayune,* June 8, 1882; June 8, 17, 29, 1884; March 13, 1885; New Orleans *Times-Democrat,* March 26, 1885.

27 New Orleans *Daily Picayune,* March 20, February 6, 1885.

28 Adams, "New Orleans as the National Center of Boxing," 21; New Orleans *Daily Picayune,* February 8, 1886; January 17, 1887.

thrown in my way by jealous people who thought there was big money in these affairs"; he particularly resented the requirement that he "donate" from twenty-five to fifty dollars to the city for fight permits. Notwithstanding such difficulties, the city's lenience made it possible for prize fighting to continue. Authorities periodically enforced the ban on boxing, but for the most part those members of the sporting community who patronized prize fights had many opportunities to indulge their proclivities for rowdy amusement.[29]

While advocates and foes of prize fighting arranged an uneasy truce, fans everywhere focused their attention on the man who had revived interest in the sport in 1882. Following his victory over Ryan, Sullivan defended his title against all challengers. "There is hardly a more disreputable ruffian now breathing than this same Sullivan," the New York *Tribune* once said, "but with all his brutality, his coarseness, and his vices, he certainly is not afraid of meeting any living man with bare fists." But even as Sullivan repeatedly proved his prowess in the ring, editor Richard Fox schemed to dethrone him. He imported numerous fighters, including "Tug" Wilson and Herbert "Maori" Slade, all of whom the Boston Strong Boy easily conquered. Then in the early summer of 1887, Fox attempted to arrange a championship bout between Sullivan and Jake Kilrain, an Irish-American from Baltimore. When Sullivan ignored the challenge and instead went to France to fight England's Charlie Mitchell, Fox gave the *National Police Gazette*'s Diamond Belt, emblematic of the heavyweight championship, to Kilrain. Prodded by his manager Billy Madden and by William Muldoon, the Boston Strong Boy at last agreed to fight Kilrain in July, 1889. Seven years after his conquest of Ryan, he returned to New Orleans for what was to be the last bareknuckle championship fight in America.[30]

Conditioning Sullivan for the match proved to be a monumental undertaking. High living and two-fisted drinking had steadily eroded the champion's body until many doubted his ability to defend his famous boast that he could "lick any son of a bitch in the world." Mul-

[29] New Orleans *Daily Picayune,* March 27, December 24, 1885; January 3, February 1, 1886; January 17, 1887; June 17, 1889; *National Police Gazette,* XLIII (April 18, 1885), 11.

[30] New York *Tribune,* December 30, 1887, quoted in Paxson, "The Rise of Sport," 150–51; *National Police Gazette,* XLIX (May 14, 1887), 2; XLIX (June 18, 1887), 2; Johnston, *Ten—And Out!,* 75.

doon, who was as well known as a physical culturist as for his wrestling ability, forced Sullivan to follow a strict regimen of exercise that soon restored his failing powers. At his training camp near Belfast, New York, Sullivan's day began with dumbbell exercises and a twelve-to-fourteen-mile walk. In the afternoon he swam, punched the light bag, and threw a ten-pound medicine ball. After the evening meal, the champion relaxed "by playing billiards, pool, or cards, or with some other pastime or sport." Before retiring, the Boston Strong Boy fortified himself with a heroic physic "which consists of about fifty cents' worth each of zinnia, salts, manna, black stick licorice" put into two quarts of liquid and boiled down to one. Muldoon's success in rejuvenating Sullivan came as a surprise to many observers, including a reporter for the New York *Sun:* "If severe physical discipline can work such wonders with the wreck that Sullivan was when Muldoon took him in hand, what may not be done with hundreds of less aggravated cases of men who are worth infinitely more to their friends, society and the world in general than an army of Sullivans?" [31]

Interest in the fight increased steadily in the early months of 1889. The country's major dailies carried lengthy accounts of the fighters' training activities; and when Sullivan and Kilrain left their training camps for New Orleans, these newspapers published daily reports of the fighters' progress and of the enthusiastic receptions that greeted the gladiators along the way. Out-of-town fans flooded into the city. To accommodate the great crowd coming from New York, Richard Fox arranged for the Baltimore and Ohio and the Queen and Crescent railroads to run a special train to New Orleans. When tickets went on sale in June, promoters Bud Renaud and Pat Duffy had no difficulty finding buyers, who paid ten dollars for general admission and fifteen dollars for seats in a "charmed circle" around the ring. Such was the state of excitement that the issuance of executive orders against the fight by Governors Francis T. Nicholls of Louisiana and Robert Lowry of Mississippi had no perceptible effect. "The city is fighting mad," the *Picayune* announced on the morning of the match. "Everybody has the fever and is talking Sullivan and Kilrain. Ladies discussed it in street cars, men talked and

31 Sullivan, *Life and Reminiscences*, 254–62; New York *Sun*, July 10, 1889, quoted in Van Every, *Muldoon, the Solid Man of Sport*, 131; Fleischer, *John L. Sullivan*, 119–23.

argued about it in places which had never heard pugilism mentioned before." A resident confirmed this opinion. "No one thinks of opening his mouth in these degenerate days, but to ask or to answer questions about the coming fight," Brooks A. Colomb wrote to a friend. "Sullivan is largely in favor here. May be Jake's stock will go up when the people see him. I am inclined to think his feet will go up when John L. begins to brush flies from him and play a little Solo on his anatomy with both hands." [32]

On the day before the fight three special trains, one for the fighters and two for the fans, left New Orleans for Richburg, Mississippi. Promoters kept the destination secret until the journey began in order to elude militia units alerted by the executives of Louisiana and Mississippi to prevent the match. After an uncomfortable night in the hamlet of Richburg, more than two thousand spectators, including reporters from New York, Chicago, Boston, and Cincinnati, gathered around a ring located several hundred yards from the railroad track.

Sullivan and Kilrain began their struggle for national supremacy at 10:30 in the morning. Through seventy-five rounds, which lasted two hours, sixteen minutes, and twenty-three seconds, the country's leading heavyweights fought a grueling battle under a sun that sent the temperature soaring well over one hundred degrees. Both fighters imbibed freely; one reporter estimated that Kilrain consumed a quart of whisky during the fight. Sullivan dominated the contest throughout, but according to Richard Fox a draught of tea and whisky almost proved his undoing in the forty-fourth round: "Sullivan began to vomit, and to those who had known him for years this appeared to be proof that his stomach was gone." But he quickly recovered and slowly destroyed his opponent. After round seventy-five, Kilrain's ringside representative "threw up the sponge." Kilrain protested this

[32] *National Police Gazette,* LIV (June 15, 1889), 6; LIV (June 22, 1889), 10; LIV (June 29, 1889), 3; LIV (July 6, 1889), 2–3, 8–9; LIV (July 13, 1889), 6–9; New York *Sun,* June 30, July 1, 2, 3, 4, 5, 6, 7, 1889; New York *Times,* July 6, 7, 1889; New York *Herald,* July 1, 2, 3, 4, 5, 6, 7, 8, 1889; Chicago *Tribune,* July 1, 2, 3, 4, 5, 6, 7, 8, 1899; Boston *Globe,* July 1, 2, 4, 5, 8, 1899; Cincinnati *Enquirer,* July 2, 3, 4, 5, 6, 7, 8, 1889; Dallas *Morning News,* July 4, 5, 6, 7, 8, 1889; New Orleans *Daily Picayune,* June 27, July 2, 8, 1889; Van Every, *Muldoon, the Solid Man of Sport,* 150; Fox, *Life of . . . Sullivan,* 80. The quotations in this paragraph are from the New Orleans *Daily Picayune,* July 8, 1889; and Brooks A. Colomb to "My Dear Old Pard" [Browse Bringier], July 5, 1889, Louis A. Bringier Papers.

signal of surrender, the *Picayune* reported, but his second "said that he did not wish to be a party to murder." [33]

Sullivan's popularity exceeded all bounds after his conquest of Kilrain. Local newspapers gave the fight unprecedented coverage, devoting their entire first and second pages to what the *Picayune* called the "greatest prize fight of the century." Cities throughout the country received telegraphic notification of the result of the fight and reported engrossing interest among all classes of society. The New York *Times*, long an opponent of the prize ring, conceded that the event had aroused tremendous enthusiasm. "Never, during even a Presidential election, has there been so much excitement as there is here now, even when the brutal exhibition is over and it is known that Sullivan was successful and that seventy-five rounds were necessary to 'knock out' Kilrain." The *National Police Gazette*, which had endeavored to build the interest of its readers for weeks before the fight, began its story of Sullivan's victory with a typical headline: "KILRAIN KIBOSHED; Sick and Sore Science Succumbs to Scarifying Sockdolagers; FEARFULLY FURIOUS FIGHTING; Tenacious and Terribly Tempestuous Trial of the Titans; EXCORIATION EXTRAORDINARY; Battering Blows that Bedizened the Brave Baltimore Boy; ASTOUNDING ASSAULTS; How the Hard-Fisted Hubite Hammered the Hero's Heart; ROUSING, RIBROASTING ROUNDS." Sullivan himself modestly acknowledged that the fight was the best since Tom Hyer had met Yankee Sullivan, adding that "he could lick all the champions ever born." Few men doubted the boast. If his personal conduct left much to be desired, Sullivan's bearing in the ring was gradually and inexorably helping to make professional boxing a sport that drew support from all ranks. Generations of Americans to come would be to told of that day in 1889 when

> Nigh New Orleans
> Upon an emerald plain
> John L. Sullivan
> The strong boy
> Of Boston
> Fought seventy five red rounds with Jake Kilrain.[34]

33 Fox, *Life of . . . Sullivan,* 90; New Orleans *Daily Picayune,* July 9, 1889; Dibble, *John L. Sullivan,* 90.

34 Quotations in this paragraph, in the order cited, are from the New Orleans *Daily Picayune,* July 10, 1889; New York *Times,* July 9, 1889; *National Police*

Sullivan's convincing victory gave prize fighting a great boost in New Orleans. Capitalizing on the enthusiasm generated by the match, professional promoters held a number of bouts in succeeding months. One of the best indications of boxing's changing status was its growing appeal among members of the socially prominent Young Men's Gymnastic and Southern Athletic clubs. Composed of the "silk stocking element in local athletics," these organizations at first confined their pugilistic proclivities to amateur contests between members who learned boxing skills from professional instructors employed by the clubs. But late in 1889 the Young Men's Gymnastic Club and the Southern Athletic Club began to sponsor professional bouts, hoping, as a spokesman for the Gymnastic Club explained, to give fans an opportunity to see prize fights conducted without rowdyism and "to prevent the manly art of self-defense from falling into complete disgrace through the tactics of money-making professionals." [35] Newspapers soon acknowledged, albeit somewhat reluctantly, that "pugilism has the town in its grasp. Steady business men, society bloods, and in fact, all classes of citizens are eager and anxious to spend their wealth to see a glove contest." [36]

Opponents of prize fighting, alarmed by this activity, appealed to city and state officials. Mayor Joseph A. Shakspeare tried to strangle the sport by refusing permits for glove contests, but his efforts proved futile. In January, 1890, council members yielded to requests from ring enthusiasts and amended the city ordinance to permit sparring exhibitions; in March the council issued a revised ordinance that permitted all regularly chartered athletic clubs to sponsor "glove contests," implying that there was a substantial difference between this type of exhibition and prize fights, which remained illegal. The *Picayune*, warning that "every time a prize fight takes place it will

---

Gazette, LIV (July 27, 1889), 2; New Orleans *Daily Picayune*, July 10, 1889; and Hazelton Spencer (ed.), *Selected Poems of Vachel Lindsay* (New York, 1931), 177. See also New Orleans *Daily Picayune*, July 9, 13, 1889; New Orleans *Times-Democrat*, July 9, 1889; New York *Sun*, July 9, 1889; New York *Herald*, July 9, 1889; Chicago *Tribune*, July 9, 1889; Boston *Globe*, July 9, 1889; Cincinnati *Enquirer*, July 9, 1889.

[35] New Orleans *Daily Picayune*, April 28, December 31, 1889; February 1, 1890.

[36] New Orleans *Daily States*, January 3, 1890, quoted in Adams, "New Orleans as the National Center of Boxing," 21.

always be given by a so-called athletic club until a state law shall put a stop to the business," asked Governor Nicholls to intervene. In May the governor recommended that the legislature update the law of 1882, cited earlier, which merely outlawed "personal combat with fists." When the legislature acted in June, however, friends of the ring inserted a section in the statute which, like the city ordinance, permitted glove contests in regularly chartered clubs. Enraged by this proviso, Nicholls refused to sign the law but allowed it to take effect without his signature.[37]

After state and city laws tacitly approved prize fighting under the euphemistic description of glove contests, a number of athletic clubs began to sponsor matches. Some of these associations, such as the Olympic Club, had existed for several years and first moved into the field of prize fighting as a side line; others, like the New Orleans Athletic Club, came into existence during the latter part of 1889 when interest in the sport began to mount; and still others, such as the West End Athletic, Columbia Athletic, and Metropolitan clubs, appeared after the removal of legal restrictions. These groups soon altered the traditional method of promoting fights. Until the latter part of the 1880s, managers of fighters or intermediaries such as Richard K. Fox arranged contests. Prize money came almost exclusively from side bets; gate receipts seldom amounted to much except in a few instances such as the Sullivan-Kilrain match. However, when athletic associations promoted fights, they provided the purses in order to gain the right to stage bouts. As the number of clubs multiplied, both in New Orleans and throughout the country, competition for fights inevitably developed, and the size of purses spiraled upward. By the mid-nineties prominent fighters in all divisions were battling for thousands of dollars in prize money.

After competing successfully with athletic clubs in the East and West, local organizations were able to schedule a number of important "glove contests" that made the city the hub of the American ring. In February, 1890, the Southern Athletic Club arranged the

---

[37] New Orleans *Daily Picayune,* January 1, 7, 10, 28, February 7, 1890; New Orleans *Times-Democrat,* January 10, 1890; *Acts Passed by the General Assembly of the State of Louisiana, 1890* (New Orleans, 1890), 19; *Southern Reporter,* XV (St. Paul, Minn., 1894), 192. The quotation from the *Picayune* is from New Orleans *Daily Picayune,* June 4, 1890.

bout between Jake Kilrain and James J. Corbett that first thrust Corbett into national prominence.[38] Five months later the Audubon Athletic Association sponsored a fight between Arthur Upham and a recent arrival from Australia, Robert Fitzsimmons.[39] Bob Fitzsimmons had fought only once before in the United States, and this match with Upham helped to establish his reputation as a middleweight. Other well-known fighters who appeared in New Orleans in the early 1890s were Billy Myer, Jimmy Carroll, Peter Maher, Charlie Mitchell, and Frank Slavin.[40] Most of these outstanding pugilists came from out of town, but the Crescent City also produced one of the country's best lightweights—Andy Bowen.[41] Known as the Louisiana Tornado, he battled his way to prominence in the late 1880s. By 1890 the *National Police Gazette* recognized Bowen as champion of the South.[42]

[38] New Orleans *Daily Picayune,* February 18, 1890; *National Police Gazette,* LV (March 8, 1890), 10; New York *Herald,* February 18, 1890; Cincinnati *Enquirer,* February 18, 1890; Dallas *Morning News,* February 18, 1890; Richard K. Fox, *Life and Battles of James J. Corbett: Champion of the World* (London, 1894), 21. Fox said that before his victory over Kilrain, Corbett "was not known outside of the Pacific Slope; but the fact that he had defeated Kilrain . . . gave Corbett a world-wide reputation. Many looked upon him as an ideal fighting man and a coming champion."

[39] New Orleans *Daily Picayune,* July 29, 1890; *National Police Gazette,* LVI (August 16, 1890), 10; Cincinnati *Enquirer,* July 29, 1890; Dallas *Morning News,* July 29, 1890.

[40] New Orleans *Daily Picayune,* May 23, September 17, 1890; May 20, December 21, 1891; March 3, 1892; *Wilkes' Spirit of the Times,* CXXIII (March 5, 1892), 261.

[41] Historians of the ring, including Nat S. Fleischer (*Black Dynamite: The Story of the Negro in the Prize Ring from 1782 to 1938;* [New York, 1938], IV, 236), E. B. Henderson (*The Negro in Sports* [2d ed.; Washington, D.C., 1939] 25 and Johnston (*Ten—And Out!,* 323), have described Bowen as a Negro. Bowen, however, fought as a white man. The New Orleans press said he was "of Irish-Spanish extraction" (New Orleans *Times Democrat,* September 17, 1890). That some doubt existed concerning his racial origins became clear when he died. The New York *Sun* of December 16, 1894, observed: "He was very swarthy, and it was often said that he had negro blood in his veins. He always denied this, and was ready to fight whenever the subject was brought to his notice." Bowen may well have been a Negro (or a mulatto, as he is usually identified) who chose to pass as a white man so that he could perform before the members of exclusive athletic clubs. At any rate, accounts of his fights indicate that both fans and reporters accepted his assertion that he was white. Consequently, without proof of his racial background, his career sheds little light on the subject of interracial sporting contests.

[42] New Orleans *Daily Picayune,* February 1, 1886; December 23, 1889; February 1, May 23, September 17, 1890; May 20, December 30, 1891; *National Police Gazette,* LVI (August 9, 1890), 11.

Prior to September, 1892, the most important fight to occur in the city was the Jack Dempsey-Bob Fitzsimmons match for the middleweight championship of the world. Bidding against three other clubs, including Long Island's Puritan Athletic Club, the Olympic Club won the right to sponsor the fight by promising the winner a purse of twelve thousand dollars, the largest offered in the United States up to that time. This contest generated almost as much national interest as the Sullivan-Kilrain bout and attracted "sports" and reporters from virtually every large city. On the evening of January 14, 1891, the Nonpareil, champion since 1884, faced the challenger from Australia in the Olympic Club's sawdust arena which was surrounded by nearly five thousand spectators. "Eight arc lights and a dozen or more powerful lamps gave out a glare almost equal to that of the noon day sun," the *Picayune* said. Fitzsimmons, who carried the flesh of a middleweight on the frame of a heavyweight, "looked like a colossal skeleton, padded with broad, powerful flexible muscles." The challenger controlled the fight throughout. By the thirteenth round, when Fitzsimmons knocked out his opponent, Dempsey "was more than whipped. Both eyes were cut, nose and mouth cut and swollen, his neck and ribs around the heart and the stomach were raw from punching. He was covered with blood and mud." [43]

This battle established the Olympic Club as the city's leading promoter of prize fights. Founded in 1883 as an athletic association for young men in the Third District, the club had first shown an interest in boxing in 1889 when members employed as an instructor of boxing, John Duffy, who later became one of the country's leading referees. In July, 1890, after city and state officials approved glove contests, the organization leased a cotton press yard on Royal Street, erected an enclosed arena equipped with electric lights and "a ring on turf covered with sawdust and canvas," and began to sponsor fights. After a few financially successful minor bouts in 1890, the association moved into national focus with the Dempsey-Fitzsimmons fight. Trading on the reputation gained from this match, the club sent representatives

[43] New Orleans *Daily Picayune,* January 15, 1891. For national and local interest in the fight, see *ibid.,* September 13, 14, 21, December 15, 1890; *National Police Gazette,* LVII (January 24, 1891), 2–3; New York *Herald,* January 12, 13, 14, 15, 1891; New York *Sun,* January 15, 1891; Chicago *Tribune,* January 11, 12, 13, 14, 15, 1891; Cincinnati *Enquirer,* January 15, 1891; Dallas *Morning News,* January 15, 1891.

throughout the country to arrange other bouts. A "prominent New Yorker," disappointed by legal problems and police interference in the East, telegraphed Harry McEnery, a sports reporter for the *Picayune:* "The fairness of New Orleans' sporting people is on the tongue of the universe, and no club now in existence enjoys the reputation of the Olympic." [44]

Only one hurdle blocked the Olympic's path to national supremacy—the legal absurdity that allowed glove contests but prohibited prize fights. If either state or city officials chose to interpret Olympic-sponsored glove contests as prize fights, which they were, the dream of pugilistic riches would vanish. To avoid this possibility, the Olympic Club decided to test the state law in September, 1891. The organization scheduled a fight between Cal McCarthy and Tommy Warren that was openly advertised as a fight to the finish for a prize. McCarthy and Warren were arrested and charged with prize fighting. However, at the trial which followed, a number of prominent citizens testified that Olympic Club matches, although fought for prizes, were glove contests as defined by city and state laws. W. H. Williams, sporting editor of the *Times-Democrat,* said: "Prize fights are always on the turf." A jury of McCarthy's and Warren's peers remained in their seats and deliberated only five minutes before declaring the defendants not guilty.[45]

Having swept away legal obstacles, the Olympic Club was free to develop the business of prize fighting. The club promoted a few matches in the autumn of 1891 and then began to concentrate on arranging a fight for the heavyweight championship. Since his match with Kilrain in 1889, Sullivan had devoted much of his time to touring with theatrical troupes, but in March, 1892, the champion agreed to defend his title against any and all challengers, except Negroes, at the Olympic Club for a purse of $25,000 and "an outside bet" of $10,000. James J. Corbett, who had wanted to fight Sullivan for months, eagerly accepted the offer. The Olympic Club fulfilled its share of the contract by providing $25,000 in prize money.[46]

[44] New Orleans *Daily Picayune,* September 15, 1889; July 12, 1890; January 11, July 8, 1891; March 1, 1893. The telegraph message is quoted in *ibid.,* September 13, 1891.

[45] *Ibid.,* September 19, 30, 1891.

[46] Fox, *Life of . . . Corbett,* 44; New Orleans *Daily Picayune,* March 6, 20, 1892; William A. Brady, *Showman* (New York, 1937), 85. Brady was a theatrical

After completing arrangements for the Sullivan-Corbett fight, the Olympic Club negotiated with other leading pugilists. By the summer of 1892, the contest committee of the club had arranged a prize-fighting festival that would include a lightweight championship fight between Jack McAuliffe and Billy Myer, a featherweight championship bout matching George "Little Chocolate" Dixon, a Negro, against Jack Skelly, and the Sullivan-Corbett contest.

Scheduled for September 5, 6, and 7, 1892, the Triple Event released a wave of boxing enthusiasm throughout the country. For weeks before the fights, local papers carried lengthy accounts of the fighters' training activities; merchants displayed portraits of the contestants in shop windows to draw attention to their wares; and street peddlers hawked photographs and scarves dyed to represent the battle colors of each fighter. Many out-of-town newspapers sent reporters to the city; a writer for the *National Police Gazette* contended that "the whole civilized world" was anxiously awaiting the results of "the greatest pugilistic carnival in the history of the world." The amount of space devoted to the contests moved a correspondent for *Frank Leslie's Illustrated* to complain that the leading dailies had "scant space to give to the movements and utterances of the Presidential nominees," Benjamin Harrison and Grover Cleveland. Railroads cooperated with the Olympic Club by offering to take special parties to New Orleans at reduced rates, by selling tickets to the fights, and by advertising the pugilistic carnival. When the fighters themselves started South, newspapers printed telegraphic reports of their progress. Interest in the matches at all levels of society confirmed the New York *Herald*'s observation that "the odium which rested upon the prize ring and the majority of its exponents a decade or two ago, because of the disgraceful occurrences connected with it, have in a measure been removed, until now the events on hand are of national and international importance." [47]

---

producer who hoped to direct Corbett to the world championship and then feature him in stage plays in much the same way that Sullivan had done in the 1880s and early 1890s.

[47] Quotations in this paragraph are from the *National Police Gazette,* LX (September 10, 1892), 2; *Frank Leslie's Illustrated,* LXXV (September 1, 1892), 163; New York *Herald,* August 28, 1892. For examples of the coverage of the fights by major dailies, see New York *Sun,* August 25–September 5, 1892; New York *Times,* September 1–5, 1892; New York *Herald,* August 28–September 5, 1892; Chicago *Tribune,* August 28–September 5, 1892; Cincinnati *Enquirer,* Sep-

On the night of September 5, a capacity crowd jammed the Olympic Club's arena for the first installment of the Triple Event—the McAuliffe-Myer fight. "Conspicuous among the seats were a number of mahogany chairs, which . . . were filled by the members of the Boston Club, each wearing a buttonaire [*sic*], neat but not gaudy." McAuliffe, who had claimed the lightweight title since 1884 when Dempsey advanced to the middleweight class, had previously fought Myer, known as the Streator Cyclone, on February 13, 1889. Battling for fifty-six rounds with a broken right arm, he had fought Myer to a sixty-four-round draw. At the Olympic Club, McAuliffe proved again that bare-fisted or with gloves, "he is the greatest fighter in his class that the world ever saw." Wearing gloves "of a pea green color, laced with red tape," he bombarded his plucky opponent with blows that "cut Myer all up and seemed like the noise made by a brass drummer in a country band as they rolled in on Myer's head and ribs. McAuliffe's friends shouted: 'Whoop! whoop! ain't that a beauty? Is it not a daisy? O, knock him out Jack! Don't give him another chance.' " The champion responded to the exhortations in the fifteenth round. He floored Myer with a powerful right, and when the Streator Cyclone arose, McAuliffe, who was poised over him, struck the groggy challenger immediately, knocking him unconscious. The first fight of the Triple Event had ended in a manner highly satisfactory to the capacity crowd and to the unnumbered thousands who gathered at newspaper offices throughout the country for round-by-round reports telegraphed directly from ringside.[48]

Thousands of fans again filled the Olympic arena for the Dixon-Skelly fight. For the first time, the club admitted Negro fans, who watched from a special section reserved for them. Dixon, one of the greatest small fighters of modern times, had won the featherweight title the preceding year and was to retain it until 1899 when he lost to Terry McGovern. Local and out-of-town newspapers reported that many observers feared Dixon's race would make it impossible for the

---

tember 1–5, 1892; New Orleans *Times-Democrat,* September 3, 4, 5, 1892; and New Orleans *Daily Picayune,* August 25, September 5, 6, 1892.

[48] Quotations in this paragraph are from the New Orleans *Daily Picayune,* September 6, 1892; New York *Sun,* September 6, 1892; Dallas *Morning News,* September 6, 1892; Chicago *Tribune,* September 6, 1892. See also New Orleans *Times-Democrat,* September 6, 1892; New York *Herald,* September 6, 1892; New York *Times,* September 6, 1892; Cincinnati *Enquirer,* September 6, 1892; Johnston, *Ten—And Out!,* 316–20.

champion to receive fair treatment in New Orleans. But as the New York *Herald* said, the Olympic Club was "made up of business men and the club conducted on business principles." The promoters would permit no acts of racial discrimination that might affect gate receipts then or in the future. A description of Dixon's conquest of Skelly left no doubt that "Little Chocolate" clearly deserved his title: "What with bruises, lacerations and coagulated blood, Skelly's nose, mouth and eye presented a horrible spectacle, and as the poor fellow staggered about almost helpless, even some of the most blasé at the ringside were heard to shudder, and some even turned away their heads in disgust, as they saw Dixon savagely chopping away at that face already disfigured past recognition, and heard the ugly half-splashing sound as his blood-soaked gloves again and again visited the bleeding wounds that had drenched them." A reporter for the Chicago *Tribune* observed that many white fans "winced every time Dixon landed on Skelly. The sight was repugnant to some of the men from the South. A darky is all right in his place here, but the idea of sitting quietly by and seeing a colored boy pommel a white lad grates on Southerners." But if the sight angered southern fans, they controlled their impulses. No one attempted to stop the fight, and when Skelly went down in the eighth, the crowd gave Dixon a great ovation.[49]

Southern feelings, however, came to the fore in the local press. Dixon's bloody victory immediately raised questions about the propriety of Negro-white contests. The editor of the *Times-Democrat* declared unequivocally that it was "a mistake to match a negro and a white man, a mistake to bring the races together on any terms of equality, even in the prize ring." Concerned that Dixon's victory would stimulate what he regarded as an unfounded belief in racial equality, the writer directed the main part of his attack against the policy of admitting Negro spectators and against the attitude of many whites present at the fight. "It was not pleasant to see white men applaud a negro for knocking another white man out," he wrote. "It was not pleasant to see them crowding around 'Mr.'

---

[49] Quotations are from the New York *Herald,* September 5, 1892; New Orleans *Times-Democrat,* September 7, 1892; and Chicago *Tribune,* September 7, 1892. See also New Orleans *Times-Democrat,* September 7, 1892; New Orleans *Daily Picayune,* September 7, 1892.

Dixon to congratulate him on his victory, to seek an introduction
with 'the distinguished colored gentleman' while he puffed his cigar
and lay back like a prince receiving his subjects." The *Picayune*, less
vitriolic than its rival, agreed that the Dixon-Skelly fight had been a
serious blunder but noted approvingly that the Olympic Club had
resolved "to permit no more matches to be fought there, which ignore
or disregard the color line." Dixon made no reply to the criticism of
the interracial bout, but a writer for the Chicago *Tribune* reported
that the champion "had nothing but words of praise for the treatment he had received and was in excellent humor, because he had been
warned not to come south owing to race prejudice. He found better
treatment here than in the North and in the West." Dixon told a
writer for the *Picayune* that he "was agreeably surprised at the way
the whites here . . . treated him" and that he would be willing to
fight in New Orleans again.[50]

Such outspoken concern about Dixon's race and the presence of
Negro spectators as that voiced by the *Times-Democrat* and the
Picayune marked a fairly sudden shift in attitudes toward racially
mixed matches and crowds. Local Negroes had fought professionally
since the sixties without eliciting condemnations from the press,[51]
and in the mid-eighties promoters occasionally staged bouts pitting
whites against Negroes. In June, 1884, for example, a mulatto fought
a white in Carver Park on Canal Street. When the mulatto won, the
press engaged in no preachments about the unwisdom of interracial
prize fights. Instead, the *Picayune* simply noted that the winner was
"very clever with his hands." Negroes seldom if ever attended bouts
involving only white fighters, but racially integrated crowds frequently congregated to watch Negro pugilists. In 1890 the *Times-
Democrat* reported a fight between black gladiators at the Spanish
Cockpit. Describing the crowd, which consisted of businessmen and
representatives of the best society as well as professional sports, the
reporter observed: "There were dudes of all shades, from the most
pronounced blonde with a snowy necktie and a pink and white flannel
lawn tennis coat, to the dandy of ebony hue, whose blackness was

[50] New Orleans *Times-Democrat*, September 8, 1892; New Orleans *Daily
Picayune*, September 11, 1892; Chicago *Tribune*, September 8, 1892; New Orleans
Daily Picayune, September 10, 1892. Quotations are in the order cited.

[51] New Orleans *Times*, June 9, 1868; New Orleans *Daily Picayune*, June 9,
1868.

emphasized by a scarlet and yellow cravat, dove-colored waistcoat, lavender trousers and dark blue coat." [52]

In spite of these indications of racial harmony, segregation soon invaded the prize ring. Dixon's victory, although not solely responsible for the *volte-face*, evidently accelerated the acceptance of racial separatism in this sport. His victory over his white opponent inflamed local prejudices and antagonized residents of a section in which separation of the races was rapidly becoming the accepted southern way of life. After 1892 promoters ceased to arrange interracial bouts, a policy that continued well into the twentieth century. Those who violated the rule did so at their own peril. In 1897 an organization known as the Mississippi Pleasure Company sponsored a match for Joe Green, a Negro, and a white pugilist who fought under the name of "the Swede." Shortly after the action began, Henry Long, "a loyal Southerner," stopped the contest, exclaiming: "The idea of niggers fighting white men. Why, if that darned scoundrel would beat that white boy the niggers would never stop gloating over it, and, as it is, we have enough trouble with them." [53] Promoters continued to arrange bouts matching Negro against Negro, but crowds attended such events on a segregated basis.

While editorial writers pondered the ramifications of Dixon's triumph, a "cosmopolitan" crowd of ten thousand assembled for the last segment of the Triple Event—the Sullivan-Corbett fight. The majority of those present had come to see what people throughout the country assumed would be Sullivan's third victory in the city. As people of all classes sat cheek by jowl, "party differences and sectional lines were obliterated, presidential candidates were forgotten, businesses were neglected, and the police of other cities lost their best customers and felt relieved." [54]

Those thousands who cheered Sullivan's ascent into the ring were to be sorely disappointed, for Corbett outfought the champion from the beginning. In his prime the Boston Strong Boy might have anni-

52 New Orleans *Daily Picayune*, June 16, 1884; New Orleans *Times-Democrat*, August 3, 1890. For other examples of integrated crowds at Negro fights, see New Orleans *Daily Picayune*, June 8, 1884; August 31, 1890. White sportsmen also served on occasion as seconds for Negro fighters, which is still another indication of the racial harmony that existed in and around the prize ring before 1892. New Orleans *Daily Picayune*, June 8, 1884.

53 New Orleans *Daily Picayune*, January 25, 1897.

54 *Ibid.*, September 8, 1892.

hilated "Gentleman Jim," but a debilitated Sullivan, weighing a flabby 212 pounds, was no match for his younger opponent, who weighed a trim 187 pounds. As the fighters went out for the twenty-first round, the challenger "rushed in and planted blow after blow on Sullivan's face and neck. The champion . . . lowered his guard from sheer exhaustion, and catching a fearful smash on the jaw, reached to the ropes, and the blood poured down his face in torrents and made a crimson river across his broad chest. His eyes were glassy, and it was a mournful act when the young Californian shot his right across the jaw and Sullivan fell like an ox." Dumfounded by the unexpected conclusion, the spectators sat silent as John Duffy counted ten; then, grasping the result, they rent the air with cheers for Corbett. The new champion later recalled that he was not particularly elated by the sudden enthusiasm: "I was actually disgusted with the crowd. . . . It struck me as sad to see all those thousands who had given him such a wonderful ovation when he entered the ring turning it to me now that he was down and out." [55]

Reactions to the fight varied widely. A writer for the Chicago *Tribune* noted that Corbett's victory "was a triumph of youth, skill, agility, intelligence, and good generalship over age, lack of science, and brute force; of one athlete who has taken care of himself, or at least has not had the experience in alcoholic dissipation of the other, over another who has recklessly abused by liquor the vast strength and sound constitution which he possessed." The New York *Times* declared Sullivan's defeat a positive blessing. "For a decade or more Sullivan has been swaggering about as an unconquerable person, and . . . the dethronement of a mean and cowardly bully as the idol of the barrooms is a public good that is a fit subject for public congratulations." At the site of the match, the *Picayune*, long a foe of prize fighting, chose to stress the ex-champion's contributions to American pugilism. "Although Sullivan has thrice defended the championship with bare knuckles under London prize ring rules, he was the virtual inventor of the modern glove contest," a local writer stated, citing Sullivan's use of gloves in his numerous four-round contests in the 1880s. By popularizing Marquis of Queensbury regulations, the report continued, "He Americanized the manly art, de-

[55] Fox, *Life of . . . Corbett*, 55; James J. Corbett, *The Roar of the Crowd: The True Tale of the Rise and Fall of a Champion* (New York, 1925), 201.

prived it of much of the brutality and made it possible to decide championships before athletic clubs under the best auspices, before classes of people who formerly took little interest in the sport." [56]

Whatever the reason for Corbett's victory and whatever its desirability, there was no disputing the rousing reception given news of the fight throughout the country. Boston fans received the news soberly, but in San Francisco, Corbett's home, crowds danced in the streets. In New York thousands gathered in Printing House Square and at major hotels for telegraphic reports. Round-by-round progress was also announced from the stages of the city's theaters. Chicago, St. Louis, Cincinnati, and Pittsburgh reported "intense" and "unprecedented" interest in the bout; and a story from Washington, D.C., said: "There was a larger crowd around the bulletin boards in this city last night to catch news of the fight than usually turns out for presidential elections." Illustrative of the appeal of this match and of the progress prize fighting had made toward respectability during Sullivan's reign was a story told by Professor William Lyon Phelps of Yale about the reaction of his father, a clergyman: "In 1892 I was reading aloud the news to my father. My father was an orthodox Baptist minister; he was a good man and is now with God. I had never heard him mention a prize fight and did not suppose he knew anything on that subject, or cared anything about it. So when I came to the headline CORBETT DEFEATS SULLIVAN I read that aloud and turned the page. My father leaned forward and said earnestly 'Read it by rounds!' " [57]

Aside from its importance to the history of American prize fighting, the Triple Event was a great financial success. After paying all

[56] Chicago *Tribune,* September 9, 1892; New York *Times,* September 8, 1892; New Orleans *Daily Picayune,* September 8, 1892. For other contemporary observations, see New Orleans *Times-Democrat,* September 8, 1892; and the New York *Herald,* September 8, 1892. For later analyses, see Johnston, *Ten—And Out!,* 98; and Fleischer, *The Heavyweight Championship,* 102.

[57] Quotations in this paragraph are from New Orleans *Daily Picayune,* September 8, 1892; and William Lyon Phelps, *Autobiography with Letters* (New York, 1939), 356. See also *National Police Gazette,* LXI (October 1, 1892), 2; New York *Sun,* September 8, 1892; New York *Times,* September 8, 1892; New York *Herald,* September 8, 1892; New York *Tribune,* September 8, 1892; Chicago *Tribune,* September 8, 1892; Cincinnati *Enquirer,* September 8, 1892; Dallas *Morning News,* September 8, 1892; *Kate Field's Washington,* VI (September 14, 1892), 162–63, quoted in Frank Luther Mott, *A History of American Magazines, 1885–1905* (Cambridge, Mass., 1957), 371.

expenses, the Olympic Club cleared more than $50,000. Moreover the influx of several thousand visitors pumped thousands of dollars into the city's economy. Gambling profits had also been high as an estimated $500,000 changed hands on the results of the contests.[58] Despite these indications of success, however, New Orleans soon lost its position as the center of American ring activity.

Among the first signs of trouble was a schism in the Olympic Club. A group of members led by Charles Noel wanted to follow up the pugilistic carnival by arranging other fights for equally large purses. When more conservative members hesitated, Noel and his followers organized the rival Crescent City Athletic Club, a promoting company capitalized at $100,000. Charles Dickson, president of the Olympic, said his club would continue to sponsor fights, adding that the association "will not pay such extraordinary big prices, but will give a reasonable amount." [59]

For the next several months, the Crescent City and Olympic clubs engaged in a bitter struggle for control of prize fighting. In the early months of 1893, both organizations arranged several bouts that drew crowds large enough to justify the supposition that two clubs could operate profitably in New Orleans.[60] But the battle soon proved financially disastrous to the Crescent City Athletic Club. Shortly after its founding, the club offered a purse of forty thousand dollars for a middleweight championship fight between Fitzsimmons and Jim Hall. "The enterprise of the new club is wonderful," the *Picayune* cautioned, "but the standard set will make glove contests an expensive luxury." The match aroused a great deal of national attention, but because of the high price of tickets local fans showed little enthusiasm for the championship contest. On the night of the Fitzsimmons-Hall fight, fewer than five thousand people filed into the Crescent City arena, which had a capacity of thirteen thousand. Failing to meet expenses, the club gave Fitzsimmons only part of the forty thousand dollars. He sued for the balance and the Crescent City Athletic Club went into receivership.[61]

58 New Orleans *Daily Picayune,* September 9, 1892.

59 *Ibid.,* November 5, 17, 29, 1892. The quote is from *ibid.,* November 17, 1892.

60 *Ibid.,* January 6, 22, 25, February 3, 27, March 3, 4, 6, 8, 1893; *National Police Gazette,* LXI (March 4, 1893), 10–11; LXII (March 18, 1893), 11.

61 New Orleans *Daily Picayune,* November 5, 1892; March 9, 1893; *National Police Gazette,* LXII (March 25, 1893), 2–3, 8–9; New York *Times,* March 9,

Following the demise of its rival, the Olympic Club attempted to retrieve its diminishing prestige. In the spring and summer of 1893, the contest committee scheduled a series of fights involving Andy Bowen. A bout between the Louisiana Tornado and Jack Burke in April of 1893 for $2,500 and the championship of the South attracted nine thousand fans who saw a drawn contest that went 110 rounds in seven hours and nineteen minutes, the longest fight on record under Marquis of Queensbury rules. The large attendance, said the *Picayune*, proved that "the successful and profitable contest is one for which a fair purse is offered and to which a moderate price of admission is charged." [62]

Before the Olympic Club fully regained its former stature, legal obstacles once more loomed in prize fighting's path. In November, 1893, the state attorney general brought suit against the Olympic Club on the grounds that the club had violated its charter and the Louisiana law of 1890 by sponsoring prize fights under the name of glove contests. At the civil court in New Orleans, a jury listened to the testimony of several prominent citizens, deliberated "a few minutes," and passed judgment in favor of the Olympic Club. When the attorney general appealed to the state supreme court, Justice Lyman B. Watkins, speaking for the majority, agreed that Olympic matches were glove contests within the meaning of the law and upheld the lower court. But the court granted the state a rehearing after deciding that expert testimony had been improperly admitted. [63]

Before the case came to trial again, prize fighting continued as usual. The Olympic Club sponsored a series of contests in the spring and summer of 1894, including a fight between Fitzsimmons and Dan Creedon for the middleweight championship. [64] Members of the bankrupt Crescent City Athletic Club reorganized as the Auditorium Athletic Club and also began to stage matches. In December, 1894, this

---

1893; Cincinnati *Enquirer,* March 9, 1893; Dallas *Morning News,* March 9, 1893; New Orleans *Times-Democrat,* October 12, 1893; Adams, "New Orleans as the National Center of Boxing," 49.

[62] New Orleans *Daily Picayune,* April 8, June 1, 1893. Bowen and Burke still hold the record for the longest fight under Marquis of Queensbury rules. Menke (ed.), *The Encyclopedia of Sports,* 279.

[63] New Orleans *Daily Picayune,* November 11, 26, December 16, 1893; April 24, 1894; *Southern Reporter,* XV, 190–99.

[64] New Orleans *Daily Picayune,* June 3, August 21, September 25, 26, 27, 1894; *National Police Gazette,* LXV (October 13, 1894), 2–3; New York *Times,* September 25, 26, 27, 1894.

association offered fans a triple event that contributed heavily to the downfall of prize fighting in the city. The first fight, which matched James Barry against Kid Madden, was canceled as a result of Madden's "showing the white feather." In the second fight, George "Kid" Lavigne, the lightweight champion since McAuliffe's retirement in 1893, knocked Andy Bowen unconscious in the eighteenth round. When Bowen fell, his head hit the hard floor and the fighter died from a brain concussion the next morning. Bowen's death unleashed a torrent of criticism that forced the cancellation of the third fight, a welterweight championship match featuring Tommy Ryan and Jack Dempsey.[65]

Several months after Bowen's death, the attorney general's case against the Olympic Club came before the state supreme court once again. In the lower court, a jury had for a second time acquitted the club, but Justice Samuel D. McEnery ruled: "Fighting in the arena of the club, as described in the record, is prize fighting, and no other description can be given to it." This decision destroyed the legal fiction that had enabled athletic clubs in New Orleans to promote prize fights and thus ended the city's supremacy as the national center of ring activity.[66]

Efforts to revive professional boxing in the next several years came to nought as officials in the city and in surrounding parishes took stringent action to ban the sport. Occasionally the authorities permitted exhibitions that lasted a specified number of rounds, but they consistently refused to grant permits for genuine prize fights. State representatives also intervened to squash projected bouts. As a result of this united front, prize fighting gradually disappeared. By the turn of the century, boxing was limited to infrequent amateur contests sponsored by athletic clubs.[67]

During New Orleans' tenure as the national center of prize fightting, the sport changed in a number of ways. It had become, like horse

---

65 New Orleans *Daily Picayune,* July 7, August 9, September 4, 6, December 12, 15, 16, 17, 1894. The quote regarding Madden is from *ibid.,* December 12, 1894.

66 *Southern Reporter,* XVIII (St. Paul, Minn., 1895), 600. Bowen's death also arrested the development of prize fighting in other cities, particularly Chicago. See Chicago *Tribune,* December 16, 1894; and New York *Sun,* December 17, 1894.

67 New Orleans *Daily Picayune,* August 3, 1897; March 28, December 13, 1898; December 29, 1899; May 20, July 1, 1900.

racing and baseball, a commercial pastime for urban residents of all ranks. Its decline in the late 1890s could in no way obscure its progress from a despised amusement for the lower classes to a sport patronized by fans from all levels of society. Prize fighting's transformation resulted in large part from the support given by gentlemen's athletic clubs. The Young Men's Gymnastic, the Southern Athletic, and the Olympic clubs, all composed of men of high social standing, had assumed a major role in regulating local ring activity after the Sullivan-Kilrain fight and had thereby given the sport society's seal of approval.

Athletic clubs made it possible for respectable citizens to support the sport by encouraging acceptance of reforms that made fighting less brutal than it had once been. When these clubs began to sponsor matches, they required combatants to follow Marquis of Queensbury rules, and they empowered referees to stop fights when it became obviously dangerous for one of the contestants to continue.[68] Another improvement that developed during the age of the athletic association was the practice of fighting for a specified number of rounds. Promoters had temporarily experimented with this idea when they came under attack after the Sullivan-Kilrain fight in 1889, and when legal problems increased in the mid-nineties, they returned to limited-round matches.[69] Initially fighters agreed that if the fight went the specified number of rounds without a knockout, it would be declared a draw, but agreements of this sort proved unacceptable to spectators. As the *Picayune* said, "Even if the men fail to knock out in the limited time the contest should be decided on its merits." [70] While the idea of limiting the number of rounds had not been nationally accepted by 1900, the desire to escape legal extinction gradually made this type of match more palatable. In the opening decades of the twentieth century, promoters and pugilists throughout the country abandoned fights to the finish.

Athletic associations also facilitated the acceptance of weight divisions for pugilists. Prior to the Civil War and for several years

---

68 *Ibid.,* February 2, 1891.
69 *Ibid.,* September 15, 1889; February 3, 1890; August 9, September 25, 26, 1894; October 25, 1895; August 31, December 2, 1897.
70 *Ibid.,* September 26, 1894.

afterwards, fighters were designated as either lightweights or heavy-weights. But in the 1860s, new classifications began to emerge; by 1890 most of the modern divisions had taken shape. When the Young Men's Gymnastic Club entered the promotion business, it recognized six ranks—heavyweights, middleweights, welterweights, lightweights, featherweights, and bantamweights.[71] National champions had been recognized in most of these divisions in the 1880s, largely through the work of Richard K. Fox, but in many cases claims were shadowy. Athletic clubs helped to remove confusion by insisting that fighters compete in accordance with recognized classifications. When the Audubon Athletic Association arranged a match for middleweights Bob Fitzsimmons and Arthur Upham, the club stipulated: "The men must weigh 154 pounds, give or take two pounds."[72] Similarly, when Andy Bowen and Jimmy Carroll agreed to fight at one hundred and thirty-five pounds in the Olympic Club, the contest committee warned that if either fighter weighed over the limit, he would be fined $750.[73]

In addition to updating the technical aspects of fighting, athletic clubs pioneered in the field of fight promotion, replacing the challenge system employed by fighters for years. Formal organizations worked actively to secure fights by pledging gate receipts for purses, dispatching agents to bargain with fighters, and making all local arrangements for bouts, including travel accommodations and news coverage. To cite an example of this last function, prior to the 1891 fight between Billy Myer and Jimmy Carroll, members of the Olympic Club gave a banquet for visiting reporters "in return for the courteous manner in which they have been treated."[74] By the turn of the century, the mechanics of promotion had been fully developed by athletic clubs.

While it would be misleading to imply that athletic clubs in New Orleans singlehandedly transformed the face of prize fighting, they obviously contributed immeasurably to the emergence of modern pugilism. With professional boxing under attack throughout the country, New Orleans served as a mecca for fighters in the 1880s and 1890s. The sudden influx of professional gladiators presented local promoters an opportunity to which they proved more than equal. In

[71] *Ibid.*, December 31, 1889.
[73] *Ibid.*, September 17, 1890.
[72] *Ibid.*, July 17, 1890.
[74] *Ibid.*, November 29, 1891.

their enthusiastic efforts to sponsor fights for fun and profit, agencies such as the Olympic Club gave shape and substance to cloudy features of the American ring. By 1900 the city's golden age of prize fighting had come to an end, but local clubs had written their names indelibly on the pages of the history of the sport.

Chapter IX
SPORTS
FOR ALL

When organized sports rose to prominence in the late nineteenth century, critics often complained that sports, along with other urban pastimes, made spectators of the masses. American Jeremiahs argued that the rural tradition of universal participation had been lost in the mad rush toward cities. In its place, they said, had arisen passive observation, which hardened no muscles. The criticism had some validity in the early days of organized sports, but after 1865 the argument lost whatever merit it had once possessed. Sports assumed major importance in American life in the late nineteenth century not only because they entertained urban crowds with commercial spectacles such as professional baseball, horse racing, and prize fighting, but also because they gave people a chance to participate actively. Several of the activities described earlier, including baseball, swimming, and rowing, gave urbanites opportunities to become players, but because they were seasonal pursuits, they could not completely satisfy the desire for participant sports. People patronized these activities, but they also looked to other sports in the quest for year-round recreation.

A series of sporting crazes swept New Orleans and other American cities after the Civil War. Diversions ranging from billiards and croquet to tennis and target-shooting found thousands of votaries in a country already becoming noted for its preoccupation with sports. Some of these leisure outlets dated from the antebellum period, but Americans also experimented with new games, many of which were imported from Europe. None of these sports threatened to dislodge baseball as the country's favorite pastime, but a few, such as billiards, captivated large segments of the sporting community before receding into the ranks of minor sports. Some new games, particularly golf and tennis, struck responsive chords in American life and began their rise to prominence. Above all, these various activities gave urban residents a wide choice of sports that invited active participation.

Like the citizens of other cities, New Orleanians seized upon most of the sporting fads. They revived games that had been popular in the 1850s, including the city's own sport *raquette*, but they also accepted new sports as they came into vogue. Careworn, workworn, bored, or simply gluttons for recreation, people from all ranks of society experimented with a variety of sports in their pursuit of pleasure.

The type of sports that appealed to New Orleanians was determined in part by the nature of the city's population. In the antebellum period, when male residents outnumbered females, the "bachelor subculture" referred to earlier was responsible for the popularity of many predominantly male sports, such as hunting, fishing, billiards, and bowling. However, after the war males lost their majority as New Orleans became a settled and mature city and as its rate of growth declined. By 1870 the city had as many women as men; by 1900 female residents substantially outnumbered males. Moreover the marriage rate increased. Together, these changes in the population diminished the role of the bachelor subculture in the city's sporting habits. The increase in the numerical strength of female inhabitants and in the relative number of married men expanded the power of women to influence the city's leisure activities.[1]

Female emancipation further undermined men's control of sporting pastimes. When women in New Orleans and throughout the country began to assert themselves in the late nineteenth century, their struggle was accompanied by attacks on many male institutions, such as the saloon, and by efforts to participate in sports, a field of activity once monopolized by men. All-male gathering places and predominantly male sports survived, if for no other reason than because they offered harassed men temporary escapes from the company of

[1] United States Bureau of the Census, *Ninth Census* (1870): *The Statistics of the Population of the United States*, Vol. 1 (Washington, D.C., 1872), 645; United States Bureau of the Census, *Twelfth Census* (1900): *Population*, Vol. II (Washington, D.C., 1901), 331; Paul Jacobson, *American Marriage and Divorce* (New York, 1959), 21–22; United States Bureau of the Census, *Marriage and Divorce, 1887–1906* (Washington, D.C., 1908), 36–37; Polsky, *Hustlers, Beats, and Others,* 21–24.

women; but by 1900 many of these diversions and retreats had lost much of their importance and a large share of the popularity they had possessed in an age of male supremacy. In their place came new sporting pastimes that respectable women could play without in any way jeopardizing their social standing or their personal reputations. The role that women were to play in determining the sporting tastes of the city was not readily apparent for several years after the war because sportsmen first revived sports that had been popular before 1861, such as billiards, hunting and fishing, target shooting, animal sports, and several ball games. But by the end of the century, a number of these pastimes had declined sharply in appeal, while sports that invited female participation, such as tennis, roller skating, and croquet, were either rising in popularity or had temporarily overshadowed older activities.

Billiards and bowling, indoor sports that had claimed many devotees in the antebellum period, remained part of the city's sporting pastimes after 1865. Until late in the century, however, bowling's following continued to shrink, as it had before the war. Travel accounts indicate that tenpin alleys existed throughout the period, usually in connection with saloons, but the press ignored the sport. The New Orleans Bicycle Club and the Young Men's Gymnastic Club built bowling alleys in the 1890s and attempted to stimulate enthusiasm for this formerly all-male sport by setting aside Thursday nights for "lady bowlers," but their efforts brought few results before 1900.[2]

While bowling struggled along, billiards became one of the great postwar sporting fads. Throughout the country knocking balls about a felt-covered table so enthralled people of all classes that in 1865 a writer for the magazine *Round Table* complained: "There is no more exquisite foolery of our day than the mania for playing billiards which has developed itself in this country in the last five or six years."[3] For a quarter of a century after the war, the game captivated the sporting world. Everyone, it seemed, took up the cue. Champion play-

[2] J. Milton Mackie, *From Cape Cod to Dixie and the Tropics* (New York, 1864), 163; Sala, *America Revisited,* 332; *Bicycling World,* XIX (May 17, 1889), 63; New Orleans *Daily Picayune,* January 11, December 4, 1892; January 1, 8, 1894; January 19, 1895; *American Clubman* (New Orleans), I (March, 1897), 6.

[3] *Round Table,* II (October 14, 1865), 88, quoted in Frank Luther Mott, *A History of American Magazines, 1850–1865* (Cambridge, Mass., 1938), 203.

ers occupied a position roughly equivalent to that accorded champion golfers today.

New Orleans experienced the mania for billiards as fully as any city in America. Billiard halls and saloons that provided tables for the convenience of sporting tipplers abounded in the city. The most prominent parlor was the Crescent City Billiard Hall, built in 1865 by A. W. Merriam and described by the *Times* as "the largest and most elegantly fitted Billiard Hall in the United States." Humorously referred to by a reporter as "one of the most seductive pastimes known to the experience of the average youth of the period," billiards attracted all classes of people from the "man of wealth and leisure" to the "industrious and plodding merchant and merchant's clerk." Such was the appeal of the game, said one writer, that it intensified "the human passion for the credit system." Poorly paid employees often spent more than their weekly salaries while playing billiards and had to resort to a "fashion, long extant, which is known as 'marking down.' " As before the war, the game was played on two distinct social levels. Gentlemen ordinarily wielded cues in the privacy of their homes or in the rooms of their exclusive associations, such as the Boston and Pickwick clubs. Rank-and-file residents usually flocked to the public parlors.[4]

Negroes as well as whites played billiards, but black players evidently participated on a racially segregated basis. The *Louisianian* reported in 1872 that Louis Kenner, a Negro, had opened "a first rate drinking saloon, a fine airy and comfortable billiard room with one of 'Phelan and Collander's' best tables and fixings." Several years later the same newspaper called attention to another new parlor for blacks: "Our 'Young bloods' can now enjoy a first class game of billiards without any fear of 'consequences.' " The Negro community apparently had a number of "young bloods," for on one occasion a black reporter observed: "Billiard matches are all the rage now." In the late 1880s, James Cooper, "the best colored billiard player in the United States," came to the city for a series of exhibition games.[5]

4 New Orleans *Times,* January 16, 1866; October 11, 1875; New Orleans *Weekly Crescent,* February 17, 1866; New Orleans *Times,* October 11, 1875. Quotations are in the order cited.

5 New Orleans *Weekly Louisianian,* August 3, 1872; November 8, 1879; March 6, 1880; New Orleans *Weekly Pelican,* November 5, 1887.

Proprietors of billiard parlors sustained interest in the sport in two ways—by sponsoring contests for local players and by bringing professionals to town for exhibitions. In the 1870s owners began to schedule matches for the state championship, a practice that continued through the 1890s.[6] Although winners of these tournaments often received cash prizes, the press almost invariably described them as amateurs for they did not play billiards for a living. Several players, including Henry Miller and Frank Maggioli, became professionals after acquiring reputations in local play.[7]

Games involving visiting players aroused the greatest enthusiasm among local fans. For several years after the war, a number of the country's leading "knights of the cue" came to the city for matches.[8] The interest generated by these touring professionals once moved the *Picayune* to declare that "the passion that prompts us to witness an accomplished player has made the name of [Pierre] Carmé, [A. P.] Rodolph, [John] Deery and [Joseph] Dion almost as well known as those finished stars that give popularity to the drama." Although billiards did not easily lend itself to mass observation, matches featuring renowned experts attracted as many as a thousand spectators, including a few curious ladies who desired to see a "great billiard player handle the cue." [9]

Touring billiard professionals, like nomadic baseball teams, introduced new developments in the game. Expert players showed novices special techniques like the massé shot and popularized new games like balkline and pocket billiards, which were first played in the seventies and eighties. The most unusual exhibition staged in New Orleans was a match with Professor Robert, the "champion nose player." A wit-

6 New Orleans *Daily Picayune,* May 19, 28, October 28, November 11, 1873; April 26, 1874; December 4, 1881; January 5, 1885; January 3, 1890; November 13, 1893; January 23, 1900. New Orleans *Times,* May 29, 1873; July 11, 1875; *Wilkes' Spirit of the Times,* XXVIII (May 24, 1873); 227; XXVIII (May 31, 1873), 243; XXVIII (June 7, 1873), 269; XXIX (August 23, 1873), 33.

7 New Orleans *Times,* April 25, September 10, 12, 1875; New Orleans *Bulletin,* April 4, May 18, 1875; New Orleans *Daily Picayune* December 10, 1875; February 3, 1886; April 1, 1887; January 10, 1891; January 14, 1895.

8 New Orleans *Weekly Crescent,* October 27, 1866; New Orleans *Daily Crescent,* April 14, 1867; New Orleans *Daily Picayune,* November 19, 1871; December 18, 1873; January 11, March 15, 1874; November 17, 1876; December 30, 1877; January 11, 12, 13, 14, 15, 18, 19, 1878.

9 New Orleans *Daily Picayune,* March 22, 1870; November 27, 30, 1876; New Orleans *Times,* April 15, 16, 1873.

ness related: "The precision with which Professor Robert plays with his nose is really wonderful. He plays cushion shots, follow, etc., with as much force and accuracy as an expert with cue." [10]

By the 1890s interest in billiards was slowly subsiding, probably a reflection of the diminishing size and influence of the bachelor community as well as an indication of the competition of other participant sports. Residents continued to play, but not in sufficient numbers to sustain what one player called "the old-time interest in the scientific game." A series of exhibitions in 1900 by Willie Hoppe, "the boy billiard champion," attracted several hundred spectators, but the time had passed when a thousand or more people would assemble daily for week-long tournaments. By the turn of the century, billiards had settled into the ranks of minor sports.[11]

While billiards provided pleasure for laborers, clerks, merchants, and businessmen, residents who preferred outdoor recreation turned to hunting and fishing. These sports, which had long been popular in New Orleans and throughout the South, had large and devoted followings in the postwar period. Hunting was a pastime of the cooler months. From mid-September until early May, local sportsmen took up their guns and rifles in quest of deer, rabbits, squirrels, ducks, geese, quail, and other game in the area. Like baseball players, the owners of thoroughbred horses, and other participants, they benefited from improved transportation facilities. As the *Picayune* explained in 1883: "The opening of several new railroads from New Orleans has opened up a vast area of new hunting grounds to the enthusiastic Nimrods of the South." Summer months always found residents turning their attention to fishing. "When the wild fowl which in winter frequent the lakes and marshes of the Mississippi have winged their flight to cooler climes," a local writer observed, "the veteran sportsman tenderly puts away his gun and diligently prepares his fishing tackle." Anglers fished in Lake Pontchartrain, rode "excursion trains" to promising sites along the Gulf Coast, or sailed on "schooners" to the islands bordering the Mississippi Sound. Black citizens also enjoyed fishing. The *Pelican*, a Negro newspaper, reported in May,

10 New Orleans *Daily Picayune*, March 22, 1870; March 31, 1873; March 16, April 5, October 14, 1883; New Orleans *Times-Democrat*, March 24, 1885. Robert's match is described in the New Orleans *Daily Picayune*, May 10, 1878.
11 New Orleans *Daily Picayune*, November 13, 1893; January 22, 1900.

1887: "Disciples of old Uncle Isaak Walton have put into shape for use their hooks, lines, reels, flies and rods, and are seeking the haunts of the finny tribe who are showing an inclination to bite." [12]

Hunting and fishing, like many sports, ceased to be as casual as they had been before 1861. Sportsmen founded a number of rod and gun clubs in the late nineteenth century to encourage interest in outdoor sports. These clubs generally drew their members from the city's "prominent business men," but associations existed for people of nearly all ranks. Rod and gun organizations had a number of functions. They built clubhouses on nearby lakes and bayous where members could stay while on hunting and fishing expeditions and where they could partake of the club's social life. An advertisement in a pamphlet issued by the Orleans Gun and Rod Club advised: "All Shooters Drink Finnin's Celebrated Cocktails, A Delightful Drink for Ladies," and "No Fishing Party is Complete without a Bottle of Finnin's Imperial Cocktails." Clubs also sponsored trapshooting contests, but they placed heavy emphasis on social obligations.[13]

One of the major objectives of several rod and gun associations was to secure passage of state laws to protect game from indiscriminate slaughter. "Everywhere in the South the gentlemen's gun club is the terror of poachers and reckless law-breakers," a writer for the *Times-Democrat* observed. But Louisiana responded slowly to pressure for game laws, for it was not until the mid-eighties that the state regulated the hunting season and set limits on various types of game. Many hunters who supported regulatory laws appear to have had less interest in protecting wildlife than in safeguarding hunting as a sport for the well-to-do. Like Englishmen who used their country's game laws to preserve hunting as a sport for the upper classes, such hunters were not genuine conservationists but rather men who thought of themselves as gentlemen sportsmen. In February, 1876, "a party of noted sportsmen of this city met in the gentlemen's parlor of the

12 *Ibid.*, November 20, 1883; June 12, 1876; New Orleans *Weekly Pelican*, May 7, 1887.

13 "Orleans Gun and Rod Club," *Sport in Dixie* (New Orleans), I (May, 1909), 45; *Orleans Gun and Rod Club, North Shore, Louisiana* (New Orleans, 1909; tournament program), n.p. See also *Stranger's Guide of New Orleans, Mardi Gras, 1890* (New Orleans, 1890), 15; New Orleans *Daily Picayune*, April 9, 1875; February 14, 1876; October 6, 1879; January 5, 1886; Crescent Gun and Rod Club, Membership Certificate, 1899 (Special Collections, Tulane University Library).

St. Charles Hotel" where they founded the Southern Sportsmen's Association, "the object of which is the establishing of proper laws for the protection of game, and also to conserve the interests of sportsmen in general throughout the State." That some of the members lacked a convincing commitment to conservation was indicated by their participation in a "grand game match" between two teams of hunters in March the following year. The object of the contest was to defeat the opposition by killing a greater quantity of game birds and animals.[14]

As in many areas of Louisiana life in the late nineteenth century, the campaign to regulate hunting encountered the race issue. By the 1880s the state's tardiness in passing game laws had resulted in a critical situation. Game animals which had once been plentiful, such as bear, deer, and wild hogs, had either disappeared or seemed likely to; other game animals and birds were available in smaller quantities than before the Civil War. When racial tensions deepened in the late 1880s, white sportsmen, with the assistance of the local press, attributed the decline in game to Negro hunters. A local reporter, writing for *Outing* magazine, observed in March, 1888, that Louisiana had game in abundance until the 1860s. But, he continued: "The emancipation of the negro changed all this. The first idea of the free negro was to become possessed of an old shot gun of some kind, a rejected army musket or rifle. This was proof of positive freedom, since no slave was allowed to keep a weapon of any kind." Thus armed, said the writer, "the negroes and their dogs" began to kill "everything that can be styled game." Negro sportsmen vigorously rejected this explanation. In response to a similar charge by an editorial writer for the *Times-Democrat*, the *Pelican* contended that Negroes hunted only for "venison, ducks, snipe or partridge, such game as only an educated palate can appreciate." Game had been destroyed, said the writer, mainly by the "lean, lank, drawling, yellowish looking white man or boy, who living on the hillsides, and in the swamps, shoot such poor game as mocking birds, etc. . . . If the onorous [*sic*] of killing off the game is to be borne by the poor white

---

14 R. A. Wilkinson, *The Gulf Coast: Letters Written for the New Orleans "Times-Democrat"* (Louisville, 1886), 60; New Orleans *Daily Picayune,* February 14, 1876; March 6, 1877. See also *ibid.,* April 9, 1875; January 5, 1886; "Our Monthly Record," *Outing,* V (October, 1884), 75; "Game Preserving in Louisiana," *Outing,* XI (March, 1888), 532–35.

man and the black man, let the major portion of the blame rest where it rightfully belongs, viz., on the poor white man. He is capable of doing everything low, mean and contemptible." Mutual recriminations, of course, contributed little to the conservation of game. By 1900 it was evident that rather than poor whites or blacks, weak and poorly enforced state laws were responsible for the annihilation of game. Since the beginning of the century the state has improved its laws and its method of enforcement to safeguard Louisiana's reputation as the "sportsman's paradise." [15]

Whatever the traditional appeal of hunting, urban conditions hindered and sometimes prevented participation in this sport by many residents. Limitations on time, the requirements of work, and the cost of long hunting expeditions encouraged some sportsmen with a fondness for outdoor pastimes to develop substitutes. Trapshooting and rifle shooting—two sporting fads of the postwar period—rose in popularity in large part because they offered urban dwellers suitable replacements for venturing into the open fields. Trapshooting, which had emerged as a recognizable sport before the Civil War when improvements in gunmaking made possible effective wing shooting, gained thousand of adherents after 1865. Technological contributions, such as better traps and mass-produced clay pigeons to replace live birds, facilitated nationwide participation. Rifle shooting, like trapshooting, was an antebellum urban substitute for hunting, but the popularity of this sport stemmed also from efforts to encourage skill with small arms. Convinced that the introduction of long-range breechloaders in the 1860s made marksmanship a necessity in wartime, military officers and private citizens throughout the country organized clubs, including the National Rifle Association (1871), to stimulate interest in sharpshooting.

Residents in New Orleans joined actively in these sports. They began to form shooting clubs in the late 1860s and by the turn of the century had founded more than twenty associations dedicated to trapshooting and rifle practice. The Crescent City Rifle Club, organized in 1869, was, according to *Wilkes' Spirit of the Times*, one of the first groups in America "to recognize the fact that long-range rifle shooting could be perfected by close care and steady practice."

[15] "Game Preserving in Louisiana," 532; New Orleans *Weekly Pelican*, February 26, 1887; New Orleans *Daily Picayune*, July 24, 1900.

Clubs were composed chiefly of middle- and upper-class residents who, like hunters, attempted to cultivate the qualities of gentlemen sportsmen. A rule of the Roman Rifle Club, as an example, encouraged members to participate for pleasure rather than for profit: "Betting on skill, efficiency and on any other qualification of members among themselves is strictly forbidden." Some clubs organized along ethnic lines, such as the Swiss Rifle Club and the New Orleans Rifle Club, a German-American association.[16]

Both trapshooting and rifle shooting had large followings among the city's sportsmen, but rifle shooting had added appeal for people who lived in a section with a traditional fondness for military activities. The South, though soundly defeated in war, remained militant; southerners continued to send many of their sons to military schools, into the army, and into local militia units. For such people rifle shooting was a sport, but it was also preparation for armed conflict. Rifle clubs in Louisiana apparently played no part in the overthrow of the state's Reconstruction government, as was the case with similar groups in South Carolina and Mississippi, but they had military aspects. The New Orleans *Bulletin* once suggested that the top prize in a rifle contest be given for off-hand shooting rather than for shooting at rest: "The cases in actual warfare, in which rest shooting is possible, are comparatively rare," a reporter observed, "while the opportunities for picking off an officer or man, off-hand, are numerous." This attitude pervaded the activities of new groups, such as the Roman Rifle Club, whose officials held military titles, and of the city's old and established military units, such as the Continental Guards and the Washington Artillery, which sponsored shooting contests regularly in the 1880s. Negroes also had military organizations and on summer Sundays, said a black journalist, "the m'lish" made "the air resonant with the rattle of musketry and the plaudits of the fair." [17]

Riflemen and trapshooters exhibited their skills frequently

16 *Wilkes' Spirit of the Times,* XCII (October 21, 1876), 283; *Rules and Regulations of the Roman Rifle Club of New Orleans, La.* (New Orleans, 1874), 5; New Orleans *Times,* September 21, 1869; July 24, 1871; September 28, 1875; New Orleans *Daily Picayune,* June 21, 1870; July 2, 1872; December 20, 1875; June 6, 1881; August 4, 1885; May 3, 1886; April 29, 1889; May 5, 1890; *Sport in Dixie,* I (May, 1909), 45.

17 New Orleans *Bulletin,* July 27, 1875; New Orleans *Weekly Pelican,* May 7, 1887; *Rules . . . of the Roman Rifle Club,* 3–4; New Orleans *Daily Picayune,*

throughout the year. Newspaper accounts indicate that large crowds gathered to watch the weekly slaughter of pigeons and the puncturing of targets. Women often attended, and, said the *Picayune,* "it is not an infrequent occurrence for some of the fair ones to try the quickness of the trigger with their delicate touch." The New Orleans Rifle Club prepared a special target for ladies and reported that it was "well patronized." [18] Clubs also arranged matches for their members who shot for prizes that ranged from a silver service given by Republican Governor Henry Clay Warmoth to a "silver-mounted Evans patent magazine rifle" presented by William F. "Buffalo Bill" Cody and John B. "Texas Jack" Omohundro while Buffalo Bill's Wild West Show was in the city in December, 1875. Manufacturers such as the DuPont Powder Company, the Sharp's Rifle Company, and LeRoy Shot and Lead Company offered firearms, sacks of shot, and kegs of powder to encourage marksmen to use their products.[19] Intraclub contests dominated local shooting activities until the 1890s, when the rifle teams of several athletic clubs began to sponsor matches for the state championship, a practice that continued until the end of the century.[20]

Local marksmen also had many opportunities to compare skills with trapshooters and riflemen from other cities. On several occasions in the 1870s, New Orleans riflemen attended matches in other cities, including Mobile, Montgomery, and Baltimore.[21] In 1877 the Crescent City Rifle Club sent a team to the National Rifle Association's national tournament at Creedmoor, Long Island, New York. The local riflemen placed third in team competition and Dudley Selph, the club's best shot, won the national championship at one thousand yards. When Selph received the winner's trophy, Sir Henry Halford of England's national team "styled him 'the greatest shot in the world.' " [22] Improved rail travel, of course, made such ventures pos-

---

October 8, December 3, 1877; July 19, September 6, 1880; March 27, May 9, 16, October 24, 1881; September 18, 25, October 9, 16, 1882.

18 New Orleans *Daily Picayune,* January 24, 1876; June 21, 1870.

19 *Ibid.,* July 2, 1872; December 20, 1875; January 22, June 18, 1877; February 25, 1879; September 18, 1882.

20 *Ibid.,* April 29, 1889; May 5, June 16, July 14, 1890; May 3, 1891; June 25, July 2, 1894; June 22, 29, November 8, 1896.

21 *Ibid.,* August 25, 1872; July 2, 18, 1878; New Orleans *Times,* August 19, 1874.

22 New York *Times,* September 16, 1877; *Wilkes' Spirit of the Times,* XCIV

sible, but if local shooters were unable to travel to other cities, they could turn to another technological wonder of the nineteenth century—the telegraph. The Crescent City Rifle Club in October, 1876, arranged a "telegraph match" in which teams from cities throughout the country shot on their home ranges and then reported their scores by wire. The Crescent City team vanquished all rivals, including the Amateur Rifle Club of New York.[23]

While local marksmen journeyed for competition, sharpshooters from other cities also came to New Orleans. Captain A. H. Bogardus, who won the national trapshooting championship in 1871, inaugurated this practice when he came to the city in December, 1873, for a series of exhibitions. Bogardus was one of the first sportsmen to utilize rail transportation for a nationwide tour. In the quarter century after the visit, local trapshooters sponsored several intercity tournaments that attracted sportsmen from throughout the country.[24] Their most successful match was the International Clay Pigeon Tournament in 1885. Arranged by the managers of the World's Cotton Centennial and Industrial Exposition, this event drew large crowds who gathered to see the country's best trapshooters shatter clay pigeons and to witness Boston's team capture the national championship. During the course of the tournament, a number of participants met at Richard Rhodes' Gun Store to found the National Gun Association. This organization lasted only a short time, but it represented the first attempt to establish national rules and regulations for American trapshooters. It was soon replaced by the Interstate Association of Trapshooters, organized about 1889, which governed the sport until 1900 when it yielded to the American Trapshooting Association.[25]

Intersectional competition in shooting, as in other sports, helped

(September 15, 1877), 169; XCIV (September 22, 1877), 192; New Orleans *Daily Picayune,* September 13, 17, 18, 1877.

[23] New Orleans *Daily Picayune,* October 13, 14, 1876; *Wilkes' Spirit of the Times,* XCII (October 21, 1876), 283, 288; New York *Times,* October 13, 1876.

[24] New Orleans *Times,* December 10, 15, 22, 1873; New Orleans *Daily Picayune,* February 26, 27, 28, March 1, 2, 3, 1876; February 8, 9, 10, 1891; August 10, 1895; New York *Herald,* March 2, 1876; Chicago *Tribune,* February 27, 1876; January 11, 1891; *Wilkes' Spirit of the Times,* XCI (March 4, 1876), 85; XCI (March 11, 1876), 110.

[25] New Orleans *Times-Democrat,* February 11, 12, 14, 1885; New Orleans *Daily Picayune,* February 11, 1885; August 10, 1895; Menke (ed.), *The Encyclopedia of Sports,* 784.

to reunite the country. When the National Rifle Association announced plans for an intersectional match in July, 1875, the New York *Times* commended the idea: "If at Creedmoor teams from Maine, Louisiana, New York, South Carolina, Massachusetts, and Georgia could meet in friendly contest, all their rifles pointed one way, it would tend immensely to increase that kind feeling among the people which now only wants better acquaintance to be enduring forever." Similarly, when the selection committee of the National Rifle Association invited Dudley Selph to join the American rifle team for international competition in 1877, the committee stressed national unity: "As a Southerner, you will appreciate how much more natural the team will be with you on it than if it be made up solely with riflemen from the Eastern and Middle States, and how much such a union in a national contest will help to revive the feelings of fraternity between the North and South, which we are all anxious to promote and foster." [26]

New Orleans' interest in organized rifle shooting and trapshooting dropped sharply in the 1890s. Most shooting groups disbanded as members and spectators found new sporting fads or returned to older pastimes. By 1900 only a half-dozen rifle clubs and one gun club held regular contests. Hunting remained a popular sport, but shooting at inanimate objects, whether moving clay pigeons or stationary paper targets, had few votaries as the city entered a new century.[27]

Among the city's rowdier elements animal sports had a large following. Bull and bear contests and bullfights failed to survive the war, but sporting men had many opportunities to attend dogfights and cockfights. Cockpits operated primarily in the downtown area. The Spanish Cockpit on Columbus Street and the Louisiana Cockpit on Dumaine Street, which was the "scene of hundreds of desperate combats," were the major arenas.[28] Partisans of canine battles generally patronized Thomas Hanley's establishment on Baronne Street, where he pitted his dogs against all comers before "motley" crowds. A reporter for the *Picayune* observed of one dogfight audience: "Kid gloved gentlemen, with shimmering beavers and light canes, jostled

26 New York *Times,* July 20, 1875; New Orleans *Daily Picayune,* July 30, 1877.

27 New Orleans *Daily Picayune,* September 6, 1897; May 7, 14, 21, 1900; *Southern Sportsman* (New Orleans), II (January, 1899), 17.

28 New Orleans *Daily Picayune,* April 9, 1871; December 22, 1878.

against squalid negroes and spoiled the immaculate sheen of their boots with incrustations of saw-dust, and the whole concourse was one of immense and uproarious confusion." [29] Cockfights also attracted mixed crowds. A visitor who attended a "main" (cockfighting match) in 1867 reported: "The place was crowded with people of the lower class." But the *Picayune* later insisted that "some of the most influential persons of our population" witnessed matches at the Louisiana Cockpit.[30]

The *Picayune* may have exaggerated the caliber of the crowd, but cockfighting attained a much higher standing in the 1870s than ever before. Turfmen who were eminently respectable (judged by the Gilded Age's rather shoddy standards) brought gamecocks to fight in local pits when they came to race meetings at the Metairie or Fair Grounds tracks. Reflecting a tendency in all sports, they often employed their bellicose fowls to settle intercity and interstate rivalries. In 1870 turfmen arranged a "great chicken main" between cocks representing Louisiana and Kentucky. During the two-day contest, local birds won the majority of the fights. Kentuckians returned the following year with a fresh batch of chickens and evened the score by winning ten of fourteen bouts. The last match was not atypical: "For this battle the Louisianians again staked their money . . . only to lose in less than a minute, for Kentucky's cock in the first fly took out both the white cock's eyes, and in the next brained him." [31]

Both cockfighting and dogfighting encountered strong opposition in the 1870s. The Louisiana State Association for the Prevention and Suppression of Cruelty to Animals, founded in 1873, launched an assault on the Spanish Cockpit in 1874. The association charged the proprietor with violation of a recently passed law prohibiting cruelty to animals. Such attacks did not end the sport, but they reduced its popularity. By the mid-eighties the Spanish Cockpit and several lesser-known arenas had passed out of existence. Within a few years, the Louisiana Cockpit also ran afoul of animal lovers. By the turn

29 New Orleans *Times,* November 17, 1873; New Orleans *Daily Picayune,* December 21, 1874; Herbert Asbury, *The French Quarter: An Informal History of the New Orleans Underworld* (New York, 1936), 332.

30 Guilio Adamoli, "New Orleans in 1867," *Louisiana Historical Quarterly,* VI (April, 1923), 277; New Orleans *Daily Picayune,* March 21, 1875.

31 New Orleans *Daily Picayune,* April 3, 5, 6, 1870; April 11, 1871; April 12, 1879; New Orleans *Times,* 1873. The quote is from the New Orleans *Daily Picayune,* April 11, 1871.

of the century, cockfighting enthusiasts had taken their sport from the center of the city to Hogan's Alley in St. Bernard Parish and to a pit in the suburb of Carrollton which held Sunday mains.[32] In the meantime the Association for the Prevention and Suppression of Cruelty to Animals had put Hanley's Dogpit out of business. When the famous dogfighter Harry Jennings of New York came to the city to open an arena in 1879, members of the Society for the Prevention of Cruelty to Animals throughout the country sent letters to the local chief of police, who agreed to arrest the intruder if he staged a fight. Jennings returned to New York where he told a reporter for the *Sun* that his venture had cost him two thousand dollars. Dogfighting disappeared altogether after this unsuccessful effort to revive the sport, a casualty in the crusade against the mistreatment of animals.[33]

While professional sportsmen relied upon traditional pastimes such as cockfighting and dogfighting for recreation, a few athletically inclined young men tried to resuscitate cricket, *raquette*, and Irish football, all games which had been played by the city's youth in the 1850s. None of these activities gained large followings after the war, but they occasionally aroused enthusiasm among particular groups of people.

Cricket, which had rivaled baseball in popularity in the 1850s, returned early in 1866 when several young athletes reorganized the Crescent City Cricket Club.[34] Members conducted games with the aristocratic features that had characterized antebellum matches. They played on weekdays while ladies and other invited guests watched from beneath tents provided by the club; "the best Champagne punch, ice cream and confections . . . were supplied without stint. For the gentlemen guests a large stock of more substantial refreshments were

32 New Orleans *Times*, May 10, June 8, 1874; New Orleans *Times-Democrat*, April 17, 1885; James A. Zacharie, *New Orleans Guide, with Descriptions of the Routes to New Orleans, Sights of the City Arranged Alphabetically, and Other Information Useful to Travellers; Also, Outlines of the History of Louisiana* (New Orleans, 1885), 33; James A. Zacharie, *New Orleans Guide, with Descriptions of the Routes to New Orleans, Sights of the City Arranged Alphabetically, and Other Information Useful to Travellers; Also, Outlines of the History of Louisiana* (New Orleans, 1902), 106; New Orleans *Daily Picayune*, January 24, 1898.

33 New Orleans *Daily Picayune*, February 18, 1879; New York *Sun*, March 10, April 1, 1879.

34 New Orleans *Times*, January 16, 1866.

provided." Since playing on working days before such select audiences gave the club a relatively small source of supporters, their efforts "to keep alive and foster an amusement so beneficial to health and mind" failed; by 1869 the Crescent City Cricket Club had disbanded.[35]

Upper-class players again attempted to revive interest in the game in the 1870s. Players organized the New Orleans and Louisiana cricket clubs, which were composed mainly of English residents and Americans who had been educated in England and included "the names of very many gentlemen well known in prominent business circles." Spurred by the activity of their fellow cricket players, members of the Crescent City Cricket Club resumed competition. In the mid-seventies, these three clubs played a number of matches that attracted small crowds who came to see "some of the most brilliant play on record." But when the *Picayune* reported unruly spectators who interfered with the game and refused to stay off the playing field, it was evident that times had changed. "As this is not a characteristic of a New Orleans assemblage," a reporter noted, "we must suppose that the latter class brought their manners from a distance (probably in carpet-bags), and express a hope that their visit will not be unnecessarily prolonged." Of course, the withdrawal of such fans would not have rescued the sport. Interest in cricket faded because some players, such as William F. Tracy, exchanged cricket equipment for baseball uniforms and because small attendance by the local gentry discouraged other players. Several Englishmen fielded a team in the late 1890s, but it lasted only a short time.[36]

Irish football, which the *Picayune* referred to in August, 1872, as "that genuine and exciting old Louisiana sport," came to the city with immigrants before the war and continued to amuse Irish residents in the 1860s and 1870s. Although players displayed no abiding interest in permanent teams, Irish fire companies, the Hibernian Benevolent and Mutual Aid Association, the Irish Rifles, the Ancient

[35] *Ibid.,* April 25, 1866; New Orleans *Daily Picayune,* February 4, 1866; New Orleans *Daily Crescent,* April 11, 26, 1866.

[36] New Orleans *Times,* March 9, 1873; New Orleans *Daily Picayune,* April 7, 1874; April 27, 1873. Quotations are in the order cited. See also New Orleans *Times,* February 23, April 6, 1873; New Orleans *Daily Picayune,* May 19, 27, June 22, 1897; October 17, November 25, 26, 1897; March 27, August 7, 1898; April 14, 1900.

Order of Hibernians, and even the Harmony Club, a predominantly German-American group, scheduled football matches at day-long festivals that also featured "stone throwing," "pig catching," "ROOSTER IN THE POT," and "SAUSAGE SNAPPING." Participants in this arduous game, a rough version of soccer, reportedly played "with a relish which betokened an almost poetic love for the traditions of the native soil." Football enthusiasts may also have had more than a passing interest in the standard reward for the victors: "One Barrel Chicago Lager Beer." Interest in Irish football declined in the eighties, but in the mid-nineties, after American football's rise to prominence, local Irish nationalists organized two short-lived teams, Erin go Bragh and Faugh a Ballagh, which played "in the most scientific manner." [37]

Raquette, played by both whites and Negroes in the 1850s, also returned soon after the war. In the summer of 1865, large crowds gathered to watch this traditional sport played by the Bayou and LaVille teams. For several weeks whites and Negroes played together without incident, but on September 10, 1865, a minor riot occurred that resulted in the death of one person and led military authorities to prohibit *raquette* games for several months.[38] When competition resumed late in 1865, whites at first refused to participate "because . . . negroes play the same game," but in the latter part of the 1860s a few white youths occasionally violated their pledge and played *raquette* at Sunday festivals.[39]

For the remainder of the century, *raquette* occupied a lowly position among local sports. During the 1870s the game was "supplanted by the foot-ball playing." In the next decade, black players once again reorganized the Bayous and LaVilles, but the teams failed to arouse much of a following; the game had again disappeared by 1890. Then, in 1897 the *Picayune* published a brief history of this old Louisiana sport and stimulated a revival of the Bayou and LaVille teams. Composed of whites, the organizations played frequently until after

[37] Quotations in this paragraph, in the order cited, are from the New Orleans *Daily Picayune*, August 12, 1872; July 6, 1876; April 26, 1875; June 19, 1876; August 15, 1869; February 5, 1894. See also *ibid.*, July 4, 1871; August 12, 1872; May 12, 1874; April 25, 1875; June 25, 1876; February 19, 20, 1893.

[38] New Orleans *Times*, September 15, 16, 1865.

[39] *Ibid.*, November 23, 1865; May 29, 1868; October 10, 1869; New Orleans *Daily Picayune*, May 29, 1868.

the turn of the century. When the games first resumed, as many as five thousand people went to City Park, the site of most matches, but after the "novelty" of the sport wore off, crowds dwindled. *Raquette* became one of several summer sports that failed to compete successfully with baseball.[40]

Residents after 1865 showed a continuing interest in pastimes that had been popular in the antebellum period, but they also manifested a willingness to participate in new sports introduced in the postwar years. As a variety of new activities became available in the late nineteenth century, thousands of New Orleanians succumbed to the appeal of these sporting pastimes. It was in the introduction and popularization of new sports that the influence of women was most strongly felt in sporting developments in the late nineteenth century.

Middle- and upper-class residents, many of whom shunned other sports, sought pleasure in lawn games that became popular after the Civil War—croquet, archery, and lawn tennis. These sports, which began as fads in the East, were among the first games played extensively by both men and women. All three came into vogue in England and in the sixties and seventies were exported to the United States, where fashionable society quickly demonstrated enthusiasm for them.

Croquet, which the *Crescent* described as "a kind of out-door feminine billiards," was the first sport imported from England after the war. So widespread was its appeal that in 1866 the *Nation* announced that "of all the epidemics that have swept over our land, the swiftest and most infectious is croquet." The activity fascinated people because it was not only a game but also a social function that permitted young people to meet in unfettered social intercourse.[41]

Croquet came to New Orleans soon after its conquest of the East. A report in 1868 said the game was "very extensively patronized by *le bon ton* of our city." The game became highly popular among younger residents of both sexes and for several years was a regular accompaniment to spring. "Since the advent of the delightful spring weather," the *Picayune* reported in March, 1869, "croquet parties

---

[40] New Orleans *Daily Picayune,* May 30, 1875; May 31, June 7, August 30, 1897; May 16, 1898; May 28, 1900; Eagleson, "Some Aspects of the Social Life of the New Orleans Negro in the 1880's," 97.

[41] New Orleans *Daily Crescent,* May 28, 1868; *Nation,* August 8, 1866, p. 113, quoted in Frank L. Mott, *A History of American Magazines, 1865–1885* (Cambridge, Mass., 1938), 219.

have again come into vogue—especially in the Fourth District, where almost every residence has a green lawn excellently adapted to the game. There are few prettier sights than a number of young ladies and gentlemen upon some level green sward pursuing a painted croquet ball, and entering fully into the spirit of the game. The dresses worn by the ladies on these occasions are usually of some bright material, and cut short to allow perfect freedom of action." [42]

Archery also appealed to both men and women. Like several other pastimes, this sport was first introduced to many residents at the festivals of social and charitable clubs which awarded prizes to the winners of archery contests. Several young ladies organized the Crescent City Female Archery Club in the 1870s and occasionally staged exhibitions at state fairs and picnics. Another group of girls founded the Pearl Archery Club in 1880. Negro archers also showed an interest in the sport; in May, 1880, the *Louisianian* reported that "young ladies are anxious to form an Archery Club." None of these associations was excessively active, but their existence indicated that women were showing a much greater desire to participate in sports. [43]

Of the lawn sports introduced in the sixties and seventies, none gained a more lasting popularity than lawn tennis. Allegedly brought to this country in 1874 by Mary Ewing Outerbridge, who had played it in Bermuda, the game became popular at fashionable eastern resorts in the late seventies. When confusion developed regarding rules, equipment, and procedures, players in 1881 created the United States Lawn Tennis Association, the sport's ruling body since that time. Interest in tennis developed slowly for the remainder of the century, mainly because men often scorned tennis as a game for women. Defenders of the sport argued that lawn tennis, "although a good game for ladies, is not a 'ladies' game,' as some sarcastic people were once wont to call it," but old prejudices lingered for years. Tennis did not achieve a mass following until after the turn of the century. [44]

The history of lawn tennis in New Orleans clearly indicated that

[42] New Orleans *Daily Crescent*, May 28, 1868; New Orleans *Daily Picayune*, March 29, 1869.

[43] New Orleans *Daily Crescent*, May 27, 28, 29, 31, 1868; New Orleans *Daily Picayune*, February 9, 22, 1879; May 16, 1880; New Orleans *Weekly Louisianian*, May 1, 1880.

[44] Henry W. Slocum, Jr., "Lawn Tennis as a Game for Women," *Outing*, XIV (July, 1889), 289; Menke (ed.) *The Encyclopedia of Sports*, 897–98; Dulles, *A History of Recreation*, 240.

local sportsmen had no need to rely exclusively on easterners to introduce new sports. While tennis slowly gained adherents in the East, it developed independently in New Orleans. In the mid-seventies, soon after Walter C. Wingfield drew up the first rules for lawn tennis in England, several English residents marked out a tennis court in the uptown section where they played regularly. In 1876, five years before the organization of the United States Lawn Tennis Association, local players founded the New Orleans Lawn Tennis Club, the oldest society of its kind in the country.[45]

For several years the game claimed few participants outside the New Orleans Lawn Tennis Club, which limited its membership to men. But in the mid-eighties, the appeal of the sport increased when residents discovered that tennis, despite its apparent effeminacy, could be an enjoyable and healthy activity. One supporter recommended tennis because it was played in the open air "where the lungs can breathe in no impurities as is the case in crowded, over-heated ball-rooms, theatres and halls." Several citizens built private courts, and, as a local sporting journal suggested, "The laying out of the 'garden district' . . . makes possible many more private courts than in most large cities." Members of social and athletic clubs also began to play tennis. Both the New Orleans Bicycle Club and the Metropolitan Athletic Club marked out courts on clubhouse lawns that formerly had been devoted exclusively to croquet. Tennis also became the first sporting interest of the Elks and Linwood clubs, which were primarily social organizations.[46]

One of the best attributes of tennis, according to many advocates of the sport, was its appeal to women. A writer for *Outing* magazine maintained that when a young woman sought "a game in which the elements of exercise and competition are combined, lawn tennis seems to be her only refuge. It is the one athletic game which women may enjoy without being subjected to sundry insinuations of rompish-ness." When local women became unrelentingly curious about the game, the New Orleans Lawn Tennis Club reluctantly opened its courts to them. In the mid-eighties the club allowed women to play

[45] *Spirit of the South* (New Orleans), February 2, 1889; New Orleans *Daily Picayune,* December 1, 1896; February 24, 1898.

[46] *Spirit of the South,* February 2, 1889; *Bicycling World,* XVIII (March 1, 1889), 292; XIX (May 17, 1889), 63; New Orleans *Daily Picayune,* January 16, 1890; May 16, 1892.

on the mornings of specified days, " 'no heeled shoes' being the one condition attached to the invitation." "Ladies' Days" and "Tennis Teas," which became regular practices, "evolved out of this generous sacrifice on the part of its members." Several years later the club advanced another step by admitting a few female players as associate members.[47]

When interest in tennis intensified, club members soon decided to formalize competition. The New Orleans Club in 1890 inaugurated an annual tournament to determine the association's best player. The club later divided competition into four categories—men's and women's singles, men's doubles, and mixed doubles. After intraclub contests had become a regular feature of the New Orleans Lawn Tennis Club, members began to compete with players outside the group. In 1898 a tournament was arranged with members of the Cotton Exchange, and in 1900 two local enthusiasts ventured to Atlanta to play for the southern championship.[48]

Tennis also attracted collegians in the 1890s. Tulane University had two teams, the Varsity and Tulane Tennis clubs, which held intraclub matches. Members of the Varsity Tennis Club played the South's first intercollegiate tennis contest in November, 1895, when they met representatives of the University of Mississippi in singles and doubles matches. Newcomb girls adopted the sport about the same time as Tulane students, and when the boys suggested a "mixed tournament," the *Picayune* warned: "Several of these young women have become very skillful in tennis and will compel the boys of Tulane to play hard to win." With the adoption of tennis as a collegiate sport as well as a pastime for members of social and athletic clubs, its future seemed assured. At the turn of the century, play was generally limited to members of exclusive clubs and college students, but it appeared likely that the sport would follow the course of other activities and soon acquire a more broadly based following.[49]

While many residents took to their lawns for amusement, others succumbed to another craze imported from the East—roller skating.

[47] Slocum, "Lawn Tennis," 289; *Spirit of the South,* February 2, 1889; New Orleans *Daily Picayune,* December 1, 1896.

[48] New Orleans *Daily Picayune,* May 23, 1897; February 24, April 10, 13, May 21, 1898; January 14, 1899; August 4, 7, 8, 9, 10, 11, 1900.

[49] *Ibid.,* May 28, 29, November 30, 1895. The quotation is from *ibid.,* May 29, 1895.

After its invention by the Englishman James L. Plimpton, roller skating was quickly adopted by New York's social leaders, who attempted to restrict it to "the educated and refined classes." [50] But gliding along on wheels appealed to all classes of people. Promoters soon built skating rinks in every major city in the country, and Americans embraced another sporting fad.

New Orleanians welcomed roller skating soon after it made its appearance in the East. In 1869 Major E. D. Lawrence, owner of Mechanics' Institute Hall on Dryades Street (site of the 1866 riot), converted the building into a skating rink and sent four thousand invitations to the "best families in the city." On November 1 a fashionable assemblage crowded into the hall to watch "any number of skaters on the floor, among whom were some fifteen or twenty ladies," sailing along to tunes played by a "fine band of music." The *Times* predicted "that this graceful amusement has every chance of becoming popular in our fashionable circles," but the *Picayune* casually dismissed it as a "nine days' wonder." [51]

Roller skating instantly met with success. The sport, said one reporter, attracted all "thinking people who needed healthful and delightful exercise." Mechanics' Hall encouraged participation by charging low rates of admission (fifty cents for adults, twenty-five cents for children), renting skates for twenty-five cents, and offering free instruction. The rink also had private rooms for novices who wished to avoid embarrassment. Within a few weeks of the opening of the rink, the *Picayune* reversed its earlier position and commended the rink's proprietor, "who has placed before the Southern public an amusement heretofore monopolized by the North." [52]

When roller skating invaded the city, local social leaders, like their counterparts in the East, tried to restrict participation to the upper strata of society. Major Lawrence initially encouraged this exclusiveness by passing judgment on all who entered Mechanics' Hall. Managers of the rink, said the *Picayune*, "are determined to make each assembly as select as any parlor entertainment." As was true

[50] Pamphlet material on James L. Plimpton in the New York Public Library, cited in Dulles, *A History of Recreation*, 193.

[51] New Orleans *Daily Picayune*, November 2, 1869; New Orleans *Times*, November 3, 1869.

[52] New Orleans *Daily Picayune*, November 7, 28, 1869; New Orleans *Times*, November 3, 1869.

elsewhere, the social elite's efforts to monopolize roller skating met defeat. In the early 1870s, the *Turnverein* built its own rink and formed the Skating Rink Club. Skaters who patronized the Lawrence rink organized the Southern Roller Skating Association and the Orleans Roller Skating Club, which popularized the sport by giving public demonstrations at the skating rink and at Sunday festivals. Negro Odd Fellows also sponsored a skating tournament in May, 1879. Roller skating clearly was available to anyone who wished to participate.[53]

Until the mid-eighties roller skating claimed many followers in the city. Occasional reports in the newspapers indicated that the Lawrence rink attracted many fans and participants each night. Such was the popularity of the sport that in 1885, "Professor" Ira W. Daniels of New York came to the city to open a new arena, the Crescent City Roller Skating Rink, which the press called the "Largest and Most Complete Rink IN THE UNITED STATES." But Daniels had misread the city's mood. The roller skating craze was dying, and by 1888, when several young men met in the Crescent City Roller Skating Rink to organize the Southern Athletic Club, "the rink was inhabited by nothing but cobwebs and a few enterprising bats." After experimenting with the sport for almost twenty years, residents rejected indoor roller skating in favor of other athletic pastimes.[54]

Another sport that enjoyed a brief vogue was the ring tournament. This social import from Europe had been popular in parts of the South during the antebellum period when the much-vaunted southern chivalry and Sir Walter Scott's books were both in fashion. After the war the sport spread throughout the section. In ring tournaments contestants armed with lances rode horseback along a prescribed course and attempted to pierce rings suspended above the track on frames resembling gallows. When conducted seriously, a great deal of pageantry accompanied the "jousts." Horsemen, who called them-

[53] New Orleans *Daily Picayune*, November 28, 1869; New Orleans *Times*, February 26, 1871; January 20, 1873; New Orleans *Bulletin*, July 25, 1875; New Orleans *Weekly Louisianian*, May 17, 1879.

[54] New Orleans *Daily Picayune*, February 9, 1879; February 15, 1880; January 6, 1885; *A Souvenir of the Southern Athletic Club of New Orleans, La.* (New Orleans, 1895), 7. Hogan, "Sin and Sports," pages 129–30, indicates that the religious press elsewhere in 1885 conducted a vigorous campaign against roller skating. It was described as an "epidemic," which was "our greatest national evil."

selves knights, rode for the honor of fair southern maidens. After each tournament the winner invariably chose a Queen of Love and Beauty.[55]

Ring tournaments first came to New Orleans in the late 1860s when fraternal societies began to sponsor this equine sport. Bearing titles such as "Knight of the Southern Cross," "Chevalier de la Belle Creole," and "Knight of the Slim Chance," riders reportedly rode before as many as twenty thousand spectators. They vied for the right to nominate a Queen of Love and Beauty, as well as for more tangible prizes such as a "silver cross of honor" and silver spurs.[56]

Participants elsewhere generally regarded ring tournaments as serious affairs, but local sportsmen could not resist the obvious opportunity to caricature these spectacles. Several firemen in 1875 staged a ring tournament with each contestant mounted on a mule and dressed in burlesque style. Some years later the *Times-Democrat* reported a ring tournament that was held as part of the Mardi Gras festivities. Ignoring the pageantry, most spectators flocked to the betting stands. "Books were opened on the tournament and considerable sums changed hands on the result," a reporter noted.[57]

Although ring tournaments occasionally drew several thousand fans, local sports fans staged few such contests. Ring tournaments were popular mainly in the rural South. In southern cities, and especially in New Orleans with its great variety of sporting pastimes, participants and spectators usually preferred other activities.

Toward the end of the nineteenth century, when many sporting fads had run their course, Americans suddenly showed an interest in still another imported sport—golf. Although there is some evidence that golf was played in this country in the latter part of the eighteenth century, the sport did not acquire a permanent following until the 1880s when Americans who had traveled in Scotland and Scots visiting in the United States gradually aroused support for it. Throughout the 1890s and well into the present century, it was a pastime for members of exclusive clubs, but over a period of years it

55 Esther J. Crooks and Ruth W. Crooks, *The Ring Tournament in the United States* (Richmond, 1936), *passim.*

56 New Orleans *Daily Crescent,* May 31, 1868; New Orleans *Daily Picayune,* October 5, 1869.

57 Both tournaments are discussed in Crooks and Crooks, *The Ring Tournament,* 119–20.

has, like so many sports, submitted to a degree of democratization.[58]

Golf arrived in New Orleans in the mid-nineties when several residents formed a country club. This short-lived organization was primarily a fashionable social club with a casual interest in bicycle riding, but one of its founders, Hugh L. Bayne, had learned golf in the North and he taught his fellow members the fundamentals. "Golf has been started here by the Country Club and should be followed by others," a writer for a local weekly magazine wrote in 1897. "Golf is a great sport and very popular North. If our young ladies understood the game it would immediately become popular here. Why not form several good Golf clubs so New Orleans will have a real aristocratic air." But for all the optimism, this first attempt to introduce the game failed miserably. Country Club members could find no suitable ground for a course, and early in 1897 the club itself disbanded.[59]

But one local enthusiast soon renewed efforts to bring Scotland's sport to the city. During the summer of 1897, John F. Tobin played golf while vacationing in Chattanooga. When he returned to the city, he endeavored to awaken interest among other people who had seen or played the game. In November, 1898, he persuaded several other golfers to organize the Audubon Golf Club, which engaged William E. Stoddart, "a young Scotchman and one of the best known professional golf players in the country," as instructor and grounds keeper. After a three-month stay, Stoddart was to return to his place of permanent employment, the Brookline Country Club of Boston.[60]

The Audubon Golf Club placed the game on a firm basis in New Orleans. Members played in a number of tournaments on their nine-hole course in Audubon Park, and in 1900 the club formed a five-man team for intercity competition.[61] The Audubons went to Georgia in that year to play teams in Macon, Savannah, and Atlanta. After they beat Macon's Greyfield Golf Club "thirty up," a reporter noted, "The tremendous drives of the New Orleans men electrified the Maconites." [62]

[58] Harry B. Martin, *Fifty Years of American Golf* (New York, 1936), 10–14; Charles B. Macdonald, *Scotland's Gift: Golf* (New York, 1928), 78–81.

[59] *Club Life* (New Orleans), III (January 24, 1897), 2; John F. Tobin, "The Genesis of New Orleans Golf," *Dixie Golfer,* I (January, 1922), 6–7.

[60] New Orleans *Daily Picayune,* November 28, December 11, 1897; November 2, 1898; January 14, 1899; Tobin, "The Genesis of New Orleans Golf," 7–8.

[61] New Orleans *Daily Picayune,* December 23, 26, 1900.

[62] *Ibid.,* December 30, 1900; January 1, 2, 1901.

This jaunt to Georgia underscored the strides that golf had made in only a few years. In 1900 the Audubon Golf Club had approximately two hundred and fifty members, including "some of the finest players in this section." [63] Although participation was still restricted almost entirely to wealthy residents, the game had demonstrated its fascinating appeal and was steadily amassing the following that would subsequently make it such a successful middle-class pastime.

Although none of the sporting activities discussed in this chapter consistently rivaled baseball or other major sports in popularity, the existence of so many diversions indicated the growing importance that sports played in the city's leisure habits. During any season of the year, people could avail themselves of a variety of sporting pastimes in keeping with their social and economic status. Experimentation with so many sports might have been symptomatic of urban restlessness or of a desire to forget crowded streets and the pressures of work; but whatever the underlying cause, New Orleanians, like city dwellers everywhere, were laying the foundation for a fuller, more satisfying existence for residents of all classes. While baseball, horse racing, and prize fighting made spectators of countless thousands, other sports represented a conscious effort to find acceptable forms of exercise and amusement for everyone.

Some of these sports also rose to prominence because of their appeal to women. The American woman, trying to free herself from the confining aspects of Victorian society, saw participation in sports as a convenient method of vivifying her struggle for equality with men. Croquet, tennis, archery, and even golf were activities that permitted women to disport themselves as actively as men. These sports also contributed to the crusade for dress reform. When athletic females took to the playing field, they found the cumbersome and bulky clothes of the period ill suited to sporting contests. To allow greater freedom of movement, they shortened skirts and wore fewer petticoats. However, in the movement to modernize dress, as well as in the effort to stimulate mass participation in sports, nothing was to have a more profound impact than technology's child, the bicycle.

[63] *Ibid.,* December 23, 26, 1900.

Chapter X
A CITY
ON WHEELS

Nineteenth century Americans showed an ingenious ability to utilize technology in their search for sport. A thick-spun web of railroad tracks enabled participants and spectators to shuttle from city to city for special events; telegraph wires draped from coast to coast allowed fans to participate vicariously in sporting exploits hundreds of miles away; and the glow of electric lights illuminated new possibilities in mass indoor recreation. One of the best indications of technology's partnership with sport was the development of the bicycle.[1] For the athletically inclined, the bicycle offered a pleasurable type of exercise, a passport to the tonic freshness of the open countryside, a speedy racing machine, and a low-cost, convenient mode of transportation. In the age of the automobile, the bicycle's appeal seems limited and remote, but during the height of the cycling craze in the 1890s, a writer for *Munsey's Magazine* assigned this conveyance a high position on his century's honor roll: "Today, in reckoning the achievements of the nineteenth century, to such epoch making discoveries as the railroad, the steamship, the telegraph, and the telephone, we can hardly refuse to add, as the latest item on the list, the bicycle." A commentator for *Forum* echoed this judgment in observing: "When the social and economic history of the nineteenth century comes to be written, the historian cannot ignore the invention and development of the bicycle." [2]

The bicycle used in the 1890s was the result of almost a century

---

[1] For accounts of cycling in America and the evolution of the bicycle, see Arthur J. Palmer, *Riding High: The Story of the Bicycle* (New York, 1956); and Norman L. Dunham, "The Bicycle Era in American History" (Ph.D. dissertation, Harvard University, 1956).

[2] "The World Awheel," *Munsey's Magazine*, XV (May, 1896), 131; *Forum*, XX (January, 1896), 578, quoted in Mott, *A History of American Magazines, 1885–1905,* 377.

of experimentation. In 1816 Baron Karl von Drais of Germany invented a wooden velocipede shaped something like a modern bicycle without pedals. The *Draisine* enjoyed only a brief vogue, but the concept of self-propelled transportation fired the imagination of inventors, who continued to tinker with the contraption. In the 1850s two Frenchmen, Ernest Michaux and Pierre Lallement, developed a wooden velocipede with pedals attached to the hub of the front wheel. Described by the New York *Times* as "every man's horse and every man's gymnasium," the velocipede attracted ardent devotees throughout America in 1868 and 1869. Henry Ward Beecher, inclined to wax enthusiastic about anything that smacked of progress, predicted that soon "devout worshippers" would be "propelling themselves with all due gravity and decorum to church on Sunday." Interest in the machine subsided when velocipedists found their machines ill suited to outdoor rambles.[3]

Enthusiasm for self-propelled transportation revived in the 1870s when British inventors perfected the high-wheeled bicycle, known as the "ordinary," which Americans first saw at Philadelphia's Centennial Exposition in 1876. Since the front wheel had a much greater diameter than the rear one, the ordinary was difficult to mount and not entirely comfortable to ride. Nevertheless, the high-wheeler established a taste for cycling that was to be universally gratified after further technical improvements. By the mid-eighties British mechanics had developed the "Rover," a chain-driven vehicle with wheels of equal size known as the "safety." The Overman Wheel Company began to produce "Victor" safeties in the United States in 1887, and other manufacturers, including Colonel Albert A. Pope, soon followed. After the introduction of the pneumatic tire in 1889, the bicycle had practically assumed its modern form.

Safety bicycles made cycling less a sport for specialists and more a general pastime. Soon men and women of all ages were pedaling the highways of the country to the tune of "Daisy Bell," "My Love's a Cyclist," "A Merry Cyclist," and countless other period songs that reflected mass interest in the sport. In 1892 Luther H. Porter, a national authority on the wheel, announced: "Within the last five years cycling has attained the dignity of being the most popular

3 New York *Times,* September 5, 1868; "Velocipede Notes," *Scientific American,* XX (February 27, 1869), 131.

form of outdoor recreation indulged in by Americans as well as by Englishmen." Technical improvements and mass production had given the country a sporting pastime and a utilitarian means of transportation that amused millions of people until it fell victim to a new craze—the automobile.[4]

Residents of New Orleans first evinced a desire for two-wheeled transportation during the velocipede mania that swept the country in the late 1860s. Several months after the craze conquered New York, it struck the Crescent City. In February, 1869, a local paper reported that officials proposed to buy twenty-five velocipedes for each of the city's fire companies. In the following month, a few daring young men imported several of the novelties and opened a school to give indoor exhibitions and to instruct anyone interested in mastering the new art. "The school," said the *Picayune*, "is the resort of our most elegant and fashionable young men, and each evening numbers of ladies assemble to witness the performances." Following demonstrations of "fancy riding," riders and spectators devoted the evening to the safer pastime of dancing. More intrepid enthusiasts ventured outdoors with their machines. Riders frequently labored along outlying roads, and the press reported that some could "make their mile in four minutes on the Shell Road, if not in faster time." During the summer firemen featured velocipede races at their Sunday outings.[5]

Pedaling over dirt and oyster-shell roads soon disclosed the deficiencies of the velocipede. Known as the "boneshaker," this forerunner of the modern bicycle was often painful to ride and always difficult to maneuver. As velocipedists discovered the shortcomings of their toys, they abandoned the sport. Benevolent societies sponsored races as late as 1871, but these infrequent contests did not reflect widespread interest in the velocipede.[6]

Residents returned to cycling only after the introduction of the high-wheeler. Even then interest mounted slowly. In the East the ordinary attracted thousands of cyclists in the late 1870s, but New Orleanians showed no desire for cycling until 1880. In May of that

[4] *Bicycling World*, XXIV (March 4, 1892), 551; Luther H. Porter, *Wheels and Wheeling: An Indispensable Handbook for Cyclists* (Boston, 1892), vii.

[5] New Orleans *Daily Picayune*, March 20, 29, July 4, 13, August 1, 1869; "Velocipede Notes," 131.

[6] New Orleans *Daily Picayune*, June 25, 1871.

year, at about the time eastern sportsmen were organizing the League of American Wheelmen, the *Picayune* lamented the indifference of local athletes: "It is remarkable that the exercise has not found favor in New Orleans, as the various shellroads offer rare advantages for bicycle practice." [7]

Shortly after the *Picayune*'s appeal, "a few gentlemen who were considered cranks on the subject" founded the New Orleans Bicycle Club.[8] This association was an elite social group that included many professional men and merchants—all "men of affairs of relatively high standing." In a period when bicycles cost from one hundred to two hundred dollars, a club spokesman said: "The fundamental principle, that personal ownership of a wheel is a requisite for membership, acts in itself as a sort of check against indiscriminate applications for admission." And the club adopted a "rigid rule" making "two black balls sufficient cause for the indefinite rejection of a candidate." [9] Toward the end of the high-wheel era, a group of independent cyclists organized the Louisiana Cycling Club, a society that became important after the introduction of safety bicycles.[10]

For several years after its founding, the New Orleans Bicycle Club sponsored only a few formal activities. Members devoted most of their riding time to individual jaunts around the city or to nearby amusement places like Milneburg. Among the more popular events sanctioned by the club were those involving visiting cyclists. In 1882 the club brought Elsa Von Blumen, the "White Fawn," to the city for a race against a trotter and a pacer. Elsa, champion female cyclist of the ordinary era, won two of three heats held at the Fair Grounds. Early in 1885 the World's Cotton Centennial and Industrial Exposition cooperated with the New Orleans club to arrange a race between John Prince, "champion bicyclist of America," and W. M. Woodside, "the Irish champion." After defeating Woodside, Prince claimed the title of world's champion.[11]

Cycling received a great boost in the mid-eighties when members

7 *Ibid.,* May 16, 1880.

8 *Ibid.,* January 11, 1892; *Bicycling World,* IV (December 2, 1881), 42.

9 *L. A. W.* [League of American Wheelmen] *Bulletin,* III (August 27, 1886), 204.

10 *Ibid.,* V (July 22, 1887), 41.

11 New Orleans *Daily Picayune,* February 20, 1882; September 20, 1884; February 12, 14, 15, March 9, 1885; *Bicycling World,* IV (March 10, 1882), 209; Palmer, *Riding High,* 182.

of the New Orleans Bicycle Club decided to join the League of American Wheelmen, which had been created in May, 1880. As stated in its constitution, the league's purposes were "to promote the general interests of bicycling, to ascertain, defend and protect the rights of wheelmen, and to encourage and facilitate touring." [12] When the New Orleans club joined its ranks, the league had more than thirty-five hundred members, representing about 10 percent of the cyclists in America. After joining the league, local cyclists showed a marked increase in dedication to their pastime. In December, 1884, E. W. Hunter and Charles Genslinger, former president of the New Orleans Bicycle Club, began publication of the monthly *Bicycle South*. By 1886 this paper reportedly had eighteen hundred subscribers. As the official organ of the Louisiana Division of the league, *Bicycle South* kept members abreast of national developments by publishing news about cycling in cities throughout the country. [13]

Like all league affiliates, the Louisiana Division held annual races for local championships. During the high-wheel period, members of the league (most of whom also belonged to the New Orleans Bicycle Club) sponsored three meetings to determine divisional supremacy. The Louisiana Cycling Club also participated in 1887, but its members made a poor showing against the more experienced riders of the New Orleans Bicycle Club. Cyclists practiced strenuously for these meets wherever they could find level ground—in the yards of cotton presses, on shell roads, or on the city's few asphalt streets. The lack of paved thoroughfares prompted the *Picayune* to observe in August, 1886, "It is a sad commentary on the administration of this city that the bicyclists can find no fit road upon which to have their races." In spite of the discouraging conditions under which the races were held, as many as thirty-five hundred spectators assembled for championship contests. [14]

Interest in league activities subsided suddenly in the early 1890s when southern wheelmen confronted the spectre of Negro member-

12 Quoted in Dunham, "The Bicycle Era," 203.

13 *Bicycling World*, VIII (March 7, 1884), 223; Dunham, "The Bicycle Era," 203; Karl Kron, pseud. [Lyman H. Bagg], *Ten Thousand Miles on a Bicycle* (New York 1887), 654, 670; *Bicycle South*, II (May, 1886), *passim*.

14 New Orleans *Daily Picayune*, May 4, 1885; August 27, 1886; *L. A. W. Bulletin*, V (September 30, 1887), 205.

ship. In the 1880s many members of the New Orleans Bicycle Club had opposed the club's affiliation with the league because they objected to the stringency of national regulations. Nevertheless, the number of members in the Louisiana Division had slowly mounted to a peak of about 150 in 1892.[15] However, in the summer of that year the chief consul (president) of the Louisiana Division, W. C. Grivot, sent the national organization a vigorous protest against "forcing obnoxious company upon southern wheelmen" by admitting black cyclists and threatened to dissolve the state association unless the league changed its admission policies. H. E. Raymond, chairman of the league's racing board, sent a lengthy reply fully explaining the position of the League of American Wheelmen:

While I am a thorough Northerner I can still appreciate the feelings of the southern wheelmen on the negro question, and . . . with the class distinction so arbitrary in your section, it would be most unwise for the league to accept applications of negroes for members in any of the southern states.

It is at the same time more or less unfair to ask us to cut out the negro up here, where he is not so obnoxious and does not rub up against us as frequently as he does in the south.

. . .

There is no question of our accepting the negro in preference to the white wheelmen of the south. If it should be narrowed down to a question such as that, we should undoubtedly decide that we want our southern brothers in the league in preference to the negroes of the country.

. . .

We, all of us, both north and south, have a feeling of antipathy towards the colored brother, but he is not so prominent or so likely to apply for membership in the L. A. W. in the north as he is in the south.[16]

While the league debated the Negro question, southern wheelmen began to resign from the association. By June, 1893, only fifty-four members remained in the Louisiana Division, and by November only nine belonged to the once-thriving organization. Alarmed by dwindling support in the South, the league sought to improve conditions by expelling its few black members. At a national convention in November, anti-Negro delegates fell only a few votes short of securing the two-thirds majority necessary to revise membership requirements.

15 *L. A. W. Bulletin,* V (July 22, 1887), 39; *Bicycling World,* XXIV (February 19, 1892), 468.
16 New Orleans *Daily Picayune,* August 16, 1892.

But at the next quarterly meeting, in February, 1894, the Negro-phobes successfully inserted the word "white" in the section of the constitution outlining qualifications for membership. This decision ultimately made possible the revival of the Louisiana Division in the mid-nineties.[17]

Although enthusiasm for the League of American Wheelmen waned for several years after 1890, cycling attracted scores of riders in this period. As the safety bicycle came into universal usage and as its price declined, many people who had formerly disdained the sport now manifested a sudden desire for wheels. Ordinary bicycles had discouraged participation in the sport, not only because they were difficult to mount and to ride, but also because they were regarded as physically dangerous. As one doctor said, "We have pressure where pressure should never be made, . . . aggravated by the jolting motion, causing a series of rapid concussions." Opposition to cycling on these grounds gradually evaporated, but local cyclists occasionally complained about "old fat-heads who . . . prate about bow legs and crook-spines." And as late as 1895 the *Picayune* cited a "medical man" as its authority in observing: "Now that bicycle riding has become so universal it is feared that the result of the craze will be a race of hunchbacks." Despite such dire predictions, cycling continued to fascinate people of both sexes and all ages.[18]

The growing appeal of cycling was reflected in a flurry of activity among local enthusiasts. Novices emulated veteran riders and formed several new clubs to encourage racing, pleasure riding, and social gatherings.[19] In 1891 Bert Spring established a cycling school for men and women to teach riding and to sponsor tours around the city. Reporting one of Spring's excursions, the *Picayune* said: "Soda water and chewing gum was the menu of a feast after the ride." [20] By far the most popular activities were the races sponsored by the older clubs. Both the New Orleans Bicycle Club and the Louisiana Cycling Club arranged a number of races for prizes donated by mem-

17 *Ibid.*, June 12, November 29, 1893; February 21, 1894.

18 Robert P. Scott, *Cycling Art, Energy, and Locomotion: A Series of Remarks on the Development of Bicycles, Tricycles and Man-Motor Carriages* (Philadelphia, 1889), 96, quoted in Dunham, "The Bicycle Era," 403; New Orleans *Daily Picayune*, June 21, 1891; April 23, 1895.

19 New Orleans *Daily Picayune*, June 15, 1890; January 7, 9, April 26, June 22, 1891.

20 *Ibid.*, June 22, 1891.

bers.[21] A few New Orleanians also ventured to other cities for cycling events in the 1880s and 1890s, but cyclists did not display as much interest in intercity competition as athletes in other sports.[22]

Clubs often encouraged tours to various watering places and other retreats in the vicinity of the city. During the high-wheel era, riders usually journeyed only as far as the lakefront resorts, but as they mounted safety bicycles, they pedaled longer distances. In 1888 a local rider reported: "Club runs to the sugar plantations above and below the city are all the go now, and many a pleasant Sunday has been spent among the immense fields of sugar cane and in the sugar houses of the hospitable planters." Bicycle associations also began to sponsor expeditions to Gulf cities such as Mobile and Biloxi. On one such excursion in June, 1891, three New Orleanians were lost for two days with only corn bread, fat meat, and creek water to sustain them until they returned to civilization.[23]

Cycling beyond the confines of the city occasionally presented more serious problems. Nonparticipants throughout the country complained that bicycles frightened livestock, cluttered the roads, and endangered the lives of pedestrians. City councils and state legislatures listened attentively to grievances and often passed laws to drive bicycles from public thoroughfares.[24] Local riders encountered a great deal of hostility, but in 1887, Harry Hodgson, chief consul of the league's Louisiana Division, reported: "There is a better feeling now towards wheelmen than ever before," for citizens "who formerly regarded the wheel as a toy, or child's sport, . . . have begun to realize that the wheel as practical mode of travelling is a fixed fact." City officials, said Hodgson, gave cyclists "a fair and impartial show" when they clashed with the ubiquitous "Road Hog." The state legislature recognized cycling's status in 1890 by awarding riders "the same rights upon the public highways of this state as are prescribed by law in the cases of persons using carriages drawn by horses." The

21 *Bicycling World,* XVIII (March 29, 1889), 388, 391; New Orleans *Daily Picayune,* August 3, 1891.

22 New Orleans *Daily Picayune,* April 26, May 25, 1886; September 29, 1891; August 10, 1896; *L. A. W. Bulletin,* III (November 19, 1886), 511; *Bicycling World,* XVIII (November 16, 1888), 40.

23 *Bicycling World,* XVIII (November 2, 1888), 8; *L. A. W. Bulletin,* III (August 27, 1886), 204; New Orleans *Daily Picayune,* June 2, August 16, 23, 1891.

24 Dunham, "The Bicycle Era," 241–74.

city council in the mid-nineties adopted a code of traffic regulations
for bicycle riders requiring wheelmen to carry lanterns after dark,
to keep one hand on the handle bars at all times, to stay on the right
side of the street, to avoid riding on sidewalks, and to go no more
than ten miles per hour in town.[25]

Statutes alone could not entirely solve the problems that confronted cyclists. Although city and state officials accorded riders full
legal rights, private citizens continued to make riding a difficult and
sometimes dangerous pastime. "The bicycling population is up in
arms against two very disagreeable forms of men who ought to be
put down with all possible speed," the *Picayune* announced in July of
1891. "The first and worst is known as the 'road hog,' a class of
drivers who are unwilling to give a wheelman sufficient room to pass
them on a public thoroughfare." The second type of offender was the
person who acted maliciously by attacking cyclists or by setting dogs
loose on them. In August, 1891, while local riders were riding in Mississippi, Charles Cox of Biloxi "attempted to bite off the finger" of
one of the excursionists. Cox was convicted of assault, a decision the
Picayune believed would serve as an object lesson to the "few inhos-
pitable residents still in Biloxi." [26]

For many cyclists the social aspects of club membership were as
attractive as participation in the sport. In 1889 the New Orleans
Bicycle Club constructed a spacious clubhouse on the corner of Pry-
tania and Valence streets. Equipped with bowling alleys and a large
lawn for croquet and tennis, it was described as "the nicest and
coziest house they have ever had." Members of both the founding club
and the Louisiana Cycling Club held "stag smokers" as well as social
gatherings for both sexes. When Colonel Albert A. Pope came to New
Orleans in December, 1890, all cyclists pooled their efforts to enter-
tain the "Father of the American Bicycle." [27]

Although cycling seemed to be progressing from a young man's
fad to a universal mania, enthusiasm suddenly waned in the autumn
of 1892. As one resident explained, New Orleans had as many cyclists
as any city of comparable size, but "riders seem to be contented to

25 *L. A. W. Bulletin,* V (September 2, 1887), 133; New Orleans *Daily Picayune,* June 16, 1890; June 24, 1896.

26 New Orleans *Daily Picayune,* July 18, August 23, 1891.

27 *Bicycling World,* XVIII (March 1, 1889), 292; XIX (May 17, 1889), 63;
New Orleans *Daily Picayune,* May 4, 5, December 25, 1890.

pedal them to and from their place of business. Such a thing as getting up a race meet . . . is seldom thought of." Another resident strenuously denied this report, but the decline of cycling news in the local press and the collapse of many bicycle clubs told a graphic story. In March of the following year, the *Picayune* lamented, "The sport has almost ceased to exist in this city." [28]

Cycling interest continued at low ebb for two years. Wheel owners used their conveyances almost exclusively for necessary transportation, taking part in few races or pleasure excursions. But in 1895 a cycling revival occurred, inspired by a surging interest throughout the country and by a handful of local enthusiasts who formed the Crescent Wheelmen to infuse new life into the pastime by sponsoring races.[29] The *Picayune* marveled at the "sudden craze for wheels" as hundreds of residents, both male and female, organized new cycling clubs and reactivated older ones.[30]

Interest in cycling surpassed anything the city had witnessed before. Clubs of the 1880s and early 1890s had been fortunate to attract a hundred members; the new associations admitted as many as seven hundred riders. As cycling enthusiasm grew, William E. Meyers and G. Abbott Waterman began publication of the *Southern Cyclist*, a periodical issued weekly "in the interest of the Sport and Trade." Surprised by the sudden preoccupation with two-wheeled vehicles, a writer for the *Picayune* noted in September, 1896: "Within a little year the bicycle, from a modest institution in the community, has become one of the powers of progress. It has become a factor for pleasure as well as business and is here to stay." [31]

During the next few years, it appeared the *Picayune*'s analysis might prove correct as cycling clubs scheduled scores of races that attracted thousands of spectators. The most active of these groups was the Southern Wheelmen, a stock company capitalized at twenty thousand dollars. Charles H. Fourton initiated this club to finance construction of a race track in the city. Cyclists had complained for

---

28 *Bicycling World*, XXV (October 28, 1892), 119; XXV (November 11, 1892), 151; New Orleans *Daily Picayune*, March 29, May 20, 21, 28, 1893.

29 New Orleans *Daily Picayune*, October 24, 1894; April 10, 1895.

30 *Ibid.*, July 7, 1895. For the organization of clubs, see *ibid.*, May 13, 18, June 2, 14, October 13, 1895; May 28, August 31, Setember 1, 21, 27, 1896.

31 *Southern Cyclist*, II (February 12, 1896), 2; New Orleans *Daily Picayune*, September 1, 1896.

years about the poor roads available for racing, and the Southern Wheelmen proposed to remedy the situation by building a cement oval. In October, 1895, members opened their track at the corner of Carrollton Avenue and Common Street (later Tulane Avenue).[32]

For the remainder of the decade, this cement track was the site of the city's major races. Local cyclists competed there frequently, sometimes drawing more than a thousand onlookers. Track managers also induced professional and amateur riders from other cities to come South. In December, 1895, Peter J. Berlo, a touring professional, raced in the city and set three world records, thus proving "the local race course was the fastest in the union." In the following year, a group of promoters persuaded the League of American Wheelman to hold one of its meets in the city. The league was then sanctioning a series of professional and amateur races from coast to coast, and New Orleans became one stop on the circuit in June of 1896. Two of the traveling professionals, Otto Ziegler and Arthur Gardiner, once again demonstrated the advantages of the local track by setting world records.[33]

Relations with the league had not always been so amicable. Since its formation in 1880, the national association had gradually assumed the right to regulate all races in which members participated. League supervision was usually regarded as a valuable asset because contests sanctioned by the association permitted "nothing that smacks of the race track or professionalism, and each event [is] won on true merit and grit."[34] But the Southern Wheelmen objected to the league's definition of amateurism. Until 1894 the league defined an amateur in accordance with the credo of the gentleman player as a person "who has never engaged in, nor assisted in, nor taught cycling, nor any recognized athletic exercise for money, or other remuneration, nor knowingly competed with or against a professional for a prize of any description."[35] While this rule remained in force, league members found it easy to guard against professionalism. "Of all athletic

<hr>

[32] New Orleans *Daily Picayune*, June 2, 14, October 17, 18, 1895.

[33] *Ibid.*, October 18, 26, December 14, 1895; June 14, 1896.

[34] *Ibid.*, June 8, 1890.

[35] *Bicycling World,* XVIII (February 22, 1889), 279. An earlier rule, promulgated in 1889, defined an amateur in approximately the same terms, but members considered the rule vague. *Ibid.*, I (October 2, 1880), 399; IV (March 10, 1882), 207.

sports," the *Picayune* once declared, "bicycle racing is the purest." [36]

But in spite of amateur vigilance, professionalism gradually crept into the sport. In the 1880s "amateurs" competed for valuable prizes and were often paid by manufacturers to ride specified makes of bicycles. In 1886 the league ruled that all riders who received fees from manufacturers were professionals, but this pronouncement did not prevent cyclists from making secret arrangements and thereby preserving their amateur status. As the situation worsened in the 1890s, the league attempted to bring order out of chaos by creating two classes of amateurs. Class A included genuine amateurs who raced only for pleasure; class B consisted of riders who were paid by bicycle companies but were not professionals since they did not receive cash prizes in competition.[37]

Complaints about this classification system precipitated a serious clash between the league and the Southern Wheelmen. When the local club began to sponsor races in 1895, it scheduled contests for both Class A and Class B amateurs. Local riders competed in Class A races until August, 1895, when the league classified two members of the Southern Wheelmen as Class B amateurs, thus compelling them to ride against men who received salaries from manufacturers. The club objected to this decision and threatened to ignore league regulations. But after the Southern Wheelmen opened the cement track in October, they returned to league control in order to attract cyclists racing on the League of American Wheelmen tour. Further difficulty was averted when the national association abolished the dual classification and returned to the policy of designating racers as either amateurs or professionals.[38]

Shortly after the amateur-professional problem was laid to rest, cyclists encountered another objectionable feature of league control. In July, 1896, the association suspended eight local men for racing on Sunday, a violation of league rules. Sunday recreation had of course been a feature of the city's social life for more than a century; when the league, which was dominated by eastern members who had yet to shed their puritanical notions about Sunday amusements, re-

---

[36] New Orleans *Daily Picayune*, June 8, 1890. For an example of the enforcement of these rules, see *ibid.*, September 15, 30, 1889.

[37] Dunham, "The Bicycle Era," 346–82, 457.

[38] New Orleans *Daily Picayune*, August 11, October 26, 1895; *Southern Cyclist*, II (February 12, 1896), 14.

fused to allow local option on the question, New Orleans clubs ceased to follow national rules. Managers of the concrete track continued to sanction Sunday races, and in May of the next year several wheelmen formed the Southern Cyclists' Association to control racing in the city. The new association soon extended its influence beyond New Orleans by admitting clubs from adjacent states. European wheel associations expressed sympathy for the cause of Sunday racing, and in January, 1898, the *Picayune* reported that the German Cycling Association had recognized the southern club "as a contemporary cycling government." Faced with similar rebellions throughout the country, the league gradually relinquished control of racing. In 1900 the association voted to devote its full attention to the campaign for good roads.[39]

While racing cyclists struggled with league rules, the majority of riders who participated in the sport in the mid-nineties amused themselves with pleasure riding and social gatherings. Members of the New Louisiana Jockey Club founded the Country Club, an exclusive society that frequently went on "bicycle runs." In August, 1896, another group of cyclists formed the Sunday Riding League, a club "devoted solely to Sunday riding and recreation." The Louisiana Road Club sponsored numerous excursions to Bay St. Louis, Abita Springs, Baton Rouge, and other towns in Louisiana and Mississippi. This organization also arranged dances and other evening amusements. On one occasion members decided to attend a football game between Tennessee and the Southern Athletic Club *en masse*. Charles H. Fenner, president of the road club, advised the cyclists to have their "vocal organs in trim to Root for our boys." [40]

As scores of riders pedaled city streets and country roads, complaints about the condition of public thoroughfares inevitably developed. Local cyclists had displayed some interest in the national movement to improve the country's highways in the 1880s. The Louisiana Division of the League of American Wheelmen maintained a standing committee on Roads and Road Improvements, and all riders

[39] New Orleans *Daily Picayune,* July 22, October 25, 1896; May 18, 1897; January 23, February 13, 1898; Dunham, "The Bicycle Era," 459–60.

[40] *The Picayune's Guide to New Orleans* (3d ed.; New Orleans, 1897), 39; New Orleans *Daily Picayune,* August 31, October 19, 1896; Louisiania Road Club Broadsides, 1889–98, Kuntz Collection (Special Collections, Tulane University Library), *passim.* The quotation is from the broadside dated December 25, 1897.

supported attempts to pass drainage and paving taxes. But neither city nor state officials followed a systematic program of road betterment. Thus, when the cycling craze reached its zenith in the midnineties, riders once again attacked the problem. The Louisiana Road Club was formed in June, 1896, expressly "for the purpose of improving the roads of this state." When the Louisiana Division of the national association was reactivated, members devoted much of their attention to the crusade for paved streets. In August, for example, Harry Hodgson distributed three hundred aprons for horses which bore the inscription, "I Want Good Roads." By September the Louisiana Division had recruited more than two hundred members who, said Hodgson, "have begun to understand that nothing of importance can be secured without organization." Although it would be a gross exaggeration to maintain that cycilsts singlehandedly brought about macadamized streets and highways, they nevertheless launched a campaign that quite literally paved the way for the automobile.[41]

During its heyday cycling had a far-reaching impact on American life. Like many popular pastimes, the sport had its detractors as well as its advocates. Carriage makers and horse traders complained that the sale of bicycles ruined their businesses; and ministers, alarmed by declining church attendance, warned that Sunday riders were pedaling straight to perdition. But even the staunchest critic could not fail to perceive some of the benefits derived from cycling.

Economically, cycling gave the country a booming industry. If the carriage trade suffered the loss of thousands of dollars in trade, bicycle manufacturers more than compensated for this reduction by selling equipment that cost buyers millions of dollars. At its height the manufacturing of bicycles reportedly represented an investment of a hundred million dollars. The *Picayune*, in a summary of the cycle industry, estimated in 1895 that Americans spent fifty million dollars each year for bicycles and related equipment: "Besides making millionaires of the manufacturers, this sum supports an industry which gives employment to thousands of bread-winners." [42]

41 *L. A. W. Bulletin*, V (July 29, 1887), 59; *Bicycling World*, XIX (May 17, 1889), 63; New Orleans *Daily Picayune*, June 28, August 12, 14, September 19, 1896. See also Philip P. Mason, "The League of American Wheelman and the Good-Roads Movement, 1880–1905" (Ph.D. dissertation, University of Michigan, 1957).

42 New Orleans *Daily Picayune*, August 4, 1895; Betts, "The Technological Revolution and the Rise of Sport, 1850–1900," 251.

In New Orleans, retail outlets for bicycles were among the first businesses to exploit fully the demand for sporting wares. Before the rise of cycling, agents for billiard, baseball, and aquatic equipment had found the sale of sporting goods a lucrative enterprise, but these dealers fell far short of the net sales registered by firms supplying the middle class with a new device for travel and pleasure. By the mid-nineties the city had more than a dozen dealers acting as agents for national manufacturing companies. At the peak of the bicycle craze, the *Southern Cyclist* reported that residents had purchased five thousand bicycles in a three-month period, and "there would be twice as many sold if the agent received any assistance from the manufacturer" in the form of advertising.[43]

Manufacturers advertised only in national periodicals, such as *Bicycling World*, but local agents hawked their products extensively in newspapers, trade journals, and club magazines. Hodgin's Riding Academy on St. Charles Avenue offered bicycles for both sexes—the Napoleon for men and the Josephine for women. The Jackson Cycle Company, agent for Stern's Bicycles, told prospective clients: "The only way to do it is to do it on a Stern's." This company also offered a bicycle with yellow rims on the wheels, and advertisements clearly indicated that the company was courting female riders: "Golden Tresses, Girls so Neat; Yellow Rims on Wheels that Beat." [44]

Agents often utilized promotional gimmicks to gain support for their wheeels. H. D. Folsom Arms Company offered new bicycles "at cut prices." Another dealer advertised a three-hundred-dollar prize for the rider who registered the most mileage on a Rambler bicycle between April 1 and December 1, 1896, and two hundred dollars for the most miles ridden on any type of bicycle with Gormully and Jeffery pneumatic tires. In February, 1896, all agents in the city cooperated to sponsor a cycle show at Washington Artillery Hall. With exhibits illuminated by electric lights, salesmen showed residents the latest in bicycling equipment, including ball-bearing shoes guaranteed to make pedaling easier. Automobile dealers today know few

43 *Southern Cyclist*, II (February 12, 1896), 2.

44 *Ibid.*, III (July 14, 1896), 2; *Official Programme of the Southern Athletic Club, Spring Games, at Athletic Park, Saturday, May 2nd, 1896, 3 P. M.* (New Orleans, 1896), n.p. Hereafter cited as *Spring Games, 1896.*

sales tricks that had not been developed by bicycle companies in the late nineteenth century.[45]

Dealers derived most of their income from the sale of bicycles, but many businessmen also relied heavily on the sale of related goods and services. Most agents advertised lamps, bells, and other gadgets for safety-conscious riders. Folsom Arms Company sold all the "latest Bicycle Novelties," such as women's skirt holders and ladies' stocking leggings—"The Latest Parisian Novelty." Dry-goods merchant Leon Godchaux found it profitable to act as the official tailor for the Louisiana Division of the League of American Wheelmen, because all members bought special uniforms. Edward G. Stoddard, an agent for Pope Manufacturing Company, made money by renting bicycles to those unwilling or unable to buy machines. He was also, according to his advertisements, the "only repair man with factory experience in the City." While it is impossible to give a detailed accounting of the importance of the cycling industry in New Orleans, the proliferation of dealers and the variety of bicycles and related equipment available indicate that the city's economy profited substantially from the growing appeal of wheeling.[46]

Socially, cycling also exerted a tremendous influence. In a period when many sports made spectators of the masses, bicycle riding encouraged universal participation. Sedentary businessmen and bored juveniles found cycling an attractive pastime offering both exercise and recreation. The best indication of the social impact of the sport was its appeal to women. Like croquet, tennis, archery, and golf, cycling was a sport in which women could participate as actively as men. Few women ventured to the lofty perch of a high wheeler, but with the introduction of safety wheels and the drop frame, the bicycle attracted droves of skirted riders. Conservative elements at first questioned the propriety of a woman on wheels, but this opposition faded as people recognized the salubrious effects of cycling. "The bicycle," asserted one free spirit, "is one of the few out-of-door sports open to

[45] *Official Programme of the Southern Athletic Club, Spring Games, Saturday, May 4th, 1895, 3 P. M.* (New Orleans, 1895), 14, hereinafter cited as *Spring Games, 1895; Spring Games, 1896,* n.p.; *Southern Cyclist,* II (February 12, 1896), 2–3.

[46] *Bicycle South,* III (May, 1886), 13, 15; *Spring Games, 1896,* n.p.; *Spring Games, 1895,* 6.

the average woman by reason of its convenience, comparative inexpensiveness, and pleasure." On the open road astride her wheels, the athletic female soon became the symbol of emancipated womanhood. Mrs. Reginald de Koven wrote in *Cosmopolitan* in 1895: "To men, rich and poor, the bicycle is an unmixed blessing; but to woman it is deliverance, revolution, salvation. It is well nigh impossible to overestimate . . . its influence in the matters of dress and social reform." [47]

Women in New Orleans turned to cycling soon after the invention of the drop-frame safety. "The ladies' safety is commencing to loom up," a correspondent told the editor of *Bicycling World* in 1889. "Two months ago there wasn't a rider, now there are three. . . . They are all delighted, too, with their wheels, though that mount does worry 'em considerably." Easily shocked residents blanched as southern belles embraced what many prudent citizens regarded as an essentially unladylike sport, but a local girl who frequently rode devised a formula to ward off adverse comments: "Sit straight, ride slowly, have the saddle high enough, use short cranks, never, never chew gum, conduct yourself altogether in a ladylike manner and sensible people will not shake their heads in disapproval when you ride." When the bicycle craze gripped the city in the mid-nineties, the *Picayune* reported that "hundreds of women" could be seen riding daily. Girls from Newcomb College joined the movement, and those who did not own bicycles said they intended to "torment their papas to death until they had one." Many teachers rode bicycles to school to save carfare. Ida Barrow, who taught at Girls' High School, declared: "I don't think anything is so beneficial to a woman's health and nerves as a long spin in the open air." Another female cyclist simply stated that women were "better and happier for the wheel." [48]

Male riders accepted female cyclists reluctantly at first, but as they discovered the pleasures of mixed cycling parties, their reservations vanished. In the early 1890s, the New Orleans Bicycle and Louisiana Cycling clubs sponsored "ladies' nights" at their meeting

---

[47] Mary Taylor Bissell, "Athletics for City Girls," *Popular Science Monthly,* XLVI (December, 1894), 149; *Cosmopolitan Magazine,* XIX (August, 1895), 386, quoted in Mott, *A History of American Magazines, 1885–1905,* 378.

[48] *Bicycling World,* XIX (July 5, 1889), 269: New Orleans *Daily Picayune,* August 9, 1891; October 7, September 21, October 7, 1895. Quotations in the order cited.

halls "to reward the ladies for the great interest they have taken in the club." [49] The New Orleans Bicycle Club even considered the formation of a "ladies' auxiliary to assimilate with the organization." [50] When the cycling fad reached its peak in 1895 and 1896, both the Southern Wheelmen and the Crescent City Cycling Club agreed to admit ladies to full membership, a feature of these associations which the *Picayune* described as "especially adroit." The Crescent City Club had two undeniably sound reasons for opening membership to both sexes. Members first conceded "that man had never created anything great without the assistance of his natural helpmate in life" and then added that "if it be desirous that a club should be made known to the world there was no advertising medium in the world to rival the tongue that forever wags." [51] Those ladies who failed to secure a place in one of the predominantly male clubs could join the Olympic Cycling Club, a group composed exclusively of women.[52]

Besides giving women an opportunity to participate in sports, the bicycle mania aided in the reform of women's dress. As women everywhere fell prey to the wheel, it became obvious that fashion changes were in order; the bulky skirts so long favored by the American woman were palpably ill suited to cycling. When women began to abandon trailing skirts and tightly corseted waists, the bicycle was recognized as the catalyst of change. Said a writer for *Puck* in 1892: "The bicycle makers have accomplished more for dress reform in two years than the preachers of that cult have accomplished since clothes began to be the fashion. Today, thanks to the bicycle, there is every prospect that woman will soon be able to dress sensibly, comfortably, and modestly, all at the same time." [53] Thus the bicycle, which at first attracted women because it symbolized their desire for freedom, assisted in the struggle; the bicycle's appeal to women was both a reflection of, and a stimulus to, the cause of female emancipation.

Like their counterparts in other cities, female cyclists in New Orleans found bulky skirts an acute problem. In 1891 the *Picayune* reported: "Ladies are puzzling their brains to know what to wear

49 New Orleans *Daily Picayune,* November 13, 1891.

50 *Ibid.,* January 11, 1892. 51 *Ibid.,* July 7, 1895; August 25, 1896.

52 Ibid., December 4, 1896.

53 *Puck,* XXXVII (August 7, 1895), 391, quoted in Mott, *A History of American Magazines, 1885–1905,* 359.

on a wheel. . . . If any lady can suggest a becoming and suitable costume for the southern wheelwoman, she will confer a great favor upon many of her sex who ride the wheel, and also many more who are very anxious to ride, but find the question of skirts a burden to manage." Although conservative elements scorned the bloomers adopted by girls in the East, local women soon capitulated. By the mid-nineties numerous female cyclists were to be seen wearing bloomers, divided skirts, or other garments that resembled men's pants. The discriminating woman at first covered herself with a cloak because "she looks queer in her divided skirt or knicks," but as the novelty wore off, false modesty also disappeared. By 1897 the *Picayune*, which at first opposed what it regarded as immodest clothing, conceded that the style made famous by Amelia Bloomer in the 1850s had at last gained public acceptance. In its fashion column of February 27, the paper included a pattern for bloomers accompanied by the observation that "if bloomers are to be, then this pattern is certainly preferable to immodishly scant ones." [54]

In spite of cycling's importance to society in the 1890s, the sport's appeal had declined noticeably by century's end. As the electric streetcar came into wide usage and the automobile made its appearance, the bicycle era drew to a close. By the 1920s the League of American Wheelmen had collapsed, cycle racing had all but disappeared, and riding had become a source of amusement primarily for young boys. Although the craze was short lived, cycling accustomed people to individual transportation and a higher degree of mobility than they had ever known. As an agent of social change, this middle-class pastime occupied an important position in the history of the late nineteenth century.

[54] New Orleans *Daily Picayune,* July 18, 1891; September 10, 1894; February 27, 1897.

Chapter XI
THE DAY OF THE
ATHLETIC CLUB

The commercialization and professionalization of sports in the nineteenth century attracted thousands of participants and spectators and helped to meet the cities' need for recreation, but these developments also drove many athletes from the playing field. Players from the upper classes surrendered sport after sport to professionals and "amateurs" who participated for money. Clinging tenaciously to the credo of the gentleman sportsman, which they had imported from England before the Civil War, they refused to play for financial rewards or to court spectators for profit. This code, which the English traveler James F. Muirhead expressed succinctly in the 1890s, emphasized participation in sports for the pure love of play: "Sport, to be sport, must jealously shun all attempts to make it a business; the more there is of the spirit of professionalism in any game or athletic exercise, the less it deserves to be called a sport. A sport in the true sense of the word must be practised for fun or glory, not for dollars and cents; and the desire to win must be very strictly subordinated to the sense of honour and fair play." [1]

America's sporting elite adhered fairly rigidly to the idea that participating for money deprived a player of both his amateur status and his claim to gentlemanliness, and in the process robbed athletic contests of their sporting nature. They placed a greater emphasis on winning than did English sportsmen, but on both sides of the Atlantic, Anglo-Saxon gentlemen played sports solely for pleasure. Walter Camp, who spent the better part of his life spreading the gospel of the gentleman amateur, spoke for these people when he decreed: "A gentleman never competes for money, directly or indirectly. Make no

[1] James F. Muirhead, *The Land of Contrasts: A Briton's View of His American Kin* (Boston, 1898), 107.

mistake about this. No matter how winding the road may be that eventually brings the sovereign into the pocket, it is the price of what should be dearer to you than anything else,—your honor." When the honorable athlete competes, Camp continued, "he plays as a gentleman, and not as a professional; he plays for victory, not for money; and whatever bruises he may have in his flesh, his heart is right, and he can look you in the eye as a gentleman should." [2] Because this concept dictated that simon-pure amateurs resist when professionals or shady amateurs invaded sports, gentlemen players founded several organizations, such as the National Association of Base Ball Players (1858), the National Association of Amateur Oarsmen (1872), the League of American Wheelmen (1880), the United States Lawn Tennis Association (1881), and the United States Golf Association (1894), to prevent or to eliminate what they regarded as the stench of professionalism by restricting competition to amateurs. They sometimes fought a losing campaign, as the collapse of the National Association of Base Ball Players indicated, but they consistently resisted the pressures that produced the commercialization and professionalization of many sports after 1865.

In the quest to cleanse sports no agency exerted a greater influence than urban athletic clubs. These groups, which appeared throughout the country in the quarter century after the founding of the New York Athletic Club in 1866, made it possible for their middle- and upper-class members to participate in sports by defining amateurism in accordance with the code of the gentleman player. In 1879 several athletic clubs in the East organized the National Association of Amateur Athletes of America to strengthen the attack on professionalism. This federation adopted a strict definition of amateurism, patterned after that of the National Association of Amateur Oarsmen, but it failed to enforce the code to the satisfaction of members. Led by the New York Athletic Club, disgruntled clubs withdrew and in 1888 formed the Amateur Athletic Union, which became the most prominent defender of amateurism in the country until the founding of the National Collegiate Athletic Association. After 1905 the AAU and the NCAA gradually devised the complicated system of dual super-

---

[2] Walter Camp, *The Book of Foot-Ball* (New York, 1910), xiii, xx. See also Keating, "Sportsmanship as a Moral Category," 25–35.

vision that still confounds and befuddles contemporary fans and players.[3]

New Orleans' interest in athletic clubs developed at a leisurely pace for several years after the war. The impetus for such groups came in large part from a growing concern about the physical debility of urban residents, a concern that became pronounced in the sixties and seventies. The *Picayune* observed in November, 1873: "The interest taken in athletics in this country is largely on the increase. The necessity for developing our muscular organism has been fully appreciated by the public, and everywhere is to be seen the effect of this new era of physical training." [4] The *Turnvereins* had demonstrated the value of gymnastic exercises before the war, and their example inspired widespread imitation in the postbellum period. Shortly before the conclusion of hostilities, Jim Roper opened a public gymnasium on Perdido Street, which was equipped with rings, pulleys, swings, and parallel bars. "If you want to keep sick and weak, and careless of life and cross and dyspeptic, don't go to Roper's Gymnasium," the *Picayune* advised, ". . . for Jim Roper will have it all out of you before you know where you are." [5] The turners reorganized the *Turnvereins* in 1866 and resumed the annual *Volksfests*, which included exhibitions of gymnastic exercises. They united as the *Turngemeinde* (or gymnastic union) in 1869 and constructed a new gymnasium where they met for regular exercise and periodic public demonstrations.[6] In 1873 the Clerks' Benevolent Association, primarily a social organization, opened a gymnasium on St. Charles Avenue "where Clerks, Book-keepers, Lawyers, Doctors, Students, and all of sedentary pursuits may resort for healthy exercise." [7] Several years later the Young Men's Christian Association also built a gymnasium as a weapon in

[3] For a summary of the development of amateur associations, see Arnold W. Flath, "A History of Relations Between the National Collegiate Athletic Association and the Amateur Athletic Union of the United States, 1905–1963" (Ph.D. dissertation, University of Michigan, 1963).

[4] New Orleans *Daily Picayune,* November 30, 1873. See also *ibid.,* December 7, 1873.

[5] *Ibid.,* December 30, 1866; New Orleans *Times,* November 9, 1864; April 23, 1865; March 4, 1866.

[6] New Orleans *Daily Crescent,* May 7, 1866; February 23, 1869; New Orleans *Times,* May 7, 1866; New Orleans *Daily Picayune,* March 4, 5, April 8, 1871.

[7] New Orleans *Times,* November 30, 1873; New Orleans *Daily Picayune,* September 30, 1873.

its war to protect "young men cut off entirely from the tender yet powerful restraints" of home and family "in a city renowned for its gaiety, love of amusement and reckless dissipation." [8] Henry Hammerly caught the full spirit of the rage for gymnastics when he opened a "Calisthenic and Orthosomic Institute" which women patronized for the "prevention and cure of Chronic Diseases by movements" under the watchful care of Hammerly "and LADY." [9]

As the number of gymnasiums multiplied, gymnasts began to organize clubs to supervise participation. For some time the *Turnvereins* were the only associations devoted to physical training, but in 1869 several youths formed the short-lived New Orleans Gymnastic Club under the direction of Professor J. R. Judd. Three years later thirteen "young gentlemen" founded the Young Men's Gymnastic Club, which became one of the city's leading athletic associations. Throughout the 1870s this club and the *Turngemeinde* gave frequent demonstrations of gymnastic exercises in their clubhouses and at weekend outings.[10]

Although local gymnasts displayed "remarkable skill and ability," observers soon tired of the exhibitions. Reporting an event sponsored by the Young Men's Gymnastic Club in May, 1880, the *Picayune* commended the participants for popularizing gymnastics, but, swallowing its sectional pride, asked the club in the future to "diversify the programme by introducing the features which characterize the performances of athletic associations in the North, such as foot racing, pedestrianism, leaping, throwing heavy weights, etc." Athletic clubs in the East had sponsored such activities for some time, but the southern group ignored the *Picayune*'s suggestion until 1886 when the club arranged an athletic and gymnastic festival that included a number of track and field events as well as boxing, wrestling, bicycling, and gymnastic exercises. The two-day meet attracted fairly large crowds and aroused an interest in track and field athletics among the city's youth who began to form additional athletic clubs.[11]

---

[8] New Orleans *Daily Picayune,* June 2, 1878; December 14, 1879.

[9] *Ibid.,* October 14, 1875; February 4, 1877.

[10] *Ibid.,* March 21, September 14, 1869; May 17, 1870; March 4, 1871; September 4, 1876; May 28, 1877; January 11, 1885. After the turn of the century the Young Men's Gymnastic Club became the New Orleans Athletic Club, which is still in existence.

[11] *Ibid.,* September 4, 1876; May 31, 1880; January 10, May 30, 31, 1886.

For almost two decades after the Civil War, amateur athletics generated little enthusiasm outside a few cities in the Northeast, but in the 1880s the movement swept the country. One writer observed in 1887: "Athletic clubs are now springing into existence in the United States in such profusion as to baffle the effort to enumerate them. Scarce a city can be found having a population of more than 30,000 inhabitants, in which there is not at least one club of this class." Young New Orleanians were carried along by this latest athletic craze and in the last fifteen years of the nineteenth century organized more than twenty associations "for the advancement of physical culture and introduction of athletic sports." Clubs existed for people of all classes, but these groups drew mostly middle- and upper-class residents who were attracted by the strict compliance with the standards of amateurism promulgated by the National Association of Amateur Athletes of America and the Amateur Athletic Union. What these clubs prized was the young man of high social standing who was physically fit, morally sound, and athletically incorruptible—the gentleman player. Following national trends in business, a number of athletic associations secured corporate charters and required members to buy at least one share of stock, which cost as much as fifty dollars. Such a policy had a dual purpose: it facilitated the process of social winnowing since few working-class youths could afford the fee; and it permitted members to construct elaborate gymnasiums, which few people could afford to do individually.[12]

Athletic clubs also organized along racial lines. In a period when separation of the races was becoming both harsher and more rigid, white clubs resolutely closed their doors to Negroes. Black youths responded by forming their own athletic associations. These clubs, though apparently less prosperous than the white clubs, built and maintained gymnasiums for members. They also sponsored public exhibitions. However, there is no evidence that blacks and whites ever participated together at such demonstrations or in any of the city's gymnasiums, as had been the case in sports discussed in earlier chap-

12 Henry Hall (ed.), *The Tribune Book of Open-Air Sports* (New York, 1887), 332–36, quoted in Betts, "Organized Sport in Industrial America," 82–83; New Orleans *Daily Picayune*, March 21, 1887; *Charter, Constitution, and By-Laws of the Young Men's Gymnastic Club, of New Orleans, La.* (New Orleans, 1892), 5–13; *A Souvenir of the Southern Athletic Club of New Orleans, La.* (New Orleans, 1895), 13, 43.

ters. By the late 1880s, white racists in the South were becoming increasingly militant in their efforts to prevent violations of the color line; white athletic clubs, which boasted memberships drawn from the best elements in society, willingly reflected and contributed to this crusade.[13]

By far the most successful athletic associations in New Orleans were the Young Men's Gymnastic Club and the Southern Athletic Club. In the 1890s each of these societies had more than a thousand members representing the "first young men of the city." They restricted membership to the social elite by requiring recommendations from three members and by blackballing undesirable applicants. A member could be expelled, according to the by-laws of the Gymnastic Club, "for conducting [himself] in a manner unbecoming a gentleman." Although both clubs occupied high social positions, the Southern Athletic Club included a larger number of professional men and probably outranked its rival. A club pamphlet described that group's officers as men who were among "the best and most influential" people in the city.[14]

Both organizations pursued athletics zealously. They constructed elaborate gymnasiums equipped with swimming pools, exercise rooms, billiard and card parlors, and indoor running tracks. Members employed professional instructors for many activities, especially for boxing and gymnastics, and they formed teams to compete in a variety of sports, including rowing and baseball. In the 1890s these clubs also tried, with indifferent success, to introduce new sports such as association football (soccer) and ladies' basketball. Most important, they enthusiastically encouraged participation in track and field and American football.[15]

Before gentlemen's athletic clubs adopted the sport, track and

13 New Orleans *Weekly Pelican,* January 12, February 16, April 6, August 10, 24, 31, November 9, 1889.

14 *The Picayune's Guide to New Orleans* (2d ed.; New Orleans, 1896), 28; James S. Zacharie, *New Orleans Guide, with Descriptions of the Routes to New Orleans, Sights of the City Arranged Alphabetically, and Other Information Useful to Travellers; Also, Outlines of the History of Louisiana* (New Orleans, 1893), 54; *Charter . . . of the Young Men's Gymnastic Club,* 22; *Souvenir of the Southern Athletic Club,* 13.

15 *Souvenir of the Southern Athletic Club,* 21–25; Zacharie, *New Orleans Guide* (1893), 54; *The Picayune's Guide* (1896), 28; *Charter . . . of the Young Men's Gymnastic Club,* 5; New Orleans *Daily Picayune,* August 11, 1885; May 2, 1889; March 14, 1895; January 20, December 7, 1896.

field had consisted only of running and walking contests, the latter a national fad of the 1870s and early 1880s. Both types of pedestrianism were dominated by traveling professionals and local "amateurs," usually workingmen, who competed for money, thus precluding participation by respectable middle- and upper-class citizens.[16] Foot racing drew little support after the war, but matches involving professional walkers, such as the "ex-champion of the world" Dan O'Leary, occasionally attracted large crowds.[17]

But interest in pedestrianism generally remained slight until athletic clubs adopted the sport. Shortly after the Young Men's Gymnastic Club held its outdoor festival in 1886, athletic associations took control of track and field. By the 1890s several clubs, such as the Southern Athletic, the Young Men's Gymnastic, and the American Athletic clubs, were sponsoring annual track meets at either Audubon Park or the Fair Grounds. Like athletic organizations in the East, they scheduled running races, pole vaulting, broad jumping, high jumping, shot putting, and hammer throwing. The spring games of most groups seldom aroused much enthusiasm outside the club, but the meetings of the Southern Athletic and the Young Men's Gymnastic clubs soon became extremely popular social events. Women particularly flocked to these exhibitions, thus underscoring the observations of psychologists that demonstrations of power and strength play a strong role in sexual attraction. The success of these affairs, said the *Picayune*, indicated that "New Orleans, so long backward, is making rapid strides toward the front ranks of amateur athletics." Local clubs produced a number of outstanding athletes, who sometimes attended regional and national meets in other cities. In 1896, for example, E. J. Miltenberger of the Young Men's Gymnastic Club won third place in both the sixteen-pound hammer throw and the fifty-six pound weight throw at the AAU championship meet in New York.[18]

The popularity of track meets in the early 1890s encouraged the

16 New Orleans *Times*, August 18, 1873; New Orleans *Daily Picayune*, July 26, 1875; January 23, February 6, 9, 10, March 11, 1878.

17 New Orleans *Daily Picayune*, February 6, 10, 20, 1882.

18 *Ibid.*, May 18, 1890; May 24, 1891; June 6, 1892; May 29, October 26, 1893; September 16, 20, 22, 1894; August 8, September 6, 13, 1896; New York *Sun*, September 13, 1896; *Wilkes' Spirit of the Times*, CXXXII (September 19, 1896), 305. The quotation is from the New Orleans *Daily Picayune*, May 24, 1891.

leading clubs to unite for joint competition. In May, 1893, after a year's deliberation, the Southern Athletic, the Young Men's Gymnastic, and the American Athletic clubs, founded the Southern Amateur Athletic Union, an organization designed to "foster and improve amateur athletics . . . in accordance with the standards and under the rules prescribed by the Amateur Athletic Union." By October the SAAU had established a legitimate claim to its sectional title by admitting athletic clubs from Louisville, Chattanooga, Birmingham, and San Antonio. The association then became a divisional member of the AAU, the final step in purifying local athletics as practiced by gentlemen players.[19]

The SAAU's main function was to sponsor annual track and field meets. The first of these, held at the Fair Grounds on October 28, 1893, won widespread support. Railroads gave special discounts of four cents a mile to enable what the press called "foreign" teams from Louisville, Chattanooga, Birmingham, and San Antonio to attend the meet, and merchants declared a half-holiday so that their employees could witness the games. Before a crowd estimated at eight thousand, "the supremacy of New Orleans in all matters pertaining to amateur athletics in the south was put beyond the possibility of a question." In twenty events local clubs won seventeen firsts, sixteen seconds, and sixteen thirds. Later meets drew fewer visiting athletes, but the SAAU's spring games, like the meetings of individual clubs, continued throughout the 1890s.[20]

Interest in track and field competition reached its peak in May, 1898, when the AAU selected New Orleans as the site for its annual spring meet. Since the AAU's final championships were to be determined that summer in Chicago, only the New York and Birmingham athletic clubs sent teams to compete with local athletes. Nevertheless, the *Picayune* greeted the meeting as the "most important amateur athletic event of the year." The Southern Athletic Club won the team title because it had the most entries, but few spectators doubted the superiority of the New Yorkers, who won every event they entered. In New York, the *Herald* reported that members of the New York

Athletic Club were "highly elated" by the success of their representatives.[21]

Track and field lost much of its local support after the AAU meet. Athletic clubs held fewer contests, and the public generally ignored those that occurred. Moreover, the SAAU foundered on the reef of internal dissension. In December, 1898, the Young Men's Gymnastic Club, apparently disturbed by flagging attendance, suggested that the association adopt a businesslike approach to the spring meetings so that affiliated clubs would not lose money through failure to attract large crowds. Members of the Southern Athletic Club balked at this idea, however, because they believed the SAAU should be a nonprofit organization whose only purpose was to encourage sports among gentlemen, a group of pure, self-sacrificing athletes who scorned money as something for merchants to fret about. By 1900 idealism had triumphed over practicality, for when the SAAU held its annual meet, the Southern Athletic Club fielded the only team in competition. Attendance at the association's spring games declined thereafter as track and field became a pastime primarily for a few dedicated participants.[22]

While gentlemen's athletic clubs in New Orleans and elsewhere endeavored to foster an interest in amateur sports among society's upper strata, college students throughout the country further expanded the athletic movement. Students in the East first showed an interest in sports before the Civil War when they formed clubs and teams for intercollegiate competition in rowing and baseball. In the 1860s and 1870s, they added football and track and field to their list of intercollegiate activities. Prior to the formation of teams for competition with other colleges, students had engaged in few athletic contests, but intercollegiate struggles stimulated the adoption of sports as campus and intramural pastimes. By the 1870s most of the leading colleges in the East had well-established athletic programs. In other parts of the country, however, sports failed to arouse more than fleeting attention until the last quarter of the nineteenth century. The popularity of sports soared during this period for several reasons. Competitive sports enabled college students, like other ath-

21 *Ibid.*, February 27, May 14, 15, 1898; New York *Herald,* May 16, 1898; *Wilkes' Spirit of the Times,* CXXXV (May 21, 1898), 543.
22 New Orleans *Daily Picayune,* December 9, 1898; April 27, May 6, 1900.

letes, to assert their individualism in an increasingly mass society and to engage in what Theodore Roosevelt called the "strenuous life," which was itself a reaction against the inactivity and the boredom that accompanied industrialism. Changes in the nature of higher education also encouraged the development of collegiate athletics. The introduction of the elective system, emphasis on graduate education, the proliferation of medical and law schools, the beginnings of business education, and increased enrollments all tended to destroy college unity. Students everywhere lamented the decline of "college spirit" and took steps to counteract this trend. The most successful antidote to the atomization of college life was the rise of collegiate and intercollegiate sports. If collegians no longer sat in the same classes or belonged to the same clubs, they at least joined together to cheer for the varsity teams. Students in the East, after several years of informal competition, began to form associations patterned after gentlemen's athletic clubs to sponsor campus sports and intercollegiate matches in the late 1860s and early 1870s. Then in 1875 athletic clubs representing several eastern schools organized the Intercollegiate Association of Amateur Athletes of America to supervise intercollegiate contests. The ICAAAA, the first of several regional associations that foreshadowed the formation of the National Collegiate Athletic Association in 1905, maintained the same high standards of amateurism later promulgated by the National Association of Amateur Athletes of America and the Amateur Athletic Union.

The rage for competitive athletics began in the East because students there first experienced the disruptive changes in the educational process, but the movement steadily became nationwide. Small student enrollments, a money shortage that existed for many years after the war, and the difficulty of procuring qualified coaches and players retarded athletic progress in southern schools, but by the late 1880s these barriers had vanished. State and private colleges throughout the South began to give vigorous and active support to collegiate sports. Casper Whitney, a writer for *Harper's Weekly*, praised these schools in December, 1893, for undertaking a program that would undoubtedly improve the character of their students. "The Southerner is prone to 'drifting,' and by the pleasantest route," he observed. "The athletic wave that has swept over the South has put new spirit into the young men, and lessened the receipts of saloons to an appreciable degree." By century's end sporting events had become such overpowering features of student life in every section of the country that to many critics it appeared that American colleges and universities had been transformed into training schools for athletic gladiators.[23]

Collegiate sports came to New Orleans in the late eighties for reasons similar to those that encouraged athletics elsewhere. In the mid-eighties student life at Tulane University, the city's major institution of higher learning, became considerably more fragmented than it had been earlier. As the University of Louisiana, the school had been small and traditional in its approach to advanced education. But when Paul Tulane's endowment made possible the creation of Tulane University in 1884, the school changed rapidly. Tulane soon had an undergraduate division, law and medical colleges, a graduate program, and a college for women (Newcomb College, which was founded in 1887). Furthermore, Tulane President William Preston Johnston (1884–99) introduced a variation of the elective system for undergraduates, which permitted them to take any one of four prescribed courses leading to a baccalaureate degree. The establishment of a College of Technology in 1894 also contributed to the growing diversity of life at the university. As a result of these changes, students lost the sense of unity that had formerly existed. In the late eighties, they began to react to this development in much the same way as students in the East, but efforts to restore college spirit encountered obstacles peculiar to Tulane. The school had no dormitories until 1902 because most students were residents of New Orleans; out-of-town students lived in boarding houses throughout the city. Thus, the students came together only for classes. In addition Tulane was located in the downtown business district until 1894 and had no campus, a deficiency that obviously hindered the growth of an extracurriculum. Finally, President Johnston frowned on attempts to promote student solidarity. "The 'College Spirit,' so much

[23] Casper W. Whitney, "Amateur Sport," *Harper's Weekly*, XXXVII (December 23, 1893), 1239; Guy Lewis, "The Beginnings of Organized Collegiate Sport," *American Quarterly*, XXII (Summer, 1970), 222–29; Frederick Rudolph, *The American College and University: A History* (New York, 1962), 375–82; Ernest Earnest, *Academic Procession: An Informal History of the American College, 1636–1953* (Indianapolis, 1953), 206–207, 220–21.

vaunted, is too often alcoholic," he wrote in 1899. In spite of these barriers, students tried to unify members of Tulane's various classes and colleges. Social, academic, drama, and music clubs appeared in profusion in the late nineteenth century; student publications, such as the *Rat*, the *Tulane Collegian, College Spirit*, and the *Olive and Blue*, exhorted students in the 1890s to support school projects and athletic teams; and in 1898 former students who wished to perpetuate school ties formed the Alumni Association to consolidate existing alumni groups from Tulane's individual colleges. As was true elsewhere, collegiate sports were by far the most effective stimulus in arousing school spirit throughout the university.[24]

Students at Tulane began to express a desire for athletic teams in the late 1880s. This interest led first to the formation of a baseball team in the spring of 1887. Then, in the fall of that year, Erasmus Darwin Fenner and several other students laid a solid foundation for the growth of sports by organizing the Tulane Athletic Association. These students intended to encourage a variety of sports, but initially they concentrated on track and field, an indication of the influence of gentlemen's athletic clubs in the early development of collegiate sports. The association sponsored Tulane's first spring track meet in 1887 and after a year's hiatus scheduled annual track contests throughout the 1890s. Entries competed in events similar to those introduced by athletic clubs, including running, high jumping, broad jumping, and shot putting. On the occasion of the first meeting, the *Picayune* announced: "The curriculum of Tulane University is now complete. Its promising pupils have organized an athletic association, and now the development of the body keeps pace with the improvement of the mind." [25]

For several years track and field offered the major outlet for students with a fondness for organized athletic competition. The spring meet, as one student said, was "the one oasis in our athletic desert, and athletic enthusiasm rose and fell with the consummation

[24] Nuhrah, "Tulane University," 727; John P. Dyer, *Tulane: The Biography of a University* (New York, 1966), 64–90; 153–67.

[25] Nuhrah, "Tulane University," 773–74; New Orleans *Daily Picayune*, April 29, 1888. Until 1891 all students were members of the Tulane Athletic Association, but when the cost of promoting athletics mounted and threatened to stifle collegiate sports, officers of the association restricted membership to those who paid monthly dues of twenty-five cents, a nominal levy that discouraged few sports enthusiasts. *Tulane Collegian*, I (December 25, 1891), 50.

of that event." At these annual games, dozens of aspiring athletes performed for their respective classes in "showy uniforms, appropriate to the occasion, and some of them strikingly handsome." As many as six thousand spectators attended the meets, including Newcomb girls and fraternity members, who gave gold medals to the victors. The faculty, which exercised practically no control over athletics until the late 1890s, generally ignored the events, although on at least one occasion, Professor Brandt V. B. Dixon, president of Newcomb College, officiated at the spring games.[26]

Baseball also became a popular spring pastime at Tulane in the early 1890s. Students had periodically fielded teams in the late 1880s, but these nines played few games. In May, 1887, the *Picayune* reported: "The Tulane 'Varsity Nine played its first game at the New Orleans Park, against a nine from the Crescent Light Guards." The players were then idle until January of the following year when they defeated a team from Louisiana State University.[27] After this date baseball steadily gained a following at Tulane, and within a few years the school had an active intramural program. Fraternities, individual classes, and the medical and "academical" colleges organized teams and played regularly during each school year. Newcomb girls took an avid interest in these contests and formed an early version of the cheering section. A writer for the *Tulane Collegian* observed: "With our fair friends near by we are inspired to be heroes in the base ball strife; particularly when said friends are in delightful ignorance of all rules, and applaud heartily with their daintily gloved hands bad and good plays alike." Baseball competition gradually settled into an established pattern. Activity began with a series of games to determine the undergraduate championship. Following completion of the intramural season, the best players from the class and fraternity teams and from the law and medical colleges formed a university nine for intercollegiate competition.[28]

26 *Tulane Collegian,* II (December 25, 1892), 26; New Orleans *Daily Picayune,* May 11, 1890; May 1, 1892; April 30, 1893.

27 New Orleans *Daily Picayune,* May 31, 1887; January 8, 1888.

28 *Ibid.,* April 13, 1890; October 23, 1892; March 24, 1895; April 13, 1898; *Tulane Collegian,* II (December 25, 1892), 26, 28; *College Spirit* (New Orleans), May 21, 1896; February 5, 1897; *Olive and Blue* (New Orleans), March 9, 16, April 6, 1898; March 8, 15, 1899; January 18, February 22, 1900; *Club Life,* III (January 24, 1897), 3. The quotation is from the *Tulane Collegian,* II (December 25, 1892), 40.

Although track and field and baseball first aroused enthusiasm for sports at Tulane, both yielded in the mid-nineties to a game that was quickly to become synonymous with collegiate athletics—American football. Football's rise to prominence began when Rutgers and Princeton played an intercollegiate soccer match in 1869. In succeeding years other eastern colleges and athletic clubs adopted this English game or the kindred pastime rugby, which more nearly resembled American football because players were allowed to run with the ball. The inability of players to agree on a single game was largely responsible for the formation of the Intercollegiate Association of Amateur Athletes of America, which helped to standardize the game and to clarify the rules. Blending English regulations with American innovations, players produced a distinctively American sport. Theodore A. Cook, an English sports writer, described the game in the 1890s as "absolutely different" from its English ancestors. "The American love of systematisation," he said, "has—to my mind—ruined a fine game. . . . The transatlantic changes in our regulations about offside, scrimmages, and what they call 'interference,' resulted . . . in a most lamentable development." [29] American football was thus a cultural adaptation of an English game. [30]

While American football disgusted British purists, it possessed a number of features that recommended it to Americans. Like baseball, it offered opportunities for individual achievement in a setting of team competition under explicit rules. Football also added other ingredients that appealed to sportsmen in this country: ruggedness and strenuous physical activity. "Football," proclaimed an editorial in the Chicago *Graphic*, "is typical of all that is heroic in American sport." Finally, the game climbed in popularity because it meshed neatly with the most salient features of national life in the eighties and nineties. Few sports captured as vividly as this sport the busi-

[29] Theodore A. Cook, *The Sunlit Hours: A Record of Sport and Life* (New York, 1925), 189. For a similar, but less critical, view, see Muirhead, *The Land of Contrasts*, 113–14. Muirhead, "accustomed to the sparse, spontaneous, and independent applause of an English crowd," regarded as particularly strange the "concerted cheering of the students of each university, led by a regular fugleman, marking time with voice and arms."

[30] For accounts of the development of football, see Allison Danzig, *The History of American Football: Its Great Teams, Players, and Coaches* (Englewood Cliffs, 1956); Camp, *The Book of Foot-Ball;* and David Riesman and Reuel Denney, "Football in America: A Study in Culture Diffusion," *American Quarterly,* III (Winter, 1951), 309–25.

ness ethics and the martial spirit of the period. Both football coach Walter Camp and Social Darwinist William Graham Sumner inspired their students at Yale to harden themselves for the rigors of competition. Football, most observers agreed, seemed to cultivate the qualities that would empower a man to survive the ruthlessness of the business world or, as a writer for the *Saturday Evening Post* declared, "that would enable a man to lead a charge up San Juan Hill or guide the *Merrimac* into Santiago Harbor." With so many appealing characteristics, the game blanketed the country in the last quarter of the nineteenth century. Southern colleges adopted the sport later than most, but in 1893 Walter Camp could write with no fear of contradiction "that the game prevails from Atlantic to Pacific and from Canada to the Gulf." [31]

Football was much more dangerous in the 1880s and the 1890s than it is today. Mass plays like the flying wedge and flying interference exposed participants to unlimited possibilities for bodily harm, particularly since they wore little protective clothing. Players performed in canvas or leather jackets and pants with a minimum of padding, and until the introduction of leather helmets in the late 1890s they played without head coverings. Athletes compensated for their bareheadedness by letting their hair grow in order to fashion hirsute cushions, but this precaution did little to reduce serious injuries. By the early years of the twentieth century football competition had crippled, maimed, or killed so many players that observers such as President Theodore Roosevelt demanded that the game be humanized or abandoned. This ultimatum led to the formation of the National Collegiate Athletic Association, which modified the rules to lessen the chances of injury. But the reform movement, coming when it did, afforded small solace to those shaggy nineteenth century gladiators who had popularized the game.

New Orleans shared the South's lack of interest in football in its initial decades. Local athletes played Irish football and soccer before and after the Civil War, but only a few showed any inclination to try the American game before the 1890s. Elsewhere football was popu-

---

[31] Chicago *Graphic,* VII (December 3, 1892), 408, quoted in Mott, *A History of American Magazines, 1885–1905,* 375; *Saturday Evening Post,* CLXXI (November 19, 1898), 330, quoted in *ibid.;* Walter Camp, "Football: Retrospective and Prospective," *Outing,* XXIII (November, 1893), 126.

larized by colleges, but in the Crescent City an athletic club first awakened the sporting community to the excitement of gridiron competition. Several members of the Southern Athletic Club, including Thomas L. and Hugh L. Bayne, had played football at eastern colleges. After the club was firmly established, the Bayne brothers encouraged several of "the stoutest and most active" members to join them in a few impromptu games in the fall of 1889. There were only enough players to staff two five-man teams, but the club tried to entice other residents onto the field by "instructing recruits at every game." [32]

The Southern Athletic Club made few converts among the citizenry, but it discovered willing allies among local collegians who came home from eastern schools for the Christmas holidays in December, 1889. Tom Bayne conceived the idea of a New Year's Day game of football "with the object of having the young athletes of our city take hold of it, and attain the same perfection, and have the game as popular as it is in the north." [33] A reporter predicted the city's "first intercollegiate football game" would be "one of the famous society events of the season" because the "participants are all in the very tip-top niches of social life." On the day of the game, the grandstand at Sportsman's Park was "filled with the choicest flowers of New Orleans society." Employing a mixture of players from Princeton, Yale, Massachusetts Institute of Technology, Virginia, Notre Dame, and Tulane, Bayne fielded two teams which he called "Princeton" and "Yale." The *Picayune* reported that "the collisions between the teams were true tests of strength, skill and endurance." After a scoreless first half, Yale scored a touchdown and a goal after touchdown to win, 6–0. The game ended several minutes early, because in making the goal a Yale player kicked the only ball into the canal that bordered the park.[34]

For almost three years after the Yale-Princeton game, the Southern Athletic Club limited its football activity to informal intraclub contests. No effort was made to organize a permanent team until December, 1892, when the club agreed to play the Birmingham Ath-

[32] New Orleans *Daily Picayune*, December 2, 1889; Whitney, "Amateur Sport," 1239.

[33] New Orleans *Daily Picayune*, December 31, 1889.

[34] *Ibid.*, December 30, 1889; January 2, 1890; New Orleans *Times-Democrat*, January 2, 1890.

letic Club at Sportsman's Park. "The Birminghams were selected," a spokesman later asserted, "because they were of the class of athletes who compose the New Orleans organization"—gentlemen amateurs.[35] For several weeks the players, coached by Tom Bayne, practiced intensively for their first formal game. The *Picayune* cooperated with the effort to stimulate interest in the match by publishing the rules as explained by Walter Camp in one of his books about football.[36] When the game began on a cold, rainy day, "Birmingham was given the ball and the local athletes braced themselves to resist the first rush." The Alabamans formed a flying wedge "and charged without delay." The New Orleans team withstood the onslaught and when they took possession of the ball, scored a touchdown and a goal to win, 6–0. At game's end, a reporter observed: "The men were masked with mud and trembling with cold, all had proven their pluck and endurance, the teams cheered each other and then limped from the field." [37]

Interest in football rose quickly after the Southern Athletic Club's conquest of Birmingham. Players practiced regularly and began to challenge athletic clubs and colleges throughout the South. By the fall of 1893, the New Orleans group had won recognition as one of the two best teams in the lower South, the other being the University of Mississippi. On Thanksgiving Day, 1893, these teams clashed for the "championship of the South." Before approximately two thousand fans, the Southern Athletic Club defeated the Oxford players, 24–0.[38]

New Orleans' "magnificent Foot Ball team" retained its championship two years. The team willingly met all challengers during this period, but they were unable to schedule more than a few games, an indication that football had yet to capture the entire South. In 1894, for example, their only contest was a game with Sewanee, won by the Southern Athletic Club. On January 1, 1896, the undefeated New Orleanians at last met their superiors when they played the Memphis Athletic Club and lost, 10–0. The report of the game indicated that the Crescent City's gentlemen players found defeat a chafing experience: "At several junctures fighting was imminent between members

35 *Souvenir of the Southern Athletic Club,* 33.

36 New Orleans *Daily Picayune,* December 9, 11, 18, 19, 1892; January 1, 1893.

37 *Ibid.,* January 1, 1893.

38 *Ibid.,* January 26, 29, December 1, 1893; Whitney, "Amateur Sport," 1239; *Souvenir of the Southern Athletic Club,* 33.

of the opposing teams, and for the first time on a local field was there a noticeable amount of what is called 'dirty playing.' . . . A number of the home boys unfortunately lost their tempers, and said naughty things so that the ladies heard them sometimes." Following its loss to Memphis, the Southern Athletic Club claimed the championship of Louisiana, Mississippi, and Alabama, but in November, 1896, Louisiana State University sent a team to New Orleans that defeated the local team, 6–0. The "long-haired players from the State capital" thus won the title of "tri-State champions." [39]

Sportsmen from the Southern Athletic Club remained active on the football field during the remainder of the century. Playing three or four games each year against athletic clubs, college teams, and elevens from military camps, the city's oldest team performed creditably, but as athletes throughout the South adopted the sport, the club's relative superiority vanished. Football in the 1890s became primarily a college sport and, as a result, the team that introduced the game to New Orleans never regained the regional championship it had once possessed.[40] Nevertheless, the club had the satisfaction of firmly implanting football in New Orleans. Before 1900 the city had more than a half dozen teams, including those of the Young Men's Gymnastic Club, Soule Commercial College, Chenet Commercial Institute, and Jesuit College (High School).[41] Most of these elevens were less active than the Southern Athletic Club, but their existence demonstrated football's increasingly broad appeal.

By far the most enthusiastic convert to football was Tulane University. In the late 1880s, students learned the rules of the game from athletic club members who had attended colleges in the East, particularly the Bayne brothers who had played for Walter Camp at Yale. As early as 1890, several Tulane novices organized teams to play informal games at Sportsman's Park, a practice that continued until players devised a more orderly system. Following a pattern established by baseball players and track and field contestants, foot-

[39] *Souvenir of the Southern Athletic Club,* 33, 37; New Orleans *Daily Picayune,* November 20, 1894; January 2, 1896; New Orleans *Times-Democrat,* November 29, 1896.

[40] New Orleans *Daily Picayune,* December 26, 1896; January 2, November 26, December 19, 26, 1897; January 2, 30, November 13, 25, December 27, 1898; November 19, 30, 1900.

[41] *Ibid.,* December 31, 1893; January 14, December 23, 1894; November 25, 1898.

ball players in the early 1890s formed class and club teams to struggle for the intramural championship. They made no effort to field a team for intercollegiate matches until 1893. After the Southern Athletic Club's game with Birmingham in January of that year, several transfer students from schools such as Garfield University, Massachusetts Institute of Technology, and the "preparatory school of Yale College" hurriedly formed an eleven to enter the football wars. Since the team appeared late in the season, its only game was a practice match with the athletic club, but football had clearly arrived as a collegiate sport.[42]

By the mid-nineties sports had become a prominent feature of student life at Tulane University. Administrators conceded as much when the university moved from the downtown area to its present campus on St. Charles Avenue, across from Audubon Park. In support of the move, United States Senator Randall Lee Gibson, a member of the Board of Administrators, emphasized the importance of acquiring "ample space for all our buildings . . . for the accommodation of faculties and students, with homes and grounds for recreation and physical training, which has become an indispensable part of education." Tulane athletes had formerly scheduled most of their events at the Fair Grounds, but after the move the Tulane Athletic Association marked off playing fields behind the main building for track and field, baseball, and football. These fields were used for both intramural and intercollegiate competition. The Carrollton Railroad, which ran along St. Charles, financed a grandstand for two thousand people because holding games at the university instead of at the Fair Grounds would bring the company additional traffic.[43]

Interest in all sports surged upwards when Tulane began to compete regularly with other colleges. The athletic movement aroused support throughout the South in the late 1880s and early 1890s. Schools of the upper South, such as Virginia, North Carolina, Vanderbilt, and the University of the South (Sewanee), pioneered in the introduction of organized sports, but they were soon joined by schools in the lower South, such as Georgia, Georgia Tech, Alabama

42 *Ibid.*, January 10, 16, 1890; January 4, 1893; *Tulane Collegian,* II (February 25, 1893), 90; Nuhrah, "Tulane University," 787.

43 Gibson's remarks are quoted in Dyer, *Tulane,* 80. See also *College Spirit,* April 3, 17, May 1, 1895; New Orleans *Daily Picayune,* April 18, 1895.

Polytechnic Institute (now Auburn), Alabama, Mississippi, and Louisiana State University, as well as Tulane. Intercollegiate competition, long a feature of collegiate sports in the East, grew naturally out of this enthusiasm for athletics. By the end of the century, players were regularly traveling hundreds of miles to run and jump, to clout baseballs, or, in the words of one beleaguered college president, "to agitate a bag of wind." [44]

Baseball gave Tulane students their first experience with intercollegiate competition. In January, 1888, players traveled to Baton Rouge where they defeated a nine representing Louisiana State University "by better base running" in the state's first intercollegiate contest. A member of the freshman class of 1889 later recalled that students "thought in reverent terms of those heroes who journeyed all the way to Baton Rouge to play a game of baseball." After a lapse of five years, intercollegiate sports resumed when the baseball team returned to Baton Rouge and lost to Louisiana State University, 10–8. "At last athletics have taken a firm hold on the students of Tulane," the *Tulane Collegian* declared, "and for the second time in the history of the college there has been an inter-collegiate contest." [45]

Within two years of this second match with its upriver rival, the university team began to compete against other southern colleges with some frequency. The varsity in the 1890s gradually expanded its season to include games with players from the universities of Alabama, Mississippi, and Texas, as well as Louisiana State University. [46] These teams sometimes came to New Orleans, but the Tulane nine had no reservations about venturing to Tuscaloosa, Alabama, or Oxford, Mississippi. Faculty members voiced no serious objections if the team received prior authorization from university officials. Students often accompanied players on shorter journeys. Shortly before a game in Baton Rouge in 1895, the *College Spirit*, the Tulane newspaper, announced: "An excursion will be run on Saturday in order

---

44 Whitney, "Amateur Sports," 1239; Camp, "Football," 126; J. Breckinridge Robertson, "Foot Ball in the South," *Southern Magazine* (Louisville), III (January 1894), 631–45; Rudolph, *The American College and University*, 374.

45 New Orleans *Daily Picayune,* January 8, 1888; Nuhrah, "Tulane University," 779–80; *Tulane Collegian,* II (May 25, 1893), 139, 142.

46 *College Spirit,* April 10, May 29, 1895; April 26, May 24, 1897; *Olive and Blue,* April 27, May 4, 11, 25, 1898; April 19, 26, May 3, 17, 24, 31, 1899; May 3, 17, 31, 1900.

that the 'rooters' can be represented." [47] Intercollegiate baseball clearly helped to restore college unity, as the students themselves realized. When several medical students announced plans to form a team for their college in 1894, *College Spirit* quickly squelched the idea: "If the students of the medical department want to play baseball, let them come out and try for the 'Varsity team." [48]

Track and field also became an important intercollegiate sport in the 1890s. When other schools in the South began to conduct meets, Tulane athletes soon expressed a desire to attend. Five students entrained for Tuscaloosa in 1894 to participate in the University of Alabama's spring games. Competing against representatives of Alabama and Vanderbilt, the Tulane contestants won seven events. Edward Rightor of New Orleans was declared the best all-round athlete and given a gold medal to signify his supremacy. [49]

Impressed by the success of these students, the Tulane Athletic Association decided to make intercollegiate competition a regular feature of track and field athletics. Prior to the spring meet of 1895, the TAA announced that "as an incentive to competition and hard training it is intended to send the best team that can be gotten together off to some inter-collegiate games." [50] In the spring of 1895, local athletes attended meets sponsored by Vanderbilt University and Sewanee. [51] When they performed poorly, the editor of *College Spirit* castigated Vanderbilt for inviting twelve colleges to compete on a track only ten feet wide and admonished Sewanee's athletic committee for having "cheek enough to invite the leading Southern colleges to contest on a track that does not rise to the dignity of a cow path." [52] Tulane also invited other athletic associations to participate in its spring games. Louisiana State University sent a team to the city in 1897. After the Tulanians easily vanquished their rivals, the losers "showed themselves true sportsmen and accepted defeat philosophically." The Baton Rouge trackmen returned the next year, but after they again performed poorly, this intrastate rivalry was temporarily

47 *College Spirit,* May 15, 1895; Nuhrah, "Tulane University," 781.
48 *College Spirit,* December 19, 1894.
49 New Orleans *Daily Picayune,* May 3, 5, 1894.
50 *College Spirit,* April 10, 1895.
51 *Ibid.,* May 15, 22, 1895; New Orleans *Daily Picayune,* May 17, 18, 1895.
52 *College Spirit,* June 5, 1895.

discontinued. In 1899 Tulane began to participate in the annual meets of the Southern Intercollegiate Athletic Association. Two years later the SIAA held its sixth annual spring games in New Orleans. Tulane won three of twelve events and placed third in team competition to the representatives of North Carolina and Vanderbilt.[53]

Football in the meantime had begun to surpass both baseball and track in popularity. Intercollegiate battles began in the fall of 1893 when the Tulane Athletic Association scheduled games with Louisiana State University and Mississippi. Tom Bayne of the Southern Athletic Club volunteered to coach the team. The school's gladiators drilled for two months and concluded their preliminary training with a practice game against the athletic club. Like Tulane, Louisiana State University had only recently organized a varsity team, and the meeting at Sportsman's Park was the first intercollegiate football game for both universities. Fifteen hundred spectators, including several hundred from Baton Rouge, assembled on November 25 to watch the local eleven win easily, 34–0. Tulane's first season ended with the Mississippi match the following week. The *Picayune* reported that the contest, which Tulane lost, was virtually devoid of interest: "All that was visible from the benches were twenty-two long-haired and unkempt youths rushing wildly to a common center, animated by an insane desire to make pemmican of each other." [54]

Despite its brevity, the first season established football as the major intercollegiate sport at Tulane. Each year students scheduled four or five games with athletic clubs or other southern colleges, including Mississippi, Alabama, Texas, and Louisiana State University. Many of these contests occurred in New Orleans, but players traveled to Baton Rouge, Tuscaloosa, Oxford, and Austin for games. Tulane athletes pursued football unremittingly in the 1890s, but they fared poorly. In 1894 and 1899, the team lost every contest. After the first of these disastrous seasons, the *Picayune* published a cartoon

[53] *Ibid.,* February 13, 1895; *Daily College Spirit,* May 3, 1897; New Orleans *Daily Picayune,* May 1, 1898; May 20, 1900; *Olive and Blue,* May 4, 1898; May 24, 1899; John W. Bailey, *Handbook of Southern Intercollegiate and Field Athletics, 1894–1924* (A. and M. College, Miss., 1924), 38.

[54] New Orleans *Daily Picayune,* October 22, November 18, 19, 26, December 3, 1893; H. Warren Taylor, *Forty-Two Years on the Tiger Gridiron: A History of Football at the Louisiana State University, 1893–1935* (Baton Rouge, 1936), 17.

recommending that Tulane's gladiators abandon football for the more suitable diversions of marbles and croquet.[55] Before the start of the 1895 season, the Sewanee student newspaper said: "Taken all in all, foot-ball at Tulane seems to be in a pretty bad way, and Tulane's chances for the booby prize to amount to what is known as a cinch." [56] Ignoring the taunts, Tulane's supporters seized upon infrequent triumphs as cause for jubilation. When the 1895 team won the school's first victory in two years, a writer for *College Spirit* declared: "No longer will the Tulane foot-ball team and defeat be synonymous. No longer can our ungenerous rivals ridicule our team." [57] But the *College Spirit*'s effusive confidence proved unfounded, for through 1900 the university had winning seasons in only two years, 1895 and 1900. The success of this last season was attributable primarily to the efforts of Tulane President Edwin A. Alderman, who had assumed office the preceding year. He urged all qualified students to offer their services, a plea that prompted an increased number of Tulanians to report for practice. The team won all its games in 1900 without yielding a point. When the players defeated their Baton Rouge rivals for the first time since 1893, Coach H. T. Summersgill said, "The Tulane team covered itself with glory" by beating "the gridiron gods of Louisiana State University." [58] This undefeated season was the last for Tulane until 1925.

Although the team won few games, football quickly overshadowed other sports at Tulane. Support of the gridiron game became synonymous with college spirit, and the success of the varsity became a major factor in determining the university's reputation. If Tulane and other southern colleges lacked the resources to equal the academic achievements of schools in the East, they could at least attempt to match their athletic accomplishments. To some extent the present preoccupation of southern colleges with football stems from a desire to prove their equality (or even superiority) in the only way possible—through prowess of the football field. "We cannot impress too strongly upon the men the importance of the Sewanee game," the editor of *College Spirit* cautioned before a game with the University

---

55 New Orleans *Daily Picayune*, December 2, 1894.
56 Quoted in *College Spirit*, November 14, 1895.
57 *Ibid.*, November 21, 1895.
58 New Orleans *Daily Picayune*, November 18, 1900; *Olive and Blue*, October 11, 18, 1900; *Highlights of* [Tulane] *Football* (New Orleans, 1932), *passim*.

of the South in 1894. "Our future may be said to hinge on the result of the game, financially and otherwise, and this in itself should be an incentive to work hard." On the eve of the 1896 season, a writer for the same student newspaper declared: "Foot-ball has become an essential part of College life at Tulane. Without this most interesting and thrilling athletic sport we have come to feel we could not exist. The same sweeping yet true statement may be made about the manly game at any of the great progressive Colleges of America." Residents of the city had evidently reached the same conclusion, for they flocked in ever larger numbers to Tulane games. In November, 1900, Mrs. Charles E. A. Gayarré, widow of the nationally known historian and jurist, wrote to a friend that on the day of a game with Louisiana State University a meeting of her social club attracted "a rather sparse collection of the members for it seems that [football] has for our Ladies now more attraction than intellectual entertainments. It was a contest between Tulane and State University. Of course Tulane triumphed." [59]

While students explained the value of football and townspeople assembled for games, faculty members and administrators had some reservations about the latest athletic craze. When it announced the 1895 schedule of games, the student press reported that it had been arranged so that players would miss only two days of classes. "To fix it in this way has been a source of considerable trouble, but, since the faculty are opposed to having athletics interfere in any way with the college duties, it is no doubt well worth the trouble to have so arranged matters." [60] Aside from taking the unreasonable position that athletes should attend classes with some regularity, the faculty generally approved (or ignored) the rise of football. The same could not be said of William Preston Johnston. He recognized the advantages of physical exercise, but football seemed unlikely to provide beneficial or desirable training. His initial reaction to the game, which he regarded as "extremely rough and to some extent dangerous," was a

---

[59] *College Spirit,* November 16, 1894; October 1, 1896; Mrs. Charles Gayarré to Mrs. B. W. McDowell, November 23, 1900, Charles E. A. Gayarré Papers, Grace King Collection (Department of Archives and Manuscripts, Louisiana State University). Mrs. Gayarré wrote the word "baseball" rather than football, but the date of the letter clearly indicates that this wording was merely a slip of the pen.

[60] *College Spirit,* May 29, 1895.

pledge to control it or get rid of it. But he soon conceded that he was powerless to stem student interest in football. On December 9, 1895, Johnston told the Board of Administrators: "A morbid craving for excitement has come to demand alleged games not essentially different from gladiatorial contests from youths dedicated to a higher and nobler plane of existence. Football is in my mind, and it has been pursued with a reckless disregard of human suffering and even of life that justly brands it as brutalizing as at present practiced. But so great and strong is the tide of public feeling, in which parents as well as students are swept away, that I am convinced that no attempt by us to abolish it would be successful." [61]

After Johnston's death in 1899 the administration's attitude changed perceptibly. His successor, Edwin A. Alderman, actively encouraged all sports, particularly football. In contrast to Johnston's description of the game as brutalizing, Alderman once declared: "I should rather see a boy of mine on the rush line, fighting for his team, than on the sideline, smoking a cigarette." On another occasion he asked members of the Tulane Athletic Association, of which he was president, "to keep their eyes open for good men and use every effort to secure good material for our teams." Alderman said he believed in promoting athletic competition "not only because it benefits a man physically and helps to make him to have a strong mind, but also because it helps to build up a college and to promote true college spirit." [62]

Football, like baseball and track and field, contributed to the reunification of the student body. *College Spirit* consistently urged students in all departments and schools to "show that spirit and enthusiasm that is essential to the modern American college student" by supporting the football team as players or as rooters. The idea soon developed that athletes played not only for their own benefit; they also performed for the school. Thus, games assumed added importance; they ceased to be simply amusing diversions. In the midst of one dismal season, a student reporter chastised the Tulane players for their poor showing: "The reason is that the men take the matter in a playful manner. They will not train. . . . We appeal to these men's spirit of patriotism, to their spirit of enthusiasm . . . to take

---

[61] Quoted in Nuhrah, "Tulane University," 786.
[62] *Ibid.*, 809; *Olive and Blue*, October 11, 1900.

matters more seriously." If the athletes responded to the repeated exhortations, students were as quick to praise as to condemn. Reporting the practice sessions before a game with Mississippi in 1894, *College Spirit* observed: "To use a slang expression, the boys have gotten more ginger in them. They play with a snap and are especially vicious." [63]

The growing emphasis on winning not only encouraged students to take play seriously; it also facilitated the acceptance of a questionable ethic of success. Students began to cross what the historian Samuel Eliot Morison has called "the almost invisible line between clever tactics and foul play." During the Tulane-Texas game of 1896, for example, Tulane introduced a trick play, which the referee disallowed. When he returned to Austin, the captain of the Texas team complained about "Tulane trickery" and the "petty maliciousness which emanates from lack of courage and manliness." The *Olive and Blue*, which succeeded *College Spirit* as the student newspaper, replied that the "trick-play that Tulane worked so successfully on their dull-witted antagonists was perfectly legitimate, and was not allowed simply because of a technicality." When students lost sight of the difference between legal and illegal plays, when they bent rules and stretched regulations and talked about "technicalities," they merely reflected the values of their parents, who had difficulty distinguishing good from bad trusts, ethical from unethical businessmen, and honest from dishonest politicians. Football seemed, in fact, to reinforce values the players learned from their parents. Some critics recognized this feature of the game and began to question the benefit of a sport that encouraged and elevated such standards of behavior. "Men trained in such methods through all the years of school and college life may become future leaders," one observer noted, "but they will be leaders in the art of evading taxes, manipulating courts, and outwitting the law of the land." Of course, football was not alone responsible for developing such attitudes, but no other college sport inspired such an overwhelming desire for success. [64]

If players sometimes sacrificed ethics for victory, noncombatants

[63] *College Spirit,* November 16, 28, 1894.

[64] Samuel Eliot Morison, *Three Centuries of Harvard, 1636–1936* (Cambridge, Mass., 1936), 406; *Olive and Blue,* November 17, December 1, 1896; Clarence F. Birdseye, *Individual Training in Our Colleges* (New York, 1907), 162, quoted in Rudolph, *The American College and University,* 382.

proved no less dedicated to winning. The student newspaper periodically admonished collegians in all departments to attend games, and at the site of the struggle they were expected to voice loudly their support of the team. "If we are winning," said the *Olive and Blue*, "incite the 'Varsity to greater efforts; if we are losing, revive their spirits by cheers of encouragement." [65] Accounts of the games indicate that students obeyed the admonition. Newcomb girls "came in solid bodies, and their presence, and incidentally horns, cow bells and other like musical instruments, urged the players to special efforts." [66] Medical students missed classes to attend contests, and on at least one occasion they hired a brass band that marched around the field before the game.[67] In 1900 Louis Bush, captain of the 1896 team, organized the university's first "Rooter's Club" for the Louisiana State University game. Bush "was armed with a huge megaphone, through which he issued orders to the faithful." [68] Cheering thus lost whatever spontaneity it had once possessed; henceforth rooting was as synchronized as the movements of the players on the field. One formal cheer popular in the 1890s was first employed during a game with Louisiana State University in 1896:

> Rah! Rah! Siz! Boom! Ah! Rah! Rah! Tulane!
> Hippety Huss Hippety Huss!
> What in ──── is the matter with us!

A shocked reporter noted in his account of the game that the yell was "faithfully given as sung before a thousand ladies yesterday." [69]

Besides rendering vocal support to the university's representatives, students also tried to find suitable players. During one losing season, they concluded that Tulane's lack of success was attributable to the loss of well-trained players: "Each year we have to start anew and build up our athletic teams of new material, the players of the former years either leaving college by graduation or other causes, or refusing to play." [70] Enthusiastic boosters endeavored to overcome the shortage of well-versed warriors by promoting the game among high-school students. In the early 1890s, local high schools formed their own athletic associations to participate first in track and field

65 *Olive and Blue*, November 1, 1899.   66 *Ibid.*, November 30, 1898.
67 *Ibid.*, December 14, 1898; November 22, 1900.
68 New Orleans *Daily Picayune*, November 18, 1900.
69 *Ibid.*, October 25, 1896.   70 *College Spirit*, February 27, 1896.

and then in football.[71] In December, 1895, the Tulane Athletic Association organized the Interscholastic Football League, which included Dyer Academy, Boys' High School, Ferrell Academy, Jesuit College, and the Rugby School. According to the *Picayune,* Tulane students sponsored this league because "they realize that by the constant practice and training there will be in the future a large field of players to draw from." The Interscholastic Football League later became the Interscholastic Athletic Association, which promoted all athletic sports, but the primary objective remained the development of football skills.[72]

Students also attempted to improve the conditions under which players labored. After Tulane lost all its games in 1894, the student newspaper suggested construction of a special dormitory for athletes. "Under this system the men live together. They eat at a training table, and are always under the eyes of their coach. Whereas, with us our men are scattered in different quarters of the city. They do not follow a regular diet and in fact are free from any restrictions whatever." Several weeks later the paper asked students to contribute money for this purpose and also to employ a professional coach, preferably "a man fresh from this year's game, and thoroughly familiar with the new plays and schemes that have come into effect." A month later students had contributed only twenty-five dollars to improve athletics.[73]

Tulane's team played without a professional coach until the season of 1896. In its first three seasons, the university relied on part-time instructors such as Tom Bayne, who coached the team without remuneration. But before the school's fourth season, the Tulane Athletic Association, whose income came from monthly dues paid by members and from gate receipts at all college athletic events, engaged Harry W. Baum, an Illinois graduate, to instruct the athletes. Baum directed the team through a mediocre season during which Tulane won two games and lost two. As will be explained, the university had no team in 1897, and Baum left the city.[74]

For the remainder of the century, the Tulane team played without

71 New Orleans *Daily Picayune,* June 12, 1892; April 22, 1894.

72 *Ibid.,* December 5, 8, 1895; May 17, 1896; *Olive and Blue,* December 8, 1896; *Daily College Spirit,* April 12, 1897.

73 *College Spirit,* December 12, 1894; February 20, March 13, 1895.

74 *Ibid.,* October 1, 15, 1896.

a full-time professional coach. John Lombard, who played on the school's first team in 1893, coached the team in 1898 and 1899 as part of his duties as director of physical education. After his graduation from Tulane, Lombard had been sent to Harvard by President Johnston to master the elements of college athletics. He took charge of Tulane's athletic program when he returned. In addition to supervising courses in physical education, Lombard coached football and track and field. When his duties proved too extensive, however, he resigned as football coach. In 1900 Tulane employed another part-time coach, H. T. Summersgill, a medical student who guided the team for one year. Under President Alderman the university administration supported the hiring of a permanent professional coach; in the early years of the twentieth century, the school embarked on the course students had advocated through the 1890s.[75]

The rapid growth of collegiate and intercollegiate sports in the 1890s brought basic changes in the control of this activity. For several years student athletic associations maintained nearly absolute responsibility for college sports. They supervised intramural programs, scheduled intercollegiate contests, and attempted to prohibit participation by professionals or ineligible students. In the East the Intercollegiate Association of Amateur Athletes of America facilitated the task of athletic management; elsewhere student groups devised their own regulations or accepted the standards of the Amateur Athletic Union. But collegiate athletics soon became too burdensome and too complex for students to manage alone. Problems such as increased costs, covert professionalism, and the use of nonstudent players forced students to share their authority with administrators, faculty, and alumni. This shift in supervisory power ultimately placed maximum control in the hands of money-wielding alumni whose principal desire was to field a winning team. Control passed first from the students to joint faculty-student committees and then to joint committees dominated by former students. In recent years faculty members have regained control at some schools, but they have yet to assume authority for athletics at most of the major colleges in the South.

Southern academicians began to reduce student regulation of

[75] New Orleans *Daily Picayune*, December 24, 1898; December 2, 1900; Nuhrah, "Tulane University," 793–94.

sports in the mid-nineties, at a time which similar steps were taken by administrators in the East and Midwest. The use of student athletes who had played for other colleges (Tulane's football team in 1893 included Hugh L. Bayne, a law student who had played for Yale as an undergraduate), the pirating of players from other schools, and the staffing of teams with players who were not registered in school convinced college officials and faculties everywhere in the South that student supervision had failed. Professor William L. Dudley of Vanderbilt asked all southern colleges to send faculty representatives to Atlanta in 1894 to form an association to direct intercollegiate athletics. Tulane declined the invitation, but delegates from Vanderbilt, Alabama, Auburn, Georgia, Georgia Tech, Sewanee, and North Carolina assembled to organize the Southern Intercollegiate Athletic Association, forerunner of the Southeastern Conference. A Tulane student, writing in *College Spirit*, said the SIAA was "organized simply for the purification of all athletics in the South. Its real aim is to suppress professionalism." A spokesman for the association, which Tulane joined in 1895, said the SIAA was to "occupy the same relation to the college athletic associations as the American Amateur Union does to the Athletic Clubs of the country." The organization was primarily a supervisory agency. Officials made little effort to aid schools in arranging intercollegiate contests, although representatives of Tulane and Louisiana State University consistently urged them to undertake this function. The only deviation from this policy was the SIAA's track meet, held annually beginning in 1896. While the association's influence was never as great as that of the AAU, it existed on an equal footing with other regional organizations, such as the Intercollegiate Association of Amateur Athletes of America and the Intercollegiate Conference of midwestern colleges, that was later known as the "Big Ten," which was created in 1895.[76]

The SIAA took steps soon after its founding to extricate athletics from the quagmire of hypocrisy that threatened to destroy intercollegiate competition. At the first conference, charter members of

[76] *College Spirit,* January 2, April 24, 1895; New Orleans *Daily Picayune,* December 24, 1898. For sketchy accounts of the formation of the Southern Intercollegiate Athletic Association, see Bailey, *Handbook of Southern Intercollegiate Track and Field Athletics;* and Melvin H. Gruensfelder, "A History of the Origin and Development of the Southeastern Conference" (M.S. thesis, University of Illinois, 1964).

the association limited participation in college sports to five years, prohibited remuneration for athletic activities, and restricted competition to registered students and faculty members who ranked no higher than instructor. One of the most important regulations adopted at the first meeting was the so-called migratory law: "A student who has been connected with an institution where he has participated in an intercollegiate contest shall not participate in an intercollegiate contest at any other institution in this Association until he has been a student there for one collegiate year." This rule prevented what an official of the University of Florida later called the "seasonal migration of bird-like athletes," who were cajoled from campus to campus. The SIAA subsequently promulgated other restrictions as it deemed necessary. In 1897, for example, it forbade college students to compete for athletic clubs. Tulane felt this rule immediately, because its athletes had frequently participated in SAAU contests as representatives of local athletic clubs.[77]

Tulane's most serious confrontation with the SIAA occurred as a result of a football game with Louisiana State University in 1896. The Tulane coach attempted to substitute a player who was not registered in the university. When the opposing coach objected, Tulane refused to continue the match. Although leading 2–0, the New Orleanians forfeited the game, which was logged as a 6–0 victory for Louisiana State University. The editor of *College Spirit* insisted the player in question "intends to enter the law department, and will matriculate when it opens next month," but this plea was made to no avail. When the SIAA met in December, 1896, it deprived Tulane of the right to enter a football team in intercollegiate contests during the 1897 season. The university retained the privilege of participating in baseball and track and field, but football activity in 1897 was limited to intramural games. Tulane students evidently realized the necessity for the SIAA's decision. Two days after the announcement of the suspension, the *Olive and Blue* spoke in favor of the purification of college sports: "We believe that all deception, cheating, slugging, and everything unsportsmanlike, should be rooted out of col-

---

[77] Bailey, *Handbook of Southern Intercollegiate Track and Field Athletics,* 7; *Daily College Spirit,* April 20, 1897; *College Spirit,* May 14, 1896; New Orleans *Daily Picayune,* May 10, 1896. R. E. Bering, who participated in Tulane athletics in 1894, was one of the founders of the SAAU. New Orleans *Daily Picayune,* July 22, 1893.

lege athletics, that a standard of scholarship should be established, and that all who fall below that standard should be debarred from athletic games." While the SIAA was willing to deal strongly and decisively with rule violations, it seemed likely that the editor's wish would be fulfilled.[78]

Tulane's decision to accept SIAA regulations in 1895 resulted in a shift in the control of athletics from students to faculty members and ultimately to alumni. Since the association's constitution required faculty members to enforce SIAA rules, the Tulane Athletic Association surrendered its monopolistic management of sports. In the latter part of the 1890s, university officials assigned athletic responsibility to two groups: the reorganized TAA, which retained control of sporting events involving only Tulane students (intramural athletics), and the new Athletic Advisory Committee, which supervised intercollegiate competition. The TAA under this new arrangement included faculty and alumni as well as students. All active athletes were required to join the association. The Athletic Advisory Committee, created in 1897, had a prescribed membership: three professors, two representatives of the Alumni Association, and four students.[79] Although the composition of the committee placed faculty members in a minority, the thrust of the new agency was to wrest control from students. Numerical juggling in succeeding years invested the faculty with almost absolute control of intercollegiate sports, subject only to pressures from alumni. Graduates of the institution never exercised as much influence as alumni of state schools in the South, but the problem of interference has existed in varying degrees down to the present.

While Tulane students pursued a variety of sports in the 1890s, girls at Newcomb College also began to participate in athletics during this period. Throughout the country, women were placing a growing emphasis on the benefits of physical exercise. Participation in sports, as bicycling and other activities demonstrated, gave women

---

[78] New Orleans *Daily Picayune,* October 25, December 20, 21, 1896; Taylor, *Forty-Two Years,* 20; *College Spirit,* October 29, 1896; *Olive and Blue,* December 22, 1896; December 14, 21, 1897.

[79] *Daily College Spirit,* May 5, 17, 1897; *The Register of Tulane University of Louisiana, 1900–1901* (New Orleans, 1901), 68. There had been an ineffectual faculty committee on athletics since 1890, but it did not interfere with student control of sports.

an opportunity to shed the forced languor of the Victorian era and aided their crusade for emancipation. When women recognized that other, more strenuous sports could serve the same function, the athletic female, like the female cyclist, golfer, tennis player, and archer, became a symbol of the New Woman. An amateur poet observed in *Munsey's Magazine:*

> Running, jumping, and natation, navigation, ambulation—
>   So she seeks her recreation in a whirl.
> She's a highly energetic, undissuadable, magnetic,
>   Peripatetic, athletic kind of girl.

A writer for *Woman's Home Companion* found the trend gratifying and an important stage in the liberation of the American woman: "A higher physical development is required by the rapid development of the sex in those pastimes and business pursuits formerly monopolized by men." [80]

Established in 1886, Newcomb made no formal provisions for the physical training of students until 1891. In that year Brandt V. B. Dixon, president of the college and a staunch supporter of sports at Tulane, employed Clara G. Baer to direct the recently created Department of Physical Education. Physical exercise for girls, although by no means a novelty, was a subject of considerable controversy in the 1890s. After announcing the opening of the new department, Dixon received numerous letters of protest from parents and physicians, "some on the ground of a supposed tendency to render young ladies coarse and unfeminine, others on account of health and other considerations." One outraged father said his daughter had sufficient exercise during the summer vacation to last through the year. Dixon's tongue-in-cheek reply quashed the parent's objection: "Permit me to ask the following: I presume that she has a hearty Thanksgiving dinner; is she excluded from later dinners on that account?" [81]

Clara Baer faced several tasks when she came to Newcomb. In addition to teaching gymnastics to girls who often regarded exercise as unladylike, she had to overcome the hostility of parents and slice through the Victorian modesty that required her students to wear

[80] *Munsey's Magazine,* XV (August, 1896), 633, quoted in Mott, *History of American Magazines, 1885–1905,* 370; *Woman's Home Companion,* XXIV (January, 1897), 15, quoted in *ibid.,* 370–71.

[81] Brandt V. B. Dixon, *A Brief History of H. Sophie Newcomb Memorial College, 1887–1919: A Personal Reminiscence* (New Orleans, 1928), 75.

bulky costumes that virtually precluded free exercise. Under Miss Baer's direction, however, Newcomb pioneered in the development of physical education for women in the South. A graduate of the Boston Normal School of Gymnastics, she stressed the Swedish system of exercise, which the Boston school had introduced to this country in 1889. She also used the Delsarte method of "Aesthetical gymnastics," which was designed to train students in the art of pantomime. To carry out her program she purchased a complete set of gymnastic equipment.[82]

After opposition to physical training declined, Miss Baer expanded Newcomb's program by teaching basketball. Invented in 1891 by Dr. James Naismith of the Springfield, Massachusetts, YMCA, basketball was introduced to New Orleans by Miss Baer. Other groups such as the local YMCA played the game later in the 1890s, but before the turn of the century no athletes participated more actively than the Newcomb girls. When Miss Baer first exposed her students to the game, parents protested that basketball was too dangerous for girls. The instructor thereupon revised the rules to eliminate mass rushes for the ball. The new rules called for seven players on each team—two goal-keepers, two guards, two ends, and a center. Each player was assigned a section on the court, which she could not leave. Baskets were placed at diagonal corners of the playing surface rather than at the ends of the floor as under Naismith's rules. Miss Baer wrote to Naismith asking permission to publish these rules, but he said she had created a new game and advised her to give it a name of her own selection. She called it "basquette" and published the rules in 1895.[83]

An immediate benefit of basquette was a change in the costumes worn by the young female athletes. When they first began to play the game, Newcomb's proper southern girls wore full-length dresses. Miss Baer soon required them to don bloomers with the stipulation that they were to be worn only in the gymnasium, which was closed to men. Shortly after the turn of the century, Brandt V. B. Dixon later recalled that "basket-ball and other games were played in the open with

[82] *Tulane University of Louisiana* (New Orleans, 1896), 99; Nuhrah, "Tulane University," 694–95; Dorothy A. Ainsworth, *The History of Physical Education in College for Women* (New York, 1930), 8–9.

[83] Nuhrah, "Tulane University," 695–96; *College Spirit,* March 7, 1895; New Orleans *Daily Picayune,* November 5, 1898; March 8, November 21, 1900.

use of appropriate costume; since which time false modesty has practically disappeared." This variation of basketball thus joined cycling and other sports in stimulating reform of women's apparel in New Orleans.[84]

In the mid-nineties Miss Baer invented still another game—"Newcomb." Similar to volleyball, Newcomb could be played indoors or outdoors on a court that varied in length according to the number of players on each team. A rope was stretched across the play area, and the object of the game was to throw or to bat a "large, inflated spherical ball" across the rope so that the opposing team could not return it. Any number of players from six to twelve constituted a team. Although designed as a game for both men and women, Newcomb attracted few male players.[85]

Basquette never became well-known outside New Orleans, but Newcomb spread throughout the United States. Until the 1920s it vied with volleyball in popularity. Ethel Perrin, supervisor of physical education for the Detroit public schools, said, "It is a highly organized team game and carries with it all of the character building lessons that such games imply." Such was the appeal of the game that Albert G. Spalding and Company manufactured Newcomb equipment, and in 1914 the company published the rules of the game in its "Red Cover" series of athletic handbooks.[86]

As a result of Clara Baer's crusade to introduce women to healthy exercise, Newcomb's department of physical education was as up-todate as any in the country. Girls participated in several sports, including tennis, gymnastics, basquette, Newcomb, and cycling. In addition to developing a broad program of physical education, Miss Baer quite likely converted other southern schools to the value of regular exercise for female students. Between 1895 and 1914, she published five books explaining the rules of games for women and emphasizing the value of proper physical activity.[87] Clara Baer also ex-

[84] Dixon, *Brief History of . . . Newcomb College,* 76; Nuhrah, "Tulane University," 695.

[85] Clara G. Baer, *"Newcomb": A Game for the Gymnasium and Playground* (New York, 1914), 5–11.

[86] *Ibid.,* 21 and *passim.*

[87] In addition to the book of rules for Newcomb, Clara Baer wrote *Newcomb College Basket Ball Guide for Women* (New Orleans, 1895); *Newcomb: A Game for the Gymnasium and Playground* (New Orleans, 1895); *Progressive Lessons in Physical Education: An Introductory Course of Instruction for the Home and*

erted some national influence, although not as much as in the South. The invention of Newcomb gave the country a game that amused thousands of girls for a quarter century. While the game of basquette won few followers outside New Orleans, it evidently influenced the development of women's basketball. When the representatives of several women's colleges met in June, 1899, to consider special basketball regulations for female players, they consulted all rules then in use, including the game of basquette. Moreover the rules for women's basketball adopted in 1899 bore many striking similarities to basquette.[88]

Newcomb's acceptance of sports and physical education for women completed the panorama of collegiate and intercollegiate sports. New sports such as swimming and basketball for men were introduced after the turn of the century, but the commitment to this phase of university life was made in the 1890s. During this decade Tulane students annually fielded teams for intercollegiate competition and intramural games in three sports—football, track and field, and baseball. In a fourth sport—tennis—Tulane and Newcomb students organized clubs that sponsored annual tournaments for members; but except for one match with Mississippi in 1895, the men showed little enthusiasm for intercollegiate competition until after 1900. In still another athletic pastime—golf—a few students formed a club called the "Golflings" in 1899 to awaken interest in a game that was just beginning to win a following in New Orleans.[89] Students had been mainly responsible for the rise of college sports, but the administration willingly accepted athletics. As Tulane entered a new century, an official publication of the school succinctly summed up the progress of collegiate sports: "Believing that athletics, when properly conducted, are of great benefit to the student engaged in them, and of proper interest to all right-thinking persons, encouragement is given to this side of college life, to all the extent possible with the means at command." [90]

School, Based on the Swedish System (New Orleans, 1905); and Basket Ball Rules for Women and Girls (New Orleans, 1911).

88 Senda Berenson (ed.), Line Basket Ball or Basket Ball for Women as Adopted by the Conference on Physical Training Held in June, 1899, at Springfield, Mass. (New York, 1901), passim, especially 5–6; Nuhrah, "Tulane University," 696.

89 Tulane Jambalaya (New Orleans, 1899), 165.

90 The Register of Tulane University of Louisana, 1900–1901 (New Orleans, 1901), 67–68.

Much of the credit for the development of collegiate sports was due the city's athletic clubs. When these organizations began to stress athletics in the 1880s and 1890s, they aroused an interest among literally thousands of middle- and upper-class citizens. Most important, they spurred students to develop sports as part of college life. By 1900 it was evident that the day of the gentlemen's athletic club was fading, but as these organizations limped into the twentieth century, it was also apparent that in providing a model for university students they had contributed to the addition of a new dimension to local sporting life.

Chapter XII
FINAL
INSPECTION

In the summer of 1880, General James A. Garfield, Republican candidate for President of the United States, spoke at a Chautauqua gathering in New York State. Society, Garfield said, faced "two great problems. . . . The first one is a very old struggle. It is, how shall we get any leisure? That is the problem of every hammer stroke, of every blow that labor has struck since the foundation of the world." The second "fight of civilization," the candidate continued, is "what shall we do with our leisure when we get it?" [1] In the period from 1850 to 1900, New Orleanians, in common with urbanites throughout the country, answered Garfield's query in a variety of ways. With a perpetually expanding amount of free time at their disposal, people in all ranks of society sought recreation in amusements of every description, including theaters, dances, concerts, opera, Mardi Gras, gambling parlors, and saloons. None of these pastimes claimed a larger following than did organized sports. Thousands of residents joined athletic teams and clubs, hundreds traveled to other cities for competition, and tens of thousands attended athletic events as spectators.

Organized sports grew up with the city. In the course of the nineteenth century, New Orleans advanced from a fairly small city of seven thousand people in 1803 to a metropolis of nearly three hundred thousand by 1900. As rural migrants, foreign emigrants, people from small towns and cities, businessmen from the North and South moved into the city, they experienced pressures and problems unknown in rural areas or in the relatively small cities of an earlier period. The nineteenth century, particularly after 1830, was a time of adjustment for urban Americans, a time in which they learned to live in large cities and to cope with the intricacies of their cramped

[1] Quoted in Jesse L. Hurlbut, *The Story of Chatauqua* (New York, 1921), 183–84.

environment. New Orleans by the turn of the century had better streets, improved municipal lighting, an urban transit system that enabled people to live farther from their places of employment, professional police and fire departments, better sewerage and drainage facilities, and up-to-date public health practices that had virtually eliminated yellow fever as a menace to health. The city still faced a number of problems, such as political corruption, but the changes that had occurred indicated that people were adapting well to urban conditions. Residents had also created a full complement of organized sports that constituted the city's major source of recreation. Until the 1840s horse racing was the only well-established sporting activity, but by 1900 the city featured a wide selection of highly organized and commercialized sports. Participants and spectators could easily enjoy a number of sporting amusements at all seasons of the year.

Sports rose to prominence in New Orleans and other cities in large part because they provided a social safety valve that allowed great masses of people to blow off steam in a relatively harmless way. The density of urban populations; the insistence that everyone engage in what was constantly described as the ruthless struggle for survival; the disappointment and disillusionment felt by the vast majority of people who could never hope to rise to the top rungs of the economic and social ladders; the necessity for synchronizing and regimenting the movements of people in such crowded environments; and the friction caused by the presence of thousands upon thousands of people with diverse social, economic, ethnic, and racial backgrounds produced a potentially explosive situation. Sports, along with other forms of recreation, offered an outlet for the tensions of urban life. By the closing years of the nineteenth century, city dwellers exhibited an almost insatiable craving for sports, particularly activities that emphasized speed, ruggedness, and even violence, such as cycling, football, and prize fighting. "It seems to be the weakness of the American people to take nearly everything in 'crazes,'" said a writer for the *Nation*. "There was the greenback craze, and the silver craze, and the granger craze, and the cholera craze, and now there is the athletic craze." In 1887 *Puck* magazine published a phrenological chart of Uncle Sam's head entitled "Sports on the Brain" showing a cranium covered with bumps representing approximately two dozen sports. Several years later a writer for the *Review of Reviews* insisted: "There is an open-air movement almost revolutionary in its degree. . . . People are bicycling, yachting, running, jumping, fishing, hunting, playing baseball, tennis and golf, to an extent which is new in this generation." In an essay entitled "The Reorientation of American Culture in the 1890's," historian John Higham has suggested that this boom in sports which seized Americans at the *fin de siècle*, together with nature cults, a "quickening of popular music," and an "unsettling of the condition of women," represented an attempt "to break out of the frustrations, the routine, and the sheer dullness of an urban-industrial culture." Higham exaggerates the docility with which Americans submitted to what he calls "the gathering restrictions of a highly industrialized society" before 1890, but there can be little doubt that at the turn of the century, sports occupied an unprecedented role in the daily lives of thousands of Americans. This leisure activity helped to restore a sense of individualism to people living in a mass society; it offered a degree of excitement and an element of chance to people whose lives were otherwise very orderly and highly routinized; and it directed competitive impulses into relatively harmless, if not always productive, channels.[2]

Sports also achieved importance because they captured better than many other organized amusements some of the most salient characteristics of the late nineteenth century. The rise of sports occurred in a period of rapid industrialization and at a time when the martial spirit was becoming pronounced in American life. Sports, industry, and the military possess several features in common, a fact that has made sports in the eyes of many people in both the nineteenth and twentieth centuries an ideal training ground for a career in business or in the armed forces. All three activities stress teamwork, obedience to command, careful planning, precise execution, contempt for softness, and a strong desire for victory at almost any cost. The close relationship between the attitudes fostered by sports and those encouraged by the military, which Thorstein Veblen noted more than half a century ago, probably played a key role in ensuring the popularity of sports among southerners, whose martial spirit was clearly

[2] "The Athletic Craze," *Nation*, LVII (December 7, 1893), 423; *Puck*, XXI (June 1, 1887), 236; *Review of Reviews*, XIV (July, 1896), 58, quoted in Mott, *A History of American Magazines, 1885–1905*, 369; John Higham, "The Reorientation of American Culture in the 1890's," in John Weiss (ed.), *The Origins of Modern Consciousness* (Detroit, 1965), 27.

evident throughout the nineteenth century. They supplied a dispro-
portionate share of the army's officers and men before 1900, and they
readily accepted those sports that developed or bolstered abilities
prized by the military, such as marksmanship, horsemanship, team
play, and physical courage. Thus, sports for individuals, such as
rifle shooting, trapshooting, and hunting, won a wide following in the
South, while football in 1900 was already in the process of becoming
what William James might well have regarded as "the moral equivalent of war" between southern colleges and universities. The nearly
symbiotic connection between sports and military activity has continued down to our own day when the commandants of the country's
service academies and base commanders around the world insist that
American servicemen engage actively in sports, presumably on the
grounds that if Lord Wellington's victory at Waterloo was won on
the playing fields of Eton, then Vietnam (or some other war) can be
won on the plains at West Point or in the mountains of Colorado.[3]

As sports assumed such a conspicuous place in the field of recreation, this leisure-time activity profoundly influenced and was in turn
deeply affected by the society that embraced it. Few areas of life
escaped sport's pervasive impact in the latter half of the nineteenth
century, and in turn the increasingly urban-technological environment in which sports developed thoroughly transformed many of the
activity's most prominent characteristics.

One of the more obvious results of the rise of sports was its effect
on journalism. As late as the middle decades of the last century,
American newspapers devoted little space to sporting intelligence,
but by 1900 the modern sports page had emerged, a graphic demon-
stration of sport's rising importance. The confluence of many factors
promoted this development. Sporting journals such as the *Spirit of
the Times, Wilkes' Spirit of the Times*, the New York *Clipper*, and
the *National Police Gazette* disclosed a vast audience of enthusiasts
eager for sporting news. As these journals prospered, eminent newspaper editors like the Bennetts, Richard Henry Dana, Joseph Pul-
itzer, and William Randolph Hearst, sensing an opportunity to boost

---

[3] Bil Gilbert, "Play Ball, You ?!¢%&#/S!," *Sports Illustrated,* XXIX (November 25, 1968), 74–88; Rudolph, *The American College and University,* 381. The
phrase "moral equivalent of war" is borrowed from William James's essay of the
same title, which is found in James, *Memories and Studies* (New York, 1912),
267–96.

circulation, expanded the amount of space assigned to sports in daily papers. They also placed all sporting news on the same page, created special departments under the supervision of sports editors, and employed athletic heroes to write articles for their papers. When Hearst created the separate sports section in the late nineties, this feature of the American newspaper had virtually assumed its modern form.[4]

In New Orleans the sports page evolved gradually in the last thirty years of the nineteenth century. Until the early 1870s, editors of the city's newspapers devoted few columns to sporting news. Horse racing and yachting received due attention, but other sporting events often passed unnoticed. Fans who desired an intimate knowledge of local activities found broader coverage in national journals such as the *Spirit of the Times.* When interest in sports increased, however, Crescent City newspapers reflected public enthusiasm by doubling and tripling the space allotted to local occurrences. As the use of the telegraph became general, readers also found a greater amount of national sporting news in their daily papers. The *Times* observed as early as 1870: "Latterly all descriptions of sports, from baseball to billiards, from the P. R. [prize ring] to ratting, have assumed a pseudo-national character. . . . The fame of a champion horse, or a successful pugilist, is no longer confined to the locality in which it was achieved, but is heralded and echoed through every section of the country." [5]

When the amount of sporting news multiplied, editors drifted easily into the practice of placing sports stories on the same page. In the 1850s and 1860s, sporting intelligence appeared throughout the newspaper—in columns of general local news, in the section for telegraphic dispatches, and as fillers between news stories. But in the 1870s, the city's daily papers frequently grouped all sports stories, both national and local, in one or two columns under headings such as "Sporting Notes," "Sporting News," and "Sporting Intelligence." [6]

[4] For accounts of the development of the sports page, see Betts, "Sporting Journalism in Nineteenth-Century America," 39–56; William H. Nugent, "The Sports Section," *American Mercury,* XVI (March, 1929), 329–38; and Frank Luther Mott, *American Journalism: A History of Newspapers in the United States Through 250 Years* (New York, 1941), 297–98, 443, 578–79.

[5] New Orleans *Times,* April 2, 1870.

[6] *Ibid.,* March 9, 16, 23, July 27, 1873; New Orleans *Daily Picayune,* October 11, 18, 25, November 1, 1874; New Orleans *Bulletin,* August 6, 1876.

For several years these special columns usually appeared only on Sundays and Mondays (or Tuesdays, if the paper had no Monday edition), because on these days the newspapers contained the most sporting news, but in the mid-eighties the city's two leading dailies, the *Picayune* and the *Times-Democrat*, made the sports columns a daily feature, and in the nineties two other papers, the *Daily States* and the *Item*, adopted the same practice. All four dailies steadily awarded additional space to sports, until by 1900 each paper carried a full page or more of sporting news on almost every day of the week. Editors willingly surrendered more space to sports because they realized that the sports section sold newspapers—an idea that was clearly in evidence when the *Item* courted patrons by advertising the "Cleanest, Newsiest, Best Written Sporting Page in the South." [7]

As newspaper editors enlarged the sports section, they also improved the quality of reporting. Sports writers in the 1890s supplemented racing reports with the inclusion of statistical charts of the previous day's results. The *Item* also issued a daily racing form to aid handicappers. Baseball news improved perceptibly after New Orleans joined the Southern League, for local dailies paid a great deal of attention to professional baseball in general and often published extensive reports of major league games. The *Picayune*'s accounts of the national game won praise from *Sporting Life*, the leading baseball journal of the 1890s. "It is a pleasure to read the baseball news in the Atlanta Constitution, Savannah News, New Orleans Picayune and, at times, in the Nashville American," the editor observed. "Of the other newspapers . . . the least said the better. They serve up daily a potpourri of indifferent news items, silly and uncalled-for roasts, and a mess of rot, rubbish and nonsense." [8] The *Picayune* also surpassed its rivals in another area that has since become a standard feature of the sports section—the sports column. In the 1890s Harry McEnerny, who joined the *Picayune* staff in the 1880s, wrote a column titled first "Bantam's Budget" and later "Mack's Mélange" that appeared regularly for several years.[9] According to John S. Kendall, who was associated with the *Picayune* in the 1890s, Mc-

7 New Orleans *Daily Item's Racing Form Chart* (January 25, 1896), 20.

8 Quoted in New Orleans *Daily Picayune,* June 7, 1893.

9 See, for examples, New Orleans *Daily Picayune,* November 12, 1893; September 30, October 7, 1894; July 19, 1896.

Enerny's articles were syndicated to newspapers throughout the South.[10]

Sport's influence on journalism was evident not only in the composition of the daily newspaper but also in the publication of weekly and monthly journals. Between 1884 and 1899 sportsmen in New Orleans issued at least seven periodicals devoted primarily to sports—*Bicycle South* (monthly, 1884–86), *Sporting South* (weekly, 1888), *Spirit of the South* (weekly, 1888–89), *Southern Cyclist* (weekly, 1895–96), *Club Life* (weekly, 1896–97), *American Clubman* (monthly, 1897), and *Southern Sportsman* (monthly, 1898–99). Collectively these publications gave fans news about cycling, baseball, boxing, athletic clubs, gun clubs, and other sporting activities. None of these journals enjoyed anything like solid financial success, but their existence reflected the public's hunger for sporting news. When they collapsed, it was not because they failed to feed that appetite, but because newspapers in the 1880s and 1890s showed a greater willingness to satisfy it on a day-to-day basis.

While sports wrought a change in local journalism, they also had an influence on the local economy. Between 1850 and 1900, the manufacture and sale of sporting equipment became, if not a major business, at least a lucrative one for those who exploited it. The first businessmen to take advantage of the market for sporting goods were those who sold billiard and tenpin equipment and hunting and fishing supplies. Billiard and bowling necessities could be obtained from a number of agents who represented companies like Phelan and Collender and Brunswick.[11] When the billiard craze hit the city in the late 1860s, "Messrs Willett and Co." built a "first class factory" to manufacture Phelan and Collender's "standard American billiard tables." [12] For outdoor paraphernalia New Orleans had several stores which, like Sportsman's Depot on Canal Street, sold "every article needed by the fisherman or hunter, from the fly-hook to a harpoon, from a pop-gun to a bear rifle." [13]

As sports grew in popularity, merchants who catered to billiard

10 John S. Kendall, "Journalism in New Orleans Fifty Years Ago," *Louisiana Historical Quarterly,* XXXIV (January, 1951), 11–12.

11 New Orleans *Daily Picayune,* December 18, 1860; January 9, 1861; New Orleans *Times,* July 6, 1866.

12 New Orleans *Daily Picayune,* November 7, 1869.

13 New Orleans *Bulletin,* June 2, 1874.

and tenpin players and outdoorsmen lost their monopoly on the sporting goods business. Bicycle dealers, as explained in an earlier chapter, were the first to reap large profits from the rise of sports, but they were by no means the only businessmen to sense an expanding market. In the late 1880s and 1890s, the city had at least four companies—Hunter and Genslinger, A. Runkel, Folsom Arms Company, and F. F. Hansell and Brothers—that specialized in the sale of sporting equipment.[14] Several shops also offered sporting supplies as part of their general selection of merchandise. To cite two examples, the Boston Shoe Store had a "Special Department for Tennis, Bicycle, Gymnasium and Yachting SHOES," and a newsstand on Commercial Place advertised: "All the Leading Sporting and Dramatic Papers on Sale." [15]

In addition to profiting from the demand for equipment, clever businessmen discovered that the popularity of sports could sell other goods and services. Makers of "HOME RUN CIGARETTES," a local brand, promised that smokers who selected their product "will always be first." When athletic associations sponsored track and field meets, jewelers found a lucrative market for gold medals. Athletes who lost "that old time snap and vigor" or felt "tired and unrefreshed" could find relief in "the scientific medical treatment" available at the Louisiana Medical Institute. If sportsmen were too ill or too far from New Orleans to pay personal visits to the clinic, the institute advised: "Out-of-town patients treated successfully by mail. . . . Send for symptom blank, and a letter giving advice, etc., will be returned free." Bottlers of Dr. Tichenor's Antiseptic also came to the aid of ailing athletes with the promise that this palliative would ease bruises and strained muscles. (It was also useful in the treatment of "Colic, Botts & Footevil in Horses and Mules.") To sell health aids, businessmen occasionally employed a technique that has since become commonplace—the hero's endorsement. The *Picayune* in 1900 published an advertisement that pictured Tommy Ryan, welter-

14 New Orleans *Daily Picayune*, June 6, 1886; *Spring Games, Southern Athletic Club, Fair Grounds, New Orleans, La., Saturday, May 23d, 1891* (New Orleans, 1891) n.p.; *First Meet: Southern Amateur Athletic Union. Under the Auspices of Southern Athletic Club, Young Men's Gymnastic Club, American Athletic Club, Pelican Cyclists* (New Orleans, 1893), n.p.

15 *A Souvenir of the Southern Athletic Club of New Orleans, La.* (New Orleans, 1895), 36; *First Meet: Southern Amateur Athletic Union*, n.p.

weight champion of the world, testifying to the virtues of Dr. M. S. McLaughlin's electric belt, a device guaranteed to "transform your weakened, pain-racked body into a paradise of health." [16]

Music in New Orleans also reflected the city's preoccupation with sporting amusements. In the post-Civil War period, local sheet-music publishers issued several songs suggesting an interest in sporting activities: August Davis' "Skating Rink March" (1871) ; Francis Navone's "St. John Rowing Club Heel and Toe Polka" (1880) ; N. Martinez' "Jockey Lancers" (1881), dedicated to Gustave A. Breaux of the New Louisiana Jockey Club; Thomas D. Harris' "L. C. C. Polka" (1891), written for the Louisiana Cycling Club; George L. O'Connell's "Progressive Y. M. G. C. March" (1895), composed in honor of Victor LeBeau and James J. Woulfe of the Young Men's Gymnastic Club; and William J. Voge's "Southern Wheelmen's March" (1896).[17] None of these songs altered the course of musical development in New Orleans, but they at least indicated the extent to which sports had become a part of the city's social life.

Sports had a more profound, if somewhat belated, effect on the improvement of the city's parks. Throughout most of the nineteenth century, officials made practically no effort to provide suitable parks where athletically inclined residents could play. In 1850 John McDonogh willed New Orleans a large tract of land some distance from the city's outskirts. Municipal authorities reserved the property for development as a park, but for years they made no improvements on the land. An English visitor who toured the city in 1868 observed: "Two miles from the city is a tract of land called the 'City Park.' It is at present undrained and uncared for. Near the entrance are some fine 'live' or evergreen oaks, and in fifty years it may be a pleasant place enough ; now it is a mere wilderness." In 1871 the city produced $800,000 to purchase a large plot of land fronting on the Mississippi River, which was designated "New City Park" to distinguish it from McDonogh's legacy. Like Old City Park, the new area remained un-

---

[16] *Spring Games, Southern Athletic Club* (1891), n.p.; *Program of the Annual Spring Games: Tulane Athletic Association, New Orleans, La., Tulane Field, Saturday, April 27th, 1895, 4:00 O'Clock* (New Orleans, 1895), n.p.; *First Meet: Southern Amateur Athletic Union*, n.p.; New Orleans *Daily Picayune*, December 9, 1900.

[17] Copies of these songs are available in the Louisiana Sheet Music Collection, Tulane University Library.

developed for several years, because the council appropriated no money for improvements. As late as 1880 the Census Bureau noted that the park "in its present condition is simply an expanse of inclosed common." [18]

While the city acquired hundreds of acres of unimproved land, sports enthusiasts resorted to other sites to practice their athletic skills. They visited open spaces in the sparsely populated parts of the city, such as the Delachaise and *raquette* grounds; played in public squares, like Lafayette and Congo (now Beauregard) squares; or patronized privately owned recreational facilities, including Oakland Park, just south of Metairie Cemetery, and the Fair Grounds. All of these retreats had disadvantages. The restricted size of the public squares rendered them unsuitable for ball games; privately owned parks were sometimes closed to the public, as the Fair Grounds was after it became a racecourse; and inadequately planned urban expansion swallowed up some playing fields, notably the Delachaise grounds on Louisiana Avenue and the *raquette* field, the area now bounded by Galvez, St. Bernard, North Claiborne, and Elysian Fields. As middle-income and upper-income residents, aided by transportation improvements such as horse cars and later electric trolleys, moved farther and farther from the center of town, the older sections of the city became nearly devoid of areas suitable for outdoor recreation. The decay of what is now termed the inner city clearly began in the late nineteenth century as more affluent residents retreated to the suburbs.

In the 1880s, when the exodus from the central city was already well under way, municipal authorities at last began to develop public parks. Belatedly joining a nationwide park movement that began in the 1850s when New York employed Frederick Law Olmsted to create Central Park, New Orleans in the last two decades of the nineteenth century took steps to rescue both Old City Park and New City Park from their natural states. The city spent freely to improve the riverfront tract, which contained some 250 acres, as the site of the World's Cotton Centennial and Industrial Exposition in 1884–1885. When the exposition ended, the area, renamed in honor of John James

---

[18] Greville J. Chester, *Transatlantic Sketches in the West Indies, South America, Canada, and the United States* (London, 1869), 207; Waring (comp.), *Report on the Social Statistics of Cities*, XIX, 275.

Audubon, became Audubon Park, a public facility that provided sports-minded residents with a running track, a baseball diamond, and, later, tennis courts and a golf course. After another decade of inactivity, the city in 1896 appropriated money for the improvement of Old City Park. Scant progress had been made by 1900, but in the early years of the twentieth century, work continued until City Park ultimately ranked as one of the leading parks in America.[19] Although local interest in sports was not alone responsible for encouraging city officials to improve parks, the amount of municipal land devoted to playing fields, golf courses, and tennis courts indicated that sports loomed large as a factor in the campaign for publicly owned outdoor recreational areas. Unfortunately, recognition of the need for parks came too late to prevent the inundation of open areas near the center of the city. Residents in the main part of town, who often ranked among the city's poorest people, had little choice but to play in the streets or to take a fairly long trolley ride to one of the city's parks. For Negro citizens the problem was further complicated by the practice of allowing only whites to use the parks on Sundays; black pleasure-seekers had access to local parks on weekdays, which were, of course, working days for most people.[20]

One of the more far-reaching effects of the rise of sports was its influence on women. Throughout most of the nineteenth century they were not expected to participate in sports. Bolder women occasionally ventured onto the athletic field, but references to these daring lasses implied that they were beyond the pale of respectable society. Notwithstanding such conservative opinions, opposition to feminine participation diminished in the postbellum period with the introduction of a number of new sports. Proper society decreed that croquet, archery, tennis, and cycling were acceptable pastimes for athletically inclined young ladies. The Southern Athletic Club also tried to interest the "feminine relatives of members" in gymnastic exercises. According to one of the association's pamphlets it was "the only club

[19] Waring (comp.), *Report on the Social Statistics of Cities*, XIX, 274–75; United States Bureau of the Census, *Eleventh Census* (1890): *Report on the Social Statistics of Cities in the United States at the Eleventh Census: 1890*, comp. John S. Billings (Washington, D.C., 1895), 35; Federal Writers' Project, *New Orleans City Guide* (Boston, 1952; rev. ed. by Robert Tallent), 297–98, 320.

[20] New Orleans *Weekly Louisianian*, May 10, August 2, 1879; April 23, May 7, 14, July 23, 1881; New Orleans *Weekly Pelican*, April 9, 1887.

of any prominence in the world which unselfishly encourages the attendance of women at its gymnasium." [21] Simultaneously Newcomb College brought girls into the gymnasium and exposed them to such strenuous activities as regular exercise, basketball, and the game of Newcomb. In New Orleans and other cities, female participation in sports helped to produce the revolution in clothing styles discussed earlier in connection with cycling. Excessively low hemlines crept up, the cumbersome leg-of-mutton sleeves disappeared, and women sighed as corset strings relaxed. A writer for *Business Woman's Journal* reported in 1892: "The bathing dress, the tennis suit, the mountain costume, the gym-blouse, and the divided skirt have given a brief experience of untrammeled exercise" and increased discontent with tight waists and heavy skirts.[22] Sports, particularly cycling, thus acted as catalysts in the transformation of women's fashions.

While organized sports contributed to the liberation of the American woman, they also reduced and occasionally eradicated other barriers that separated various groups of citizens. At a time when some features of urban life, such as rapid, poorly planned growth, an increase in specialization, the division of labor, and the infusion of heterogeneous elements into the city, tended to isolate people and to destroy all sense of community, sports acted as a countervailing force. The athletic arena was a great mixing bowl that brought together people of different classes and ethnic backgrounds and gave them common interests. Upper-class residents introduced and for a time tried to monopolize a number of the city's sporting pastimes, including baseball, horse racing, cycling, roller skating, tennis, golf, and American football, but they found it impossible to restrict participation and observation to people of their own station. The pressures of urban life and the perpetual desire for new forms of recreation brought about the democratization of nearly all sports and the commercialization of several of them. Foreign-born citizens who attempted to preserve their own national games found it equally difficult to bar other residents. Thus, the German-American *Volksfest* attracted people of all ranks, including Negroes,[23] and the exercises

21 *Souvenir of the Southern Athletic Club*, 25.

22 *Business Woman's Journal*, IV (January, 1892), 38, quoted in Mott, *A History of American Magazines, 1885–1905*, 358; Ernest R. Groves, *The American Woman: The Feminine Side of a Masculine Civilization* (New York, 1944), 386.

23 New Orleans *Weekly Louisianian*, May 25, 1872.

of the turners and Irish football appealed to active youngsters, regardless of their ethnic background. Sports could not fully bridge class and ethnic divisions, but they nevertheless accelerated the trend toward full democratic participation in every phase of American life.

The most conspicuous failure of sports as a social mixer was in the area of race relations. In the latter half of the nineteenth century, Negroes in New Orleans participated actively in several sports. They swam, organized baseball and *raquette* teams, hunted and fished, roller skated, handled gamecocks in local pits, practiced sharpshooting, rode thoroughbreds at the Metairie and Fair Grounds race tracks, and fought for prizes in the twenty-four-foot ring. Black athletes usually played on a racially segregated basis, but they also vied with whites. Negro baseball players frequently competed with white athletes; Negroes rode against white jockeys; and black pugilists boxed white fighters. Until the mid-eighties participants in racially mixed contests encountered little hostility. It would be erroneous to assume that white athletes accepted black players as social equals, but that the vast majority of whites discerned no inherent threat to southern society in Negro-white competition was clearly evident.

Tolerance of interracial sports vanished in the last fifteen years of the nineteenth century. In the mid-eighties, a few white baseball players threatened to boycott white teams if they competed with blacks. In the early 1890s, local cyclists withdrew from the League of American Wheelmen because it admitted Negro members in the North. And when George Dixon annihilated his white opponent during the Olympic Club's famed Triple Event in September of 1892, the *Times-Democrat* warned that it was a "mistake to match a negro and a white man." [24] The effect of such concerted opposition was to terminate contests between Negroes and whites. Black and white baseball teams went their separate (but presumably equal) ways; Negro jockeys were gradually driven off the tracks, not only in New Orleans but throughout the country; the League of American Wheelmen responded to southern pressure by expelling black cyclists; and fight promoters refrained from matching Negroes and whites. By the turn of the century, interracial sporting events had virtually disappeared.

Rigid segregation in sports was part of a general policy of racial

[24] New Orleans *Times-Democrat*, September 8, 1892.

separation that took shape in the South during this period. Throughout the antebellum era, most white residents of Louisiana saw little
need for laws to separate the races. Segregation practices have always aimed at racial control and at convincing Negroes that they are
inferior to whites. In the rural South, slavery accomplished these objectives; it was "the supreme segregator." In antebellum southern
cities, on the other hand, slavery proved inadequate as a social regu-
lator. The conditions of urban life gave slaves and free Negroes some
degree of social freedom and sorely tested assumptions of white supremacy. Whites responded with segregation laws and practices designed to establish in the city the caste system that slavery created
on the plantation. Theaters, hospitals, hotels, restaurants, saloons,
gambling parlors, and graveyards were racially segregated either by
law or by custom.[25] This system of segregation was fairly complete,
but it did not comprise, as one student of the period has concluded,
"a code of race separation as thorough as any that developed in
Louisiana after the Civil War, including the notorious 'Jim Crow'
statutes of the 1890s." [26] Frequent violations of the antebellum color
line suggest that it lacked the harshness and the rigidity of the line
established by the Jim Crow laws of the late nineteenth and early
twentieth centuries.

The collapse of the *ancien régime* brought a new era of race relations to New Orleans. From the moment the city fell to the Federals
in 1862, Negroes engaged in a campaign for equal political and civil
rights that reached a peak during Radical Reconstruction. Black
citizens did not want social equality, according to an article published
in the *Louisianian*, a Negro newspaper. "What the colored people demand is this: They demand political and civil rights in the fullest
sense. They demand political and civil equality, and they are willing,
as all persons should be, to let the question called social equality
regulate itself." They wanted access to public facilities, said a writer
for the *Tribune*, another Negro newspaper, not because they were
unable to survive without equal rights, but for a reason of a higher
order: "It is that, under the present order of things, our *manhood is*

25 Fischer, "Racial Segregation in Ante Bellum New Orleans," 926–37. For
an excellent account of slavery in the cities, see Richard C. Wade, *Slavery in the
Cities: The South, 1820–1860* (New York, 1964).

26 Roger A. Fischer, "The Segregation Struggle in Louisiana, 1850–1890"
(Ph.D. dissertation, Tulane University, 1967), 24.

sacrificed. The broad stamp of inferiority is put upon us." Under such assaults racial barriers began to crumble. The state constitution of 1868 and the state civil rights laws of 1869 and 1873 extended full political and civil rights to Negroes, temporarily ended school segregation, and granted equal access to public accommodations; a Federal Civil Rights Act of 1875 further guaranteed the rights of black citizens. Negroes still encountered a great deal of discrimination, for theaters, saloons, hotels, and restaurants often barred them in contravention of state and national laws, but the color line was frequently breached.[27]

Democratic redeemers, who took control of the state in 1877, attempted soon after taking power to establish strict separation of the races and to place Negroes in a position of complete subordination. They restored segregation in public schools, counted Negro voters out in elections, and supported segregation policies in public facilities. They nevertheless fell short of creating a complete system of segregation. During this period Negro athletes played against whites, and mixed crowds attended sporting events and other social activities. When Charles Dudley Warner visited New Orleans in 1885 to attend the Cotton Centennial and Industrial Exposition, he was surprised that "white and colored people mingled freely, talking and looking at what was of common interest. . . . On 'Louisiana Day' in the Exposition the colored citizens took their full share of the parade and the honors. Their societies marched with the others, and the races mingled on the grounds in unconscious equality of privileges." Warner also reported seeing "a colored clergyman in his surplice seated in the chancel of the most important white Episcopal church in New Orleans, assisting in the service." And when Negro residents sponsored a Colored State Fair in November, 1887, the *Pelican*, a Negro newspaper, reported similarly that "immense crowds gathered, both white and colored, to do honor to the occasion." Negroes never achieved anything like full equality, but for years they evaded vicious attempts to drive them into political, economic, and social submission. As late as 1889, R. W. Gould could say to a meeting of the Colored Screwmen's Association that the color line formerly "had been strictly drawn, but this condition of affairs has

---

[27] New Orleans *Weekly Louisianian*, May 4, 1872; New Orleans *Tribune*, February 7, 1869; Fischer, "The Segregation Struggle," 25–99.

gradually been improved and better things are looked for by the colored race." [28]

But toward the end of the nineteenth century conditions changed abruptly. Convinced that the federal government would not interfere, racists and demagogues, aided by businessmen and the press, intensified their assault on black citizens. Some public facilities, such as theaters, had been closed to Negroes since Reconstruction, and in the late 1880s virtually all public accommodations supported and encouraged racial segregation. In July, 1889, for example, the *Pelican* reported: "The Louisville and Nashville and Mississippi Valley railroads have placed separate cars on their routes for colored people." The *Picayune* candidly explained the reason for strict separation: "There is a difference between the colored man and the white man, which neither education nor law can abrogate. . . . To sit by the negro's side at a hotel table or in a concert hall would be, in the opinion of the white people, to ignore that truth." After 1890 the legislature ratified segregation practices that had become widely prevalent in the late 1880s by passing the "separate but equal" Jim Crow laws. These state statutes were patterned to a great extent after New Orleans' antebellum municipal ordinances, but the severity and harshness of segregation policies after 1890 indicated that it was a far more rigid system than anything New Orleans or Louisiana had seen before.[29]

The cessation of Negro-white athletic contests and the segregation of crowds at sporting events, occurring as they did in the late 1880s and early 1890s, reinforce the idea that although Negroes suffered discrimination before 1890, they possessed some freedom of movement, activity, and association that they lost almost altogether after the arrival of Jim Crow. For twenty-five years after the Civil War, sports brought Negro and white athletes together in friendly

28 Charles Dudley Warner, *Studies in the South and West with Comments on Canada* (New York, 1889), 13, 15, 17; New Orleans *Weekly Pelican,* November 12, 1887; June 8, 1889.

29 New Orleans *Weekly Pelican,* July 6, 1889; New Orleans *Daily Picayune,* March 13, 1888; Fischer, "The Segregation Struggle," 161–90; Henry C. Dethloff and Robert R. Jones, "Race Relations in Louisiana, 1877–98," *Louisiana History,* IX (Fall, 1968), 301–23; Eagleson, "Some Aspects of the Social Life of the New Orleans Negro in the 1880's," 103n. The best general account of the origins of modern segregation is C. Vann Woodward, *The Strange Career of Jim Crow* (2d rev. ed.; New York, 1966).

rivalry and on occasion enabled Negroes to ascend the economic lad-
der by becoming professional jockeys or ball players. The appearance
of strict and inviolable segregation practices all but eliminated these
features of organized sports. In New Orleans, throughout the South,
and everywhere in the country interracial contests disappeared, and
professional sports no longer welcomed black players. Negro baseball players organized the Negro National League, but black athletes generally discovered that the idea of equality on the playing
field was essentially a myth. Rather than make it possible for Negroes
to overcome or to escape the problems of discrimination that they
encountered elsewhere, sports merely reflected prevailing social attitudes. In the field of race relations, then, sports provided an inadequate social safety valve. The racial integration of professional
sports since World War II has encouraged the acceptance of racial
cooperation in other areas of life, but this result ought not to obscure
the equally important fact that the owners of professional teams accepted Negro players only after the national government had begun
to assail the bastions of racism in American life. Thus, the owners
could be reasonably sure that white spectators would not boycott
games. Moreover the racial integration of athletic teams has not always proceeded harmoniously. Periodic friction on professional teams
and recent accusations of exploitation by black college athletes have
once again suggested that organized sports do not provide an un-
obstructed route to acceptance by white society.

While sports modified many characteristics of the society in which
they grew to maturity, they also were strongly influenced by one of
the most striking features of nineteenth century America—technology. An expanding railroad network facilitated the travel of athletic
teams and thoroughbred horses; the stringing of telegraph wires
across the country produced instantaneous reports of sporting events,
which in turn aided the development of the sports page; mass production techniques permitted the manufacture of standardized sporting equipment; and finally, inventions such as the electric light and
the bicycle created new trends in urban recreation. Technology was
not alone responsible for the shaping and molding of sports; but as
historian John R. Betts has written, "to ignore its influence would

result only in a more or less superficial understanding of the history of one of the prominent social institutions of modern America." [30]

In New Orleans the impact of the technological revolution was abundantly evident. Telegraph lines connected the city with the East in 1848, and during the remainder of the century this instrument of progress afforded residents broad coverage of sporting activities in distant cities. For several years after its introduction in the city, the telegraph was used sparingly for sporting news because messages were costly, but after the war the keys clicked freely to supply local fans with reports of events throughout the country. The telegraph's value was made manifest in 1870 during the steamboat race between the *Robert E. Lee* and the *Natchez*. "The people of the entire Mississippi Valley have been excited about this race as they never were before by any similar event," the *Picayune* said after the completion of the contest.[31] To satisfy the curiosity of its readers, the *Picayune* published daily telegraphic accounts of the progress of the steamers. Telegraphic reports also enhanced the value of poolrooms (betting parlors), for gamblers could easily learn the latest racing results or baseball scores from around the country. For example, in April, 1886, the *Picayune* reported that races in Mobile were exciting great interest among the city's betting men. "The Turf Exchange is thronged with visitors during the running of the race," a reporter observed. "The Western Union wire runs right into the room, and people sit down and see the race going on as the various phases of the contests are told by the wires." [32]

Another invention that altered the city's sporting habits was the electric light. With the aid of this device, many outdoor activities moved inside. In 1889 John L. Sullivan fought "seventy-five red rounds" with Jake Kilrain under a Mississippi sun that raised the temperature above a hundred degrees. Three years later Sullivan met James J. Corbett in a cooler arena illuminated by electric lights. At the turn of the century, Edison's invention had not yet been adapted to some outdoor activities, such as horse racing and baseball, which required large playing areas, but it was already evident that the in-

---

30 Betts, "The Technological Revolution and the Rise of Sport, 1850–1900," 256.

31 New Orleans *Daily Picayune,* July 6, 1870.   32 *Ibid.,* April 16, 1886.

candescent bulb had greatly expanded the working citizen's ability to participate both actively and passively in sporting events.

Technology's influence upon local sports was perhaps most apparent in the use of steamboats and railroads. In the antebellum period, both modes of transportation enabled turfmen throughout the South to ship their racing stock to the Metairie and other New Orleans courses. After the war railroads and steamers continued to serve horsemen, but they also promoted intercity competition in many other sports. From the late 1860s until the end of the century, baseball teams, billiard players, oarsmen, riflemen, and other sporting enthusiasts traveled throughout the country; and sportsmen from other cities readily invaded New Orleans. Railroads occasionally encouraged sports (and, of course, helped themselves) by offering discounts to touring athletes and by advertising special events such as the Sullivan-Corbett fight.

Intersectional competition helped to nationalize American sports. As sportsmen began to compete in distant areas, they discovered that regulations often varied markedly from city to city. Racing was the first sport to confront this difficulty, but the problem also appeared in other activities, such as baseball. To surmount this obstacle, sportsmen created national associations to adopt standard rules of competition. Initially these organizations wielded little influence, but as the participants realized the value of uniform regulations, they gained recognition as the supervisory agencies of their respective sports.

New Orleanians willingly acknowledged the authority of most of these associations. Rowers accepted the principles of the National Association of Amateur Oarsmen; cyclists, those of the League of American Wheelmen; riflemen, the regulations of the National Rifle Association; athletic clubs, the standards of the Amateur Athletic Union; and turfmen, the rules of the Jockey Club. When participants adhered to national regulations, intercity competition progressed smoothly. Local athletes entering contests throughout the South, Midwest, and East traveled with the certain knowledge that their abilities would be tested against men who trained under identical rules, and out-of-town contestants who came to New Orleans experienced no untoward difficulties after the development of national regulations.

Although sportsmen quickly disposed of the impediments posed by rule variations, another vexatious problem that resulted from increased mobility defied facile solutions. As soon as sports became a popular diversion, some athletes inevitably tried to profit from the public's desire for recreation. When professionals and spurious "amateurs" who played for money on a part-time basis invaded athletics, many genuine amateurs abandoned the field. Sometimes the integrity of sports declined: because professionals derived their income from competition, many did not hesitate to assure success by prearranging, either by giving or taking bribes, the outcome of contests. By the 1870s fraud and dishonesty had become so commonplace that a reporter for the New York *Times* sneeringly referred to "that class of crimes known as athletic sports." [33]

Eliminating the problems created by professionalism and sham amateurism became the responsibility of a number of national and regional associations formed to regulate sports and to enforce amateur codes that enabled gentlemen players from the middle and upper classes to participate. Their definitions of amateurism were basically undemocratic, for they prohibited all forms of athletic profit taking, including money earned by teaching sports, and thus discriminated against less affluent athletes who could ill afford to devote much time to sports without receiving some financial rewards. From the latter half of the nineteenth century to the present, American amateur standards have penalized players from the working and lower middle classes who lack the resources to express an altruistic dedication to sports for the pure love of agnostic competition. In this way, as in the area of race relations, sports have failed again to fulfill their promises of equality on the athletic field. But sportsmen from the upper ranks of society cared little about the alleged democratizing influence of sports; their interest lay in the purification of athletics by whatever means they thought necessary. Their associations were fairly successful in eliminating professionalism from sports over which they exercised uncontested control, but many sports, including baseball, boxing, and billiards, lacked national or even regional amateur associations. Amateur groups also created problems because they failed to agree on standard definitions of amateurism and professionalism, a failure that has troubled sports down to the present.

[33] Quoted in Adams, *Grandfather Stories*, 213.

Although the amateur-professional question has increased in complexity in the twentieth century, the outlines of this dilemma were distinctly visible before 1900. In New Orleans concepts of amateurism and professionalism varied markedly in different sports. Rowers, cyclists, college athletes, and members of athletic clubs acceded to the amateur codes of their national and regional associations, but because these agencies applied their definitions differently, rules of competition were not identical. Oarsmen, cyclists, and gentlemen athletes lost their amateur standing by disporting with professionals, but the Southern Intercollegiate Athletic Association, which prescribed regulations for Tulane athletes, prohibited competition with professionals only in intercollegiate competition.

When sportsmen participated without national regulations, basic amateur standards varied even more noticeably. Turfmen seldom concerned themselves with the amateur question, but in practice a professional was a jockey who rode for pay and an amateur was a "gentleman" who rode for pleasure or the sport involved, usually to the delight of professional riders, "who enjoyed the awkward appearance of the gentlemen riders." [34] Tennis and golf, which were played by members of exclusive social clubs, were governed by amateur codes similar to those of the United States Lawn Tennis Association and the United States Golf Association, although local players did not belong to these associations. In other sports, such as baseball, billiards, and boxing, spectators and participants usually agreed that a professional made a vocation of athletics, while an amateur, though he might accept money, regularly pursued another occupation. When athletic clubs or college students participated in sports that employed these practical, but sometimes vague and poorly applied, definitions, they, of course, imposed their own rules of amateur competition.

For all the ramifications of sports, one feature of this leisure-time activity was abundantly evident as New Orleans entered a new century: people of all classes had discovered in sports broad possibilities for urban recreation. Many residents preferred to participate vicariously as spectators at commercialized sporting events, but there existed also a variety of activities for those who chose to compete ac-

[34] *Wilkes' Spirit of the Times,* XXVI (April 20, 1872), 147.

tively. Through political misfortunes, economic hardships, and natural disasters, fans and players sought and found pleasure in athletic pastimes. In a rapidly changing, increasingly complex society, sports provided a sense of orderliness, simplicity, and continuity, as well as amusement. They truly diverted the minds of careworn, workworn residents. New Orleanians were also aware that sports, coupled with other leisure outlets, made the city attractive to money-laden visitors. The *Picayune* in December, 1866, urged support of horse racing to aid the city's economic recovery: "The forlorn condition of the South will in all probability surrender the majority of the old racing grounds to the weeds and grass, but with New Orleans the case is different. It matters not what comes to pass—whether sugar cane flourishes or the cotton plant blossoms—New Orleans will be the rendezvous of gaiety for all America. . . . What is lost to the city by a crippled commerce must be gained by the patronage of a pleasure-seeking public." On another occasion the *Picayune* observed: "It is not to amuse ourselves alone that we must have theatres, and agricultural fairs, and carnival festivities, and race meetings. These are amusements, it is true; but they are amusements which bring us profit and wealth; which attract visitors, invite residents, and go far toward building up a great and prosperous city." [35] Modern business leaders who seek professional teams to make their cities more appealing to travelers, residents, and new business enterprises are merely following a pattern established a century ago.

Whether for their own pleasure or from a desire to enhance the city's value as a mecca for tourists, thousands of people encouraged the rise of sports in New Orleans in the period from 1850 to 1900. They supported traditional pastimes such as horse racing, boating, boxing, and billiards; welcomed new activities, including baseball, cycling, and American football; and competed in sports of their own invention, such as *raquette*, basquette, and Newcomb. Participation in some pastimes, notably yachting, tennis, and golf, was restricted to members of prominent social clubs, but the general trend throughout this period was for sports to submit to democracy. Although the upper class could take satisfaction in having introduced many new sports, their efforts to monopolize them generally failed ignominiously. Those sports they controlled in 1900 seemed likely to follow

[35] New Orleans *Daily Picayune*, December 18, 1866; April 10, 1875.

the paths of baseball, roller skating, and racing into the hands of the masses. Their descent would be but a predictable extension of the continuous process that had brought sports to prominence in a city renowned for its varieties of pleasure.

BIBLIOGRAPHY

MANUSCRIPTS

Gustave A. Breaux Diaries, 1859, 1863–1865. Special Collections, Tulane University Library.

Louis A. Bringier and Family Papers. Department of Archives and Manuscripts, Louisiana State University.

Burden, Edwin J. "Horse Racing in New Orleans." Special Collections, Tulane University Library.

Crescent Rod and Gun Club, Membership Certificate. Special Collections, Tulane University Library.

John G. Dunlap Papers. Special Collections, Tulane University Library.

Charles E. A. Gayarré Papers, Grace King Collection. Department of Archives and Manuscripts, Louisiana State University.

Reverend Charles W. Hilton Diary. Special Collections, Tulane University Library.

Joseph P. Horner Papers. Department of Archives and Manuscripts, Louisiana State University.

Lady of Lyons Boat Club Book, 1839–1841. Special Collections, Tulane University Library.

G. Loomis Letter, 1848. Department of Archives and Manuscripts, Louisiana State University.

Louisiana Road Club Broadsides, 1889–1898. Kuntz Collection, Tulane University Library.

William J. Minor and Family Papers. Department of Archives and Manuscripts, Louisiana State University.

Minutes, Southern Yacht Club, July, 1849–July, 1860. Southern Yacht Club, New Orleans.

New Orleans Rowing Club, Account Book and Membership Rolls, 1873–1877. Special Collections, Tulane University Library.

New Orleans Scrapbook, 1813–1865. Department of Archives and Manuscripts, Louisiana State University.

Nuhrah, Arthur G. "History of Tulane University." Special Collections, Tulane University Library.

Samuel J. Peters, Jr., Diary, 1840–1862. Department of Archives and Manuscripts, Louisiana State University.

William P. Riddell Journals, 1853–1857. Special Collections, Tulane University Library.

Duncan Shaw Diary, 1852. Special Collections, Tulane University Library.

Southern Yacht Club Regattas, August, 1849–September, 1857. Southern Yacht Club, New Orleans.

Eleanor P. Thompson Collection. Special Collections, Tulane University Library.

Thomas Kelah Wharton Diaries, 1853–1862. Microfilm in Special Collections, Tulane University Library; original in Manuscripts Division, New York Public Library.

James S. Zacharie Diary, 1863–[1864]. Department of Archives and Manuscripts, Louisiana State University.

NEWSPAPERS

Boston *Globe*
Chicago *Tribune*
Cincinnati *Enquirer*
Dallas *Morning News*
New Orleans *Bee*
New Orleans *Bulletin*
New Orleans *Daily Crescent*
New Orleans *Daily Delta*
New Orleans *Daily Orleanian*
New Orleans *Daily Picayune*
New Orleans *Daily States*
New Orleans *Item*
New Orleans *Louisianian*
New Orleans *Times*
New Orleans *Times-Democrat*
New Orleans *Tribune*
New Orleans *Weekly Crescent*
New Orleans *Weekly Pelican*
New York *Herald*
New York *Illustrated News*
New York *Sun*
New York *Times*
New York *Tribune*
Tulane University *College Spirit*
Tulane University *Olive and Blue*
L'Union (New Orleans)

Official Documents: Institutional, Municipal, State, and Federal

Acts Passed by the General Assembly of the State of Louisiana, 1890. New Orleans, 1890.

Annual Report of Wm. Preston Johnston, President, to the Board of Administrators of Tulane University of Louisiana. New Orleans, 1885.

Leovy, Henry J., comp. *The Laws and General Ordinances of the City of New Orleans, Together with the Acts of the Legislature, Decisions of the Supreme Court, and Constitutional Privileges, Relating to the City Government.* New Orleans, 1857.

Pass Christian Institute: Sea-Side Academy for Young Ladies and Girls. Pass Christian, Miss., 1891.

Register of Tulane University of Louisiana, 1900–1901. New Orleans, 1901.

Southern Reporter: Concerning All the Decisions of the Supreme Courts of Alabama, Louisiana, Florida, Mississippi. Vol. XV. St. Paul, 1894.

Southern Reporter: Concerning All the Decisions of the Supreme Courts of Alabama, Louisiana, Florida, Mississippi. Vol. XVII. St. Paul, 1895.

Tulane University of Louisiana. New Orleans, 1895.

Tulane University of Louisiana. New Orleans, 1898.

United States Bureau of the Census. *Eighth Census* (1860). *Population of the United States in 1860; Compiled from the Original Returns of the Eighth Census, under the Directorship of the Secretary of the Interior.* Washington, D.C., 1864.

——. *Eleventh Census* (1890). *Report on the Social Statistics of Cities in the United States at the Eleventh Census: 1890.* Compiled by John S. Billings. Washington, D.C., 1895.

——. *Marriage and Divorce, 1887–1906.* Washington, D.C., 1908.

——. *Ninth Census* (1870). *The Statistics of the Population of the United States.* Vol. I. Washington, D.C., 1872.

——. *Sixth Census* (1840). *Compendium of the Enumeration of the Inhabitants and Statistics of the United States, as Obtained at the Department of State, from the Returns of the Sixth Census, by Counties and Principal Towns.* Washington, D.C., 1841.

——. *Tenth Census* (1880). *Report on the Social Statistics of Cities.* Compiled by George E. Waring, Jr. Vol. XIX. Washington, D.C., 1887.

——. *Twelfth Census* (1900). *Population.* Vol. II. Washington, D.C., 1901.

United States Bureau of Labor. *A Report on Marriage and Divorce in the United States, 1867 to 1886.* Compiled by Carroll D. Wright. Washington, D.C., 1889.

PROGRAMS, MANUALS, RECORD BOOKS, AND CLUB CONSTITUTIONS

American Racing Calendar and Trotting Record. New York, 1858.

American Turf Register: A Correct Synopsis of Turf Events in the United States, Embracing Running, Trotting, and Pacing, for 1870. New York, 1871.

American Turf Register and Racing Calendar: A Correct Synopsis of Turf Events in the United States and the Dominion of Canada, Embracing Running, Trotting, and Pacing, for 1871. New York, 1872.

Baer, Clara G. *"Newcomb": A Game for the Gymnasium and Playground.* New York, 1914.

————. *Progressive Lessons in Physical Education: An Introductory Course of Instruction for the Home and School, Based on the Swedish System.* New Orleans, 1905.

Bell, Ernest, ed. *Handbook of Athletic Sports.* 6 vols. London, 1890–1892.

Berenson, Senda, ed. *Line Basket Ball or Basket Ball for Women as Adopted by the Conference on Physical Training Held in June, 1899, at Springfield, Mass.* New York, 1901.

Brunell, Frank H., ed. *The American Sporting Manual for 1901.* New York, 1901.

Charter and By-Laws of the St. John Rowing Club of New Orleans. New Orleans, 1884.

Charter, By-Laws, House Rules, Racing Rules, Sailing Directions, Etc., of the Southern Yacht Club of New Orleans, La. New Orleans, 1905.

Charter, By-Laws, Racing Rules, Table of Time Allowances, Sailing Directions, Etc., of the Southern Yacht Club of New Orleans, La. New Orleans, 1901.

Charter, By-Laws, Table of Time Allowances, Racing Rules, Etc., of the Southern Yacht Club of New Orleans, La. New Orleans, 1892.

Charter, Constitution, and By-Laws of the Young Men's Gymnastic Club of New Orleans, La. New Orleans, n.d.

Constitution and By-Laws of the Southern Association: Official General and Athletic Rules of the Amateur Athletic Union of the United States. New York, 1895.

Constitution of the Pontchartrain Regatta Association. New Orleans, 1889.

Dwight, James. *Practical Lawn Tennis.* New York, 1893.

First Meet: Southern Amateur Athletic Union. Under the Auspices of Southern Athletic Club, Young Men's Gymnastic Club, American Athletic Club, and Pelican Cyclists. New Orleans, 1893.

James, Edward. *Manual of Sporting Rules.* Twelfth Edition. New York, 1877.

Official Catalogue of the World's Industrial and Cotton Centennial Exposition, Held Under the Joint Auspices of the United States of

America, the National Cotton Planters' Association, the City of New Orleans, Louisiana, U.S.A., During the Period from the 16th of December, 1884, to the 31st of May, 1885, at New Orleans, Louisiana, U.S.A. New Orleans, 1885.

Official Programme of the Southern Athletic Club Spring Games, at Athletic Park, Saturday, May 2nd, 1896, 3 P.M. New Orleans, 1896.

Orleans Gun and Rod Club, North Shore Louisiana (Tournament Program). New Orleans, 1909.

Porter, Luther H. *Wheels and Wheeling: An Indispensable Handbook for Cyclists.* Boston, 1892.

Pratt, Charles E. *The American Bicycler: A Manual for the Observer, the Learner, and the Expert.* Second Edition. Boston, 1880.

Program of the Annual Spring Games, Tulane Athletic Association, New Orleans, La., Tulane Field, Saturday, April 27th, 1895, 4:00 O'clock. New Orleans, 1895.

Racing Rules, Regulations, and By-Laws of the New Louisiana Jockey Club. New Orleans, 1880.

Rules and Regulations for the Government of Racing, Trotting, and Betting, as Adopted by the Principal Turf Associations Throughout the United States and Canada. New York, 1866.

Rules and Regulation of the Roman Rifle Club of New Orleans, La. New Orleans, 1874.

Rules: Louisiana Jockey Club. New Orleans, 1872.

Souvenir of the Southern Athletic Club of New Orleans La. New Orleans, 1895.

Spring Games, Southern Athletic Club, Fair Grounds, New Orleans, La., Saturday, May 23d, 1891. New Orleans, 1891.

DIARIES, MEMOIRS, TRAVEL ACCOUNTS, GUIDE BOOKS, AND SERMONS

Adams, Samuel H. *Grandfather Stories.* New York, 1955.

Alexander, James E. *Transatlantic Sketches, Comprising Visits to the Most Interesting Scenes in North and South America, and the West Indies.* 2 vols. London, 1833.

Arfwedson, C. F. *The United States and Canada in 1832, 1833, and 1834.* 2 vols. London, 1834.

Blakemore, Allen Bruce. Interview conducted by D. Clive Hardy, January 18, 1960; tape recording of interview in Department of History, Tulane University.

Brady, William A. *Showman.* New York, 1937.

Buckingham, James S. *The Slave States of America.* 2 vols. London, 1842.

Buel, James W. *Metropolitan Life Unveiled; or, The Mysteries and Miseries of America's Great Cities, Embracing New York, Washington City, San Francisco, Salt Lake City, and New Orleans.* St. Louis, 1882.

Cable, George Washington, ed. "War Diary of a Union Woman in the South," in *Famous Adventures and Prison Escapes of the Civil War.* New York, 1893.

Chester, Greville J. *Transatlantic Sketches in the West Indies, South America, Canada, and the United States.* London, 1869.

Clapp, Theodore. *Autobiographical Sketches and Recollections During a Thirty-Five Years' Residence in New Orleans.* Boston, 1857.

[Coleman, William H.], ed. *Historical Sketch Book and Guide to New Orleans and Environs.* New York, 1885.

Cook, Theodore A. *The Sunlit Hours: A Record of Sport and Life.* New York, 1925.

Corbett, James J. *The Roar of the Crowd: The True Tale of the Rise and Fall of a Champion.* New York, 1925.

Creecy, James R. *Scenes in the South and Other Miscellaneous Pieces.* Washington, D.C., 1860.

Cunynghame, Arthur A. T. *A Glimpse at the Great Western Republic.* London, 1851.

Dawson, Sarah Morgan. *A Confederate Girl's Diary.* Boston, 1913.

DeLeon, Thomas C. *Four Years in Rebel Capitals: An Inside View of Life in the Southern Confederacy, from Birth to Death; from Original Notes, Collated in the Years 1861 to 1865.* Mobile, 1892.

Devol, George H. *Forty Years a Gambler on the Mississippi.* Second Edition. New York, 1892.

Dixon, Brandt V. B. *A Brief History of H. Sophie Newcomb Memorial College, 1887–1919: A Personal Reminiscence.* New Orleans, 1928.

Donald, Aïda DiPace and Donald, David, eds. *Diary of Charles Francis Adams.* 2 vols. Cambridge, Mass., 1964.

Duncan, W. C. *Ladies' Pulpit Offering.* New Orleans, 1856.

Elworth, Thomas. *Sketches of Incidents and Adventures in the Life of Thomas Elworth, the American Pedestrian.* Boston, 1844.

Federal Writers' Project. *New Orleans City Guide.* Revised by Robert Tallent. Boston, 1952.

Gohdes, Clarence, ed. *Hunting in the Old South: Original Narratives of the Hunters.* Baton Rouge, 1967.

Hall, A. Oakey. *The Manhattaner in New Orleans; or, Phases of 'Crescent City' Life.* New York, 1851.

Hardy, Lady Duffus. *Down South.* London, 1883.

Hogan, William R. and Davis, Edwin A., eds. *William Johnson's Natchez: The Ante-Bellum Diary of a Free Negro.* Baton Rouge, 1951.

Houstoun, Matilda C. F. *Hesperos; or, Travels in the West.* 2 vols. London, 1850.

———. *Texas and the Gulf of Mexico; or, Yachting in the New World.* 2 vols. London, 1844.

Ingraham, Joseph H. *The South-West. By a Yankee.* New York, 1835.

Jewell, Edwin L., ed. *Jewell's Crescent City Illustrated.* New Orleans, 1874.

Kron, Karl, pseud. [Lyman H. Bagg]. *Ten Thousand Miles on a Bicycle.* New York, 1887.

Lanman, Charles. *Adventures in the Wilds of the United States and British American Provinces.* 2 vols. Philadelphia, 1856.

Lewis, George. *Impressions of America and the American Churches.* Edinburgh, 1845.

Logan, James. *Notes of a Journey Through Canada, the United States of America, and the West Indies.* Edinburgh, 1838.

Lyell, Charles. *A Second Visit to the United States of North America.* 2 vols. London, 1849.

Mackie, J. Milton. *From Cape Cod to Dixie and the Tropics.* New York, 1864.

Marryat, Frederick. *A Diary in America with Remarks on Its Institutions.* 2 vols. Philadelphia, 1839.

Martineau, Harriet. *Retrospect of Western Travel.* 3 vols. London, 1838.

Mathews, John. *Peeps into Life: Autobiography of Rev. John Mathews, D. D., a Minister of the Gospel for Sixty Years.* n.p., 1904.

Muirhead, James F. *The Land of Contrasts: A Briton's View of His American Kin.* Boston, 1898.

Nevins, Allan, ed. *America Through British Eyes.* New York, 1948.

New Orleans As It Is: Its Manners and Customs—Morals—Fashionable Life—Profanation of the Sabbath—Prostitution—Licentiousness—Slave Markets and Slavery, &c. &c. &c. Utica, N.Y., 1849.

New Orleans Bicycle Road Guide. New Orleans, 1896.

Nichols, Thomas L. *Forty Years of American Life.* Second Edition. London, 1874.

Olmsted, Frederick Law. *A Journey in the Seaboard Slave States, with Remarks on Their Economy.* Vol. I of *Our Slave States.* New York, 1856.

Palmer, Benjamin M. *The Sabbath Was Made for Man: Sermon.* New Orleans, 1857.

———. *Sermons.* New Orleans, 1883.

Phelps, William Lyon. *Autobiography with Letters.* New York, 1939.

Picayune's Guide to New Orleans. Second Edition. New Orleans, 1896.

Picayune's Guide to New Orleans. Third Edition. New Orleans, 1897.

Picayune's Guide to New Orleans. Sixth Edition. New Orleans, 1900.

Pickett, Albert J. *Eight Days in New Orleans in February, 1847.* Montgomery, Ala., 1847.

Ralph, Julian. *Dixie; or, Southern Scenes and Sketches.* New York, 1896.

Ripley, Eliza. *Social Life in Old New Orleans, Being Recollections of My Girlhood.* New York, 1912.

Roberts, DeWitt C. *Southern Sketches; or, Eleven Years Down South, Including Three Years in Dixie.* Jacksonville, Fla., 1865.

[Robinson, William L.]. *The Diary of a Samaritan by a Member of the Howard Association of New Orleans.* New York, 1860.

Rose, George. *The Great Country; or, Impressions of America.* London, 1868.

Rowland, Kate Mason and Croxall, Mrs. Morris L., eds. *The Journal of Julia LeGrand: New Orleans, 1862–1863.* Richmond, Va., 1911.

Sala, George A. *America Revisited: From the Bay of New York to the Gulf of Mexico, and from Lake Michigan to the Pacific.* Fifth Edition. London, 1885.

Shippee, Lester B., ed. *Bishop Whipple's Southern Diary, 1843–44.* Minneapolis, 1937.

Sights and Scenes Along the Sunset Route: A Dialog. New York, 1885.

Smedes, Susan Dabney. *Memorials of a Southern Planter.* Edited by Fletcher M. Green. New York, 1965.

Stirling, James. *Letters from the Slave States.* London, 1857; reprinted, New York, 1969.

Stranger's Guide of New Orleans, Mardi Gras, 1890. New Orleans, 1890.

Souvenir Sketch Book of the Fifth Ward, 1910. New Orleans, 1910.

Souvenir Sketch Book of the Fourth Ward, 1911. New Orleans, 1911.

Sullivan, John L. *Life and Reminiscences of a 19th Century Gladiator.* Boston, 1892.

The Third Municipal District of New Orleans. New Orleans, 1910.

Van Every, Edward. *Muldoon, the Solid Man of Sport: His Amazing Story as Related for the First Time by Him to His Friend Edward Van Every.* New York, 1929.

Warner, Charles Dudley. *Studies in the South and West with Comments on Canada.* New York, 1889.

Watson, William. *Life in the Confederate Army; Being the Observations and Experiences of an Alien in the South During the American Civil War.* London, 1887.

Wilkinson, R. A. *The Gulf Coast: Letters Written for the New Orleans "Times-Democrat."* Louisville, 1886.

The Winter in New Orleans: Carnival, Racing, French Opera. Houston, 1901.

Woodruff, Hiram. *The Trotting Horse of America: How to Train and Drive Him, with Reminiscences of the Trotting Turf.* Nineteenth Edition. Philadelphia, 1877.

Wright, Louis B. and Tinling, Marion, eds. *Secret Diary of William Byrd of Westover, 1709–1712.* Richmond, Va., 1941.

Zacharie, James S. *New Orleans Guide, with Descriptions of the Routes to New Orleans, Sights of the City Arranged Alphabetically, and Other Information Useful to Travellers; Also, Outlines of the History of Louisiana.* New Orleans, 1885.

————. *New Orleans Guide, with Descriptions of the Routes to New Orleans, Sights of the City Arranged Alphabetically, and Other Information Useful to Travellers; Also, Outlines of the History of Louisiana.* New Orleans, 1893.

————. *New Orleans Guide, with Descriptions of the Routes to New Orleans, Sights of the City Arranged Alphabetically, and Other Information Useful to Travellers; Also, Outlines of the History of Louisiana.* New Orleans, 1902.

PERIODICALS

Adamoli, Guilio. "New Orleans in 1867," *Louisiana Historical Quarterly,* VI (April, 1923), 271–79.

Adams, William H. "New Orleans as the National Center of Boxing," *Louisiana Historical Quarterly,* XXXIX (January, 1956), 92–112.

American Clubman (New Orleans), Vol. I, 1897.

"The Athletic Craze," *Nation,* LVII (December 7, 1893), 422–32.

Baughman, James P. "A Southern Spa: Ante-Bellum Lake Pontchartrain," *Louisiana History,* III (Winter, 1962), 5–32.

"Before the Mast," *Barometer* (New Orleans), V (February–March, 1919), 8.

Betts, John R. "Sporting Journalism in Nineteenth-Century America," *American Quarterly,* V (Spring, 1953), 39–56.

————. "The Technological Revolution and the Rise of Sport, 1850–1900," *Mississippi Valley Historical Review,* XL (September, 1953), 231–56.

Bicycle South (New Orleans), III (May, 1886).

Bicycling World (Boston), Vols. I–XXVI, 1879–1893.

Bissell, Mary Taylor. "Athletics for City Girls," *Popular Science Monthly,* XLVI (December, 1894), 145–53.

Bryce, James. "America Revisited: The Changes of a Quarter Century," *Outlook,* LXXIX (March 25, 1905), 733–40.

Camp, Walter. "Football: Retrospective and Prospective," *Outing,* XXIII (November, 1893), 119–28.

Catton, Bruce. "The Great American Game," *American Heritage,* X (April, 1959), 16–25, 86.

Chenault, William W. and Reinders, Robert C. "The Northern-born Community of New Orleans in the 1850s," *Journal of American History,* LI (September, 1964), 232–47.

Club Life (New Orleans), III (January 24, 1897).

Coulter, E. Merton. "Boating as a Sport in the Old South," *Georgia Historical Quarterly,* XXVII (September, 1943), 231–47.

Daily Item's Racing Form Chart (New Orleans), Vols. I–II, 1896.

Dethloff, Henry C. and Jones, Robert R. "Race Relations in Louisiana, 1877–98," *Louisiana History,* IX (Fall, 1968), 301–23.

Fischer, Roger A. "Racial Segregation in Ante Bellum New Orleans," *American Historical Review,* LXXIV (February, 1969), 926–37.

"Game Preserving in Louisiana," *Outing,* XI (March, 1888), 32–35.

Gilbert, Bil. "Play Ball, You ?!¢%&#/S!," *Sports Illustrated,* XXIX (November 25, 1968), 74–88.

Good Roads (New York), Vols. I–IV, 1892–1894.

Holmes, Oliver Wendell. "The Autocrat of the Breakfast-Table," *Atlantic Monthly,* I (May, 1858), 871–82.

"The Human Wheel and Its Rival—the Velocipede Mania," *Scientific American,* XX (January 9, 1869), 25–26.

Keating, James W. "Sportsmanship as a Moral Category," *Ethics,* LXXV (October, 1964), 25–35.

Kendall, John S. "Journalism in New Orleans Between 1880 and 1900," *Louisiana Historical Quarterly,* VIII (October, 1925), 557–73.

———. "Journalism in New Orleans Fifty Years Ago," *Louisiana Historical Quarterly,* XXXIV (January, 1951), 5–24.

L. A. W. Bulletin (Boston), Vols. I–VI, 1885–1888.

Lewis, Guy. "The Beginnings of Organized Collegiate Sport," *American Quarterly,* XXII (Summer, 1970), 222–29.

National Police Gazette, Vols. XXXIX–LXV, 1882–1895.

Nugent, William H. "The Sports Section," *American Mercury,* XVI (March, 1929), 329–38.

"Orleans Gun and Rod Club," *Sport in Dixie* (New Orleans), I (May, 1909), 45.

Paxson, Frederic Logan. "The Rise of Sport," *Mississippi Valley Historical Review,* IV (September, 1917), 143–68.

Ralph, Julian. "Two Early Southwestern Beach Resorts," *Harper's Weekly,* XXXIX (September 21, 1895), 891–92.

Riesman, David and Denney, Reuel. "Football in America: A Study in Culture Diffusion," *American Quarterly,* III (Winter, 1951), 309–25.

Robertson, J. Breckinridge. "Foot Ball in the South," *Southern Magazine* (Louisville), III (January, 1894), 631–45.

Slocum, Henry W., Jr. "Lawn Tennis as a Game for Women," *Outing,* XIV (July, 1889), 289–300.

Southern Cyclist (New Orleans), Vols. II–III, 1896.

Southern Sportsman (New Orleans), Vols. I–II, 1898–1899.

Spirit of the South (New Orleans), February 2, 1889.

Spirit of the Times, Vols. XII–XXX, 1842–1861.

Sporting South (New Orleans), March 3, 17, 1888.

Tobin, John F. "The Genesis of New Orleans Golf," *Dixie Golfer* (New Orleans), I (January, 1922), 6–8, 22.

Tobin, Richard L. "Sports as an Integrator," *Saturday Review,* L (January 21, 1967), 32.

Tregle, Joseph G., Jr. "Early New Orleans Society: A Reappraisal," *Journal of Southern History,* XVIII (February, 1952), 20–36.

Tulane *Collegian,* Vols. I–IV, 1891–1895.

Tulane *Jambalaya,* 1896–1901.

"Velocipede Notes," *Scientific American,* XX (February 27, 1869), 131.

Wheel: A Journal of Cycling, Vols. IV–V, 1883–1884.

Whitney, Casper W. "Amateur Sport," *Harper's Weekly,* XXXVII (December 23, 1893), 1237–39.

Wilkes' Spirit of the Times, Vols. I–CXL, 1859–1900.

Wittke, Carl F. "Baseball in Its Adolescence," *Ohio State Archaeological and Historical Quarterly,* LXI (April, 1952), 111–27.

"World Awheel," *Munsey's Magazine,* XV (May, 1896), 131–59.

GENERAL WORKS

Ainsworth, Dorothy. *The History of Physical Education in Colleges for Women.* New York, 1930.

Akers, Dwight. *Drivers Up: The Story of American Harness Racing.* New York, 1938.

Asbury, Herbert. *The French Quarter: An Informal History of the New Orleans Underworld.* New York, 1936.

Bailey, John W. *Handbook of Southern Intercollegiate Track and Field Athletics, 1894–1924.* A. and M. College, Miss., 1924.

Bartlett, Arthur. *Baseball and Mr. Spalding.* New York, 1951.

The Baseball Encyclopedia: The Complete and Official Record of Major League Baseball. Revised Edition. New York, 1969.

Boyle, Robert H. *Sport: Mirror of American Life.* Boston, 1963.

Bragg, Jefferson Davis. *Louisiana in the Confederacy.* Baton Rouge, 1941.

Burlingame, Roger. *Engines of Democracy: Inventions and Society in Mature America.* New York, 1940.

Cady, Edwin L. *The Gentleman in America: A Literary Study in American Culture.* Syracuse, N.Y., 1949.

Camp, Walter. *The Book of Foot-Ball.* New York, 1910.

Capers, Gerald M. *Occupied City: New Orleans Under the Federals, 1862–1865.* Lexington, Ky., 1965.

Carter, Hodding, ed. *The Past as Prelude: New Orleans, 1718–1968.* New Orleans, 1968.

Castellanos, Henry C. *New Orleans as It Was: Episodes of Louisiana Life.* New Orleans, 1895.

Charlesworth, James C., ed. *Leisure in America: Blessing or Curse?* Philadelphia, 1964.

Chidsey, D. B. *John the Great.* Garden City, 1942.

Cole, Arthur C. *The Irrepressible Conflict, 1850–1865.* Vol. VII of *A History of American Life.* New York, 1934.

Coulter, E. Merton. *The Confederate States of America, 1861–1865.* Vol. VII of *A History of the South.* Baton Rouge, 1950.

Cozens, Frederick W. and Stumpf, Florence S. *Sports in American Life.* Chicago, 1953.

Cozzens, Fred S. *et al. Yachts and Yachting.* New York, 1888.

Crooks, Esther J. and Crooks, Ruth W. *The Ring Tournament in the United States.* Richmond, Va., 1936.

Crowther, Samuel and Ruhl, Arthur. *Rowing and Track Athletics.* New York, 1905.

Danzig, Allison. *The History of American Football: Its Great Teams, Players, and Coaches.* Englewood Cliffs, 1956.

———— and Brandwein, Peter, eds. *The Greatest Sports Stories from the New York Times.* New York, 1951.

———— and Reichler, J. *The History of Baseball: Its Great Players, Teams, and Managers.* Englewood Cliffs, 1959.

Davis, Edwin A. and Hogan, William R. *The Barber of Natchez.* Baton Rouge, 1954.

DeWitt, Robert M. *The American Fistiana, Showing the Progress of Pugilism in the United States from 1816–1873.* New York, 1873.

Dibble, R. F. *John L. Sullivan: An Intimate Narrative.* Boston, 1925.

Duffy, John. *Sword of Pestilence: The New Orleans Yellow Fever Epidemic of 1853.* Baton Rouge, 1966.

Dufour, Charles L. *The Night the War Was Lost.* Garden City, N.Y., 1960.

————. *Ten Flags in the Wind: The Story of Louisiana.* New York, 1967.

Dulles, Foster Rhea. *A History of Recreation: America Learns to Play.* Revised edition of *America Learns to Play: A History of Popular Recreation, 1607–1940.* New York, 1965.

Durant, John and Bettman, Otto. *Pictorial History of American Sports from Colonial Times to the Present.* New York, 1952.

Dyer, John P. *Tulane: The Biography of a University.* New York and London, 1966.

Earnest, Ernest. *Academic Procession: An Informal History of the American College, 1636–1953.* Indianapolis, 1953.

Evans, Oliver. *New Orleans.* New York, 1959.

Ficklen, John Rose. *History of Reconstruction in Louisiana (Through 1868).* Baltimore, 1910.

Fleischer, Nat S. *Black Dynamite: The Story of the Negro in the Prize Ring from 1782 to 1938.* 4 vols. New York, 1938–1947.

————. *The Heavyweight Championship: An Informal History of Boxing from 1719 to the Present Day.* New York, 1949.

————. *John L. Sullivan: Champion of Champions.* New York, 1951.

———— and Andre, Sam. *A Pictorial History of Boxing.* New York, 1959.

Fossier, Albert A. *New Orleans: The Glamour Period, 1800–1840.* New Orleans, 1957.

Fox, Richard K. *Life and Battles of Jack Dempsey: A Complete History of All the Battles Fought by the Nonpareil, Graphically Told and Handsomely Illustrated.* New York, 1889.

———. *Life and Battles of James J. Corbett: Champion of the World.* London, 1894.

———. *Life and Battles of John L. Sullivan.* Second Edition. New York, 1891.

Franklin, John Hope. *The Militant South, 1800–1861.* Cambridge, Mass., 1956.

Gibson, Nevin H. *The Encyclopedia of Golf with the Official All-Time Records.* New York, 1958.

Groves, Ernest R. *The American Woman: The Feminine Side of a Masculine Civilization.* Revised Edition. New York, 1944.

Harding, William E. *Jem Mace of Norwich, England, Champion Pugilist of the World: His Life and Battles, with Portraits and Illustrations.* New York, 1881.

Henderson, Edwin B. *The Negro in Sports.* Revised Edition. Washington, D.C., 1939.

Henderson, Robert W. *Ball, Bat, and Bishop: The Origin of Ball Games.* New York, 1947.

Hennessey, Louis J. *One Hundred Years of Yachting.* New York, 1949.

———. *The Fair Grounds Race Course: A Time-Honored American Institution.* New Orleans, 1947.

Herbert, Henry W. *Frank Forester's Horse and Horsemanship of the United States and British Provinces of North America.* 2 vols. New York, 1857.

Hervey, John. *Racing in America, 1665–1865.* 2 vols. New York, 1944.

Highlights of [Tulane] *Football History.* New Orleans, 1932.

Holliman, Jennie. *American Sports (1785–1835).* Durham, N.C., 1931.

Huizinga, Johan. *Homo Ludens: A Study of the Play Element in Culture.* Boston, 1955.

Hurlbut, Jesse L. *The Story of Chatauqua.* New York, 1921.

Hutchinson, Horace. *Golfing.* Third Edition. London, 1894.

Jackson, Joy J. *New Orleans in the Gilded Age: Politics and Urban Progress, 1880–1896.* Baton Rouge, 1969.

Jacobson, Paul H. *American Marriage and Divorce.* New York, 1959.

Jensen, Oliver. *The Revolt of American Women: A Pictorial History of the Century of Change from Bloomers to Bikinis—from Feminism to Freud.* New York, 1952.

Johnson, Thomas C. *The Life and Letters of Benjamin Morgan Palmer.* Richmond, Va., 1906.

Johnston, Alexander. *Ten—And Out! The Complete Story of the Prize Ring in America.* Third Revised Edition. New York, 1947.

Kendall, John S. *The Golden Age of the New Orleans Theater.* Baton Rouge, 1952.

———. *History of New Orleans.* 3 vols. Chicago, 1922.

King, Grace. *New Orleans: The Place and the People.* New York, 1926.

Kmen, Henry A. *Music in New Orleans: The Formative Years, 1791–1841.* Baton Rouge, 1966.

Krout, John Allen. *American Themes.* New York, 1963.

———. *Annals of American Sport.* Vol. XV of *The Pageant of America.* New Haven, 1929.

Landry, Stuart O. *History of the Boston Club.* New Orleans, 1938.

Lee, Alfred M. *The Daily Newspaper in America: The Evolution of a Social Instrument.* New York, 1937.

Lieb, Frederick G. *The Baseball Story.* New York, 1950.

Liebling, Abbott J. *The Honest Rainmaker: The Life and Times of Colonel John R. Stingo.* New York, 1953.

Macdonald, Charles B. *Scotland's Gift: Golf.* New York, 1928.

Manchester, Herbert. *Four Centuries of Sport in America, 1490–1890.* New York, 1931.

Marcott, Louis W., comp. *Membership Roster of New Orleans Clubs, 1899.* New Orleans, 1899.

Martin, Harry B. *Fifty Years of American Golf.* New York, 1936.

Menke, Frank G., ed. *The Encyclopedia of Sports.* Third Revised Edition. New York, 1963.

Morison, Samuel Eliot. *Three Centuries of Harvard, 1636–1936.* Cambridge, Mass., 1936.

Mott, Frank L. *American Journalism: A History of Newspapers in the United States through 250 Years, 1690–1940.* New York, 1941.

———. *A History of American Magazines, 1781–1850.* New York, 1930.

———. *A History of American Magazines, 1850–1865.* Cambridge, Mass., 1938.

———. *A History of American Magazines, 1865–1885.* Cambridge, Mass., 1938.

———. *A History of American Magazines, 1885–1905.* Cambridge, Mass., 1957.

Mumford, Lewis. *Technics and Civilization.* New York, 1934.

Nevins, Allan. *The Emergence of Modern America, 1865–1878.* Vol. VIII of *A History of American Life.* New York, 1927.

Palmer, Arthur J. *Riding High: The Story of the Bicycle.* New York, 1956.

Parton, James. *General Butler in New Orleans: History of the Administration of the Department of the Gulf in the Year 1862; with an Account of the Capture of New Orleans, and a Sketch of the Previous Career of the General, Civil and Military.* New York, 1864.

Paxton, Harry T., ed. *Sport U. S. A.: The Best from the Saturday Evening Post.* New York, 1961.

Polsky, Ned. *Hustlers, Beats, and Others.* Anchor Books Edition. New York, 1969.

Reed, Merl E. *New Orleans and the Railroads: The Struggle for Commercial Empire, 1830–1860.* Baton Rouge, 1966.

Reinders, Robert C. *End of an Era: New Orleans, 1850–1860.* New Orleans, 1954.

Rightor, Henry, ed. *Standard History of New Orleans, Louisiana, Giving a Description of the Natural Advantages, Natural History in Regard to the Flora and Birds, Settlement, Indians, Creoles, Municipal and Military History, Mercantile and Commercial Interests, Banking, Transportation, Struggles Against High Water, the Press, Educational Literature and Art, the Churches, Old Burying Grounds, Bench and Bar, Medical Public and Charitable Institutions, the Carnival, Amusements, Clubs, Societies, Associations, Etc.* Chicago, 1900.

Roberts, W. Adolphe. *Lake Pontchartrain.* Indianapolis, 1946.

Rudolph, Frederick. *The American College and University: A History.* New York, 1962.

Savage, Howard J., et al. *American College Athletics.* New York, 1929.

Saxon, Lyle. *Fabulous New Orleans.* New York, 1928.

Schlesinger, Arthur M. *The Rise of the City, 1878–1898.* Vol. X of *A History of American Life.* New York, 1933.

Seymour, Harold. *Baseball: The Early Years.* New York, 1960.

Shugg, Roger W. *Origins of Class Struggle in Louisiana: A Social History of White Farmers and Laborers during Slavery and After, 1840–1875.* Baton Rouge, 1939.

Siler, George and Houseman, Louis M. *The "Fight of the Century," Being a Review of the World's Championship Contest Between Robert Fitzsimmons and James J. Corbett at Carson City, Nev., March 17th, 1897.* Chicago, 1897.

Slovenko, Ralph and James A. Knight, eds. *Motivations in Play, Games, and Sports.* Springfield, Ill., 1967.

Smith, Robert. *Baseball in America.* New York, 1961.

Spalding, Albert G. *America's National Game.* New York, 1911.

Spenser, Hazelton, ed. *Selected Poems of Vachel Lindsey.* New York, 1931.

Sullivan, Mark. *The Turn of the Century.* Vol. I of *Our Times: The United States, 1900–1925.* New York, 1926.

Taylor, H. Warren. *Forty-Two Years of the Tiger Gridiron: A History of Football and the Louisiana State University, 1893–1935.* Baton Rouge, 1936.

Taylor, William H. and Rosenfeld, Stanley. *The Story of American Yachting Told in Pictures.* New York, 1958.

Tinker, Edward L. *Creole City: Its Past and People.* New York, 1953.

Toynbee, Arnold J. *A Study of History.* 11 vols. London, 1934–1959.

Trevathan, Charles E. *The American Thoroughbred.* New York, 1905.

Voigt, David Q. *Baseball: From Gentleman's Sport to the Commissioner System.* Norman, 1966.

Vosburgh, Walter S. *Racing in America, 1866–1921.* New York, 1921.

Wade, Richard C. *Slavery in the Cities: The South, 1820–1860.* New York, 1964.

Weaver, Robert B. *Amusements and Sports in American Life.* Chicago, 1939.

Wecter, Dixon. *The Saga of American Society: A Record of Social Aspirations, 1607–1937.* New York, 1937.

Weiss, John, ed. *The Origins of Modern Consciousness.* Detroit, 1965.

Wiley, Bell I. *The Life of Johnny Reb: The Common Soldier of the Confederacy.* Indianapolis, 1943.

Winters, John D. *The Civil War in Louisiana.* Baton Rouge, 1963.

Wittke, Carl F. *Refugees of Revolution: The German Forty-Eighters in America.* Philadelphia, 1952.

Woodruff, "Fuzzy." *A History of Southern Football, 1890–1928.* 3 vols. Atlanta, 1928.

Woodward, C. Vann. *The Strange Career of Jim Crow.* Second Revised Edition. New York, 1966.

Woodward, Stanley. *Sports Page.* New York, 1949.

Yates, Norris W. *William T. Porter and the* Spirit of the Times: *A Study in the Big Bear School of Humor.* Baton Rouge, 1957.

Zucker, Adolf, ed. *The Forty-Eighters: Political Refugees of the German Revolution of 1848.* New York, 1950.

THESES AND DISSERTATIONS

Adams, William H. "New Orleans as the National Center of Boxing." M. A. thesis, Louisiana State University and Agricultural and Mechanical College, 1950.

Betts, John R. "Organized Sport in Industrial America." Ph.D. dissertation, Columbia University, 1951.

Dunham, Norman L. "The Bicycle Era in American History." Ph.D. dissertation, Harvard University, 1956.

Eagleson, Dorothy R. "Some Aspects of the Social Life of the New Orleans Negro in the 1880's." M. A. thesis, Tulane University, 1961.

Fischer, Roger A. "The Segregation Struggle in Louisiana, 1850–1900." Ph.D. dissertation, Tulane University, 1967.

Flath, Arnold W. "A History of Relations Between the National Collegiate Athletic Association and the Amateur Athletic Union of the United States (1905–1963)." Ph.D. dissertation, University of Michigan, 1963.

Gruensfelder, Melvin H. "A History of the Origin and Development of the Southeastern Conference." M. S. thesis, University of Illinois, 1964.

Hoover, Francis L. "A History of the National Association of Intercollegiate Athletics." Phy. Ed.D. dissertation, Indiana University, 1958.

Jones, Ruth Irene. "Ante-Bellum Watering Places of Louisiana, Mississippi, Alabama, and Arkansas." M. A. thesis, University of Texas, 1954.

Korsgaard, Robert. "A History of the Amateur Athletic Union of the United States." Ed.D. project, Teachers College, Columbia University, 1952.

Maden, Ann. "Popular Sports in New Orleans, 1890–1900." M. A. thesis, Tulane University, 1956.

Mason, Philip P. "The League of American Wheelmen and the Good-Roads Movement, 1880–1905." Ph.D. dissertation, University of Michigan, 1957.

Reinders, Robert C. "A Social History of New Orleans, 1850–1860." Ph.D. dissertation, University of Texas, 1957.

Taylor, Arvilla. "Horse Racing in the Lower Mississippi Valley Prior to 1860." M. A. thesis, University of Texas, 1953.

INDEX

Alderman, Edwin A., 261

Allen, Tom, 162, 163

Amateurism: definitions of, 87–88, 237–38; in baseball, 116–17, 137–39; in swimming, 144–45; in yachting, 149; in rowing, 151, 155–56, 156*n.;* in bicycling, 228–29; threats to, 237; attempts to safeguard, 238–39, 293–94; and athletic clubs, 241; Young Men's Gymnastic Club and Southern Athletic Club differ over, 245; variation of from sport to sport, 294

American Athletic Club, 243, 244

Animal Sports: legal opposition to, 59, 60–61, 205–206. *See also* Bull and bear contests; Bullfighting; Cockfighting; Dogfighting

Archery, 210

Athletic Advisory Committee of Tulane University, 268

Athletic Clubs: and prize fighting, 57, 174–75, 186, 187–88, 189–91; and tennis, 211; and attempts to eliminate professionalism, 238–39; proliferation of, 241; and amateurism, 241; and attempts to encourage an interest in sports, 242; and track and field, 243–44; and introduction of football to New Orleans, 251–52; and football competition, 252–54; and development of collegiate sports, 273. *See also* Southern Athletic Club; Young Men's Gymnastic Club

Audubon Driving Club, 102–103

Audubon Golf Club, 216–17

Audubon Park, 103, 142, 283–84

Bachelor subculture: role in sports, 52–53; and popularity of billiards, 67; waning influence of, 193

Baer, Clara G., 269–72 *passim*

Baseball, 49–51, 74, 77–78, 115–39, 249, 255–56, 279

Basketball, 270

Basquette, 270

Bayne, Hugh L., 216, 252, 266

Bayne, Thomas L., 252, 264

Bicycling: popularity of in New Orleans, 218–36; legal opposition to, 225; and traffic regulations, 225–26

Billiards, 62, 66–67, 76, 78, 194–97

Bingaman, Adam L., 26, 30; Bingaman Racecourse, 26, 27

Board of Racing Stewards, 107

Boston Club: and support of horse racing, 28, 108; and billiards, 66, 195; and baseball, 118; mentioned, 8

Bowen, Andy, 176, 176*n.,* 187, 188

Bowling, 62–66, 78, 194

Boxing. *See* Prize fighting

Breaux, Gustave A., 94, 282

Brewster, Alexander, 148, 149

Bride, Ira E., 101, 102

Brooklyn Racecourse (Algiers), 102

Bull and bear contests, 59, 60

Bullfighting, 59–60

Burke, James "Deaf," 55

Butler, Benjamin F., 76, 80

Carrollton (La.), 40, 165

Cincinnati Red Stockings, 126, 127, 128

City Park (New Orleans), 282–83, 283–84

Coburn, Joe, 164

Cockfighting, 59, 60–61, 78, 204–206

Collegiate sports: origins of, 245–46; in the South, 246–47; at Tulane University, 247–49, 254–58, 272; student control of, 265; faculty and alumni control of, 265–66; mentioned, 87. *See also* Intercollegiate sports, Tulane University

Commercialism: in the pastimes of New Orleans, 8–9; in leisure-time activities, 19; in horseracing, 25, 26, 91–92, 100–101, 105–106, 109, 113–14; in